William Roscoe Thayer

The Dawn of Italian Independence - Italy from the Congress of
Vienna, 1914, to the Fall of Venice, 1849

Volume I

William Roscoe Thayer

The Dawn of Italian Independence - Italy from the Congress of Vienna, 1914, to the Fall of Venice, 1849
Volume I

ISBN/EAN: 9783337230173

Printed in Europe, USA, Canada, Australia, Japan

Cover: Foto ©ninafisch / pixelio.de

More available books at **www.hansebooks.com**

THE DAWN OF ITALIAN INDEPENDENCE

ITALY FROM THE CONGRESS OF VIENNA, 1814
TO THE FALL OF VENICE, 1849

BY

WILLIAM ROSCOE THAYER

S' io al vero son timido amico,
Temo di perder vita tra coloro
Che questo tempo chiameranno antico.
    DANTE: Paradiso, xvii, 118-120.

IN TWO VOLUMES
VOLUME I

BOSTON AND NEW YORK
HOUGHTON, MIFFLIN AND COMPANY
The Riverside Press, Cambridge
1893

CONTENTS OF VOLUME I.

BOOK FIRST.
THE INHERITANCE.

CHAP.		PAGE
I.	ROMAN AND BARBARIAN	1
II.	CHARLEMAIN AND THE SPELL OF ROME	16
III.	DEVELOPMENT OF STATE AND CHURCH	23
IV.	MANY REPUBLICS, BUT NO NATION	43
V.	DANTE	52
VI.	THE RENAISSANCE	60
VII.	REACTION AND DECLINE	72
VIII.	SCIENCE AND FOLLY	82
IX.	NEW VOICES AND REVOLUTION	95

BOOK SECOND.
THE DOOM OF TYRANNY.

I.	THE CONGRESS OF VIENNA	116
II.	THE RETURN OF THE DESPOTS, 1814-15	139
III.	FOREIGN INTRIGUES	179
IV.	CONSPIRACIES	190
V.	NAPLES IN REVOLUTION, 1820	215
VI.	THE REVOLUTION IN PIEDMONT, 1821	253
VII.	RETRIBUTION	279
VIII.	UNDERCURRENTS, 1820-30	312
IX.	THE REVOLUTIONS OF 1831	342

BOOK THIRD.
WHILE GREGORY XVI PONTIFICATES.

I.	CONSPIRACY GETS ITS LEADER	379
II.	THE DECADE OF CONTRADICTIONS, 1833-43	401
III.	THE POLITICAL REFORMERS	429

THE DAWN OF ITALIAN INDEPENDENCE.

BOOK FIRST.

THE INHERITANCE.

Ahi serva Italia, di dolore ostello,
Nave senza nocchiere in gran tempesta,
Non donna di provincie, ma bordello!
DANTE, *Purgatorio*, vi, 76–78.

CHAPTER I.

ROMAN AND BARBARIAN.

THE gradual regeneration of the Italians during the first half of the nineteenth century must be described, like the convalescence of a patient from a long sickness, by symptoms much more than by startling occurrences. We must look for signs of progress in the aspirations rather than in the achievements of any conspicuous leaders. For this movement was inward and subtle; and its outward expression in deeds was stubbornly repressed. In order, therefore, to tell truthfully this very significant episode in the life of modern Europe, I shall draw information from many sources, passing from the narration of events to the biography of a representative man, or pausing to examine a custom or a book, which may often serve better than official documents to reveal the forces working below the surface in Italy. I shall be fortunate if I succeed by any means in recalling from the " dark backward and abysm of Time" the living motives and high influences which, penetrating the Italian heart, revived self-respect in it, and courage, and slowly fitted it to rise from serfdom to independence. When a man reforms his life, and, putting away his follies, rises to take his place among the strong and righteous, we are edified: how much greater, then, should be our interest and edification at beholding an entire people, who, long sunk in moral and political misery, lift themselves into the comradeship of their best neighbors. This spectacle, the noblest that Europe has had to show in our century, unfolds itself to our view as we follow the history of the modern Italians.

It is evident that in the brotherhood of states, as in the family or the community, the welfare of all must be attained through the excellence of each of the members according to his qualities. Every weakling, every idler, diminishes the common prosperity. To develop each individual to the utmost limit compatible with the general weal is the goal towards which destiny urges mankind. Hitherto, this process has resulted in the formation of strong individuals, and in concentrating and intensifying the traits peculiar to each race; for the first commandment given to every creature in the physical world is, *Be strong, if thou wouldst survive.* But individualism, when unrestrained and unspiritualized by the recognition of a larger communion of interests, is selfish and partial; it uses its strength brutishly: its neighbor is not a brother, but an enemy, to be robbed or crippled or enslaved. The past has witnessed the endeavor of race after race to make itself supreme by absorbing all the power of its fellows and by holding them in subjection. But we stand on the threshold of a new age, in which time and distance and the barriers of Nature have been overcome; when the products of one land can be transported swiftly to other lands, and when the utterances and events in one hemisphere are known immediately in the other. And now we begin to perceive that the fate of each people is interwoven with that of all the rest. Interdependence is as necessary as independence, and whatever law of trade, whatever intriguing of diplomacy, aims only at selfish and local gain, though it seems for a time to benefit the egotist, will inevitably weaken him, because it weakens his neighbors. The swarm is harmed when a single bee is harmed. The old politics took no note of this, nor have present Ministries given heed to it; but there is the fact, and all the inventions which make commercial intercourse easy, and disseminate knowledge, are prophetic of the ultimate solidarity of mankind. A crime against one will at last be seen to be a crime against all.

This being true, how could Europe have real health, so long as one of her members — Italy — was sick? Servitude debases not only the slave, but the slave-owner and those who abet him. What wealth that Austria wrung from the Italians could compensate her for the moral slough — the cruelty and selfishness — into which she sank in order to maintain her tyranny? And what of France and England, what of Prussia and Russia, who consented to the degradation? The Italian, too, must have a voice in the Parliament of Nations; he, too, must contribute to the common treasure of humanity that which he, and no other, was peculiarly adapted to produce. But first, he must be free, Italy must be an independent nation; for no man can speak the truth that is in him when the hand of an oppressor is upon his throat.

How came it to pass, then, that the Italians at the beginning of the nineteenth century were not free? that they seemed an exhausted race, fit only to grind wheat and press out oil to enrich their taskmasters? To answer these questions, and to understand the regenerative movement which is the subject of the present work, we must take a rapid survey over the past; for in no other country was the past so tenacious and so authoritative as in Italy.

Traditions there had the force of new and irresistible impulses elsewhere; men lived by memory alone; customs, feuds, aspirations, survived to shape conduct long after the particular circumstances which begot them, or the conditions which matured them, had ceased to exist. Just as, if you drove a spade into Italian soil, you might uncover an ancient statue or the fragment of a cyclopean ruin, so if you but scraped the surface of an institution or a habit, you might find that its roots shot deep into a remote antiquity. Past and present seemed to grow side by side; you could never be sure that an influence was dead or that a trait had been forgotten. When Rienzi would have established a republic at Rome, he exhorted his hearers to be stirred by the example of their forerunners, the Gracchi, though these had been dead fourteen hundred years, and the world had been transformed. Imagine Hampden appealing to Britons by their memory of Caractacus, or Camille Desmoulins rousing the French by allusions to Vercingetorix! In Italy alone was this possible, and we need therefore to know, at least in epitome, what was the inheritance which the Italians of whom we are to treat had received from their ancestors.

From the earliest times there had never been a united Italian nation. The various tribes which occupied the peninsula were conquered one by one by the Latins, who carried Rome with them wherever they went, and who succeeded, in the reign of Augustus, in converting Italy into a uniform Roman state. After the age of the Antonines, — that Indian summer of prosperity and glory, — the empire of Rome slowly fell asunder: within, vice and luxury and civil factions corrupted its integrity and sapped its vigor; without, hosts of sturdy barbarians swept down the frontier-bulwarks and surged on Rome itself, — till at length Huns and Teutons had submerged the throne of the Cæsars, and lay like a flood over Italy. That calamity seemed to portend the ruin of the world; and, indeed, for a long time after the waters had subsided, there seemed no hope of reconstructing civilization out of the wreck. The invaders mingling with their conquered subjects bred a new race, which gradually differed in language and character both from the Latin and the barbarian; but the Latin strain predominated in this new people, which was the Italian. Our purpose does not require that we should unravel the history of the centuries of confusion and readjustment when not only Italy, but the whole Roman world was shattered, and then rudely remodeled.

Peer into that time never so hard, you will scarcely discern a recognizable human face turned towards yours. You will see only masses indistinctly, like waves through a fog. Individual names there are, but they seem rather the names of personified vices and ferocities than of rational beings. Deeds there are, but collective and ill-defined, like the forces which slowly transform autumn into winter. You know that between the fifth century and the eleventh, European society was completely resmelted; that the battered metal of Paganism, being fused in the same furnace with Catholicism and Teutonism, produced an alloy such as the world had never seen. You know the chief traits of the new civil system, the chief dogmas of the new religion; and you repeat the names of a few score kings, warriors, and popes, which stud that historical waste like surveyor's stakes to mark distances and boundaries. But to realize by the force of your imagination what an individual man thought and was, so that he lives again for you, is perhaps an impossible thing. Growth you see, and change; but you cannot quickly perceive into what, for on the surface there are only tumults and wars, chaotic and incessant. You need not look for complex motives; the recorded actions of the men and women of the Dark Age are almost always traceable to the elementary appetites of half-savage mankind,—to lust, to greed, to revenge, to love of fighting. The law of the strongest rules;

the weak can get, and he expects, no mercy. Yet above the din of clashing arms, if you listen attentively you can hear the dull tapping of myriads of mattocks on the earth, and the beating of flails on the threshing-floors, and the thud of the woodman's axe in the forest; for every year, be there quiet or carnage, the soil must be tilled, the crops sown, the harvests garnered, and the fuel stored, against the coming of winter: and the nameless multitude of serfs worked on, season after season, century after century, silent, unquestioning, without hope, grinding the grain for another to eat, pressing out the wine for another to drink. Dynasties appeared and vanished, but the race of the toilers, stretching back to the day when the first man tilled the first patch of glebe, was permanent, and the sound of its tools seemed to beat out a funeral march. The peasant literally belonged to the earth, to be treated as a natural force, like spring rains or summer heats. And a few men, like to him in shape, but as unlike him in privilege as the hawk is unlike the worm, came and took from him the product of his labor. Himself but a better tool, the peasant had spade and plough to his portion; and when, worn out with travail, he sank into the earth, or was struck down by some troop of pillagers, his sons toiled in his stead. Pathetic, unmurmuring delvers of the fields, on your humble shoulders you bore the foundations of great cities and mighty empires; you bent your backs for the arrogant tread of armies; yet you, neglected and uncivilized, were the corner-stone of civilization. How many ages should you look down along the furrow and break its clods, before you suspected that you too were human, that you too were entitled to a share, not only of the wealth you created, but also of all the excellencies of the world? Immemorial oppression has curved your spines earthwards, but the time shall come when, erect once more, you shall look any of your fellows in the eyes, and lifting your gaze upon the stars, you shall say, " We, too, are partakers in the dignity of the universal scheme, of which these are the tokens and the promise."

But during the Dark Age men dreamt not yet of this. Society grew as grows the coral : at first, a shapeless mass; after a century it has put forth little prongs and shoots ; after another, those shoots have lengthened into branches, until at last it stands there an organic growth, shapely and marvelous, with trunk and limbs and twigs. The social organism which then took shape and became dominant in Western Europe until the French Revolution was Feudalism. Its origin was Teutonic ; its fundamental principle, Force. Each German tribe elected as chief its strongest man. Part of the booty taken in war was distributed among the tribe in common ; part was reserved for him. As the tribe prospered, his power increased, and his share of plunder — land, cattle, and captive enemies — descended to his sons. Gradually, his office became hereditary, and each tribesman swore to obey him, became " his man."

In the course of three centuries the Franks had fought their way to the front of the German tribes, and Charlemain was their king. This extraordinary man, the last of a family of vigorous soldiers, is well-nigh the only being of that era whose personality can be made to live again : for he was not a monotone, nor the mere spigot of a single vice or passion, but a man of many powers, excelling as soldier, as statesman, and as patron of letters and education, very human in his defects, and almost unparalleled in his influence upon history. His genius it was which raised Feudalism into a world-system, at least for the world of Christendom. Over all France, as far south as the Ebro in Spain and as the Liris in Italy, over Germany to the Elbe and across Pannonia to the Theiss, stretched his empire. Each district was governed by a count or duke whom he appointed ; and lest the provincials should imagine that distance could dim his watchfulness or weaken his supremacy, he sent every year two *missi* or imperial inspectors among them, to report upon their condition and to see that the viceroys were faithful in their stewardship. Charlemain himself traveled constantly through his realm, to inquire into the needs of his subjects, to dispense justice, to chastise rebels, and to fortify his outposts along the borderland where his domain ended and the unexplored wilderness of the barbarians began. Merciless to his enemies, — did he not cause forty-five hundred Saxons to be beheaded at Verden? — he put aside his wrath when they submitted, and treated them as his own people, suffering them to retain their local customs, but imposing upon all a uniform scheme of government and law.

The proof of Charlemain's extraordinary genius, and of the suitableness of Feudalism to the needs of that age, lies in the fact that, before the end of his forty years' reign, a larger part of Western Europe was reduced to orderly government than had been for nearly five centuries. In an epoch when physical force was the supreme test, a system based on force came to be adopted. Charlemain had approved himself the strongest man in Christendom, as his lieutenants acknowledged by becoming his vassals. Each received his province or his estate directly from the sovereign, on condition that he should furnish a stipulated number of troops when the sovereign required them. Each great vassal, or over-lord, then subdivided his territory among other vassals on the same terms, and these again to others, down to the petty knight who had but a few score acres and half a dozen fighting retainers, and lower still to the simple freeman who had only his own sword to serve with. Below all these were the serfs, too humble to be reckoned in this scheme: like cattle, they went with the soil and were powerless to choose their masters. Force being the arbiter and self-preservation being the strongest instinct, it behooved every man to get as much force on his side as he could; the weak therefore turned to the strong and voluntarily accepted him as liege, and was promised protection in return for personal service. By this strange chain, made up of links of regularly diminishing size,— the largest firmly riveted in the suzerainty of the emperor, the smallest desperately clutched by the poor freeman, — was society once more held together. So long as the sovereign was Charlemain, a man not only preëminently strong but also just and wise withal, Feudalism was a system capable of promoting civilization by restraining the violent ; by soothing the terrors of the weak ; by uniting all classes against the attacks of their common enemies, the Huns on the east and the Saracens on the south; by awakening in all that sense of mutual interdependence without which nations can be neither compact nor concordant ; and by affording a ready means of communication between the head and the members. A beneficial system, we must pronounce it, so long as the head was strong and just ; when, however, the head was weak or wicked, or both, as soon came to pass, Feudalism proved most efficacious in exasperating the very evils it should have quelled.

Feudalism is the contribution made by the Teutonic races to the art of government. At the time when it reached its growth under Charlemain, another power, different alike in origin and nature, but even more tremendous in its effects, rose to share the dominion of the western world. This power was Roman Christianity. The teachings of Christ, early transplanted to Rome, grew up there in a form determined by the character of the Romans. Their genius, markedly administrative and legal, imposed upon the new church an intricate system of government and a sharply defined, dogmatic expression. The necessities of those early Christians, who were now tolerated under sufferance and now persecuted without mercy, intensified their natural tendency as Romans towards a compact organization and a rigid creed. You will look in vain among the recorded utterances of Jesus for any sanction of a hierarchy, for any authorization of papal or ecclesiastical rule. You will find that Christ invariably addressed the individual conscience. He came to call sinners to repentance, not by scaring them into heaven through a fear of hell, but by revealing to them that righteousness alone can give lasting peace and strength to the soul. And he spoke not according to tradition, after the manner of Scribes and Pharisees, but out of his immediate conviction that virtue and right and love are absolute and eternal, not to be affected nor diminished by the opinions men may hold about them. The assent of Moses or Solomon could not make truth one jot more true; nor could the decree of the Sanhedrim make an unjust act just. Spiritual laws are absolute; they operate immediately, whether we attend to them or not; they were in the past, from the beginning; they are in the present; they will be in the future; they pervade all time, but they are above time. And just as the physical laws discovered by Kepler and Newton were not born at the moment of discovery, so the spiritual laws unfolded by Christ did not originate with him; better than any one else, he knew that their authority came not from him, but from the Centre and Source of Life. By a method which has fitly been called the method of " sweet reasonableness," he explained these spiritual verities, and, what was immeasurably more important, he illustrated them by the example of his own life. Let us not suppose that virtue was first taught by the gentle Galilean, — wise men had long before confessed her in many lands, and many men had led good and noble lives, — but Jesus proclaimed that all men are equal before God, and that the individual conscience is judged directly by the eternal laws of the Spirit. You are better or worse, not in proportion as men think well or ill of you, but as you obey or disobey the Inner Voice. The rank and prestige of the individual avail nothing in the presence of these impartial laws. He who follows them, though he be a slave, has the spiritual strength which they alone can bestow; he who departs from them, though he be a Cæsar, loses their support, and in that deprivation is punished. The equality of the moral law and the judgment of conscience,— these are Christ's teachings, and they condemn the interposition of any third party, any church or spiritual attorney. I can as soon picture him being borne in gorgeous papal apparel into St. Peter's, or, disguised in the worldly pomp of the Archbishop of Canterbury, holding a levee at Lambeth Palace, as I can believe he meant to sanction the clerical machinery and dogmas which grew up under his name, and which, under various forms, still pass for Christianity.

Christ appealed at first to simple, earnest men, who needed but to have the truth put clearly, and to see it exemplified in his actions, in order to accept it. No miracles, the stage-thunder of religion, were necessary to persuade them; those were later devices for terrifying or astonishing minds less spiritual into belief,— minds that required a sign, minds that could be convinced that Jesus was the Lord, as they heard him called, only after they were assured that he had turned natural laws topsy-turvy and wrought wonders more amazing than those attributed to the gods of other nations. As if the recognition that, in both the spiritual and physical world, harmony and order prevail to attest the majesty and wisdom of God were not immeasurably more religious than the belief in any scheme of afterthoughts, interruptions, and whims! As if the turning of water into wine, or the feeding of a multitude with a few loaves and fishes, were comparable to the miracle of that career of holiness and self-abnegation, or to that Sermon on the Mount which has furnished food to millions of souls, yet cannot be exhausted! But men cannot long live the free life of the spirit, in which virtue is its own witness and justification; before the end of the first century, Christianity had fallen from its pure, spontaneous estate. The fiery genius of Paul had molten the spiritual ore and cast it into metaphysical moulds, and the Christian communities which sprang up in various parts of the Roman Empire made doctrinal agreement, rather than conduct, the test of orthodoxy. Paul, be it never forgotten, was the Oriental dragoman who interpreted Christ's message to the Greek and Latin world; and Paul, preëminently an orator and a logician, could not help adding arguments, the character of which was determined by his temperament, as he translated. Christ, a Jew, with the Jewish power of illustrating abstract truths by vivid concrete examples, had often spoken in parables; but over and over again he had warned his disciples that the truth lay in the spirit and not in the letter. Nevertheless, owing partly to the natural tendency of men to mistake the symbol for the reality, and partly to the fact that an uncritical age attaches fantastic and mystical significance to the plainest words and deeds, Christianity soon began to petrify into literalism.

Nowhere was this more apparent than among the Romans, masters in rules and codes. During the first three centuries the Roman bishop enjoyed no acknowledged precedence over the bishops of Africa and the East; but when Christianity was decreed by Constantine to be the State religion, the authority of the Roman bishop gained great prestige in fact, if not in the official recognition of the other churches. The Bishop of Antioch or of Alexandria might still claim independence, but the Bishop of Rome spoke from the capital of the Empire, and he already represented a larger number of Christians than belonged to any other diocese. The rapid increase in the membership of the Roman Church required a strong organization; and whereas in early days each community had chosen its minister, the power to elect now passed out of the hands of the congregation and was usurped by the priests, who elected their superiors, and these in their turn elected the

Bishop of Rome. Then sprang up a sacerdotal clan, which arrogated to itself complete jurisdiction over the government and tenets of the church. A chasm as wide as that which separates the pariah from the brahmin separated priest from layman in this hierarchical system modeled upon Roman imperialism.

When the Empire was divided by the establishment of a second capital at Byzantium, the authority of the Pope over Italy and Western Europe was naturally extended, and when the Western Empire fell asunder, it was equally natural that the people of Rome and its neighborhood should rally to the spiritual head of Rome for that protection which the civil government could no longer give. Even the barbarians respected him, and as they settled on Italian soil and became Christians, they turned to him as their religious arbiter and guide. Nominally, the emperor at Constantinople protected the church at Rome, but actually the Romans in those grievous days had to protect themselves, whether by propitiating the temporary conqueror or by striving to resist him. Among the incessant tumults and changes, nothing was stable, nothing permanent, except the rule of the Pope. His spiritual authority, transmitted from successor to successor, could not be affected by temporal vicissitudes. The man might be driven from Rome, but the office embodied in him was beyond the hazard of his personal fortunes. Privileges and property once acquired by or bequeathed to the church did not lapse, for the church was perpetual.

From the fifth to the eighth century, the Bishops of Rome established their spiritual supremacy in Italy. Even the Iconoclastic Controversy in which they engaged with the Eastern Church ended in strengthening them. The Greek Christians were the more speculative and mystical; was it not natural that the religion of a land where the language and literature of the race which had excelled in philosophy still flourished should be clothed upon with philosophical wraps? The Latins, on the contrary, had produced no philosopher; they were logical and practical, caring more for things than for thoughts; they knew the value of visible images and symbols in helping dull imaginations to perceive religious dogmas. The Popes who refused to prohibit the use of idols acted in harmony with the genius of the Latin people, and they lightened the task of converting the heathen natives of Western Europe to Christianity. A missionary who could show an image of St. Peter or of Christ to the Teutonic barbarian was much more likely to be understood than another who labored with words to make abstractions plain.

This assertion of independence not only enhanced the prestige of the Roman bishop, but also fixed upon the Roman Church that reverence for symbols which, exaggerated at later periods, became the substitutes for inner spiritual devoutness. But the Popes soon had to cope with nearer and more dangerous enemies than the Byzantine emperor. They were hard bestead by the Lombards, those long-bearded warriors who conquered Northern Italy in the sixth century, and spreading southward to Spoleto and Benevento menaced the patrimony of St. Peter itself. There being no champion for him in Italy, the Pope sought succor across the Alps of Charles Martel, king in all but name of the Frankish nation. Before Charles could descend into Lombardy and punish the tormentors of the Pope, he died. His son, Pepin the Short, succeeded him; deposed Childeric III, last of the do-nothing kings of the Merovingian line (752); was crowned by the Archbishop of Mayence, the Pope's representative; and erelong he compelled the Lombards to submit. This league of amity between the Popes and the Carolingians is the most important fact in the history of that age. It confirmed the papal power in Italy: it established the precedent that the Pope's sanction of a monarch beyond the Alps was, if not absolutely indispensable, a source of strength and dignity; it showed that the influence of the Byzantine emperors over the affairs of Western Europe was virtually dead; it fixed Roman Christianity, to the exclusion of Arianism, on the west. Ambition would doubtless have been a sufficient motive for urging the Frankish kings to subdue the Lombards; but this league, by making them the champions and defenders of the Roman Church, gave to their ambition a holier aspect, and thenceforward the spread of Christianity coincided with the extension of their dominion over the barbaric tribes.

CHAPTER II.

CHARLEMAIN AND THE SPELL OF ROME.

PEPIN was followed by his greater son Charlemain, who, as we have seen, brought Central and Western Europe under his sway and organized Feudalism as an imperial system. His genius, his methods, his traditions were Teutonic, but these did not prevent him from feeling the spell of an influence which had begun to fascinate the imaginations of men long before Teuton or Hun had emerged from primitive savagery. " What's in a name ? " exclaimed the lovesick heroine of Verona. " Everything ! " experience might have replied to her; for " the generality of mankind is wholly and absolutely governed by words and names, without — nay, for the most part, even against — the knowledge men have of things."[1] The name which captivated Charlemain, which dazzled the world for well-nigh two thousand years, — from the fifth century before to the fifteenth century after Christ, — was Rome. Among all the names uttered by men, only one other has been more potent.

ROMA ! There is the history of our Western races in these four letters. The stories of Greece and Palestine, of Carthage and Egypt, are as rivers which flow down from remote regions into a great lake called *Rome*. Antiquity is a vast ravine, from one side of which to the other reverberates the magic word *Rome*. A hundred and sixty years before the Christian era, the fame of the Romans was sounding through all the lands then known. Tribes which had never seen them knew that " they were mighty

[1] Robert South, *A Sermon preached May* 9, 1686.

and valiant men." Judas Maccabæus, the last hero of Jewish independence, bade his countrymen in their distress to seek the friendship of that invulnerable people who had their citadel on the distant Tiber. He related how "they destroyed and brought under their dominion all other kingdoms and isles that at any time resisted them, but with their friends and such as relied upon them they kept amity; and that they had conquered kingdoms both far and nigh, insomuch as all that heard of their name were afraid of them; also that, whom they would help to a kingdom, those reign; and whom again they would, they displace; finally, that they were greatly exalted; yet for all this none of them wore a crown, or was clothed in purple to be magnified."[1] Thereafter, during more than four hundred years, victory upon victory, advance upon advance, added significance and lustre to the name of Rome, until the Pict among the chilly mists of Shetland, and the Hindoo in the jungles of Bengal, had seen the flash of Roman breastplates; and the nomads of Yemen and Sahara knew that far away in the centre of the world there was a nation invincible and terrible, whose arm was long and whose grasp was firm. This wonderful nation had taken up the gate-posts of civilization and set them down many hundred leagues ahead. Kingdoms which had sufficed for the ambition of Darius or the Ptolemies were mere segments in the great circle which Rome described upon three continents. The empire of Alexander was but a province; the realm of Hannibal was but a proconsulate. Rivers and mountains were no barriers to her; over those leaped her bridges, over these wound her highways. She penetrated forests and left them cornfields behind her. Her ships rode supreme in every port. It seemed that genius through all the past had been unconsciously working for her embellishment; that the Athenian sculptors had wrought statues to adorn her palaces, and that The-

[1] 1 Maccabees, viii. 11-14.

ban Pharaohs had hewn obelisks to commemorate her triumphs.

Think of the thirty generations which went into the augmenting of that power which we sum up in the single word *Rome!* Think of the reputations, each a splendid star, whose several brightness was merged into the brightness of his fellows, to compose that galaxy which spread over a large part of the firmament of history, and will excite the wonder of mankind forever. Regulus and Collatinus, the Scipios and the Gracchi, Marius and Sulla, Cato and Cicero, Cæsar and Pompey, Augustus and Hadrian, Trajan, Agricola and Aurelius, — these are but a few whose magnitude we have measured and named. But in the sound of that word *Rome* there is also the tramp of a thousand legions, there is the din of countless victories, there are the commands of dauntless forgotten generals and the decrees of innumerable lawgivers. No single genius lifted the fame of Rome to the stars, but the valor and energy and patience of a whole people, the concerted effort of nameless multitudes, who were not impelled by a sudden frenzy of conquest nor disheartened by a lost campaign, but who advanced slowly, steadily, rhythmically, as with the step of Fate. Rome conquered because she was strong; and she drew her strength from the integrity and patriotism of her sons during many successive generations. So strong was she that even her decline bore witness to her deep-rooted grandeur. Alexander, Napoleon, ceased to be, and their empire was as if they had never been; but Rome in her dissolution threatened the ruin of the world. Gradually, through four hundred years, luxury and vice stole vigor from her body and resoluteness from her soul, yet men still believed that she could not die; and she had lain dead in her palace already for a long season ere the barbarians dared to enter and look upon her corpse.[1]

[1] The real fall of Rome was in A. D. 397, when Theodosius died. Alaric, the first invader who had entered the city since Brennus, just eight hundred

But even death could not destroy the magic of the name of Rome. Freed from the limitations of fact, it lived as a disembodied spirit with an immortal existence which could not be assailed by the shock of mortal change. It had now, like a Miltonic archangel, that attribute of vagueness through which conceptions too vast for precise statement loom terrible or sublime. The visible empire still survived at Constantinople, but how weak and narrow it was compared with that idea of empire in which all that Rome had been was expressed! The degenerate Romans, and the barbarians who settled among them, alike deemed that idea to be a part of the universal order, just as the sun and seasons were; even though now invisible, they thought that it still held mankind together. The northern savages showed their reverence for it by the eagerness with which they sought to legitimize their conquests by obtaining for themselves the title of Roman Patrician; but they did not yet dare to assume the title of Emperor, although had one of them — Odoacer, for instance — done so, he could hardly have been prevented.

In the ears of Charlemain, however, that name *Roma* was continually resounding, and before his mind's eye that ideal of empire kept passing, vivid and seductive. He was more than king, for he had many kings to his vassals: he had reduced under his sway a large part of what had been the Roman Empire, and had established therein a uniform, stern government. He was, moreover, the champion of the religion which, spreading from Rome, was fast converting the West. All that he needed was the prestige of that title with which were associated the highest reach of human power and the maintenance of civilization itself. And when the Pope, representing the citizens of Rome, declared that the legitimate line of Eastern emperors had lapsed through the crimes of Irene, a woman who had

years before, sacked Rome in 410. Romulus Augustulus, the last phantom emperor, was deposed by Odoacer in 476.

usurped the Byzantine throne, and that the Romans, exercising their ancestral right to elect an emperor, had chosen Charlemain, the ambition of the Frankish conqueror was realized. Just what motives led to this epoch-making act we cannot say. The Pope may have been moved by gratitude for a monarch by whom he had been succored; he may have hoped to secure good-will and protection for the future; he may have wished to assert in this decisive fashion the independence of the Western Church from the nominal dictation of the Eastern emperors; or he may have merely intended to acknowledge that one who deserved the title of emperor should wear it. Certainly, had Charlemain commanded, nobody could have resisted him. The most natural reasons are probably nearest the truth. In after times, when history was rewritten by papal partisans, who, disregarding fact and unabashed by anachronisms, assigned purposes retrospectively, so as to give present issues the semblance of past authority, they claimed that Charlemain derived his imperial rights from the Pope, and that the emperors were therefore subordinate to the Popes. But we may well doubt whether Charlemain would have admitted or Stephen have pressed this claim on that Christmas day, A. D. 800, when the pontiff, rising in the basilica of St. Peter's, " advanced to where Charles, who had exchanged his simple Frankish dress for the sandals and the chlamys of a Roman patrician, knelt in prayer by the high altar, and as, in the sight of all, he placed upon the brow of the barbarian chieftain the diadem of the Cæsars, then bent in obeisance before him, the church rang to the shouts of the multitude, again free, again the lords and centre of the world, '*Karolo Augusto a Deo coronato magno et pacifico imperatori vita et victoria.*'"[1]

The consequences of this act have not yet ceased to be felt. Its immediate effect was to confirm and extend the power of the Pope. The Roman form of Christianity

[1] Bryce, *Holy Roman Empire*, p. 49.

became thenceforth established as the State religion of the West, and the Roman Church had the aid of the secular ruler in stamping out heresy and in pushing its missions heathenwards. The Emperor gained on his side whatever advantage imagination and tradition attached to his title; he gained also in being the official champion of the Church. His wars of conquest might now be defended by the plea of religious zeal, and he might strengthen his administration by persuading the Pope to punish with spiritual instruments the refractory subjects who would not obey the imperial command.

This partnership on equal terms between Church and State was very simple in theory. God, it was believed, had intrusted the governing of mankind to two heads, one of whom, the Pope, should direct the spiritual, while the other, the Emperor, should direct the temporal affairs of men. Each should be supreme in his own province; but since the spiritual and the temporal are as closely allied as body and soul, their governments must be harmonious, one supplementing and propping that of the other. These twin monarchs were equally necessary and equally venerable, and only in the sense that the soul is higher than the body could the Pope be said to be superior to the Emperor. God is universal; therefore the government which represents Him on earth must be universal. In antiquity only one nation succeeded in mastering the then known world; that nation was the Roman, and the breadth and power of its empire proved that God ordained it to be the model of civil government. Later, when He had revealed His scheme of salvation, He confided it to the Roman Church to preserve and disseminate. Since that scheme applied to all men, the Church must be universal, eternal, and catholic; and as there was but one scheme, there could be but one true religion: the Roman was therefore the sole guardian of orthodoxy.

Thus, at the beginning of the ninth century, we find

society in Western Christendom constituted under two strangely derived systems, that of Feudalism, Teutonic in origin and nature, but now popularly supposed to be the perpetuator of the Roman Empire ; and that of Christianity, a Hebrew product, transformed through the genius of the Latin race into a genuine Roman institution. Rome had never created a world-religion. She imposed her laws, but not her creed, upon the tribes she overcame. She had persecuted the early Christians, not because they held odd doctrines, but because they denied the authority and disturbed the peace of the Roman State. Yet now, the real Rome being dead, her spirit was to circulate among mankind in a world-religion, and the mere tradition of her grandeur was to give lustre to an empire utterly unlike her own. Marvelous people of the Tiber, none other that ever trod the earth has left upon it footprints so deep as yours! Dead but sceptred kings, who from your urns have ruled the spirits of a long posterity, the might of your genius shall be active among men until the last Romish priest shall have said his last mass, and the last candle shall flicker on the altar.

CHAPTER III.

DEVELOPMENT OF STATE AND CHURCH.

AT the beginning of the ninth century, therefore, Western Europe has issued from chaos, and feels the need and benefit of a dual restraint. It looks up to a Roman Pope and a German-Roman Emperor. There exists at Constantinople another Emperor calling himself Roman, and a Church claiming to be Christian and catholic; but the Western Emperor troubles himself little about the former, and the Pope brands the latter as schismatic. Local interests tend more and more to separate the East from the West in spirit, and a broad zone inhabited by barbarians keeps them asunder in fact. European history, so far as it concerns us, is henceforth the history of the West, and if we think of the Byzantine Empire at all, we think of it as sinking deeper and deeper into Asiatic lethargy, which the terrible warriors of Othman shall at last plunge into the sleep from which no man wakes. Of the events in Western Europe itself that belong to the Middle Age, the epoch between Charlemain and Dante, we can refer to only a few of the most important which directly or indirectly moulded the destiny of Italy.

Imperialism and Catholicism, whose compact had been so joyfully celebrated, worked together as allies but a short time, then their separate ambitions and their conflicting interests goaded them to internecine rivalry. Soon after Charlemain's death the empire was split into three fragments. The western portion, comprising Neustria and Aquitaine, — a considerable part of what was later France, — fell to Charles the Bald; a central strip, running from the North Sea to what was anciently Latium and including the two imperial capitals, Aix-la-Chapelle and Rome, was given to Lothair; the provinces east of the Rhine were the share of Louis, surnamed the German. These three rulers were the grandsons of Charlemain. Lothair had the title of Emperor and of King of Italy. And now it was seen that the feudal system could not, in spite of Charlemain's precautions and foresight, maintain a uniform government over Western Europe. Not only did the mutual jealousy of the three brothers prevent them from forming a common union, but also centrifugal forces too strong to be overcome had been set in motion in each kingdom. The great feudatories, who as dukes, counts, and marquises, had governed the outlying provinces of the Empire and had been checked by Charlemain, now, under weaker sovereigns, established themselves as hereditary lords, and aspired to independence. The king, whether in France or in Germany, had a smaller territory than that of his great vassals; he could keep them obedient only by keeping them disunited. On the whole, the royal power expanded in France and dwindled in Germany; and for this reason, — the king of the former was hereditary, of the latter elective.

While the Capetians were slowly subduing their great vassals and bringing more and more land to the royal domain, the German monarchs had to cope not only with refractory nobles at home, but also with Huns, Slavs, and Scandinavians abroad. The sceptre passed from family to family; those who failed to receive it by election envied the successful and resisted their efforts to erect a dynasty. Perhaps it was still more important that the German king was also the Holy Roman Emperor: for this union of offices involved him in difficulties with the Pope, and it further embarrassed him with the affairs of Italy. Having been chosen by the electors, he must proceed to Milan to be crowned with the Iron Crown of the Lombard kings, and

thence to Rome to be anointed Emperor by the Pope.
Time wrought swift changes in the land south of the
Alps. New States grew up, each craving independence,
and the interval between one imperial visit and the next
being often long, the Italians began to lose respect for the
nominal suzerainty of their foreign Emperor. But the
spell of Italy had a fatal fascination for those German
kings. They pursued the southward-flying phantom, leaving in the Alpine passes and on the Italian plains the
withered flower of their armies. That will-o'-the-wisp
enticed them on and on, but always settled at last over a
graveyard.

What was the magic by which Power — the reality
they pursued — eluded them? Italy seemed to flourish
in spite of internal discord ; proud cities and fertile plan-
tations covered the peninsula, and the Italians who enjoyed them were merchants and prelates rather than warriors. Yet when the Emperor came to demand them as
his due, they slipped from his grasp. The oily state-craft
of the Italians countervailed the slow force of the Germans ; the subtle sunshine of the South bred a pestilence
more deadly than an armored foe, and whom pestilence
spared, voluptuousness dispatched. Hannibal, too, had
found the ease of Capua more formidable than Scipio's
legions at Cannæ. Nevertheless, though baffled time after
time and undone, the German kings persisted in their
hopeless task; when the vision of Italy hovered before
them, like men in whom the desire for strong drink returns too tempting to be controlled, they gave up all for
that. Triumphs they had, indeed, but they were temporary triumphs ; for while the German sovereign was
making or deposing Popes, and forcing the Italians to do
him homage, his restless vassals and enemies at home
seized the occasion of his absence to sow sedition or to
hasten attack. The league between the Empire and the

Church inevitably brought blight and disaster to the Empire.[1]

The power which circumvented the Emperors in Italy, the power with which southern sunshine and voluptuousness seemed to connive, was the Papacy, the most adroit, the most plausible institution which has ever influenced for ages together the fortunes of men. In its effects material, in its essence intangible, the Church of Rome forfeited the high prerogative of spirituality and preferred worldliness, from the day when a Pope first thrust himself into competition with temporal rulers. "Where your treasure is, there will your heart be also," is Christ's warning; the treasure which, for a thousand years past, the Popes have coveted and hoarded has been of the earth, and here have been their hearts. "No man can serve two masters: for either he will hate the one and love the other, or else he will hold to the one and despise the other. Ye cannot serve God and Mammon."[2] During more than a millennium the Papacy has been engaged in reconciling its service of two masters; while raising one hand in the worship of God, it has stretched forth the other to catch the bounty of Mammon, and in this conflict of allegiance, its zeal, except at rare intervals, has been on the side of God's adversary. But the purpose of the historian is not merely to pass verdicts on creeds and systems; it is rather to study the conditions amid which these rose and flourished, in order the better to understand that elemental human nature from which all religions and polities spring, and to furnish examples for the instruction of our own and after times. Little will it profit us if we imagine that Feudalism or Papalism, which to-day we have reason to condemn, was never useful. For better or for worse, these and all other systems were once the best,

---

[1] Four emperors died in Italy: two others just after they had recrossed the Alps.

[2] Matthew, vi, 24.

and by their scope and effects we can measure the period in which they were the best. We may prefer June to December, but December also has its bleak chapter in the chronicle of the year.

The expansion of the Roman Church into the Roman Papacy was as natural as the expansion of the bishopric of Rome into the spiritual dictatorship of Western Christendom. The Church early acquired property in and near the Holy City, and wherever a monastery was founded it owned and tilled land. Princes made propitiatory gifts; the faithful bequeathed money and estates. Charlemain exacted the payment of tithes to the priesthood, and in other ways fostered the institution of which he was proud to call himself the defender. The Popes soon exercised a moral influence in temporal concerns; they settled quarrels between rival claimants, and their sanction often outweighed military force. It was of course inevitable that their decision should be biased by their interests, that they should sincerely favor those who favored the Church. In theory the Empire was universal, coextensive with the Church, but its early partition, leaving the Emperor suzerain of but a portion of Charlemain's realm, created local and mutually hostile interests, while the Church remained unchanged, and had everywhere the same work to accomplish. It was a corporation with a perpetual charter, and it guarded its temporal possessions with a spiritual authority which even violent men in lawless times rarely dared to attack. And since the German king must be consecrated by the Pope before he could legally bear the title of Holy Roman Emperor, the idea of equality soon gave place to the assumption that the Emperor was inferior to the Pope; and lesser kings sometimes acknowledged their inferiority by receiving their crowns from the Roman legate. A strong Emperor might deny the assumptions of the Pope, and might make good his own supremacy, but his strength died with him; whereas the Romish power had a continuous life. The great ecclesiastics — the archbishops, bishops, and abbots — were both temporal and spiritual lords. Their clerical office or benefice was bestowed by the Pope; to the Emperor they did homage for their secular possessions; but in their allegiance they were clerics who labored at all times to magnify the Church. In acquiring, they were indifferently ecclesiastics or laymen; in holding, they were always ecclesiastics. If the secular sovereign arraigned them as vassals, they took refuge behind their inviolability as churchmen. Moreover, being often foreigners sent from Rome to promote Rome's interests, their resistance to the temporal sovereign was all the more bitter, in case of conflict between him and the Pope.

Evidently, the dual control as planned by Charlemain and Stephen worked unequally. Feudalism, on which the integrity of the empire was staked, proved too weak to bind the members together subordinate to one head; whereas the organization of the Roman Church spread in all directions, yet at the farthest point it was firmly connected with the centre. The chief instrument in solidifying the Church was the celibacy of the clergy. Whether priest or friar, the churchman was forbidden to marry; freed, therefore, from the ties of home and the distractions and ambitions of family, he could devote his zeal wholly to the Church. Whatever his nationality by birth, he became by ordination a citizen of spiritual Rome. He eschewed his native tongue and adopted Latin, the language of the Church. His allegiance to a temporal prince he exchanged for obedience, utter and unquestioning, to the Pope. And when you multiply this churchman by thousands, and multiply those thousands by hundreds, you can estimate the vast army of clerical soldiers, all inspired by the same purpose and drilled in the same tactics, that made it possible for the Roman hierarchy to set up and maintain its supremacy in every country of Western Europe. Thanks to that rule of celibacy, Romanism kept its uniformity during the Middle Age, while Christendom was gradually breaking up, through the ambition of dynasties and development of nationalities, into separate States. Had it not been for a celibate clergy, Britain and France and Germany might each have had its national church, with its native head and clergy, independent of the Pope at Rome, whose jurisdiction would have been confined to Italy.

This monstrous rule, whose influence on the politics and morals of Christendom cannot be overestimated, must not be passed by with a mere allusion, although this is not the place in which to do more than indicate its effects. Wherever you lay your finger on the degeneracy of Italian character, there you will find evidence of the perniciousness of sacerdotal celibacy which the Roman Church adopted and still makes compulsory. It came into Europe from the far East in the days of the early Christians. Asceticism commended itself to men who believed the world of Matter to be the creation and province of Satan, as the world of Spirit was of God, and that Satan was sleeplessly busy in devising lures to entice souls into his power. To resist Satan by renouncing the material world became, therefore, the aim of the early Christians: and how could they show their devotion to Christ more plainly than by denying that instinct, which is, next to self-preservation, the strongest and commonest of the natural passions? The zealot who succeeded in mortifying the flesh might well feel himself secure against the other wiles of the fiend. A fashion of asceticism as intemperate as licentiousness took possession of the Church; and presently whoever aspired to the reputation of devoutness must conform to the practice of the most fanatical. If a clergyman married, it was taken as proof that he had not conquered his animal nature; that he was not satisfied with a spiritual bride, the Church, and with spiritual children, his parishioners. So extravagant was the delusion, that worthy fathers feared lest everybody, clericals and laymen alike, would adopt celibacy and thus cut off the race; but Jerome, one of the fiercest advocates of the practice, dispelled their fears by pointing out that virginity is a most difficult state to preserve, and that there would always be enough backsliders to people the earth.[1] And in truth many of the brethren and sisters married and bred children; but while their weakness was condoned, it was still deemed a weakness. Christ had never married; therefore, it was urged, he held celibacy to be the higher state.

In this way, many causes contributed to convert what had been voluntary self-denial into a rigid law which churchmen must obey and laymen would strive to obey. Men whose pure lives excluded the suspicion that they pleaded from low motives protested against this unnatural prohibition. " Deprive the Church of honorable marriage," exclaimed the austere St. Bernard, " and you fill her with concubinage, incest, and all manner of nameless vice and uncleanness."[2] But the ascetics prevailed. Sacerdotal celibacy widened the gulf which already separated clergy from laity; and since the monks had taken the vow of chastity, pride forced the secular clergy to appear not less self-renouncing than they. For generations together they did indeed resist the ordinance and married; but the Popes, whether impelled, as was sometimes the case, by a desire to reform the morals of the Church, or, as was usually the case, by ambition, persevered, and finally declared sacerdotal celibacy to be the irrevocable law. And then Nature, who never forgets to punish men, whether they err through ignorance or by intent, took a terrible revenge. The very rule by which misguided zealots expected to attain purity, and by which haughty ecclesiastics schemed to lift themselves above laymen, this rule Nature turned

---

[1] Hieron. ad Jov. i, 36, quoted by H. C. Lea, *History of Sacerdotal Celibacy* (Philadelphia, 1884), p. 624.
[2] *Ibid*, 331.

into an instrument of foulness and degradation. Age after age, St. Bernard's prophecy has been fulfilled.

In times and countries that looked lightly on sexual immorality, ecclesiastics took no pains to conceal their profligacy; but in more recent times, among communities that assume the virtue of purity, even though they have it not, clerical debauch has been less open. *Si non caste, saltem caute*, is the convenient rule. Doubtless, there have always been honest men and women in the Church, for no system is so bad that it can vitiate some temperaments; but we speak not of Francis and Theresa, nor of their similars, we speak of the great body by whose conduct the Church is judged. This is corroded by hypocrisy; and hypocrisy in the priest has created easy-going indifference to virtue and skeptical distrust of things spiritual in the parish. Men who have no faith in the sincerity and uprightness of their religious guides, to whom nevertheless they attribute a mysterious sanctity which does not depend upon personal goodness, are apt to deem it unimportant that they themselves be upright and sincere. And Nature has indeed taken a terrible revenge! Her law to-day is as inflexible as it was fifteen centuries ago, when Jerome and Origen, in their errant enthusiasm, thought that it could be curbed or annulled by a papal decree: ignorance led them astray, but the guilt of the Church has been increased just in proportion as experience has proved, generation after generation, that their purpose was monstrous and unattainable. As well might the Pope stand on the brink of Niagara and command the waters not to fall as bid Nature to withdraw her vital instinct from every man who puts on the priest's gown or the monk's frock.

Nevertheless, this rule which sensualizes the clergy and corrupts the laity — this rule which conflicts with Nature and is the cause of patent hypocrisy — this it was that upheld the worldly sway of the Roman hierarchy and furnished agents to build up the edifice of the Papacy. It completed the organization of that distinct clerical caste which carried one language and one policy into many lands; a caste of religious Janissaries, of unattached bachelors, who, bound by no love to mother or wife, were pledged body and soul to obey their pontiff. And when at last there came a Pope whose strength equaled his ambition, he found that army of trained soldiers ready to do his will. That Pope was Gregory VII, popularly called Hildebrand, the first in time and among the most eminent in rank of the men of genius of the modern Italian race. He conceived a system of world-government even more wonderful than that of Charlemain and Stephen; for he dreamed of replacing the joint control of Emperor and Pope by a single control, the Pope's.

Theocracy is the legitimate ideal of any Church which pretends to be universal and infallible. Granting that men's souls must be saved, and that God has ordained one Church for their salvation, how can she fulfil her mission if the temporal government be in the hands of a ruler of whom she does not approve, or if the civil laws be not in harmony with her spiritual laws? Man has not two separate beings; his acts in mundane affairs cannot be set apart; and since all his acts have a moral significance, all contribute to purify or stain his soul. The State, which regards only his worldly life, is evidently incompetent, unless it be guided by the Church, to lead that life into the path of salvation. The State, therefore, must be the steward of the Church. If any precedents were needed they could be quickly found; did not the Old Testament record the dealings of God with his chosen people, whose government was theocratic? and even among the pagan Romans, was not the Emperor *pontifex maximus*, the nominal religious head of the Empire? And to the record of history the Roman hierarchs had already begun to add the authority of forged decretals, and had concocted traditions which an uncritical age easily mistook for genuine.

Many things combined to make Hildebrand's scheme appear realizable. The Church had already large possessions in Italy, over which she ruled as temporal sovereign. The creation of the College of Cardinals in 1059 permanently established a small and exclusive aristocracy in the Church, and seemed to assure the election of Popes who would carry out a uniform policy. The rise of several independent kingdoms over which the Emperor could not maintain his sovereignty tempted the Church to usurp the position of arbiter and peacemaker among them. The Emperors themselves seemed to acknowledge, in the ceremony of consecration, that they derived their authority from the spiritual power. Hildebrand, quick to perceive the opportunity which two centuries had slowly prepared, was quick to seize it. He boldly proclaimed his theocratic system.

Thus rose the Papacy, a temporal institution governed by ecclesiastics, who in their struggle for its aggrandizement equipped themselves with weapons spiritual and weapons material. At first they hoped to bring all Western Europe under their sway, but gradually they had to content themselves with the possession of a part of Central Italy. The Emperors from the outset resisted their encroachment. They refused to confirm bishops whom the Popes installed in German dioceses contrary to their wishes; again and again they descended with strong armies into Italy, to compel the arrogant pontiff to retreat into his legitimate position. Many the expeditions, long the wars over investitures, varying the fortunes; but on the whole, the Popes triumphed. They did not, indeed, win the temporal control over the northern kingdoms, but they retained their mastery over the ecclesiastical organization in them, and prevented the formation of national churches. Hildebrand kept Henry IV barefoot and shivering for three days and nights at Canossa, ere he would allow him to appear in his presence and beg for forgiveness. Frederick Barbarossa, the most puissant monarch since Charlemain, was haughty in defiance; yet he too humbled himself, and on the steps of the Church of St. Mark in Venice he fell at the feet of Alexander III and was granted pardon.[1] A strenuous Emperor might depose a hostile Pope, but his victory was only transient; for the Emperors were confronted by an invisible policy, — the same yesterday, to-day, and forever, and not to be exterminated by the displacement of whosoever happened to be its temporary spokesman. In every diocese, in every parish, were the upholders of that policy, and they could not be silenced. On the whole, then, the prestige of the Empire was shattered against the invisible armor of Rome, but the spiritual influence of the Popes declined in proportion as they rose to be worldly monarchs. The idea of the Papacy, shorn and discredited, has survived down to the present time, although there have been but six or seven Popes in as many centuries with sufficient personal force to realize in small measure, and for a brief season, the earth-embracing dream of Hildebrand.

When at length Western Christendom emerged from the Middle Age, what was the condition of its inhabitants? With what power did men battle with this life? With what faith did they apprehend the life to come? How had a thousand years of Roman Christianity and half as many years of Feudalism left them? There can be no doubt, I think, that the average European of the thirteenth century was on a lower plane than the Roman citizen of the second century had been. He had a smaller respect for law, a duller sense of justice. He had not yet learned to curb his brutal passions: he still relied upon

---

[1] In much later times, Joseph II of Austria thought that he could strengthen his empire by breaking free from Roman interference; but after a few years he surrendered, and Austria has been since then the most servile daughter of the Church. Even Napoleon, even Bismarck, after a highhanded resistance, saw the advantage, if not the need, of compromising with the Vatican.

physical strength as the test of right and the criterion of honor. He was cut off from political activity; he had almost wholly lost touch with nature. His religion was partly superstitious, partly fanatical, administered by a corrupt or an ignorant priesthood, who made piety to consist in the performance of certain stipulated outward acts. The Popes, like the Roman Emperors, had arrogated to themselves a sort of divinity. The religious rites were, to the eye of Reason, not a whit less fantastic than the sacrifice of the flamens or the auspices of the augurs. The pagan worship of minor gods was perpetuated in the Catholic worship of saints. The subtle, circular arguments of the theologians — the speculations as to the color of God's beard, and as to whether Christ ascended naked or clothed into Heaven — were sterile and foolish compared with the spiritual discussions of the Neo-platonists and the ethical precepts of the later Stoics. If the Church restrained society at all, hers was a restraint of terror. She scared men with menaces of damnation, rather than drew them to virtue by the sweet persuasiveness of love. Hell seemed so inevitable that it became necessary to build an antechamber to it, a Purgatory, whence souls had a chance to escape, in spite of their sinfulness, into Heaven. Fear lies very deep in the human heart, so deep as to be an elemental instinct; no wonder, therefore, that Romanism and Calvinism — the two forms of Christianity that have bound men most firmly — clinched their doctrinal fetters in this instinct of fear. God a tyrant, religion a terror, — that is the upshot of mediæval Christianity. Neither poet, nor seer, nor saint, has yet drawn a picture of Heaven that satisfies the soul: nothing better have they foreshadowed than an eternity spent in playing harps, wearing crowns, and singing hosannas. And, indeed, no prognostic can be drawn of everlasting bliss, because the divine desire of the soul yearns for infinite expansion in ways which it cannot even surmise:

whereas the outlines of the theologic vision are finite, fixed, monotonous, — and bliss shuns limits and monotony. But of Hell, on the other hand, representations so vivid have been conceived, that millions with but a vague notion of Heaven have believed in the reality of Hell. Hell is material and physical, and since the first man scorched his fingers in fire, the dullest have understood that a place in which flames rage forever and burn without destroying the whole body is a place to be avoided. By keeping this terror vividly present, the Roman Church became and has remained a dominant religion, and it was in possessing this dread that the mediæval man differed most widely from the man of pagan Rome.

In spite of this deterrent neither the mediæval man, nor his posterity for many generations, rose in many respects above the plane where natural passions have full sway: his lust, his anger, his selfishness, his pride, his cunning, were the impulses he obeyed. Seldom can you find, in all the wars and intrigues which make up the history of a long period, motives higher than those of a well-developed animal. Emerging from the Middle Age, man was losing that religious enthusiasm which expressed itself in the building of cathedrals and in the Crusades; his creed which, so long as it had been unreflectingly emotional, had not wanted picturesqueness, was now poured into the rigid matrix of theology. Superstition, which like the naïve guesses of children had had a certain charm, was now, through the casuistry of schoolmen's logic, declared to be demonstrable truth. Faith had become a dogma, and worship was becoming a commercial transaction. The Church had marked off a little patch of knowledge, beyond which there was nothing to know: in that the inquirer might get what fodder he could, although, truth to tell, the grass had long since been nibbled to the roots. Or we may picture him as a caged squirrel, whirling in his wire wheel and never advancing, while just outside is freedom, — the broad branches of the pines, the shagbarks with their nuts, the oaks with their acorns. To wonder why he was content with this confinement, why the universe could not stir his curiosity, is to fail to comprehend him; the mediæval man was bent on getting to heaven, and was taught that everything of earth would delay his journey thither; the Church knew the mystic watchword, the *Open sesame* which would unlock Peter's door; to know that rendered all other knowledge as unnecessary as would be a whole dictionary of words to a merchant who knew the combination of letters which unlocks the safe where his treasure is stored. The layman lacked even the formal juiceless training of the clerics; many of the princes whose renown still survives could not write their names. The earth, whose laws it behooves us to study if we would not be crushed by them, was still under the ban. The Mosaic fables and the Ptolemaic guesses were the only keys to nature's mysteries. Science, whether of experiment or observation, was not: criticism was not: because tradition, which acts on the reason like laughing-gas on the brain, put the reason to sleep and produced phantasmagoric dreaming. The curious who pried into physical secrets were accused of practicing the Black Art, because Satan alone, it was believed, knew the mechanism of the physical world. Sorcery, witchcraft, ordeals, alchemy, astrology, — these are some of the rubrics under which the superstitions of that age might be described. This uncritical state of mind fostered the growth of all sorts of incongruities, of miracles in religion, of legends in history. The Church was the sole judge of truth, and she quashed any investigation that might conflict with her assumptions. Much that was fanciful and picturesque casts a glamour over this strange period, in which romancers have found those contrasts which surprise and charm the imagination; but it was, nevertheless, a period of passage which bequeathed to posterity no information in religion, politics, or sociology, by which later men could steer with profit. Those are the great epochs, and those only, in which Reason, untrammeled by arbitrary tethers, unprejudiced by partisanship and tradition, looks Fact squarely in the eyes and discovers Truth there; and the truths so discovered are of imperishable value to mankind.

It is a law of human progress that a strong habit or institution can be overcome only by something stronger. On this principle depends the conservation of society and the sequence of character; for if men and nations changed suddenly, either for better or worse, life would be unstable, lawless, a thing of weather-cocks. Furthermore, a system which may have been the best possible in one era — and we cannot deny that Feudalism and Catholicism were such — becomes harmful and a hindrance when altered conditions have suggested a system better adapted to the new needs and ideals of mankind. Modern history narrates the struggle between men bent on reorganizing society according to new ideals, and men who, satisfied with the old, regard the new as dangerous. To the former, change wears the aspect of life and growth, to the latter of dissolution and death.

The inventory of the legacies bequeathed by the Middle Age to the modern world contains first a Church claiming to be catholic and infallible. The product of a semi-barbarous and uncritical age, — the fruit of Hebraism grafted on the decaying trunk of Roman Imperialism, — she preserved the dogmas and discipline which enabled her to overcome myth-beguiled and violent barbarians. After the fourth century, when the old Roman civilization dissolved and the very existence of social order was imperiled, this Church tamed the hordes which repeopled Europe and diffused principles of unity among them. These conditions no longer exist. Reason and not Authority is now the rule by which, in theory at least, men govern their affairs; but in the course of this history we shall see how the Roman Church, still clinging to the methods which proved potent over the heathen of the sixth century, and sufficed for the monks and schoolmen of the twelfth, erects her authority in the face of the nineteenth century, and forgets that only by Reason can Reason be vanquished. And as if it were not labor enough to fight with antiquated weapons for her spiritual supremacy, she would compel the modern world to recognize her carnal offspring, the temporal Papacy, begotten amid conditions long ago obsolete.

The second mediæval heirloom is the idea of monarchical government: the assumption that a king rules by divine right, that he is the fountain of honor and source of justice, that his will is absolute law, so that he may dispose of the service, property, and lives of his subjects as suits his whim. As a corollary from this is the division of society into three classes, nobility and clergy forming the privileged class, merchants or bourgeoisie the middle class, and peasants and common laborers the lowest or servile class. Only the king is his own master; all the others in some sense belong to him.

A wonderful scheme. Upper class did not work, unless the performance of Church ceremonies and the fighting of battles were work: yet both nobles and clergy, whether they were idle or diligent, received tithes and taxes. Middle class worked with the head, and enjoyed what wealth remained to it after paying tribute to king, count, and Church. Lower class worked with the hand, yet was of no more account than cattle which worked with the hoof; for all its products, after deducting enough wool for its homespun jerkin and enough wheat for its daily loaf, passed upward to enrich its superiors. Labor is the law of life; every man must earn his food, apparel, and lodging; the gods do not give, they lend, and men must repay their loan; happiness itself, if attained at all, can be attained only through work; but the Feudal scheme bestowed the highest rewards on those who did not toil, while demeaning the many who with head or hand toiled for the privileged few. The law of primogeniture kept great estates intact, and transmitted titles to idleness from generation to generation, by making birth a lottery, in which the first-born drew the grand prize and his younger brothers drew blanks. Finally, woman held a position inferior to man in society and before the law; the singers of chivalry had lifted her above the level of mere sexual companionship, but she was in fact treated as a subordinate, and could not be treated otherwise in a system framed by men who, as warriors, looked upon women as weak but pleasant solaces during the unheroic interludes of peace, or who, as priests, regarded them as decoys set by the Devil to entrap pilgrims on their way to heaven.

These are among the bequests and posthumous influences which the modern world has received from mediæval times, ancestral taints and hereditary diseases from which Europe has not yet wholly purged herself. What was beneficent died with its season, leaving its husk, its symbol, to deceive mankind. When the Cid was dead, they clad his body in his armor, and put his good sword Colada in his hand, and set him upon his steed Bavieca, and then, a squire sustaining the corpse on each side, they led him forth from the city; and at sight of him approaching, the army of the Saracens were seized with fear and fled while the hero was still afar off. Verily, most tenacious among men is the worship of a symbol after its reality has vanished. Look at Europe at any moment during the past ages, and see how ghosts bearing great names and dummies dressed in royal garments have lorded it over her. At Rome, for instance, see the mightiest symbol,— the Pope; in reality he should be meek, unselfish, pure, spiritual, as becomes the successor of Peter the Fisherman and the representative of Jesus of Nazareth; but

Popes long since exchanged humility for a monarch's pomp; they have been by turns worldly, proud, licentious, cruel, ignorant, — as far removed from the Christlike ideal as their hell from heaven; and yet being clothed in the symbol, they have had the reverence which the reality once drew to it. The pontiff cannot foretell whether he shall live to behold to-morrow's sun, nevertheless the keys of eternity jangle on his girdle. Or look at that other symbol, — the Holy Roman Emperor; that, too, was a reality in Charlemain; it meant an invincible conqueror, a wise legislator; it meant a ruler strong enough to yoke order upon the turbulence of Western Christendom; it stood for prudent counsel and power to enforce it. But when Charlemain died, only his name, like a mantle, survived, to be worn by men who had barely a province loyal to them, or by weaklings unfit for camp and council, until even boys were swaddled in its folds. And yet the sight of that symbol inspired some of that awe which originally only Charlemain could inspire, as if some of his vigor had been diffused through his imperial robes, there to lie latent for ages. And only a little while ago men were among us who as schoolboys learned the name of the then reigning Emperor, and who remembered when the news came that the very symbol of the Holy Roman Empire was no more. And so with the other titles which distinguish the peerage of modern Europe: the duke was originally the leader of an army, a skilful general and brave fighter; the count was the Emperor's companion, chosen for valor or shrewdness; the marquis was the Emperor's deputy, charged to defend the march between the Empire and barbarians. But these titles became hereditary, and sons who had no soldierly qualities decked themselves in symbols their sires had made significant; till by and by the court dandies and rich merchants and the bastards of royal mistresses wore the honors once intended for champions in war. The Emperor likewise was served by a cupbearer, a steward, a marshal, and a chamberlain; and these titles also were bestowed later upon courtiers who had never raised a goblet (except to their own lips), or borne a platter, or groomed a horse, or made a bed. In many other instances we might point out how Reality slipped away from its symbol, with the consequent perversion and misapplication of symbols, and the gradual dulling of the senses to Reality; but in the Roman Church, as elaborated by mediæval theologians, and in the monarchical institution of modern times, we have the best illustrations of the pertinacity of symbols. The veneration paid to the relics of departed saints, and to the robes and titles of living potentates, is the expression of one of the strongest instincts of human nature, — the tendency, that is, to mistake the symbol for the reality, the body for the soul, the letter for the spirit. Nevertheless, " the letter killeth, but the spirit giveth life."

CHAPTER IV.

MANY REPUBLICS, BUT NO NATION.

WE have thus far measured roughly the trunk of that new society which sprang up in Europe after the fall of the Western Empire, — a tree rooted in the soil of Teutonism and manured by the decaying Roman civilization: for Providence, to whom nothing is waste, uses corrupt races, like dead leaves, to fertilize exhausted human nature for other crops. We must now examine more particularly the branch which earliest stretched out from that trunk; we must confine ourselves to the development of the Italian people. Why was it that Italy, the first country to revive, did not revive as a nation? We see plainly enough that the principle of nationality was shaping the people of the North into distinct States, and that, by the end of the Middle Age, these States had a recognized existence: why was it that the Italians, so superior to the northerners at the start, failed to attain national unity? Three causes opposed the tendency to a national union in Italy and doomed her to a thousand years of thraldom, discord, and shame: these were first, the Papacy, which, in spite of its Italian origin and methods, strove to extend its sway over Christendom, instead of confining itself to the peninsula; second, the Empire, whose head, a foreigner, being the nominal King of Italy, brooked no native rival; and third, the astonishingly rapid development of small States, from the Alps to Sicily.

In no other country in the world, not even in Greece, has a race manifested so varied a sensibility as in Italy. The wonderful keenness, delicacy, and energy of the Italian character, responsive to the smallest diversity of place and condition, blossomed in new forms of individuality, each differing from the rest. At a time when England or France had hardly one centre from which the national life-blood pulsated through all the members of the people, in Italy there were a score of such centres, each distinct, each throbbing with life. Indeed, there were too many hearts, too many little republics; the competition among them was too incessant; the area from which each drew its sustenance was too narrow. Having exhausted their own store, they fell to devouring each other, till tyrants mightier and more rapacious than they came and found them an easy quarry. This marvelous individuality, so intense and productive of splendid monuments in art, in religion, in government, in literature, was the glory of Italy, and insured for her the everlasting interest of men. But she bought distinction at the expense of her political independence, and she, who led the nations to that modern civilization out of which they have drawn their freedom, was destined not to be free. Like a discoverer, whose genius had added to the power and wealth and happiness of mankind, she was condemned to live poor and forlorn.

More than once in the early age was she teased by the delusive prospect of independence. At the dissolution of the Western Empire, Odoacer united the peninsula in his Ostrogothic kingdom, which Theodoric, the first of the barbarians who displayed talents of administration, strengthened. But at his death, Justinian, the Eastern Emperor, reasserted his claims in Italy, and dispatched thither first Belisarius and then Narses, who routed Theodoric's heirs and brought their possessions under the rule of Byzantine exarchs. Justinian died, and another Teutonic tribe, the Lombards, settled in Northern Italy; they were fierce and lawless, but nevertheless they had force, — the first element of superiority, — and they might in time have been tamed into civilization through the influence of the people they had conquered. But just as they were becoming paramount, the Pope, harassed and terrified by their encroachments, sent over the Alps and besought Charles Martel to hasten to his assistance. Gregory III is the name of this pontiff who set the example of calling foreigners into Italy, — a precedent followed century after century, till the ruin of the country was complete. Charles Martel died before he could punish the Lombards, but his son Pepin, and his grandson Charlemain, obeyed similar calls, and reduced the Lombards to the condition of vassals. Italy became a fief of the Emperor, who was crowned king at Milan. When Charlemain's dominion fell in pieces, Italy was left in confusion; almost abandoned by her nominal sovereign, she was the victim of the ambition of her native princes, who fought to possess her. Again it seemed likely that an Italian, descended from the Lombard princes, would establish himself as king; but a strong Emperor, Otto I, marched against him, humbled him, renewed the compact between the Empire and the Church, and left a terrible warning for all future aspirants. Otto it was who fixed those relations between the Emperor and the Pope which formed the basis of mediæval polity and were the cause of mediæval conflicts. The Popes, as we have seen, gained in this struggle; but they had the aggrandizement of the Papacy, and not the welfare of Italy, in view. Had they dreamed of uniting the Italians in one State, they would have been prevented by the Italians themselves; for local competition was too vehement to allow the republics to merge their individual privileges for the sake of a larger collective freedom. To secure advantages for itself, by propitiating now the Emperor and now the Pope, according as the one or the other happened to be uppermost, was therefore the policy of each republic.

Thus in Italy there was no general movement towards national coherence. There sprang up no dynasty, — like that of the Capets in France, or of Wessex in England, or of the Saxons in Germany, — to arouse in the Italians the sense of a common fatherland, broader than the frontiers of any province, and including the interests of every district. There was, instead, a bourgeoning of many separate communities, in almost any one of which flourished a higher civilization than could then be found north of the Alps. As early as the time of Charlemain, the Greek cities of Southern Italy prospered. Their ships traded with Constantinople and the Levant. The coin of Amalfi passed current along the shores of the Mediterranean. The School of Medicine at Salerno [1] had already, in the ninth century, a wide reputation. When the Norman invasion crippled these southern States, — so small, but sturdy, — others came to their growth in the north, Pisa first, then Genoa and Venice. The sea wonderfully promotes enterprises in those who dwell along its shores. Its paths lead to all countries; its severities and dangers toughen the body and call forth presence of mind and fortitude. Thus its children, the seafaring nations, have been brave and alert, and by their intercourse with other people they have escaped the stagnation of pastoral life. Amalfi and Pisa, Genoa and Venice, these were the mediæval children of the sea: breathing its strong salt air and shrinking not from its stern hazards, they acquired some of the inexhaustible energy of the ocean itself. Each was an example of the quickness and sane vigor with which the new Italian race threw itself into the work of mastering the obstacles amid which it was placed, and of drawing from them, as from a quarry, the materials of a new civilization.

But not alone along its seaboard was Italy active. Her inland towns had suffered less than her rural districts from the Teutonic inundation. It is a common error to

---

[1] For an account of this earliest European university, see Coppi: *Le Università Italiane nel Medio Evo* (Florence. 1880).

suppose that the barbarians exterminated the peoples
whom they conquered; nowhere was this true, in Italy
least of all. Their position there has been aptly likened
to that of the English conquerors in India, under the
Mogul Empire; "they were in it, but not of it."[1] Inferior in numbers to their subjects, they gradually became
fused with them. The Teuton was merely a fighter, but
he quickly perceived that the wealth which was his prize
in Italy depended upon the preservation of a system of
agriculture, industry, and law that had been perfected by
the vanquished race. He was shrewd enough not to destroy those who possessed the key to this system, — a key
which unlocked the treasure he coveted. He had brought
his own tribal laws, but these, complicated, fluctuating,
and unwritten, disappeared before the permanent and
clearly codified laws of Rome. He had brought his own
gods, but these, too, vanished before the new religion of
Rome. He felt the mighty spell of learning, — that intangible power which survives the shock of armies and
looks disdainfully upon the rude triumphs of brute force,
— and he knew that only from his subjects was that
learning to be had. A king he was, but a king dependent upon counselors who excelled him in everything
except physical strength. Thus was he moulded on all
sides by the subtle influence of the race he had overcome.
The Roman had been mastered by the culture of his
Greek bondsmen, so that the most eminent Augustan
works seem only to echo the deathless Athenian voices:
in like manner, but even more completely, the Teuton
in Italy was absorbed in the survival of Roman civilization.

In Italy, moreover, feudalism took a weaker hold than
in the Transalpine countries. The absence of a stalwart
sovereign favored the growth of many small States. The
cities had never quite lost the municipal and legal customs

[1] R. W. Church: *The Beginning of the Middle Ages*, p 19.

handed down from imperial times, and they were therefore fitted for the rapid expansion of civic life. Each city had its count, the nominal representative of the Emperor, and its bishop, who derived his authority from the Pope; and it was natural that these two rulers should strive to outwit each other, and that the burghers should gain concessions for themselves by supporting now one and now the other. Like a household in which the father and mother having quarreled, the spoilt child gets permission from one parent to do what the other forbids, so the citizens of Lombardy or Tuscany profited by the rivalry between the Empire and the Papacy. During the twelfth century the towns were, with but few exceptions, on the side of the Pope, as the master to be less feared. Frederick Barbarossa, the mediæval sovereign whom history and legend agree in honoring next after Charlemain, came into Italy to subdue the rebellious Lombard cities. At the first onset he succeeded; Milan was destroyed after a cruel siege; Crema, her ally, also fell. For Milan's neighbors, jealous of her supremacy, had looked on with malicious satisfaction while she suffered; but by the light of her burning dwellings they saw their own danger. For the first time in their history Italians forgot their local spites, recognized a common duty to each other, and formed a league. They helped to rebuild Milan, and then prepared to fight together for freedom. Frederick returned, full of wrath and confident of victory. The Milanese, who had time to summon only a few allies from Piacenza, Verona, Brescia, and Novara, met him at Legnano, May 29, 1176. The Germans had almost conquered, when they were checked by a band of brave youths, who called themselves the Company of Death. The waverers rallied; from resisting they advanced, and the Germans in their turn wavered, then retreated, then fled. Frederick himself barely escaped capture; his camp was pillaged, his army dispersed. For the first time Italians had fought man to man with foreign invaders and routed them; for the first time, and almost for the last, until the present century.

That victory of Legnano might have been the harbinger of a new era for Italy. The patriotism then kindled might have welded the States in the north into a confederation, which should have gradually stretched southward; but there were too many forces eager to shatter such a fabric. The Pope, though he rejoiced at his adversary's humiliation, in nowise intended that the cities should pass out of his own control: and the cities, having wrested large concessions from Frederick, fell to wrangling amongst themselves. The danger from abroad being surmounted, they dissolved their union, and each pressed forward in its own concerns, striving to outrun its neighbor, and unscrupulous in the choice of means by which to circumvent or to excel him. During two hundred years, Northern and Central Italy were torn by the quarrels of factions, in which city raised its arm against city, and brother against brother. It was as if a vehement wind contended against a strong tide. Two great parties — the Guelfs (Pope) and the Ghibellines (Emperor) — divided the allegiance of the contestants; but in each town local feuds and family ambitions gave a different complexion to the struggle. A tiff between lovers, a dispute between merchants, a fancied insult, a suspected encroachment, — these were trifles sufficient to set a whole province in a blaze which burned luridly long after its cause was consumed and forgotten.

Nevertheless, we can discern amid this incessant confusion that mighty changes were unfolding. The cities, despite wars, grew rich, and their control passed from the old nobles, whose titles had originated with the Pope or the Emperor, into the hands of the merchants and tradesmen. These, organizing in arts or guilds, chose representatives who administered the commonwealth and were amenable to all the citizens. The government was therefore popular, or republican, but no longer stable. The passion for freedom was impetuous, but not yet tolerant. Restless competition and pitiless strife sharpened the wits, and quickened that tendency to strong individuality which had already been set in motion by the varieties of interest, place, and tradition. Characters remarkable for their intensity, deeds conspicuous for their heroism or their wickedness, astonish us wherever we look into that epoch. The monotony of the Middle Age had been succeeded by an unexampled diversity; its grim seriousness had been broken by the loud laughter of the Goliardi; instead of masses drifting sluggishly, we behold individuals, sharply defined and strong, each rushing with the turbulence of a mountain torrent. But as civic power descended to lower and lower levels, it became more and more unstable, till at last it reached the rabble, always fickle, always ready to hearken to demagogues. Swift changes, tumults, proscriptions, and at last exhaustion, — that is the inevitable sequence in the degeneration of popular governments; and when exhaustion supervenes, the tyrant steps in. By the beginning of the fourteenth century, the energy of the Italian republics was spent: each lay panting for the strong man to come to take from it that fatal gift of liberty which it had not known how to preserve.

Yet how rich, how surpassing rich, was the Italian genius at that time! Its political experiments, so brilliant and so instructive, gave but one outlet to that versatile and fervent nature. Within a hundred years appeared Thomas Aquinas, the "angelic doctor," who dressed Roman theology in the garb it wears to-day; Niccolò the Pisan, earliest of modern sculptors; Arnolfo, the first in time and all but the first in achievement of modern architects; Giotto, who left one of the perfect buildings in the world, and whose inexhaustible imagination outlined the types for three centuries of painters; Dante, the world-poet; Petrarch, the man of universal erudition, and the singer of the deathless sonnets; Boccaccio, the father of modern prose. These are names which, viewed individually, shine among the brightest in the constellations of Art and Learning; but they represent more than themselves, more than the isolated achievements of genius.[1] A whole race expressed itself through them, — a race sensitive to the least touch of beauty, brimming with the wine of passion, trained and stimulated and disenthralled by all varieties of experience. At last, after more than a thousand years of silence or stammering, the human spirit had again a voice. It spoke through many forms of art and literature, religion was its oracle, the great universities were its mouthpieces, new forms of government were its tribune, and still there remained to it messages to be expressed through the humble daily affairs of men. The Italians were the pioneers in commerce, they organized a banking system,[2] they were probably the first to write policies of insurance. Their merchants and fabrics were known in all the marts of Europe; the florin of Florence[3] and the ducat of Venice circulated from London in the West to Samarcand in the East. Manners, which sweeten and smooth social intercourse, by marking out a neutral ground where personalities the most antagonistic can meet without clashing, were already far advanced in refinement among the Italians, at a time when German princes and English barons were still uncouth. Even upon tools and household utensils this pervasive and exuberant spirit left its mark of grace, wedding utility to beauty, were it only in the manufacture of a hinge or of a lantern. Such was the activity of the Italian spirit, in spite of incessant unrest, and of the lack of a concerted national life.

[1] Remark that all these, except St. Thomas, were Tuscans. The elder Villani, the earliest modern historian, might be added to the list.

[2] The Bank of Venice was founded in 1171.

[3] The first florin was coined in 1252.

CHAPTER V.

DANTE.

OF Dante we must speak, however briefly, because neither the character of the Italians nor the subsequent history of Italy can be understood, unless the genius and influence of Dante be in some measure computed. Whether you look at him as poet or as man, he is equally wonderful, and it was his fortune to undergo the mysteries of mortality at a unique period in the progress of mankind. Other great men, — David, Pericles, Cæsar, Shakespeare, Molière, Goethe, — coming at a great moment in their country's political or intellectual development, stand forever as its representative and epitome: but Dante is more than this; he is not only the consummation of Florentine genius, not only the exemplar of the Italian race, but he embodies one form of European civilization, and he leads the way to the next. His poem is alike the most vivid and varied record of mediæval conditions, and the noblest expression of the only European religion which has deserved the name Catholic. In that poem you may read the actual life of Dante's contemporaries and the ideal life towards which the purest of them aspired. It was possible for him to know all that was known in his time — good fortune which, owing to the continual widening and particularization of knowledge, has been denied to his successors; so we may say truly of his erudition that it was universal. But erudition of itself is impotent: how many of the erudite have we not seen bending under a huge burden of facts, but palsied in will and shriveled in heart, to die at last famished, like the ass in the fable, powerless to reach the sack of meal strapped on his back? Dante had learning and much more than learning; he had passion and imagination, the poet's supreme equipment: and he had experience with life on many levels; and thus he transmuted scholasticism, theology, statecraft, into living realities, making allegories concrete, and turning the concrete deeds of men into symbols of wide and perpetual significance.

That "Divine Comedy" of his was the emancipation and warrant of the modern intellect. Twelve hundred years had elapsed since Europe had been ennobled by a masterpiece. The colossal fragments of classical literature astonished and discouraged the mediæval mind; for the power which created them seemed to have vanished along with the youth of the world. The doom of inferiority was evident and men accepted it, until Dante's epic broke the spell of the Past. Let Greece bring her Homer and Rome her Virgil, here was their peer, who, speaking a new tongue, bore witness to a genius as inexhaustible, as lofty, as any in antiquity. Dante wavered, it is said, between writing in Latin and writing in Italian: by choosing Italian, he gave a patent of nobility to every modern language. The vernacular had been hitherto a sort of Cinderella, a household drudge, good enough for singing rustic songs and legends, good enough for kitchen gossip and peasant wooing, whilst Latin and Greek, the two proud sisters, read learned books in the parlor, and talked theology with the bishop in his palace.[1] Dante, like the prince in the fairy tale, came and made a princess of the despised one. In so doing he confirmed the European tendency towards national life, of which language is the most obvious outward sign: the popular

---

[1] I need hardly remind the reader that in Dante's time Greek was unknown to Italian scholars; they read Aristotle and Homer in Latin translations.

speech in England, France, Spain, Germany, and Italy became the vehicle for literary expression, as well as the medium for daily intercourse, and although Latin was employed by scholars down to the eighteenth century, the most precious works of literature since Dante's time have been written in the language spoken and understood by the people. The Italian sonnets of Petrarch are as fresh as the sweet notes of nightingale or throstle, whereas his Latin epic is as mute as some antediluvian bird, some epiornis, whose huge skeleton is dug from its sepulchre of primeval slime; a few ringing songs of Ulrich von Hutten outlive the learned sarcasms of Erasmus. Thus in its form "The Divine Comedy" is an epoch-making book; indeed, none other in literature so well deserves that title; for it authorized the new peoples to write after their own fashion, unabashed by antique precedents, and it determined the utterance of Chaucer and Cervantes, of Camoëns and Montaigne.

In its subject, also, it is equally original. The great poets of antiquity had sung the exploits of legendary heroes, the fortunes of princely families, the passions of very human gods: Dante wrote the epic of the human soul. Here is a theme which, for reality and interest, surpasses all the rest. The conflict in the soul between good and evil, — what Trojan War, what Battle of Giants, is so awful as that? The progress of the soul through the hell, purgatory, and paradise of earthly experience, — its wrestling with temptation, its alliance with virtue, its vision of a perfection hovering, beautiful but elusive, along the future's horizon, — what Odyssey is so impressive, so varied as that? And Dante illustrates this universal moral order, not by cold, dead abstractions, but by living examples; he shows pride and lust, loving-kindness and sanctity, as we all know them, through individuals. He ransacks past and present for specimens of every variety of character. He tells us, in words how few but how indelible, what each one did, and we know from the deed what each one was. In that work of his, Mediævalism and Catholicism are summed up: a world-polity and a world-religion utter their highest message to mankind. But there is in "The Divine Comedy" something deeper, something more permanent than any social or religious system: there is in it the imperishable substance of human nature, out of which all creeds and systems are woven, and into which they all dissolve. The Mediævalism, except as a symbol, is obsolete; the Catholicism affronts our modern reason; the philosophy sounds strange to our modern ears; but we can strip all these away without impairing the essential worth beneath; having done so, we shall perceive that under those transient forms one of the four or five men who have seen farthest and clearest into the mystery of life is dealing with that which perpetually concerns the soul. Time shall make our own conclusions on these themes ancient; the language wherein our philosophy is clothed shall look awkward and outlandish to posterity, just as the scholastic dialect looks to our eyes; but then, as now, he who studies the pages of Dante shall learn the most important of lessons, *come l' uom s' eterna*, — how man makes his life eternal, by mastering the appetites of the flesh, by denying self, and by cleaving to those ideals of the spirit which neither wane nor die, but rise in ever-widening spires towards the empyrean of all-embracing and immortal Truth; the life which lifts man above the shock and accident and baseness of earthly existence, and fits him to depart trustfully, equipped for the possibilities which eternity hides.

"Follow thou thy star, thou shalt not fail of a glorious haven,"[1] that is Dante's counsel to all men; to his countrymen he spoke further, according to their needs. It is as a national hero and an influence, rather than as a poet,

[1] *Inferno*, xv. 55, 56.

that he should be treated by the historian of modern Italy. Not only was he "the Father of the Tuscan tongue," but he was also the prophet of an Italy in which the cruelty and corruption of tyrants should cease, of an Italy in which, under one wise and just ruler, the cities of the hills and the cities of the plain and the sea should live in peace and mutual helpfulness. Dante did not, indeed, dream of a nation independent of the Empire, but he pleaded for a united nation, having its own laws and governors, guided and protected by the Emperor. And, what was most important, he denounced the temporal covetousness of the Papacy as unholy; he denounced the Decretals, not because they were forged, — that was not known in his time, — but because they degraded the Church, by converting it into a monster of simony and worldliness; he denounced the irreverence of placing Tradition on an equality with the Scriptures: he denounced the lewdness and pride of those who, sitting in the chair of St. Peter and representing Christ on earth, forsook things spiritual for things carnal, and used their sacred office as a net wherewith to catch the bribes of Mammon or as a cloak to hide their profligate lives. Graven ineffaceably in Dante's epic was this truth, reiterated by every sage and every prophet, that wealth and power, which minister to the desires of the senses, poison and pervert the spirit. This truth, easily verifiable in the case of each particular soul, Dante applied to the Church, the universal soul of Christendom. He cried out against pastors who turned their shepherd's crooks into swords, and who through avarice had become as wolves. In the circle of Hell where simoniacs are punished, he placed Nicholas III, and rebuked him and all Popes like him: "Ye have made you a god of gold and silver: and what difference is there between you and the idolater save that he worships one and ye a hundred? Ah, Constantine! of how much ill was mother, not thy conversion, but that dowry which the first rich Father received from thee!"[1]

So unerring was Dante's moral sense that hardly one of the judgments pronounced by him have been set aside. In so far as he believed that the government of the world by one spiritual and one temporal sovereign was still possible, he was the spokesman of the highest mediæval ideal; but in declaring that Church and State must be independent, and that the Pope defiled his spiritual functions in usurping the prerogatives of the Emperor, Dante was the forerunner of the wisest statesmen and purest moralists of modern times. And thus his "Divine Comedy" became to his countrymen a political Bible, in which they learned the cause of their evils and the remedies for them. It was so mighty a book that neither Popes nor tyrants nor inquisitors could suppress it. It was the delight of the scholar and the comfort of the patriot; to the earnest it brought wisdom which "is conversant with the mysteries of the knowledge of God." Its phrases became household words, and dignified the speech of peasants. No other book, except the Bible in Protestant countries, has so completely saturated the thoughts of a whole people. Wherever it was read, there were heard, as if issuing from a holy oracle, condemnation of the hate and jealousy which kept Italians asunder, and of princes who strangled liberty, and that awful judgment on Popes who made their holy offices like to the scarlet woman prophesied in the Apocalypse, "the habitation of devils, and the hold of every foul spirit, and a cage of every unclean and hateful bird: for all nations have drunk of the wine of the wrath of her fornication, and the kings of the earth have committed fornication with her, and the merchants of the earth are waxed rich through the abundance of her delicacies."[2]

[1] *Inferno*, xix, 112-117, Norton's translation.
[2] *Revelation* xviii. 2, 3.

"The Divine Comedy" became a Bible for the Italians: by that fact we measure the majesty and the wisdom and the truthfulness of the man. So firm was his integrity and so intense his spirituality, that he strengthened and purified whatsoever souls came fully under his influence. With the vehemence of Paul, he had the catholicity of Shakespeare. Men call him a Ghibelline, or a White, to specify certain phases of his activity, as they give names to the bays and inlets of the ocean; but his nature overflowed the coast-line of partisanship. During five centuries, wherever there was an Italian who amid civil discords longed for harmony and under oppression longed for freedom, and who, despite the pettiness and abominations of his time, still kept his soul pure and his aims high, there was found a disciple of Dante. The patriot, languishing in some Austrian dungeon, or wandering in exile along the banks of the Thames or the La Plata, refreshed his fortitude by the words and example of that other exile who had tasted "the salt bread of strangers" and abandoned "everything beloved," and who yet had exclaimed, "Can I not from any corner of the earth behold the sun and stars? Can I not everywhere under the heavens meditate the all-sweet truths, except I first make myself ignoble?"[1] And the statesman who was to achieve the independence and unification of Italy only summed up the policy of Dante in that phrase forever memorable, "A free Church in a free State."

Thus briefly must we speak — and on this subject much would be little — concerning the unique position of Dante in the literature of Europe and in the history of Italy, because it is more important to understand him than to know by heart the brawls and revolutions which tormented Italy from the twelfth to the sixteenth century. His influence flows, like the Nile, through each later age, ready to fertilize the souls of men. At times, his coun-

[1] Letter to a Florentine Friend (*Epistolæ*, x).

trymen, like modern Egyptians, have gazed blankly at the mighty current; at times they have drawn life-giving water from it. And the river has flowed on, majestic and too deep for noise, bearing with it a force capable of regenerating a nation, and forming not only an unbroken connection between the past and the present, but also the one bond of union, the one common object of reverent admiration for the divided and factious Italians.

CHAPTER VI.

THE RENAISSANCE.

DANTE came, indeed, at the critical moment. Fifty years later his faith must have been less complete, his statecraft less certain. For then, instead of expressing the ideals of Catholicism and of mediæval Imperialism in their purity, he would have been troubled by the stirring of new influences, whose touch could not be resisted though their import was not yet clear. He would have seen that the Empire, to which he appealed as the universal peacemaker, having hopelessly lost its universality, was shrunk to be merely the appanage of a German prince; he would have seen the Church, no longer one and catholic, but split by a schism from which she never truly recovered; he would have seen the glory of free Florence already past meridian, and her liberty handed over to a foreign lord; he would have seen the other Italian republics, exhausted by feuds, fall into the clutches of cruel, selfish despots; above all, he would have felt the first exhilaration of Humanism, of that revival of learning which truly deserves the name New Birth, because the souls of men were born anew into a life of liberty and reason, through the rediscovery of the old learning.

We have so long enjoyed the results of this spiritual revolution that we can hardly realize the enthusiasm, the wonder and delight, which swept through the hearts of those who first felt its stress. You who have known the divine fervor of a love deep, pure, and irresistible,— when the old self drops away like a clod from the soul, and the world dances in gladness, and hope is infinite, and being is suffused with the radiance and tenderness of one Beloved, — you who have known this ecstasy of passion may perhaps understand the revelation which captivated and transformed the early Humanists. To these there came, as from the heaven of Truth, an angel, a messenger, with tidings of great joy.

"You have wandered far," said the Angel: "you have been misled by false guides. That Promised Land, that Happy Country for which you yearn, lies not before, but behind you. Wearied by your march, cast down by the cheerlessness of the desert you have traversed, you have sought peace where it cannot be found. You have shut yourselves up in cloistered cells, and lo! joy was not there. You have worshiped phantoms of terror, and lo! they could not soothe your dread. The cobwebs of theology, spun athwart your window, have shut out the light. You have called yourselves the children of God, yet have you fled from yourselves as from creatures accurst. You have fixed your eyes on a life hereafter; to purchase that you sell this life, and postpone for a little while the enjoyment of those pleasures you covet now. As if God were a broker or a bailiff! The religion you profess does not comfort you: in the devout it breeds sickly foreboding and selfish piety: it connives at the sanctimoniousness of hypocrites; it stupefies the ignorant with superstitions; it restrains not the violent: it neither deters the wicked, nor touches the indifferent, nor protects the weak. You have been taught that to be saved you must become like clowns and frightened children; and having dwindled to their stature, heaven seems farther from you than ever before.

"But I bring you tidings of men who, living in the morning of the world, looked upon the earth and saw that it was fair; of men who crouched not in slavish worship of terror, nor deemed it unlawful to enjoy the largess of the gods. They opened windows in all sides of their dwelling, and Beauty greeted them wherever they gazed. They made no cage for their mind, but they bade it soar through the æther, believing that it could never outfly the boundless expanses which the Divine Planner had created, nor alight on any perch His fingers had not made. They did not cramp their powers, nor mutilate their faculties; they found health in the full use of all their gifts, and they learned that were their endowment an hundred-fold richer, it would not suffice to drain the source of joy. They were strong, and heroic were their deeds. They were wise, and cherishing Nature they learned her secrets, in order that, allied with her laws, they might confirm their footsteps and perpetuate their existence on the earth. They envisaged death without shrinking, and if they looked to an Elysian life beyond, it was because they had felt, more deeply than other men, that the life here may be elysian and divine. Emulate them. Learn from them the wonder and beauty and joy of living. Learn from them to realize one world at a time."

In this wise spake the Spirit, and it was as if a stranger should come to a community of aged folk, interned in a cheerless valley, and should tell them that just across the mountains lay a plain full of verdure and sunshine, amid which gushed the Fountain of Perpetual Youth. The best minds of Italy were aroused, and before a generation had passed, they were engaged with an eagerness never before devoted to learning, upon the collection and interpretation of that classical literature which they believed contained the precious gospel. And immeasurable were the results to which that movement led; for mankind, like Antæus, gathers fresh vigor from every contact with Nature, and till now, for more than a thousand years, mankind had ignored Nature.

The Renaissance liberated the intelligence and reinstated reason; it was, as Michelet has tersely expressed it, the discovery of man and the discovery of the world.

That theological conception of both which had grown up during the Dark and Middle Ages, and which, the Church insisted, embraced all truth, was now seen to have no basis in fact, being but a nightmare spawned by ascetic brains. The Renaissance proved the continuity of human development, — a view condemned as sacrilegious by dogmatists, who had asserted that a great and impassable gulf rolled between those who lived before Christ and those who, born since his time and believing on him, were ransomed from everlasting punishment by his sacrifice. This narrow and abominable creed, which set apart a little flock of the elect and doomed the majority of the race to perdition, inevitably exalted faith above conduct and struck at the roots of virtue by assuming that the goodness of the best of the ancients was of no avail, whereas the wickedest of moderns could from his deathbed sneak into heaven by acknowledging Christ. As if the moral laws were not eternal, but were first invented when Christ, their pure exemplar, walked among men in the reign of Tiberius! as if the Greek or Hindoo who had ordered his life by them could fail to be spiritualized by them! Error is nevertheless error, be it maintained by Jew or by Gentile, and charity is charity, whether it sweetens the heart of Samaritan or of Parsee. To this sense of the unity and continuity of mankind the Humanists gradually rose.

As long as Catholicism was the only system, who could say that it was not the best? But when the revival of the study of antiquity introduced another standard, so-called pagan, Catholicism could be compared with it, — and comparison is the mother of criticism. The intellect, after its long servitude to tyrant dogmas, rioted in its freedom and ran to the extreme of indiscriminately despising everything Catholic and of approving everything Classic.

In its intent, however, the Renaissance was not a religious revolution, like its scion the Reformation; it was an intellectual solvent. Men plunged eagerly into the newly-discovered sea and brought up pearls which they esteemed more precious than any gems in kingly crown or papal tiara. Little suspecting whither the new impulse was leading them, the highest dignitaries of the Church joined with the humblest lay scholars in pursuit of the antique ideal. To possess a classic manuscript, or to be the patron of a noted Humanist, made the reputation of a bishop; monks rummaged their archives for long-forgotten books; the recovery of a Greek tragedy or of one of Cicero's orations was hailed throughout Christendom as an incalculable benefit; copies of the classics were worth a prince's ransom; and Pope Nicholas V, in the middle of the fifteenth century, accounted it his proudest glory to be the promoter of that revived paganism which consorted strangely with the Church whose crown he wore.

The Italian intellect had at last its liberty, but this intellectual deliverance coincided with the complete political servitude of Italy. The restless republics were no longer free. Each had fallen into the control of a powerful family which strove to perpetuate its dynasty. The cry was no more "Guelf against Ghibelline," but "Visconti against Sforza," or "Medici against Pazzi." First tyrants of the strong arm; then tyrants of the long purse. Even Genoa and Venice, which retained the semblance of republics, were bound under the tyranny of small oligarchies. From the fourteenth century, citizens no longer fought for their rights, or for revenge, they hired mercenaries to fight for them; war itself became a commercial transaction, and the despot who paid best, secured the ablest *condottiere* and the most troops. Then began that shame of Switzerland, — the leasing of her freemen to crush the efforts of peoples who strove against their masters. Shame indeed, — which has been branded on every language of Europe, where the word Swiss means not only the dwellers among the Alps, but also the hirelings ever ready to sell their valor to the highest bidder, whether he were the autocrat of the Tuileries or of the Vatican. The employment of mercenaries indicates a decline in patriotism; it is the sure forerunner of servitude. In Italy, as we have seen, patriotism had never been national, but always intensely local. The Florentine, for instance, fought heroically for Florence when a rival, like Pisa or Siena, attacked her, but at home, his devotion to faction was stronger than his devotion to the State; and like the Florentine were the other Italians. Whereas the tyrant, who usually owed his power to a partisan triumph, kept it by stimulating civic vanity: he would have it believed that works whereby the strength and lustre of his house were increased were really intended for the glory of the commonwealth. How adroit they were, those tyrants! How thoroughly they understood all the wiles by which a high-spirited and suspicious people could be brought almost unawares under the yoke! The vulgar tricks — the *panem et circenses* — by which the imperial tyrants had amused and lulled the Roman populace could not have lured the intellectual Tuscans; for them the decoy must be more spiritual and more cunning. So the tyrants of the Renaissance encouraged Humanism in all its forms. They drew round themselves whosoever was eminent in letters or in art. At their courts, the manifold genius of Italy had full play to express itself in everything, except in government. Outside of this reservation, the poet, painter, or scholar was free. He was extolled; he was almost deified. Princes vied with each other to secure his services; they were ready to go to war over him. The spirit of art, which quickened Italy from the fourteenth to the sixteenth century, poured forth imperishable works, and the lords of the cities shone in the light reflected from those works. Men almost forgot that

Florence was politically enslaved, in their admiration for Lorenzo the Magnificent. He a tyrant? Why, at his symposia at Cajano you might hear him discourse as comrade and equal with Pico and Politian and the stripling Buonarotti! So at night the few bright stars impress us more than do the vast starless spaces.

These despots were so friendly to the blossoming talents of the Renaissance that some later critics have asserted that only under similar conditions can the highest arts attain full growth, and that the glorious result was well worth the price paid for it, — political freedom. But this inference is false, because it is drawn from too short a retrospect of those causes which prepared the Italians to be masters in art. It was in the earlier days of liberty, in the strife and competition of politics, in the liberalizing activity of commerce, in the spiritualizing influence of faith, that the Italian nature got its keenness, vigor, intensity and breadth, — the very qualities which prepared it for Humanism. Luxury and licentiousness can never originate great works of art; at most, they can but patronize great artists, who unconsciously derive their powers from a spiritual fund bequeathed to them by ancestors endowed with qualities which luxury does most to destroy. The splendid achievements mistakenly assigned to the patronage of Lorenzo, and Julius II and Leo X, bear witness to a bygone integrity, without which the reigns of those princes would have been as barren of artistic glory as was the reign of any Byzantine voluptuary.

The Italian genius, prevented by local conditions from pouring itself out in permanent free institutions, flowed all the more impetuously through the sluices which were open. The vision of beauty and of the hoard of knowledge captivated and for a time absorbed a race which had been tormented by fierce and inconclusive quarrels; and the tyrants under whose dominion these men fell shrewdly fostered pursuits which diverted attention from lost liberty, and which clothed tyranny itself in gorgeous robes. And thus the Renaissance — Italy's most precious gift to the modern world — failed to bring lasting benefit to the Italians, — the only modern people from whom that movement could have originated, or by whom it could have been nurtured: not from this failure, however, should we argue that the Renaissance was bad, nor that the efflorescence of the noble arts must necessarily be accompanied by a decay of character or liberty.

The fifteenth century, in which the Renaissance rose almost to its zenith in Italy, is in many respects the most important of the Christian era, unless posterity shall assign that distinction to our own century. It witnessed the close of many old influences and the beginning of many new ones which have slowly remodeled the civilized world. Among its momentous achievements were the voyages of Columbus to America and of the Portuguese to India, which not only revealed the sphericity and therefore the extent of the earth, but also threw open new continents to the enterprise and greed of Europeans. And just as Columbus by his voyage westward dispelled ignorance concerning man's terrestrial home, so Copernicus, navigating in thought the celestial spaces, ascertained that our globe and her sister planets revolve about the sun, and he surmised, further, that the solar system itself is but one among innumerable stellar families, of which each star is the parent. This discovery is the most profound that Science has ever made, if we judge it, as we should judge it, by the conclusions subsequently deduced from it concerning the position of the earth in the universe and of man's destiny on the earth; for it has swept away the Ptolemaic errors on which dogmatic Christianity had elaborated its assumptions, and it has shown the earth to be, not the centre of creation, but a tiny ball encircled by myriads of orbs inconceivably vast. As there is but one cosmos, these revelations due to the fortitude of Columbus and to the imagination of Copernicus can never be repeated, and Science since their time has but formulated the laws of the material world and of organic life, to which they furnished the clue.

These were the two supreme achievements of fifteenth century men: but there were many others, almost equally remarkable, whose effect was felt at once. There were those great agents of equality, the invention of printing and the introduction of gunpowder: the former brought the best thoughts of all times into the reach of every reader, thus breaking up the little aristocracy of learning; the latter leveled the disparity between knight and foot-soldier, by supplying the weak with a weapon which made him the peer of the strong, thus shattering a military system based on bodily force. In politics, there was the crystallization of Western Europe into those units which have existed, in spite of temporary variation, down to the present day. England, having abandoned the long struggle to maintain her sway over part of France, and having healed her internal dissensions between the Houses of York and Lancaster, became a compact nation. France, likewise, being rid of English interference, and having defeated her most dangerous vassal, the Duke of Burgundy, began her independent career. In Spain, the union of the crowns of Castile and Aragon produced a strong monarchy, destined in the next century to take the lead in Europe. All these kingdoms were ostensibly dynastic, but the dynasty in each derived its power from the fact that it had a coherent nation behind it. And now kings began to claim that they ruled by "divine right,"—a claim originally asserted by the Emperor to offset the pretensions of the Pope. In Germany, the Empire took on irrevocably the character of a local sovereignty hereditary in the House of Hapsburg, while half a score of small principalities were independent

of it in all but name. Hungary reached her highest
renown under John Hunyadi and Matthias Corvinus;
Bohemia made a magnificent effort to secure a place
among progressive and free States; and the kings of
Muscovy, by conquering some of their neighbors and by
shaking off the Turkish yoke in the South, laid the
foundation for the vast Empire of modern Russia. The
Mahometans quenched the Byzantine Empire and established themselves in Constantinople; but their advent in
Eastern Europe was soon followed by the expulsion of
the Saracens from Spain. Throughout Italy, principalities and duchies were erected on the ruins of spent republics. The Papacy, returning from its exile at Avignon,
made Rome once more the central city of Christendom,
and assumed definitively the rôle of a temporal power,
astute and unscrupulous in its political methods, and
often shockingly corrupt in its morals. The unity of the
Church was disturbed by a schism only less fatal than
that of the Reformation to its pretensions of catholicity.
The revolt of the Bohemians, one of the noblest of
religious movements, but not yet adequately esteemed;
the persecution of the Lollards in England; the first
whisperings of Luther's forerunners in Germany; the
effort of Savonarola to regenerate Florence while a Borgian Pope was bestializing Rome; the founding of the
Inquisition; — these are some of the religious symptoms
and prognostics of that prolific century.

Add to all these the fact that the Renaissance was
sweeping like a vernal influence through every part of
the Italian intellect, quickening knowledge, thawing the
frosts of dogma, dropping the pollen of new hope, and
cherishing the buds of Art and Poetry, whilst over outward Nature it breathed an atmosphere unspeakably
enchanting, and you will understand in some measure
the marvels of that time. Then originated criticism and
that curiosity which tests with the flame of reason every

phenomenon of life. Then was couched the cataract which dogma had spun, film on film, across the vision of man; he groped no longer purblind, but looked at each object point-blank and asked its meaning. He was skeptical of the old explanations, but his was the skepticism which stimulates research, in the belief that a final and satisfactory answer can be wrested from the taciturn gods, and not the skepticism of those who, having found every avenue of knowledge end at the foot of a precipice, cry out in despair that there is no thoroughfare. To the man of the fifteenth century all seemed discoverable: he had found the key to the door of the Temple of Life, and as he crossed the threshold an immense hope thrilled him. Possibly, possibly he might discover within the answers to those immemorial secrets, — human origin and destiny, and the principle of being; possibly he might in that holy of holies stand face to face with God! The quest was irresistibly enticing: men set forth on it as enthusiastically as their fathers had set forth on the Crusades; but now the universe, and not an empty sepulchre, was to be won. The Church encouraged her priests and prelates to be among the pioneers, and only when she saw that Humanism menaced her very existence did she cry halt; but it was long before she was obeyed, even in outward acts of conformity. For then it was that Nicholas V and Pius II, both intoxicated with the new paganism, derived more glory from their patronage of the classic revival than from their triple mitre. Then it was that Brunelleschi, Ghiberti, and Donatello, Masaccio, Fra Angelico, the Bellini, Carpaccio, Lippi, and Botticelli made the arts once more the interpreters of the soul; when Leonardo da Vinci, endowed with nearly every faculty, and each a master's, attained his prime; when the court of Alfonso was renowned at Naples, when the Medici gave Florence splendor in lieu of freedom, and the Visconti made Milan magnificent; then it was that Michael

Angelo, Raphael, Titian, and Giorgione were born in Italy, and when, beyond the Alps, Memling and Van Eyck flourished, and Dürer and Holbein were born; when Luther and Erasmus grew up in Germany, and Rabelais, who was to paint with sardonic humor the paradoxes of the new age, passed from boyhood to youth in France. Verily, a marvelous century! And how many of the names by which we refer to it were Italian!

CHAPTER VII.

REACTION AND DECLINE.

THE century which followed brought only disaster to Italy, — disaster embittered by the remorse which comes with the knowledge that the humiliation has been deserved, — humiliation all the deeper when contrasted with the intellectual and æsthetic superiority of the victims. The genius of Italy supplied Christendom with the priceless agents of liberty and culture, — as Greece had supplied Rome, and Rome her Teutonic conquerors, — at the very time when the Italians showed that they were incapable of using liberty, and that culture without civic and personal morals is as the apples of Sodom. During the Middle Age, Italy had been frequently ravaged by the expeditions of the German Emperors, who had at least the excuse that they came to assert their titular right. Many Popes had renewed the invitation first sent by Gregory III to Charles Martel. Charles of Anjou had established a French dynasty at Naples; John of Bohemia, the Duke of Athens, Ladislaus of Hungary, and the Aragonese princes, had each left an impress more or less ephemeral. But now, in the sixteenth century, Italy became the prey of invaders who could plead neither feudal rights nor an ill-advised invitation, — imperial burglars and royal robbers, whose sole object was to plunder the treasure which she could amass but not defend. French and German and Spaniard fought over the booty they wrested from her, turning her fertile plains into battlefields, and making her cities desolate with pillage and slaughter. Her riches and her enlightening influence passed over Alps and beyond the sea, but for her there was joy no more. And when the foreigner paused in his cruelty, the inveterate feuds of her native tyrants burst forth afresh. Her princes were no longer of the stamp of Lorenzo the Magnificent, and of Frederick of Urbino: bastard Medici were Dukes of Florence; the Farnese lorded it at Parma and Piacenza; the papal throne passed from Medici to Farnese, then to Caraffa, then to Borghese. What were the aims and methods of a tyrant you read in Machiavelli's "Prince." Perfidy and cunning were then the highest qualities of the governor; fawning and deceit, of the governed. Personal valor had departed; private morals, whether of honesty in man or chastity in woman, were not looked for. Debauch produced now imbecility and now blood-madness, — a diabolical desire to kill, which waxed greedier in killing. The records of almost any noble family at that period would furnish episodes more abominable than the delirium of a modern French novelist could invent.[1] Even the virtuous remnant held itself not aloof from the wicked majority, — a dismal and significant fact. Pietro Aretino, an epitome of foul sensuality and of intellectual effrontery, was the favorite of princes and the comrade of poets, painters, and philosophers. Titian had him for an intimate, even Michael Angelo, the austere, addressed him as "my lord and brother."[2] In Benvenuto Cellini, you have an example as distinct and amazing as in Aretino, — of the sixteenth century Italian; and in Iago, Shakespeare has immortalized another common type.

Italians in their days of bondage have been too ready to point to this era as the most splendid in their history.

[1] Eleven members of the Medici family came to violent ends between 1535 and 1585. The crimes of the Cenci, of Vittoria Accoramboni and others, were not exceptional.

[2] *Rime e Prose di M. A. Buonarotti* (Milan, 1821), p. 224. Tintoret, however, treated Aretino as he deserved; see Ridolfi's work on Venetian Painters.

How they have extolled the age of Leo the Tenth and of the House of Este, and forgotten the shame implied in the supremacy of such princes! The splendor was that of a burning edifice, which for a time illumines the twilight; then embers and flickering jets of flame; then ashes and desolation and darkness. Before the end of this century, every talent by which Italians had purchased glory was spent. Painting had descended through the stages of mannerism, coarseness, and brutality, to ineptitude; flourishing latest in Venice, where there was still a phantom of civic independence, and dying there with Tintoret, the last of the masters; to be revived now and then by some school of eclectics, who fumbled among the works of the dead for ornaments and inspiration. Poetry, already become an elegant diversion, was silent after Tasso. Classical study was fossilizing through pedantry, or volatilizing through dilettanteism. Statecraft meant bargaining with *bravi* and concocting poisons. The Renaissance, the noblest regenerative influence man had felt since the introduction of Christianity, had failed in Italy. The tidings of joy that the Angel had brought to the fourteenth century were now a mockery. Why, we ask, should this be? Why should a message of truth and life mislead men to error and death? Was it not because the message of the Renaissance had been perverted, just as Christianity itself had been perverted? Was it not because the Italian character, through lack of moral and political soundness, could absorb only what was intellectual or æsthetic in that inspiration? Under the mediæval Church, the moral nature of the Italians had sunk so low that it responded as little to the best ethics of paganism as to the precepts of Christ. Through superstition and terror, the Church could still hold the peasants, but over the educated she was powerless. They had before them the example of a profligate priesthood, to show how completely holy functions can be severed from righteous living. The Church insisted that no matter how vicious the priest, the offices performed by him could not be affected; the water was always pure, no matter how foul the vessel that held it. And the Italians came to look upon conduct as independent of principle; live how they might, they could buy indulgences, at the price fixed by the Church auctioneers. The revival of classic learning appealed, therefore, to their intellect and not to their morals; the masters of Greece and Rome stimulated their artistic instinct and whetted their wit, but failed to uplift their character; and before long it was not Æschylus nor Sophocles,[1] not Plato, nor Tacitus, nor Marcus Aurelius, to whom they listened, but Ovid and Martial and Anacreon, and those other ancients who have recorded, and in recording have gilded, the vices of Greece and Rome. And from preferring these authors, it was but a step to imitating them.

The Renaissance, then, had not in Italy a firm moral nature to build upon, nor was there any other commanding motive, such as patriotism, to counteract the tendency to local and personal selfishness. Everybody worked for his private glory and his own gain. The intellectual liberty proclaimed by the Renaissance sank into license; individualism was exaggerated to amazing proportions; not character, but success, was the object of desire, and success justified any baseness, any crime. Self-respect and its twin self-control were not; neither was there recognition of duty to others, of a common humanity and common interests, for which selfish desires must be renounced. Where could there be fellowship when each man saw in his fellow a rival, an enemy, bent on possessing the prize which both coveted, whether that prize were

---

[1] I recall no Renaissance masterpiece inspired by either of these tragedians, or by Homer. The unnatural amours of Jupiter, the antics of satyrs, nymphs and fauns of doubtful respectability, supply, on the contrary, the best masters with themes.

the tyranny of a city or the favor of a prince, the embraces of a mistress or the wide-echoing reports of fame?

The lesson of the Renaissance in Italy is plain to read. The intellectual nature divorced from the moral nature may burn never so brightly for a time, but it will surely destroy itself at last. Man may build him a palace of art or a treasury of knowledge, and shut himself in it, and declare that here is all he needs, that the interests of his fellows concern him not. But by and by those frescoed walls shall begin to contract; the light of the sun and the voices of humanity shall enter no more; the wretch shall shriek for assistance, but no one shall hear him, and that palace which was the pride of his selfishness shall fall upon him and be his tomb. In nations not less than in men, the surety of permanence is the blending of enlightenment and integrity, of mind and soul. That is not culture which does not purify and sweeten conduct, embodying in fair deeds the beauty which delights the spirit. "The beautiful is higher than the good, because it includes the good," — so runs Goethe's maxim: but, alas for the Italians of the Renaissance! their beautiful included not the good, and therefore their arts from being spiritual became intellectual, and from intellectual they became carnal.

The sixteenth century, which witnessed this culmination and decline in Italy, ushered in the Reformation beyond the Alps. The first aim of the reformers was to correct the abuses in the Church; but these were found to be so inveterate that it was impossible to say which was Church and which abuse. So the Lutherans organized a new Church to suit themselves. By this act they postulated the right of every person to liberty of conscience, the chief boon of Protestantism, although Protestants have often been as quick as Catholics to persecute dissenters. As by the revival of classical learning another standard of life had been recovered, by which to judge Catholicism, so long the only standard; so by the expansion of Protestantism, Europe had the benefit of a further comparison. We might suppose that the Italians, who had been the first to welcome the Renaissance, would have been eager to accept the Reformation, the offshoot of the Renaissance; on the contrary, they were scarcely moved by it, and for these reasons: the educated Italians were so debased that they were indifferent to religion; there were no princes who, like many in the North, espoused Protestantism for political reasons; and finally, when the hierarchy discovered that it had something more than a monkish squabble to deal with, — that, in fact, the German movement threatened the overthrow of papal power at home and abroad, — the instinct of self-preservation warned it to reject compromise and to stamp out every shoot of heresy on Italian soil. Each priest, each monk in Italy could be relied upon to uphold the institution to which he owed his livelihood; the princes, many of whom belonged to papal families, and the aristocracy, which was copartner with the Church in the enjoyment of special privileges, knew that the Church was their best friend. While in the North, therefore, political considerations had far more influence than is usually acknowledged in deciding rulers to take up the popular religious reforms as a means to their personal advancement,[1] there were lacking in Italy both popular enthusiasm and leaders to direct it.

Thus the Reformation saved the Papacy from complete collapse. Another century of uninterrupted decay, such as had gone on between 1300 and 1500, must have left it moribund. But the appearance of a rival roused it to make a desperate struggle for life. The Inquisition be-

---

[1] I need hardly refer to the motives for which Henry VIII threw over Catholicism in England. Equally worldly and striking was the conversion of Sweden to Protestantism; see P. B. Watson: *The Swedish Revolution* (Boston, 1889).

came its incomparable instrument for detecting and punishing heretics; the Company of Jesus, composed of men as subtle in intellect as they were zealous in spirit, became its chief agent in sowing the seeds of reaction. At the Council of Trent, Romanism, like the arrogant but fond Danish king, planted its throne on the beach and said to the inflowing tide, "Thus far shalt thou go and no farther;" and even to-day, although the waves have plainly swept in, engulfing that throne in their resistless rise, the Pope, from his rock of refuge farther inland, repeats that forbiddance in tones just as haughty, and there are those who would fain believe that the waters will obey him. We must not, however, deny to some of the promoters of the Catholic reaction the admiration due to sincerity; Loyola and Bellarmine were as sincerely fanatical as Calvin and Knox, Bonner was as mercilessly earnest as Cranmer or Latimer. Even the Inquisition, whose name has become loathsome to the tongue, was, from the Catholic standpoint, salutary in purpose and consistent in method: for the vitalest concern to every man is the everlasting welfare of his soul, and, once admitting that any Church controls the means to that welfare, she is in duty bound to save him from perdition by stretching him on the rack, or even by burning him, — in order that he may not corrupt other souls, if, after long persuasion, he remains incorrigible. We need waste no time in exploding this theory, which is the logical outcome of every creed pretending to be infallible, and which once seemed equally true to Puritan and Papist: we have learned that genuine devoutness cannot be superinduced by wrenching limbs asunder, nor by any physical torture, and that ideas cannot be destroyed by the fire which consumes the body: to state such beliefs is to refute them.

Just at this time, therefore, when the genius of Italy was nearing the limit of its superb artistic productiveness, when the last spark of communal liberty had been quenched, and the moral sense was dullest, the Church tightened the bonds of her authority over the minds and consciences of the Italians. Her dogmas were more formal, her rules more explicit than ever before; and she had agents more alert and powerful for seizing those who were suspected, and for punishing those convicted of heresy. As a result, she secured a general outward conformity to her commands. Skepticism and irreligion did not cease, they merely ceased from openly avowing themselves. Among a people where few had deep moral convictions, it was not to be supposed that many would jeopard their lives by proclaiming themselves unorthodox; martyrdom seemed foolish, when life and the privilege of free-thinking could be bought cheap by performing the outward acts prescribed by the Church. If with pistol cocked you spring upon an unarmed man and say, "Profess what I tell you, or die," he will probably submit, especially if he happens to have no belief which he deems worth dying for.

Catholicism, then, assumed that character in Italy which it retained down to the middle of the present century. Those who believed it at all, believed it bigotedly; the skeptical were either silent or disingenuous. For all there was a rigid formality, which the devout bowed to voluntarily, the doubting as a matter of prudence. Superstition spread. Government, intrusted to priests, or to the parasites of incapable tyrants, became as inefficient as corrupt. Nepotism controlled the Papacy. The Italian, debarred from exercising himself in civic affairs, and forbidden to use his reason outside of the pinfold of dogma, frittered away his intellect over trifles. He vaunted his recondite erudition. He amused himself by writing ponderous works on insignificant themes, carrying to an extreme that fashion of the late Renaissance which substituted Latin for Italian. To turn a period like Cicero, to mimic Martial in an epigram, were the aims of every one who pretended to cultivation. If we could believe the tablets and epitaphs which meet the stranger's eye in every town in Italy, recording that "this was the house," or "this is the tomb of So-and-So, the peer of Virgil in poetry, of Cicero in eloquence, of Horace in wit," we must conclude that the Italian intellect was never so luxuriant as in the two centuries between Tasso and Alfieri. But the great number of those immortals and the unstinted praise make us suspicious. Those little reputations of a village, those heroes of a clique, those fireflies which the uncritical mistook for stars, what were they but indications of the intellectual beggary of that time? Affectation pervaded manners and the arts. Painting still had some skill of technique, but no soul nor taste; even color, the supreme gift of the Venetians, became ashen and ghastly,[1] as if dissolution were near. Sculpture and architecture blustered in the bombast of the Baroque School, and then simpered in the puerilities of the Rococo. Yet there was endless talk about art; and the collections of paintings and statues, that are among the most precious visible products of the Renaissance, were gradually formed. Elegance of a certain pompous sort was not wanting to the intercourse of the nobility. Ecclesiastical pageants were never more magnificent. How many millions of candles — from those tallow lights at a penny which the poor burn to solace the souls of friends in Purgatory, to those huge standards of wax, too heavy for one man to carry, and kindled only on state occasions — were consumed at Italy's myriad altars every year? How many hundred millions in a century? Festivals of the Church, processions, banquets, and celebrations of the nobility, the laying out of parks, the embellishment of villas, the erection of votive chapels and mausoleums, — on ends such as

---

[1] As in the works of Tiepolo, the most prominent Venetian painter of the eighteenth century.

these prelates and nobles spent the wealth which, according to the shrewd system they maintained, flowed through the channels of privilege into their yawning coffers.

Beyond the Alps, great events and pregnant changes were to record: a Cromwell in England, a Grand Monarque in France, the sturdy independence of the Dutch, a Thirty Years' War in Germany, Sweden striding confidently into the European arena, the Electorate of Brandenburg expanding into the Kingdom of Prussia, Muscovy waxing ominously strong in the North, and in America the sapling liberty transplanted from England growing into a tree, — all this, while Italy remained inert and backward, scarcely noting what occurred. And she in her turn was forgotten by her neighbors, except when they coveted her riches or passed her provinces as marriage dowers from one prince to another. Spain was her taskmaster, — Spain the bigoted, the bloodthirsty, the corrupting. Were it not for the business and intrigues of the papal court with the rest of the Catholic world, we might declare that Italy had no concern in the international life of Europe for more than two hundred years. How, indeed, could it be otherwise? Had not the Council of Trent decreed that progress was damnable, that the Renaissance should be expunged, and that Italians should slink back into the condition of the Middle Age?

CHAPTER VIII.

SCIENCE AND FOLLY.

At last Italy seems hopelessly fallen. Corroding dogmas, tireless Jesuits, a vindictive Inquisition, and the Spaniards have like fabled vampires settled upon her exhausted body to suck out the last drop of life-blood. The mission of Spain has been to brutalize whatever people she has ruled; the Huns of old slaughtered the bodies, the modern Spaniards have spared the lives only to befoul the souls of their victims. To Italy they did, indeed, bring peace, — but what a peace! "The invasions ceased," says Balbo: "for the stranger who hectored us screened us from invaders. Intestine wars ceased: the same stranger took away their cause by bridling national ambitions. Popular revolutions ceased: the stranger bridled the peoples!"[1] From the Treaty of Cateau-Cambrésis (1559) onward, a black shadow mantled Italy, — the shadow of the iniquities of Spain.

Nevertheless, in spite of political and moral decadence, the Italian genius was not dead. It exercised itself in the Drama and in Music, — the only arts which, like exotics in a greenhouse, can flourish amid despotism. Early in the sixteenth century, dramatic literature had been revived on classic models by Machiavelli, Dovizio, and Ariosto, but the Drama, being tied to the apronstrings of its venerable nurse, — the Unities, — never learned to walk; whereas low comedy, the farce, and the burlesque, springing from humble native origin, and having neither Plautus nor Terence for sponsor, nor Aristo-

[1] Balbo: *Storia d' Italia* (10th ed.). p. 313.

tle for pedagogue, grew up to represent the life of the lower classes, and was at last introduced into polite society by Goldoni, the most genuine of comic writers. Palestrina was the earliest master of musical composition; after him Music gradually became secularized, and, in Peri's opera "Euridice," it was first wedded to the Drama.

But the most important field in which the Italian genius labored between the Council of Trent and the French Revolution was that of Science; and as if to symbolize the change from Art to Science, Galileo was born on the day of Michael Angelo's death (February 18, 1564). The men of science worked amid the greatest obstacles: on the one hand, civil and ecclesiastical rulers were united to strangle free investigation; on the other, pedants and dilettanti took no interest in and gave no encouragement to investigators. Only recently have we come to know how many of the ideas which are the leaven of our time were engendered by neglected Italians, whose fame has been inherited by more fortunate Germans, Frenchmen, or Britons. Were the cryptographic notes of Leonardo da Vinci fully edited, it would be found that he deserved to rank among the foremost inventors and natural philosophers of the world; for receptivity so universal, observation so keen, a power to specialize so perfectly blended with a power to generalize, have perhaps never been developed to so remarkable a degree as in him; but his encyclopædic discoveries were veiled for three centuries behind a cipher, and an army of investigators had caught up with and surpassed him, before his cipher was interpreted. This happened also to Giordano Bruno, the precursor of modern rationalists. His restless mind wandered through the domain of knowledge, came to the frontier beyond which the Church asserted there was nothing, crossed it as galliardly as a swallow flies over a hedge, and found a limitless, living universe, of which Christendom and the earth are but a speck. And when, in his unmethodic roaming, he returned and told of some of the wonders he had seen, the Inquisition caught him in its clutches, imprisoned him, tortured him, burnt him. A little earlier than this, Palcario, another liberal thinker who had dared to say that the "Inquisition is a poniard aimed at all writers," perished at the stake; a little later Vannini, teaching at Toulouse what we call rationalism, and the Church calls heresy, was seized and done to death. Whatever may be the value of these men's speculations, the preciousness of their example cannot be blinked; right or wrong, they died for their ideas, — and there is no higher test of sincerity than that. They by their martyrdom and others by their exile proved that Italians were capable of sacrificing everything for their convictions.[1] Bruno had declared among other "abominable heresies" that there are innumerable worlds; shortly after his death a more illustrious victim, Galileo, was threatened with torture for affirming this and other corollaries of the Copernican system. One would think that the theory of the plurality of worlds testified to the majesty of an omnipotent God, but the Inquisition thought otherwise; for the inhabitants of those other worlds must need salvation, and Christ must therefore be kept busy traveling from world to world on his redeeming mission. The doctrine of the Incarnation was sufficiently improbable when applied to the earth only; to conceive of the same process as going forward successively in all the habitable orbs of the firmament was to stretch improbability even beyond the clasp of faith. So the Church declared this new theory, which puzzled faith and degraded man from his solitary honor as the peculiar favorite of the Almighty, to be heretical. From this example we perceive how quick the Church was to scent danger in scientific investigation. Galileo was not, indeed, burned, but he was harassed until his spirit broke. Contempora-

[1] Cf. Berti: *Giordano Bruno da Nola: Sua Vita e Sua Dottrina* (1889).

neous with him, Campanella, a pioneer in scientific study, who urged that the laws of Nature must be sought in Nature, and not in Aristotle, suffered, partly for political reasons and partly for alleged heresies, an imprisonment lasting twenty-seven years. Sarpi, an eminent scholar and the best historian of his time, was secretly menaced by the Jesuits. Such the treatment awaiting men whose researches might conflict with the assumptions which the Council of Trent had mistaken for eternal truth. Brains and perseverance were not wanting in Italy; but with what cheer could they be applied when the path of Science, always arduous, led to the dungeon or the stake?[1]

Patiently, and for the most part obscurely, those disciples of science toiled; with the menace of the Inquisition always hanging over them, yet unable to frighten them from their brave and genial task. Like the earthworms, which bore underground to fertilize the soil, their invaluable work was unappreciated. On the surface, butterflies, gaudy of hue and indolent of flight, creatures without sting or industry, flitted to and fro, complacent and careless; as if the eternal forces of the universe had been in travail but to bring forth butterflies, the frail product and glory of creation. Behold the noblesse of Italy disporting itself during the eighteenth century, after the manner of jeweled insects; behold high-born and pedantic Italians reduced to silliness, yet even in silliness proving themselves masters. Every people has had its interims of affectation, its holidays of folly, its nights of moonshine and sentimentality; but the Italian Arcadians

---

[1] Among many names deserving mention, I can specify but a few: In Medicine, Falloppio and Vesalius; in Natural History and Physics, Torricelli, Cassini, Redi, Malpighi, and Magalotti; in the Philosophy of History, Vico; in Sociology, Beccaria and Bandini; in Electricity, Galvani and Volta; in Mathematics, Lagrange. Lyell (in his *Principles of Geology*) enumerates twenty-one Italians who advanced that science between the sixteenth and nineteenth centuries. See also Libri's *Histoire des Sciences Mathématiques en Italie*.

surpassed them all. And to follow the Italian genius to the end of its long pilgrimage we must now turn aside into imaginary pastures and listen to the pipings of mock-shepherds and watch the gambols of make-believe shepherdesses.

In the year 1690 some poetasters at Rome were wont to go into the neighboring country, where, reclining beneath pine or chestnut, they read their effusions to each other. Real poetry was long since dead; but now that they had nothing to say, a legion of rhymsters started up to say it. One day, a party of these having gathered in the fields beyond the Castle of St. Angelo, one of them, stirred by the conclusion of a fellow's verses, exclaimed, "Lo, Arcadia has come to life again for us!" All were delighted by this discovery, and they planned forthwith an Academy to be called "The Arcadian." Crescimbeni, whose brain the irreverent described as being "half wood and half lead," was the foremost in this enterprise. The Academy soon flourished. Everybody was eager to belong to it. Cardinals and priests, judges and cavaliers, ladies and literati, flocked to its meetings. The Arcadian community was established on republican principles, each sheep being as good as his neighbors, whatever difference in rank might separate them in the unpoetical world outside. Jesus Christ was unanimously elected the Tutelar President, and Christina, the tomboy ex-Queen of Sweden, who had died on the very day the Academy was projected, was chosen its patroness and honored with funeral rites. The Arcadians met in the parks of its illustrious members. In the Giustiniani Gardens there was an open lawny space encircled by trees, and this they called their "theatre," which they provided with two rows of seats, "simple and rustic, but pleasing and delicious, being all clothed in odorous myrtle and interwoven with green laurel." Here nymphs and shepherds listened to bucolic poets, or mingled in pastoral dances. They gave classic or mongrel-classic names to everything, and to themselves. Beautiful Faustina Maratta was "Aglaura Cidonia," Marchioness Massima was "Fidalma," Rolli was "the modern Propertius," macaw-beaked Crescimbeni was "Alfesibeo," Gravina, the learned jurisconsult, was "Opico." They proposed to themselves this task: "to exterminate bad taste, and to prevent its resurrection by pursuing it continually whithersoever it may hide or nest, even into fortresses and villas least known and least suspected." The Arcadians thought themselves crusaders: not theirs to free the Holy Sepulchre from Paynim foes, but "to redeem Parnassus, Helicon, Pindar, Hippocrene, Apollo, the Muses, and Pegasus, fallen under the bondage of Christian dogs." They reckoned by Olympiads, they celebrated Olympic games. Gravina wrote the laws of the Academy, which were engraved on tablets of marble and preserved in the *serbatojo* or sacristy. Crescimbeni not only directed the revels of the Arcadians and wrote their chronicles in many great volumes, but he also edited what we may not irreverently term the official Arcadian cook-book, containing recipes for preparing canzoni and sonnets, maggiolate, cobole, seroni, motti, mottetti, strambotti, rispetti, barzelate, disperate and contradisperate, matinades and serenades, gypsy-songs, oracles, nenie, epicedi, birthday odes, and all other varieties of Orphic pastry. Angiolo di Costanzo, a mediocre sonneteer of the sixteenth century, was singled out as the master for Arcadians to imitate, and a part of the Arcadian ceremonial was the reading of a dissertation on one of Costanzo's sonnets. The acute Crescimbeni declared that four of these sonnets contain "all that is necessary for Tuscan lyric poetry."

Dom John V of Portugal was so grateful for honors showed him at Rome by the Arcadians, that he bestowed upon them a strip of land on the Janiculum, which they named the Parrhasian Grove, and resorted to in summer.

Portraits of distinguished shepherds and shepherdesses were hung there, and when Arcadians died, — for death enters even Arcadia, — magnificent pyramids were raised to them. The fame of the Academy spread so rapidly that within two years fifty-eight colonies had been established outside of the capital, and the colonists numbered above thirteen hundred. The peninsula was infected by a species of epidemic, a Phœban influenza, whose victims sneezed in rhythm. The business of saving souls and of governing States seemed trivial and sordid to these thirteen hundred poets, amid whose twittering the notes of vulgarer Academies, like the Intronati, the Stravaganti, the Umidi, or the Imbecilli, were drowned.

What pictures the imagination paints of plump dowagers weaving laurel crowns for venerable but still amorous prelates! Of shepherds, sad, mad, passionate, disconsolate, breathing their sighs upon the zephyrs of the Villa Odescalchi or wandering rueful through the melancholy cypress-lanes of the Villa d' Este! Of pompous Gravina, quitting legal folios to chirp madrigals in Fidalma's bower! Of Crescimbeni, having piped all day on his syrinx, devoting his night to immortalizing Arcadia in his history! A herculean task he found it, for the poets to be immortalized soon numbered thousands, and new ones hourly appeared: so that in despair he wrote all their names on slips of paper, and shook them up, and drew forth a few for Fame to blazon. Can we not see Monsignor Daphnis and the Countess Chloe billing and cooing beside an Arcadian haycock, or Narcissus, — known in plain life as Abbé Frugoni, — gazing at himself in a fountain? And here His Eminence the Cardinal, transformed into Corydon, adores Her Grace the Duchess, — who as Phyllis or Dorinda tends imaginary sheep; what time the Duke, with periwig on head and crook in hand, frisks over the sward or darts into the shadowy bosks, in pursuit of some portly nymph, still coy, though the mother of many children!

Let us draw near and listen to some of these poets. Lucinio — whose real name is Meloncelli (little melons) — yearns to be turned into a swan, for no evil purpose, but simply that he may expire singing praises to the Delphic god. Siralgo wishes to be changed into a laurel, so that the Muses may come and cut the name of Delia, his mistress, on the bark. Gantila, a lachrymose, middle-aged gentleman, unable to restrain his tears night or day, forefeels that Cupid will turn him into a river; and he is not sorry, because he can then serve as a mirror to the beautiful but obdurate face which he has borne and still bears in his bosom. Thyrsis tells us that having plaited a little straw basket, he put a kiss in it and sent it to his sweetheart; but Cupid slyly hid his darts therein, and when the unwary Nigella lifted the cover, she was of course hopelessly wounded.[1] Oh edifying innocence of shepherds in broadcloth and shepherdesses in brocades! Having heard each other's idyls till their Arcadian ears were cloyed, and having gamboled till their aristocratic legs were weary, they were served a banquet of pastoral dainties, borne by lackeys into a rustic cabin.

Strange freak of fate! At a time when few or none had any more the capacity to feel passion, — whose voice is poetry, — the wit and rank of a whole people succumbed to this mild delirium, which they mistook for the divine poetic frenzy. Then, when there was no genuine sympathy for real shepherds and husbandmen, nor for any other toiler, the *élite* of Italy put on this mask of rusticity, not for once only, nor for a single carnival of silliness, but for well-nigh a century. The Arcadians exorcised Marini and all the demons of bad taste: they had their jubilees, at one of which they crowned Perfetti, who sang his improvisations to the accompaniment of a harpsichord; at another they crowned Corilla Olimpica.[2]

[1] Crescimbeni: *L' Arcadia* (Rome, 1711), pp. 310-12.
[2] Her real name was Maddalena Monelli.

a squint-eyed improvisatrice, whom Madame de Staël subsequently made the heroine of "Corinne." They importuned high and low with their honors: Goethe himself avoided the absurdity of a coronation at the Capitol only by accepting membership in their Academy and by promising to cultivate the Field of Melpomene. But alas for the ten thousand fleeting Apollos, and alas for the blissful reign of Bo-peep! Arcadia itself, its legion of poets, its bevies of shepherdesses, — "semi-nymphs, semi-nuns," — its naiads, fauns, and Pythian priestesses, faded into the inane, from which like a vapor they had emerged. Their very names are forgotten, or if one or two — Frugoni's, for instance — be remembered, it is to give personality and a semblance of life to an age of nonsense, which would otherwise seem too silly, too fantastic, to have ever been real.[1]

Nero fiddled, we are told, while Rome was burning. The aristocracy of Italy danced and piped in equal unconcern during the eighteenth century, when there was kindling a conflagration destined to consume crowns and privileges, and to singe even the vestments of the Pope. Pipe and dance, shepherds and shepherdesses! Frisk, innocent sheep, for the hour is at hand when the wolves shall come. M. Voltaire is turning not only your verses, but also your religion, into ridicule. Can your Church survive that? Contempt follows close upon sarcasm, and after contempt — what? M. Rousseau, too, is preaching a strange social doctrine; he avows that those rustics,

[1] For details see Crescimbeni; also Emiliani-Giudici and other historians of Italian literature; in English, Vernon Lee's diffuse but entertaining essay (in her *Studies of the Eighteenth Century in Italy*) should be consulted. I quote her clever summary of Arcadian bombast: "The sun cooled itself in the waters of rivers which were on fire; the celestial sieve, resplendent with shining holes, was swept by the bristly back of the Apennines; love was an infernal heaven and a celestial hell, it was burning ice and freezing fire, and was inspired by ladies made up entirely of coral, gold thread, lilies, roses, and ivory, on whose lips sat Cupids, shooting arrows which were snakes." Page 11.

whom you condescend to mimic, have hearts and souls, and that, were classes ranked according to nature and natural rights, you would not be uppermost. What if the peasants take counsel of Jean Jacques and forcibly claim their own; think you to tame their savage breasts with madrigals, or to drive them back by flourishing your ribboned crooks? Futile questions. Arcadians stoop not to such vulgar fancies; they reck not what may happen to barbarians beyond the mountains. Butterflies which come in summer believe that summer is made for them; what can they know of other seasons? Merciful nature bids numbness to precede dissolution, otherwise the agony of death would be too cruel.

And yet, even in Italy there were little signs and warnings that a calamity was approaching. Viewed on the surface, the most important change was the expulsion of the Spaniards and the accession of the Austrians, — a change of taskmaster, but not of conditions. Bourbons of the House of Austria ruled Milan and Mantua, Tuscany and the Two Sicilies. Leopold, Grand Duke of Tuscany, framed a code restricting the privilege of the Church in his dominion, and his brother, Joseph the Second, — a skeptic and cynic, — introduced into the Empire reforms that threatened to disestablish Catholicism as the State religion. But the Papacy, like an experienced coquette, knew the value of persistence, and now by upbraiding, now by caressing, and now by threatening, she recovered her ascendency. Nor should we pass by unmentioned the efforts of at least one able Pope to purify the Curia; nor the suppression of the Jesuits. But amelioration dependent on one man lasted only his lifetime, and soon the Revolution came, to make all changes suspected by the civil and hierarchical tyrants, and to reunite Rome and Austria in a communion of terror. Nevertheless, it is significant that Leopold looked to economists and philosophers, and not to churchmen, for counsel, and that he, the son of Maria Theresa, was the first ruler in Italy to respond to the changing current and to propose laws prophetic of the modern spirit.

Another symptom is the greater frequency and sincerity of the utterance by un-Arcadian Italians of their desire to be free. That desire was certainly old. It resounded from Dante's volume, like the undertone of a cataract. Dante predicted the coming of a greyhound who should put to flight the wolves that harried Italy; he believed that the Emperor could quell the strife of Guelfs and Ghibellines, restore peace and unity to the disordered land, and restrain the arrogance of the Church. But even before Dante died, the fulfilment of his dream appeared plainly improbable, and though, with the course of time, it became impossible, still the dream itself, the desire, nestled close in the hearts of the noblest Italians. They mistook the isolated and spasmodic outbursts of dying liberty for birth-throes. Petrarch lamented that Italy, "aged, otiose, and slow," seemed not to feel her ills. "Will she sleep forever, and will no one arouse her?" he exclaimed, appealing to the patriotism of Rienzi.[1] When Rienzi's brief illusion had been dispelled, the poet turned to the lords of Italy, and urged them to arm for her liberation. "Behold with pity the tears of your dolorous people, which only from you, after God, await repose; and if you show but one sign of pity, Virtue against Fury will take up arms; and short will be the combat; for the old-time valor in Italian hearts is not yet dead." A noble appeal, but the grandees heeded it not.[2] Two centuries later, Machiavelli, in closing his treatise, "The Prince," invoked Lorenzo de' Medici, to whom he dedicated that sphinx-like book, to come to the rescue of his country. "I cannot express," he writes, "with what love that redeemer would be

[1] Canzone a Cola di Rienzo.   [2] Canzone a' Grandi d' Italia.

received in all the provinces that have suffered through these foreign inundations; with what thirst for vengeance, with what stubborn faith, with what pity, with what tears. What gates would be shut against him? What peoples would deny him obedience? What envy would oppose him? What Italian would deny him homage? This foreign dominion stinketh in the nostrils of every one."[1] But the degenerate Medici could not be moved to noble action.

The plaint passed on from mouth to mouth, becoming less vehement because the belief that the future could bring succor began to wane. Only the strong heart dares to hope amid adversities. Chiabrera, the courtly verse-maker of the sixteenth century, bade his countrymen to arise, not to shake off their tyrants, but to save themselves from even worse ignominy, — the oppression of the Turks. The glory of the past, the freedom that would never return, now inspired the utterance of the few in whom a sense of the dignity of patriotism still throbbed. As among the later Jews, the voices were voices of lamentation, not of courage; what-might-have-been stifled what-shall-be. Filicaja, in a sonnet which Italians still love, poured out this despairing wail: "Italy, Italy, thou to whom fortune gave the fatal gift of beauty, whence hast thou this dower of infinite woes, which, written by great sorrow, thou bearest on thy brow? Would thou wert less beautiful, or at least more strong, so that he who seems to be destroyed by the rays of thy beauty and who yet betrays thee to Death, might fear thee more, or love thee less. For then thou wouldst not behold the army-torrents sweep down from the Alps, nor Gallic troops drink the blood-tinged waters of the Po; nor wouldst thou see thyself, girded with a sword not thine, fight with the arms of foreign peoples, to serve always,

[1] Il Principe, chap. 26.

whether victorious or vanquished."[1] It is related that when Napoleon's army was crossing the Alps, an avalanche swept a bugler from the path into a ravine far below; and his comrades heard his bugle sound, fainter and fainter, until the snows and cold silenced him: from such a depth of hopelessness, Filicaja's melancholy note floated to the ears of his countrymen; and it had many echoes.

[1] Byron paraphrased the opening of this sonnet in *Childe Harold*, iv, 42.

CHAPTER IX.

NEW VOICES AND REVOLUTION.

At last, about the time when Arcadians were growing ridiculous even to themselves, Italy was startled by a new voice, — which had in it the resonance of trumpet and drum. Here was no dirge, but a reveille, no lamentation, but a defiance, which rang through the peninsula. For the first time since Tasso, an Italian poet was heard beyond the Alps. Europe was astonished that Italy, the ancient mother of great men, should bear in her old age such a son as Alfieri; but he was plainly hers and no changeling, for in his speech, his gestures, and his mien he resembled the mighty children of her prime. In his life, Alfieri was wild and wayward; equally vehement in his appetite for women, his craze for horses, and his hatred of tyrants. He galloped over Europe from Lisbon to St. Petersburg in a coach-and-six, not to observe customs nor to admire monuments, but to ease a restlessness which could be eased only by motion. After a youth of promiscuous libertinism, he centred his affections during the last part of his life on the Countess of Albany, wife and subsequently widow of the Young Pretender. Yet his character did not lack high qualities: he was as firm in friendship as implacable in enmity; he was without sordidness; he was consistently independent even to haughtiness, in his demeanor towards princes. The pedantry and mawkishness of his contemporaries he despised, and he ridiculed alike the follies of the Arcadians and the servile imitators of the French. A rigid republican, he denounced as unrepublican the excesses into which the

French Revolution was urged by Robespierre and St. Just. His tragedies reveal the man. He took for his subjects the career of the Brutuses, of Timoleon, of Saul, and the Conspiracy of the Pazzi, or he revamped the classic legends of Agamemnon, Merope, and Antigone. Any personage, any episode, by which he could illustrate the corruption of kings and the manful resistance of citizens, set his imagination aflame. He breathed no sighs for irrevocable grandeur, no regrets for the past, he chided submissiveness, and instigated revolt. Regicide and the slaying of tyrants he extolled, if freedom could be attained by no other means.

As Italian literature had been sterile in tragedies, Alfieri, in supplying this void, was revered as the completer of the intellectual glory of his race. He seemed to tower above Sophocles and Shakespeare, and held that pinnacle until his power and art ceased to be novel. Then his critics, piqued at finding that he had been lifted higher than he deserved, set him down in a place lower than he deserved. By that time the fashion in letters had veered towards Romanticism; political events had scattered republican doctrines everywhere; men needed no longer to be aroused, but to be guided. So Alfieri's reputation suffered, as that of every author whose work has a historic rather than a literary significance must suffer: but now, neither blinded by political hopes nor biased by the appeals of a literary clique, we can judge him impartially. We see in him a man of extraordinary energy, and we may well doubt whether talents purely intellectual ever produced more splendid results. Every trick of rhetoric, every subtlety of oratory, is under Alfieri's control. His method is that of the French dramatists, who wind up their plot as a boy stretches his catapult, until it seems as if the elastic must break: and then — presto! the missile is discharged, the plot is solved. Your interest is fixed on the tension, on the strength with which the elastic is drawn, rather than on the accuracy of the aim. Alfieri wastes nothing, and tolerates no superfluities. He astonishes and excites, but does not charm us; we are dazzled, but not warmed by his genius. We may say of him what Schiller said of Madame de Staël: "In everything which we call philosophy, consequently in all the ultimate and highest stages, one is at strife with her, and remains so in spite of all discussion. But nature and feeling are in her better than her metaphysics, and her fine intellect rises to the capacity of genius. She tries to explain, to understand, and to measure everything; she admits of nothing obscure or unintelligible; and those things which cannot be illuminated by her torch have no existence for her!"[1] Qualities similar to these Alfieri possessed so abundantly that he earned a conspicuous place in literature. But it is as an historical figure in the regeneration of Italy that he most concerns us, and will be longest remembered. After two hundred years of rhyming gabblers and drowsy pedants, he came and spoke with all the vehemence and vigor of a man. The work before the Italians called for energy, and Alfieri was the trumpet through which that call, startling and metallic, was sounded. He blew a strong blast, and the effeminate guitar-strumming was heard no more.

Contemporary with Alfieri was Parini, a quiet, kindly man, the mildest of satirists, who describes dispassionately the follies of society and leaves the reader to laugh at them. The theme of his principal poem is the daily life of a fashionable young noble. In his odes and shorter pieces, he depicts the simple virtues or reveals the charms of every-day nature. He finds, for instance, in the discovery of vaccination a subject more worthy than battles or conquerors of our esteem. His influence may be compared to Cowper's in England: for he brought poetry back from extravagance and vapidity to the con-

[1] *Correspondence between Goethe and Schiller* (London, 1879), ii, 170.

templation of actual life, with its common sorrows and pleasures, — unheroic, if you will, and yet often touched by gleams of true sentiment and nobleness. Among the painted Jezebels of Arcadia, his sober Muse walked unaffectedly and at first unobserved, but after a while men turned in disgust from them to her, and made her their model. So Parini has justly been called the regenerator of modern Italian poetry.

A little younger than Alfieri and Parini were Monti and Foscolo, two men who represented so well the character of Italians at the end of the eighteenth and beginning of the nineteenth century, that in reviewing their careers, we shall best understand their countrymen at this period. Italians still spend superlative adjectives when they speak of the talents of Vincenzo Monti, and for the sake of those talents, they generously forgive the ignominy of his life; but we may doubt whether they still read his poetry with pleasure equal to their praise. Of the historical importance of Monti and his works there can be, however, no question. Born near Alfonsine, in Romagna, in the year 1754, he went to Rome to devote himself to letters. There he found the Arcadians still tending their flocks, and for a while, he chimed in with their pastoral ditties. His first effusions, like those of most receptive youths, echoed the prevailing tone of his time, but they had in them besides something original and un-Arcadian, that attracted attention. Thanks to the patronage of Cardinal Scipio Borghese, he became erelong the most popular verse-maker in Rome. His was one of those natures to whom it is easy to discover good qualities in those who feed with flattery and clothe with honors, and for fifteen years it was his agreeable duty to extol the virtues of his protector and to magnify the achievements of the Pope, by whom also he was graciously favored. There is an old story of a Christian lady so benign that she had always something kindly to say about everybody. One of her family, provoked by her uniform amiability, exclaimed at last, "But you must admit that there's nothing praiseworthy in the Devil!" "On the contrary," replied the good woman, "I think we might well take a lesson from his diligence." Monti likewise had eyes only for the excellence of the Roman court, at a time when less interested critics saw chiefly its faults. Nevertheless, he had a mind which responded quickly to high influences; he soon scorned the silliness of Arcadia and was stirred by Alfieri, Shakespeare, and Dante. He sympathized in the abstract with heroes and patriots, and expressed his sympathy so far as it was discreet to do so, by attributing to his protectors the heroic traits which he admired. Few men have been more richly gifted than he with that intellectual prudence which mixes just as much of radicalism with the antidote of conformity as will make a pleasant draught for those in power. When the French Revolution burst forth, Monti was still in Rome, writing praises of Pius VI, and when, shortly after, Ugo Bassville, a revolutionary disciple, came to the Holy City, preached republican heresies, and was killed by the mob, Monti was inspired to write one of his most famous poems, in which he reprobated the bloody events in France. Bassville, in the poem, could expiate his crime of having joined the regicides only by passing through hell and witnessing there the terrific punishments decreed for them, and by waiting at the gate of heaven until the Bourbon monarchy should be restored to France. Monti, no doubt, had planned to end his poem with a fine peroration, glittering with praise of absolute monarchs and of papal benevolence; but unfortunately for poetic symmetry, and for the repentant spirit of Bassville impatient to enter into bliss, the restoration of the Bourbons was delayed. Monti published his work without its final canto; his fame increased, but the soul of Bassville still waits.

Presently down into Italy came General Bonaparte, and changed the fashion of poetry and politics. Monti, the alert, was among the earliest to greet the rising sun. He had been deceived by the lurid flames of the Reign of Terror, which, he now saw, were but forerunners of the day of freedom; he had confused the excesses of the Revolution with its true purpose, and this was plainly enough to bring liberty and equality to all men, even to Italians. Ah, how joyfully he welcomed the effulgent deliverer, — how easy it was to indulge the sublime sentiment of patriotism, now that every one was patriotic. Wishing, he said, "to merit well of a free fatherland, by writing at last as a free man," he poured forth in a single year (1797) three canticles, entitled "Fanaticism," "Superstition," and "The Peril," in which he execrated the upholders of that Old Régime, whose bread he had eaten and whose purse he had tapped for well-nigh twenty years. And to show the thoroughness of his conversion, he addressed to Bonaparte an ode in which the young conqueror figured as Prometheus. If there be by any other man of equal rank eulogies as fulsome as those which Monti showered upon Napoleon, I have not seen them. "O illustrious God of War, for a God thou surely art!" he exclaims at one time; at another, he likens Napoleon bringing order out of chaos in France to God himself stretching forth His hand over the primeval abyss. The hyperbole of adulation could hit no higher!

When a law was passed to cut off from preferment all those who had written against liberty since 1792, Monti promptly issued a poetical apology for his Bassvillian blunder, was granted pardon, and appointed to the chair of belles-lettres at Milan. For an interval his prospects darkened, when the Austrians and Russians, profiting by Napoleon's absence in Egypt, invaded Italy: but Napoleon returned: the victory of Marengo swept the invaders back into their North, and secured to France for fourteen years the control of Italy. Monti throve exceedingly during that period. He was chosen Poet Laureate to the Cisalpine Republic, and, later, Historiographer to the Kingdom of Italy; and in order that his Pegasus might not be worn out by treadmill work, he was relieved of his duties as professor, but allowed to draw a salary therefor. Napoleon was eager to entice authors into his service; but in spite of favors and subsidies, he could command only the mediocre; Monti's reputation was the most conspicuous which he bought.[1]

When Napoleon made himself Emperor, and there was no longer a reason for cherishing the delusion that he was a disinterested champion of liberty, Monti, the official songster at Milan, moulted his democratic feathers and strutted magnificent in imperial plumage. His ardent muse could not be restrained from caroling whenever there was a Napoleonic victory or wedding or baptism to celebrate. It was marvelous how the smallest happening in the imperial family kindled his imagination; how punctually his song came, sometimes even before it had been commanded by his master! There were not lacking, of course, voices which accused him of apostasy and cringing; but then, envy is a sin to which literary men are proverbially prone, and he could console himself with the thought that his detractors would gladly have received, even from the tyrant they affected to abhor, the fat pension which came to him every month. Prosperous genius, if it be not annoyed by modesty, finds a new meaning in the fable of the Sour Grapes. Monti did feel, nevertheless, that his friends had some reason for regarding his position as ambiguous, for he wrote to Melchior Cesarotti, in 1805: "I am touching the Pindaric

---

[1] De Gubernatis, in his study of Manzoni (Florence, 1879), gives some amusing specimens of these subsidized penny-a-liners' adulation. One, Gagliuffi by name, turned the Code Napoléon into heroic couplets. See pp. 211-15.

chord for the Emperor Napoleon. The government has thus commanded me, and I must perforce obey. God grant that the love of country do not draw me to a too great liberty of thought, and that I respect the hero, without betraying the duty of a citizen. I follow a path where the desire of the nation does not accord very well with the political condition, and I am afraid of ruining myself. May St. Apollo aid me, and do you beseech me to circumspection and prudence."[1] How naïve is that prayer that his patriotism may not draw him to a too great liberty of thought!

Just when Monti intended to throw off his disguise we do not know. The fall of Napoleon gave him an opportunity of abjuring forever his gilded bondage, but he did not avail himself of it. On the contrary, he made haste, when Northern Italy passed into Austria's keeping, to ingratiate himself with the new tyrant. He greeted the Austrian Emperor as "the wise, the just, the best of kings," a whirlwind in war, a zephyr in peace. But Francis had a wholesome dread of authors: literary activity is a sign of wakeful brains, and wakeful brains are too apt to concoct incendiary thoughts, which lead the populace to revolutionary deeds. To suppress and not to encourage the intellectual life of his subjects was, therefore, the wise policy of Francis. He abolished the office of historiographer, either because he intended that his subjects should be too happy to need an annalist, or because he suspected that there might be matters which had better not be recorded. Still, he allowed Monti to draw a small pension, in return for which poetic tribute was dutifully paid. In his later years Monti harmed Italy by renewing a Dryasdust dispute concerning the purity of the Italian language, and he frittered away his talents over the questions whether Italian be Tuscan or Tuscan

---

[1] Quoted by Mestica: *Manuale della Letteratura Italiana* (Florence, 1886), i, 33.

be Italian, whether a writer should use words not found in the works of the fourteenth century, or whether words added to the vocabulary since 1400 should not also be recognized. A fine quarrel for the foremost writer of his time to engage in: worthy to be fought out by servile pedants, amid much taking of snuff and frequent rubbing of spectacles, in dim, dusty attics. An appetizing dish of chaff to set before a people who, deceived in their hope of independence, crushed to earth but not killed, were hungering for words of liberty which should be as strong wine to their resolve. The Austrians chuckled to see their bondsmen voluntarily return to the threshing of old quibbles, in which too much of the intelligence of later Italians had worn itself out. Absolutism had learned that it had nothing to fear from pedants. Monti in this fashion sank into an old age of poverty and neglect, all his trimming and talents of no avail; distrusted by his countrymen, unfeared by his countrymen's enemies, he died in 1828.

His contemporaries dubbed him Abbé Monti, Citizen Monti, Courtier Monti, to designate the different phases of his sycophancy, but the *man* Monti did not change. To his family he was kind, even tender; to his friends, he was affectionate; but he was vain and vulgarly ambitious. He loved to move among smiling faces, though they were those of flatterers; he loved to see himself the favorite of the great, though the great were tyrants. At heart, he preferred virtue and liberty, and we can imagine that he covered the margins of his Dante with approving notes: but it is one thing to be intellectually hospitable to noble thoughts, and quite another thing to obey them "in the scorn of consequence." Monti had behind him and about him a society which had long ago divorced precepts from practice; which took it for granted that the guardians and exemplars of morality would themselves be neither chaste nor humble, neither charitable nor sincere. His life, and that of most of his fellows, was of the intellect and not of the conscience, and the intellect, greedy of applause, makes worldly success a duty. Moreover, the alternative was very real, and very stern: poverty for certain, probably imprisonment, perhaps exile, possibly death, — those were the grim conditions he must choose, if he preferred independence to compromise. He exonerated himself by reflecting that his intentions and sympathies were excellent; perhaps self-deception went so far that he thought himself a martyr to circumstances, and blamed destiny for spreading ignoble nets before the steps of one who might otherwise have stridden with a regal gait through the world. He could plead that he had counteracted so far as possible the effect of his fawning poems, by sprinkling upon them patriotic sentiments, which the alert would find and interpret. "My duty as husband and father," he wrote, "made me belie my countenance and speech; listening to the voice of nature made me seem guilty; but so beautiful a fault does not merit the blush of shame."[1]

It would have been too cruel to drag Monti's delinquency again into the light, merely to illustrate the fact that intellectual ability is often without conscience. The public press furnishes daily evidence that the hand can write what the heart does not believe; so that to strengthen a statement by "the honor of a journalist" would in most cases provoke sarcastic laughter. He is condemned to live in the history of Italy's regeneration, because he was the most conspicuous of those Italians who, in spite of mental ability and good intentions, failed from lack of moral courage. The new ideals urged them forward, but the spiritual enervation of centuries held them back. Not without reason has Monti been called "the last poet of the past."

Although Monti's public career could serve but as a

[1] From his poem "La Superstizione."

warning, and although his writings were too often base, yet he did positive good to the Italian literature of his time. He wrote with force, he seized upon living subjects, he showed that the real substance of poetry lay in the great events by which men's souls were actually moved, and not in the archaic puerilities of mock shepherds and shepherdesses. The best Italian critics agree that he infused into the verse-forms he used a vigor unknown since Tasso sang. When he was not restrained by prudential motives, he could speak plainly. "Mute sittest thou," he says to Italy, at the time of the Congress of Udine; "at every shock thou castest down thy glances tremblingly; and in thy fear thou knowest not whether fetters or freedom await thee. O more vile than unfortunate! O derided slave of thy slaves! Not thus would thy countenance be dejected, nor thy feet chafed with shackles, if cowardly pride and long fornication with tyrants and Levites had not softened the sinews of thy native valor. Honored spouses these, whom thou hast preferred to Brutus and to Scipio! A fine exchange, a shrewd judgment, forsooth! She who had the universe for slave now sings psalms, and a mitre is the crest of her helmet."[1] A sad truth, we confess: but a truth that comes strangely from lips which have just lauded the mitred leader of the psalm-singing choir, and which, a little later, lauded the new tyrants. In the anthologies, Monti still holds a considerable field, and editors still append footnotes exhorting the studious youth to be thrilled at the proper passages, but to me the reading of Monti's poems gives little pleasure. The constant inversions, in imitation of Latin models, are artificial; the alleged grandeur is grandiose. Monti does not soar like a bird: he leaps like a kangaroo, and while he surprises you by the height and length of some of his bounds, you see that he is quickly on the earth again. Between

---

[1] Ode per il Congresso d' Udine, 1797.

leap and leap there is a succession of very fluent, often melodious, commonplaces. In this respect, he resembles the English poet Young; and if his verse has a larger space allotted to it in Italian manuals than Young's has in English manuals, it is not because he excels Young, but because English poetry has had many subsequent poets far superior to Young, whereas later Italy has had few superior to Monti; and because, above all, Monti is associated with a great period in Italy's growth, whereas Young speaks to us out of a period when the poetic life of England was barren.

Of different stamp was Ugo Foscolo, born in 1779 on the island of Zante, then a Venetian possession. His father, a physician, was a Venetian, his mother, Diamante Spaty, a Greek. Foscolo's first schoolbooks were Plutarch and Xenophon. After his father's death, his mother and her children settled at Venice in 1793. Ugo attended the lectures of Melchior Cesarotti at the University of Pavia; he was precocious in versifying, and was swept, while still a youth, into the current of active life by the revolutionary tumults in Italy. In a fine ode he addressed Bonaparte as the "Liberator," but when, soon afterwards, Bonaparte by the deceitful treaty of Campo Formio extinguished the Republic of Venice and sold Venetia to Austria, Foscolo's illusions as to the probity of the Liberator were dispelled. Upon Napoleon's return from Egypt, the young poet republished the ode, adding thereto a dedication in which he exhorted the victor to fulfill his mission as the bringer of liberty, and not of servitude, to the distressed nations. "Our age," he said, "will have a Tacitus, who will hand down your sentence to severe posterity." But Napoleon's ambition, having tasted power, was not to be satiated by patriotic appeals; he assumed the title of Emperor in France, and converted the Cisalpine Republic into the Kingdom of Italy, of which he was king. Foscolo tacitly submitted to the change, tacitly, but not ignobly; he served in the imperial army in France, and accepted the chair of oratory at Pavia, but thenceforth he wrote no praises of Napoleon. Indeed, he took so little pains to disguise his republican opinions that his professorship was soon abolished, and he had to shift as best he could. Literature is at all times a precarious profession, but never more precarious than when the free utterance of authors is muzzled; to Foscolo's credit be it recorded that, unlike Monti, he never spiced his speech to the taste of his censors. In 1811 he brought out at the Scala Theatre in Milan a tragedy called "Agamemnon;" the official ferrets scented in it meanings which the author disavowed: Agamemnon, they said, was intended for Napoleon, Ajax was the exiled General Moreau, and Ulysses was Fouché, Imperial Minister of Police. The play was prohibited and Foscolo banished. Three years later, when the Napoleonic kingdom was tottering, he returned to Milan and took part in the unsuccessful attempt to resist the Austrians; but when they had by craft reëstablished themselves, and required every Italian to swear allegiance to Francis, Foscolo refused and fled to Switzerland. He went thence to England, and wore out the remainder of his life in exile, writing articles for the English reviews and giving lessons in Italian. He died there in 1827.

Foscolo's poems are more genuine than Monti's, for they spring out of the man's soul, and not out of his intellect. The poet does not set traps for the approbation of critics, nor for the ducats of patrons. Patriotism finds in them nothing to blot, nothing to extenuate. When the French, in one of their democratic deliriums, were for prohibiting the erection of tombstones and other memorials to the dead, as being a custom whereby the aristocratic and rich displayed even in death a pomp and an arrogance inconsistent with poor but honest democracy, Foscolo — in his most noted poem, "The Sepulchres" —

defended the practice, and showed how the tombs of heroes keep alive the memory of noble deeds and rebuke the littleness of posterity. He described himself as a man who heard the continual rumbling of passions within him, as being "rich in vices and in virtues;" and, so bitter was exile, as being "sad for the most part and solitary, ever pensive, and incredulous alike of hope and fear." A man of great gifts, impulsive, quick to resent wrongs and quick to forgive them, although he wrote a Wertherian romance, yet he could endure to live in spite of disillusions more poignant than those which drove his hero, Jacopo Ortis, to suicide. In the weariness of exile he served his country better than he knew, by acquainting Englishmen with the genius of Dante and by showing them the almost unknown spectacle of an incorruptible Italian, who preferred banishment and poverty abroad to oppression and sycophancy at home. Italians could better spare Foscolo's writings from their literature than his example of integrity from their history.

These two men represent the two prominent classes into which Italians were divided during the Napoleonic era, and for nearly a generation beyond it. The one, facile and unscrupulous, preferred liberty in theory, but bent the pregnant hinges of the knee to any master from whom rewards and favors could be obtained; the other, setting principles above self, sacrificed self rather than submit. From the former class no good came, nor could come; by the latter was slowly accumulated that moral force which alone could make Italy worthy of freedom, and could endure all shocks, all rebuffs, until freedom was at last won. There was, besides, a third class, composed of the princes of the Old Régime and of their parasites and protégés, who were consistently and inflexibly hostile to any change which threatened to diminish their inherited privileges. The eighteenth century approached its last decade, but these deluded creatures still dwelt in their mediæval paradise, and thought it permanent.

The Revolutionary War in America set a dangerous example to Europe, but the Italians no more thought of imitating the sturdy colonists, than of flying when they saw a hawk circle above them. The existence of the American Republic doubtless made independence seem possible, but I cannot discover that it had as yet excited more than a languid interest in Italy, when the French Revolution burst forth terrific. Since the subversion of the Roman Empire under the flood of Teutonic invasion, such a catastrophe had not been known. Now, as then, a régime which had endured for so many centuries that Europeans had come to regard it as eternal, was confronted by strange, terrible enemies, who seemed to be agents of chaos and anarchy. These enemies were not Goths, nor Huns, nor Turks, but members of the very social system which had been created and held together by the Old Régime; the struggle, therefore, was not between the civilized and the barbarians, but between one class and another, between the privileged few and the unprivileged many. Aristocracy found itself set upon by its great pack of underlings, like Actæon by his hounds. No wonder that the wisest spectators of that contest failed to realize its import. Little guessed Mirabeau, when he flung down defiance to the king's messenger at the Tennis Court, whither the current was sweeping; little foresaw Burke, when he looked aghast at the orgies of the Reign of Terror, that in those convulsions, though the old world-order was passing away, a new and juster one was coming into life.

When such men were unaware of the mighty change impending, it is not to be supposed that the princes of Italy understood at first the omens flashing across the skies France-ward. Their anxiety was perhaps as great as that of one who receives news that a neighbor is suffering from an acute but not deadly fever. But when French royalty was insulted, imprisoned, and then guillotined, they realized their own danger, and prayed that the allied monarchies of Europe might dispatch the revolutionary monster at Paris. Then was the time for Italy to free herself. But those Italians who read Alfieri and dreamed of liberty were too divided, too unskilled to seize the opportunity held out to them. The habit of ten centuries made them look to foreign lands for leadership. At the most, they trusted that in the amazing changes, Fortune would assist them. The mere fact of change was a most encouraging prognostic. Like gamblers, they watched the wheel a-spinning, and relied upon their luck. And suddenly, beyond all expectations, a leader arose.

Napoleon, leaping on the back of the revolutionary Bucephalus, rode him over Europe, and where his hoofs struck, the earth quaked and thrones toppled over. Napoleon, himself an Italian, galloped down into Italy, swept the armies of Austria before him, appealed to the Italians to strike for freedom, promised them independence, and then, caught in a frenzy of selfish ambition, he broke his promise, and made Italy an appendage of his Empire. The Cisalpine Republic was transformed into a kingdom governed by his stepson Beauharnais; Etruria was a toy for his sister Eliza; the Parthenopean Republic became a kingdom ruled by his brother-in-law Murat. Napoleon undeniably betrayed the hope of the Italians, but even in betraying he benefited them. He was a great reality, stalking over Europe and exposing immemorial shams. By a stroke of the pen he signed the burial-certificate of the Holy Roman Empire; he touched the Republic of Venice, and it dissolved in ashes, as the body of a queen crumbles when its sepulchre is opened; he carried the Pope about with him, like a parrot in a cage; he made ridiculous the old tactics in war; he made obsolete the old methods in peace; he set up Merit instead of Privilege to be the ladder of promotion. While Bourbons or Hohenzollerns or Hapsburgs or Romanoffs slunk away in terror from the back door of their palace, he strode imperiously through the front portal, mounted the grand staircase, sat in the king's seat in the banqueting-hall, and slept in the royal bed. He put the Iron Crown of Charlemain on his upstart brow and distributed half the sceptres of Europe among his vulgarian relatives — that was the *reductio ad absurdum* of that old pretense, the divine right of kings. He manufactured an aristocracy as easily as he had organized an army, raising butchers' sons, taverners, and lawyers' clerks to principalities and dukedoms, and grafting them by marriage on the loftiest family trees.

The Empire he founded fell, because he, too, lost his hold upon reality and came to make compacts with impostures; but the effect of his deeds remained. Such might of pure intellect has been applied to State affairs by no other man unless by Cæsar. Astonished, you follow him through court to camp, and from camp to council, yet you have not seen his activity flag. He had time for framing codes and appointing a legion of office-holders; for building bridges and laying out roads; for scandal and amours; for reading the correspondence of numberless envoys; for deciding where a picture should be hung or a statue erected; for discussing antiquities with Denon and Champollion; for devising liveries for his lackeys and uniforms for his generals; for ridiculing his wife's dresses and his sister's manners. Nothing escaped his intellect, — it took in the most weighty business and the most trivial. In mental vigor he was a colossus, in moral character a dwarf; carnal and selfish as a man, yet imperial beyond all others as a conqueror. He did not create the Revolution, but he had the power, and he alone, to grasp the thunderbolts the Revolution had forged, and to hurl them as if he were Jove. He so identified that movement, which had been long maturing, with his personal fortunes, as to blind Europe for more than a generation to the irresistible principles behind him. She imagined that in crushing him she could crush the new world-order and restore the Past. Fame shone round him, as from a sun, lighting up all who came near him, were they friends or foes; a troop of lesser men — Wellington, Nelson, Blücher, Schwarzenberg, Archduke Charles, Wittgenstein, Kutusoff — won enduring renown merely in resisting him. But Napoleon's great achievement was to discredit the Past. Force less Titanic than his could not have broken up the petrified crust of European society. He seemed to his contemporaries a destructive whirlwind; but after he had passed, they beheld the seeds of regeneration springing up in his track.

Thus when Napoleon reconstructed Europe, Italy did not attain independence; she did not even get unity, for the master-carver cut her into several slices to feed his favorite dogs of war: nevertheless, she gained much. She woke from torpor to activity; she lived in the Present. Instead of being stranded like a rotting hulk, she was once more swept into the current of European destiny. The Napoleonic administration, though autocratic, was centuries in advance of that of Pope or Bourbon. The watchword of the new era, "*La carrière ouverte aux talents*," called for able officials; antiquated placemen were laid on the shelf. Civilians succeeded to ecclesiastics in every department of government. The Code Napoléon did away with mediaeval courts, recognized equality before the law, and promoted respect for justice. Incessant campaigns and the military conscription not only made the Italians fighters, — between 1796 and 1814, Italy furnished 360,000 soldiers to the imperial armies, — but also broke down provincial barriers and encouraged national spirit. It was something to fight for the Kingdom of Italy, though that kingdom had a foreign sovereign. The Lombard who marched side by side with the Romagnole or the Neapolitan felt that they came of the same kindred and had interests in common. Above all, Italy learned that her petty princes and even the Pope himself, whom they had regarded as necessary and incurable evils, could be ousted by a strong hand. Thus were the Italians rejuvenated by contact with the European Autocrat; thus did they store up some of the strength and courage which are given out in days of stress and mighty undertakings. Perceiving that they could not act for themselves whilst Napoleon lived, they looked forward to his death as the signal for new changes, out of which they might pluck the fulfilment of their desire.

And here we may close our retrospect of the growth of Italy. Henceforth we shall follow the Italians in their struggle to secure independence and unity by means of elements and against obstacles which many centuries had prepared for them. That struggle was all the harder because of the conflict among these elements and because the Past has had over no other European people so strong and paralyzing a hold as over the Italians. Institutions which at one era had been beneficial remained like the trunks of dead trees overgrown with living vines; how to cut down the dead and save the living was the task before Italy.

In our retrospect we have seen how the Roman Empire grew languid in prosperity, then rotted in vice, and finally fell asunder; how the Teutonic invaders, having conquered, gradually mixed with the races of western Europe, and how, from the mingling, new races were born. We have seen the Bishop of Rome lift himself into the primacy of the Christian world and unite with Charlemain to organize society under a dual government; and how the Pope stealthily reached forth his hand and surely seized temporal power. We have glanced at Feudalism, the source of mediæval and modern class distinctions; we have surveyed the rise and overweening expansion of the priesthood, with its demoralizing asceticism, — whence came the divorce between conduct and profession; we have noted the solidification of dogmas, — whence came the divorce between reason and faith. We have seen a multitude of small republics spring into nervous life, toss and waste themselves in internecine feuds and local jealousies, and remember only their mutual spites when, exhausted, they succumbed to tyrants. We have seen Italy the prey of foreign invaders, — of Saracens, Franks, Normans, Germans, French, Spaniards, who robbed her treasure and stultified her people. We have seen her genius express itself in many forms: how Italy was the pioneer in commerce and industry; how letters revived through her enthusiasm; how Dante, greatest of her sons, broke the spell of antiquity; how, having formulated and maintained the religion of Christendom, she was the first to feel the liberating breath of the Renaissance, which carried to other lands principles by which the unique tyranny of that religion was destroyed. And just as the rest of the world was becoming more tolerant, we have seen the rivets of clericalism driven deeper into her soul, — Inquisitors burning her liberal thinkers at the stake, Jesuits repressing education and controlling government. We have seen her aristocracy slip down from magnificent licentiousness to brutality, and from brutality to the emasculate follies of Arcadia. Yet we saw, too, that she put forth new branches from her aged stem, — Science, Music, the Drama, — and that each bore fruit. We have seen the dark shadows of Spain and Austria hanging like a pall over her land, and then Napoleonic clouds blown across her sky, still dark, but with fitful gleams breaking through the rifts. We have seen her debased by servitude to foreign conquerors, debased by the treachery of native tyrants, debased by the hypocrisy, worldliness, and superstition of her Church. And we have seen that from the time of Charlemain to the time of Napoleon, she was never mistress of herself, but always the victim of foreign rapacity. All this was her inheritance, when, at the beginning of the nineteenth century, she seriously resolved to be free. Like a beautiful woman under the spell of a mesmerist, she had so often sinned and been so often baffled in her efforts to recover her freedom, that she had begun to despair of her will-power: then Napoleon came and banished her Evil Genuis for a time, and the fibres of her will tingled with new strength. Can she revive? Can a nation, like a man, turn from a career of shame and rise, not only above the effects, but also above the memory of evil ways? To this question the following pages of this history will give in part an answer.

BOOK SECOND.

THE DOOM OF TYRANNY.

Libertà va cercando, che è sì cara,
Come sa chi per lei vita rifiuta.
     DANTE, *Purgatorio*, i, 71, 72.

CHAPTER I.

THE CONGRESS OF VIENNA.

IN the month of March, 1815, the Congress of Vienna had been five months in session. After twenty years of warfare, the royalties and aristocracies of Europe were assembled to celebrate the return of peace. So august a concourse had not been seen in modern times: two emperors, several kings, potentates by the dozen and diplomats by the score, with their retinues and their regiments, with women and with prelates, made boundless jubilee, and promised each other that the Old Régime thus happily restored should nevermore be disturbed. Revelry by night, endless chatter by day: monarchs amusing themselves with the dissipations of one of the naughtiest capitals of Europe; ministers inditing protocols and memoranda; courtly urbanity on the surface, reptilian intrigues and jealousies and hatreds in the depths; balls, masquerades, banquets, and hunting parties alternating with conferences and map-makings: princes, dames, milliners, pastry-cooks, and lackeys all toiling without truce in this carnival of gayety, — such was the mixture of business and play at Vienna during the winter of 1814-1815. For the Lion who had so long desolated Europe had been overpowered, and was now caged in Elba, wherefore the lesser beasts were met to carouse over his capture and to divide his booty. Reynard the Fox, his Excellency Prince Metternich, acted as master of ceremonies and distributor of spoils. But the proceedings were so slow, and so often interrupted by festivities, that one of the revelers, the cynical Prince de Ligne, declared that *"le Congrès danse, mais ne marche pas,"* "the Congress dances, but does not advance." Nevertheless, by the beginning of March, the chief topics had been discussed,[1] although the discussion had been so hot that there was immediate danger that the peacemakers would fall to fighting among themselves. Then, happily for them, news was brought that the Lion had escaped from his cage.

On the morning of March 7 a servant brought a dispatch to Prince Metternich, who was still in bed. He saw the words, "Urgent, from the Consul General at Genoa," but being sleepy, he turned over for another nap. Unable to sleep, however, he reached for the envelope, broke the seal, and read, "The English Commissary, Campbell, has just appeared in the harbor, to inquire whether Napoleon has been seen in Genoa, as he has disappeared from the Island of Elba; this question being answered in the negative, the English ship has again put out to sea." Metternich rose at once. "I was dressed in a few minutes," he says, "and before eight o'clock I was with the Emperor. He read the dispatch, and said to me quietly and calmly, as he always did on great occasions: 'Napoleon seems to wish to play the adventurer: that is his concern: ours is to secure to the world that peace which he has disturbed for years. Go

---

[1] The Congress had two sessions, namely, that of the *Five Powers* — Austria, Russia, Prussia, France, and England; and that of the *Eight Powers*, in which, besides these five, Spain, Portugal, and Sweden took part. All the smaller States had also accredited representatives.

without delay to the Emperor of Russia and the King of Prussia, and tell them that I am ready to order my army back to France. I do not doubt but that both monarchs will agree with me.' At a quarter past eight I was with the Emperor Alexander, who dismissed me with the same words as the Emperor Francis had used. At half past eight I received a similar declaration from the mouth of King Frederick William III. At nine o'clock I was at my house again, where I had directed the Field-Marshal Prince Schwarzenberg to meet me. At ten o'clock the ministers of the four Powers came at my request. At the same hour adjutants were already on their way in all directions, to order the armies to halt who were returning home. Thus war was decided on in less than an hour."[1]

From this official report we learn that in cases of emergency imperial chancellors can make haste, and that august monarchs can dispense with the usual ambages of ceremonial. History records no other instance where two emperors and a king, in night-cap and ruffled night-gown, declared war in bed at eight o'clock in the morning. But the resolve thus promptly taken was prosecuted with vigor. And while the Allied Armies were driving Napoleon to bay, the diplomats at Vienna proceeded to finish their partition of spoils. On June 9, 1815, just nine days before Waterloo, the articles of the treaty were signed, the distribution was completed, and the Congress adjourned.

The principle which guided the Congress was very simple. "We will ignore the Revolution and its results, and restore Europe to its condition previous to 1789," said the monarchs and their minions. But, as much had been destroyed which could not be replaced, and as the events of a quarter of a century had brought the various Powers into new relations, it was decided to make a fresh partition where restoration was impossible. One common in-

[1] Metternich: *Memoirs* (New York, 1881), i, 254-5.

terest, the need of exterminating the revolutionary spirit, bound the sovereigns together; after deferring to this, each grabbed as much for his private use as his neighbors would permit. The strongest took large slices; the weak, but not less greedy, snarled over the crumbs and morsels that remained. When it came to cutting up Italy, which had from time immemorial set forth a feast for foreign despots, there was much wrangling, much envy; but Metternich held the knife and carved to suit himself.

After Napoleon's first abdication in 1814, most of the Italian States saw that their old rulers would return; but Murat still held the Kingdom of Naples and Beauharnais the Northern Kingdom. Now it was decided that Austria should annex Venetia, Milan, and Mantua, together with Istria and Dalmatia on the eastern shore of the Adriatic.[1] To the Archduke Francis of Este, an Austrian, were allotted the Duchies of Modena, Reggio, and Mirandola; the Archduchess Mary Beatrix of Este received the Duchy of Massa, the Principality of Carrara, and imperial fiefs in the Lunigiana.[2] The King of Piedmont, who had lived in retreat on the island of Sardinia during the Napoleonic upheaval, had to cede a part of Savoy to the Canton of Geneva, for which he was compensated by the Republic of Genoa.[3] The Genoese protested; they pointed to their long career of liberty and to their past glory; they begged to be allowed to preserve the independent government which Lord Bentinck had recently set up. Their envoy, Marquis Brignole, pleaded eloquently, but in vain; the Powers wished to make the King of Piedmont strong enough to resist possible French invasions, and accordingly, in January, 1815, he took possession of the Genoese.[4] When it came to the question of Tuscany and Parma, the Spanish plenipotentiary Labrador and the French plenipotentiary Talleyrand fought hard for their

---

[1] Treaty of Vienna, § 93.   [2] Treaty, § 98.   [3] Treaty, §§ 80, 85.
[4] Flassan: *Histoire du Congrès de Vienne* (Paris, 1829), ii, 89.

respective governments; but Metternich stopped their arguments by bluntly declaring that "the Tuscan matter is not an object of discussion, but of war."[1] Archduke Ferdinand of Austria was therefore restored to Tuscany, with sovereignty over the Principality of Piombino, of which Prince Ludovisi Buoncompagni enjoyed the revenues; Maria Louisa, daughter of the Emperor of Austria, and wife of Napoleon, was given the Duchies of Parma, Piacenza, and Guastalla, the succession to be determined later.[2] To the other Maria Louisa, Infanta of Spain, and her son Charles Louis, was offered the Principality of Lucca together with a perpetual annuity of 500,000 livres; an offer which she, who had once enjoyed the sounding title of Queen of Etruria, at first refused, but subsequently accepted. It was agreed that at the extinction of her line, Lucca should revert to the Grand Duke of Tuscany.[3] Cardinal Consalvi urged that to the Pope be restored those possessions from which he had been driven. The Cardinal pleaded, "not from temporal motives, but for the maintenance of oaths taken by the Pontiff at his elevation, — oaths according to which he could alienate nothing from the domains of the Church, of which he was only the usufructuary."[4] The pious request was heard; the Pope was again temporal lord of the Marches, of Camerino and its dependencies, of Benevento and Ponte Corvo, — these two were embedded in Neapolitan territory, — and of the Legations, Ravenna, Bologna, Forlì, and Ferrara. But he grumbled because Avignon and the Venaissin in Southeastern France were taken from him, and because Austria, in order to complete her military frontier, insisted on keeping garrisons in Ferrara and Comacchio.[5] Ferdinand IV, who, thanks to the English, had been able to hold Sicily whilst the French were in Naples, was restored to his realm on the

---

[1] Flassan, ii, 106. [2] Treaty, §§ 99, 100. [3] Treaty, § 101.
[4] Flassan, ii, 118. [5] Treaty, § 103.

mainland. Such were the provisions, so far as concerned Italy, of the treaty signed and sealed by the European spoils-distributors, "in the name of the Most Holy and Indivisible Trinity," at Vienna, June 9, 1815.

Were the Italians satisfied? No. Had they been consulted? No. Did their dissatisfaction matter? No. That generous but deluded knight, Don Quixote, once mistook a flock of sheep for a hostile army; Metternich, the champion of the Old Régime, mistook the human populations of Europe for sheep. According to him, the Almighty was pleased to create a few privileged persons, to whom the earth and all that in it dwelt belonged. These few, with their families, their favorites and their priests, were of a different genus from the common herd of humanity. Like Shepherd-Kings, they drove their people to pasture, or to shearing, or to slaughter, without consulting them. We must confess that the people had too often, by their stupidity and compliance, justified monarchs in holding this unscientific view; but at last the unprivileged classes had, in the French Revolution, announced with sudden and unprecedented vehemence that they were bipeds and not quadrupeds, and that they, too, as sons of Adam, had human rights. Metternich and the European sovereigns regarded this assertion as proof that a strange madness had infected their sheep; and when the flocks began to run amuck at the heels of a colossal bell-wether, threatening the existence of sheep-dogs and shepherds, Metternich and his monarchs were amazed; but now, having bound the bell-wether, it was believed that the frenzy would soon subside, and that the sheep would graze as peaceably as before. During the period between 1815 and 1848 we shall often hear Metternich tell the peoples of Europe, "You are sheep," while the peoples endeavor to prove by every means in their power that they are men.

To understand this conflict we must know the character

and policy of Prince Metternich, who succeeded to the dictatorship of Europe that Napoleon lost at Waterloo. A system has rarely been so completely embodied in one man as was the revived Old Régime in Metternich, who, ruling by a few formulas, was himself a formula by whose help we can reduce to lowest terms the products of his time. Born of noble parents in 1773, in Rhineland, he studied for a while at Strasburg, just after a young Corsican named Napoleon Bonaparte had left that University; he remembered with a certain pride that the same masters taught both of them fencing and mathematics. His studies were interrupted by social distractions into which his father's position at the Viennese Court got him an early admittance. When but seventeen years old he represented the Westphalian Bench at the coronation of Emperor Leopold at Frankfort, and two years later in the same capacity he saw Francis I crowned, and he led the ball with the beautiful Princess Louise of Mecklenburg, — afterwards Queen of Prussia and mother of William, first Emperor of Germany. Then he followed his father to Belgium, but the war disturbed his studies and he went to England, where he became acquainted with the leading politicians and inspected the mechanism of Parliament, which, he says, "was not without use in his subsequent career." Returning to Austria, he married the granddaughter of Kaunitz, that statesman who had been the adviser of Maria Theresa and the antagonist of Frederick the Great. On his own avowal, Metternich had no ambition to enter public life, for he measured his abilities and found them so modest that he preferred to devote himself to a gentlemanlike pursuit of science and letters. But Emperor Francis saw promising qualities in him, and bade him to be ready against duty's summons; to which the young courtier, despite his modesty, replied that he would. His first diplomatic mission was to the Congress of Rastadt, which ended abortively through no fault of his; then, in 1801, he was appointed minister to Saxony, where he began to cultivate his peculiar powers. Dresden was one stage on the road to Berlin and St. Petersburg, and offered him rich opportunities for studying the intrigues of Prussian and Russian emissaries, and for acquainting himself with the new crop of European diplomatists. His strength lay in watching. Unimpassioned, observant, patient, he could wait, like Jason, while the dragon of the Revolution uncoiled its huge bulk before him, and then, where he saw a vital spot bared, there he plunged his sword. He knew his country's resources; he knew his adversary's preponderance; he had unfailing tact, unruffled suavity, and he risked nothing by untimely rashness. His sojourn at Dresden brought no immediate victory to Austria's schemes, but it secured his promotion to the embassy at Berlin. There, too, his achievement was seemingly barren; since he was expected to bind the fickle resolution of a king who veered now, under the instigation of Haugwitz, towards France, and now, under the instigation of Hardenberg, towards Russia. War broke out: Napoleon crushed Russia and Austria at Austerlitz, and Prussia, in spite of Metternich's efforts, had so planned that, by her insincerity and indecision, she was sure of immunity whichever might win. Still, Metternich's efforts were not forgotten. Francis nominated him ambassador to St. Petersburg, when Napoleon, who had taken a fancy to the polished young diplomatist, requested that he should be sent to represent Austria at Paris. "I do not think it was a good inspiration of Napoleon's," he writes in his "Memoirs," "which called me to functions which gave me the opportunity of appreciating his excellences, but also the possibility of discovering the faults which at last led him to ruin, and freed Europe from the oppression under which it languished." [1]

To Paris Metternich went, reluctantly, but not tim-

[1] Memoirs, 67.

idly; knowing the difficulties which lay before the Austrian ambassador at the Court of Austria's recent conqueror, but resolved to improve this occasion for studying Napoleon, "the incarnation of the Revolution," in the hope of finding his vulnerable spot. If we are to believe Metternich's "Memoirs," we must believe that already in 1806 he regarded himself as destined to humble Napoleon, and that he foresaw much that came to pass; but those "Memoirs" were written years later, when retrospect could be dressed up as foresight, with the evident intent of magnifying the wisdom of their author.[1] At the raw and gaudy Napoleonic Court he was a perfect specimen of eighteenth century aristocracy. In person not commanding yet pleasing, in manner elegant but not stiff, choosing to be deemed frivolous rather than earnest, too self-controlled to be surprised into petulance or anger, he soon shone as a star of the first magnitude in Napoleon's hastily-improvised social firmament. He did not forget that Napoleon was a parvenu, but with the tact of a man of superior breeding, he took part in the pomp, and kept his derision to himself. He was affable and insinuating, but, when occasion demanded, he showed firmness as well as pliability. He announced at the outset to Napoleon that he was charged by Emperor Francis to promote friendly relations between Austria and France, but these relations, he said, "must not be confounded with submission." So he pursued his purpose, apparently intoxicated with court gayeties, but really scrutinizing Napoleon and his satellites, sounding the temper of the French people, investigating the resources of the Empire, and picking up what hints he could of the Emperor's intentions. A high-bred libertine, his *liaisons* with the women of the French Court — among others, with Caroline Murat, Napoleon's sister — served not only to gratify his vanity

---

[1] Some specimens of Metternich's skill in editing may be found in Malleson's clear monograph: *Life of Prince Metternich* (Philadelphia, 1888).

but also to put him in possession of secrets which he could not worm from the more wary men. In brief, he played finely the part of licensed eavesdropper which diplomacy dignified by the name of ambassador. All that he knew or surmised, he reported duly to Vienna; and perhaps it was from relying too much on his information that Austria declared war in 1809. Napoleon quickly brought Austria to terms at Wagram. "We have much to retrieve," said Francis to Metternich as they witnessed the losing battle. The Emperor's first step towards retrieval was to appoint Metternich Chief Minister of the Empire. The moment was indeed black. The past ten years had been strewn with the wrecks of ambitious but unsuccessful ministers. Thugut had been discredited at Marengo, Cobenzl at Austerlitz, Stadion at Wagram; the finances verged on bankruptcy; the army was beaten and discouraged; diplomatic relations with the other Powers which had coalesced against Napoleon were frayed. But Metternich assumed his new duties, unprejudiced by responsibility for the last disaster or for the ignominious peace. His policy was to restore as rapidly and secretly as he could the finances and the army, and to reach out for new combinations with Austria's former partners. Then came the proposition that Napoleon should marry Maria Louisa, the Emperor's daughter. Metternich, seeing that Austria had much to gain and little to lose, approved of it. If Napoleon should maintain his supremacy, a Napoleonic-Hapsburger dynasty might rule Europe for generations; if he should grow weak, the mere marriage-tie would not prevent Austria from seeking alliances with Napoleon's enemies. Moreover, Napoleon was intriguing to marry a Russian grand duchess, if Maria Louisa refused, and the union of France and Russia might be fatal to Austria. Therefore, Metternich approved, Francis consented, and the old House of Hapsburg was united to the upstart House of Bonaparte.

Metternich hastened to Paris, ostensibly to escort Maria Louisa to her husband, — although he took a different route from hers, — but really to fathom the hidden plans in Napoleon's mind. He was thus occupied six months instead of six weeks, and was able on his return to Vienna to inform Francis that 1811 would be a year of outward peace, during which Napoleon might prepare for a campaign against Russia in 1812. Austria, he added, must arm and hold aloof, ready to take fortune by either hand. Thenceforward, Metternich played his rôle with consummate duplicity. He signed a treaty of alliance with Napoleon and equipped a corps of 30,000 for the right wing of the Grand Army; but at the same time he assured the Czar that Austria's feelings towards Russia were friendly, — and the Czar, believing that Metternich acted from compulsion rather than from preference, bore him no malice. When space and the elements achieved what half a dozen European coalitions had failed to achieve, — the destruction of Napoleon's army, — Metternich deemed the hour of Austria's deliverance near. He saw that Napoleon, though checked, was not yet crushed, that he would strain every sinew to retrieve in 1813 the prestige lost in 1812. Austria was still bound to France by treaty, but Metternich had no intention of respecting it. Increasing the strength of the Austrian army as quietly as possible, he announced that Austria's sole interest was to mediate between the belligerents. Napoleon, however, was suspicious and ordered his agent Otto to pin the slippery Chancellor to his obligations. But Metternich fooled Otto as easily as a juggler mystifies a child. Then Narbonne, a subtle diplomatist, was sent to Vienna, and he thrust so near the truth that Metternich was embarrassed. "Why was Austria arming? Oh, merely to be in the position where she could forcibly mediate, should her offices as peacemaker be rejected." Napoleon scented treachery, but he hoped to outstrip it. At Lützen and Bautzen he whipped the Russians and Prussians. Then there was a brief pause, for victory had been as costly to him as defeat to his enemies. Metternich, having already secretly intimated to the Allies that he intended to join them, exclaimed, "The hour has struck;" but he still delayed to take the irrevocable step, because Austria still required a few weeks to complete her armament. Summoned to Dresden to confer with Napoleon, his one purpose there was to dissemble in order to gain time. The Emperor and Chancellor met at the former's quarters in the Marcolini Garden.

That interview is surely one of the most memorable set down in human annals. On the one hand, Napoleon, a lion at bay, representing in some fashion a world-system destined to revolutionize Europe; on the other hand, Metternich, a fox, representing a world-system which but recently seemed hopelessly stricken, and now seems on the point of resurrection, — these are the speakers in the dialogue. The Lion storms, threatens, coaxes: the Fox listens calmly, almost disdainfully, calculating the strength of the trap into which his foe must fall. It is an eight-hours' parley between the Present, still confident of its superiority, and the Past, unexpectedly come back to life and covetous of its former power. The Lion roars, but the Fox does not tremble: time was when the King of Beasts did not roar but did strike, and now sound and fury signify nothing. Napoleon leads Metternich into an inner room and shows him the map of Europe: Austria, he declares, shall have this compensation and that, if she but hold true to France; for France and Austria together may laugh at coalitions. Metternich is evasive, he promises nothing; he is already thinking how long it will take his army in Bohemia to march over to the allied camp. Napoleon appeals to the pride of the Hapsburgs: was it for nothing that he wedded the Austrian archduchess? Metternich replies that family considerations cannot interfere with his master's duty to his State. Napoleon in wrath flings his hat on the floor; Metternich, leaning imperturbably against a cabinet, does not condescend to pick it up; the Old Régime no longer fears the Revolution. From noon till night the fateful encounter lasts. Neither is deceived by his antagonist's ruses; each feels that there can be no league, no compromise between the systems they represent; each knows the other too well to hope to dupe him. At last they part, the irrevocable word still unsaid. Metternich lingers yet a few days at Dresden. They agree upon a conference to be held at Prague to discuss the terms of peace, — a pretense which neither means shall be more than a pretense; but it secures for Metternich the twenty days needed for his army in Bohemia, and for Napoleon time to replete the regiments decimated in the late battles. And so, with peace on their lips, but war in their hearts, Metternich finally quits Napoleon and Dresden. The Austrian Fox has counted the allied forces, they outnumber the French three to one; he is satisfied that the Old Régime can now overwhelm this terrific "incarnation of the Revolution." Napoleon, on his side, measures the full stature of his peril, but trusts that his genius and desperation may countervail the odds against him, and resolves to die fighting as a Lion should. The sham truce ends; beacon fires flash the news from peak to peak in Bohemia that Austria has declared war against Napoleon. The Allies press on Dresden and are hurled back by a Titanic effort. For a moment it seems that Napoleon may triumph. But he fails to pursue his advantage, his generals are worsted, and he falls back on Leipzig. There, in mid-battle, the Saxons desert him. the odds are too great, and he loses. Metternich has won. His tactics in this campaign may stand forever as a pattern of the methods of the old school of diplomacy.

With equal cunning he managed the policy of the Allies during their first invasion of France. When the Prussians were too eager for vengeance, he checked them by exciting the jealousy of the Czar, and when the Czar was headstrong, he brought him to terms by threatening to withdraw the Austrian army from the Alliance. At the Congress of Vienna he was both chart-maker and pilot. He dictated his views at the session of the diplomats; he strutted with monarchs in the drawing-rooms; he dallied with duchesses in their boudoirs. When the greed of Prussia and Russia would have devoured prey which Austria, not less greedy but more circumspect, wished to keep from them, he formed a secret treaty with France and England and was prepared to resist the northern gluttons by arms. He so thwarted and badgered the Czar, that Alexander, in a passion, sent a second to him to demand an apology or a duel. What a spectacle that would have been, the Autocrat of all the Russias and the Chancellor of the Austrian State engaged in a duel, while all the monarchs and ministers of Europe looked on! Metternich would not apologize; he merely insinuated that the misunderstanding was due to the deafness of the Prussian minister, and Emperor Francis was able to patch up a reconciliation. For the sake of his *liaison* with Murat's wife, Metternich would have kept Murat on the throne of Naples, and his persistency in pressing this matter might have brought the Congress to blows, had not Murat, by untimely impetuosity, put himself beyond the pale of even Metternich's favor. Napoleon's escape from Elba caused the Powers to drop their quarrels, and to complete more harmoniously the division of their booty. Thus conniving, bullying, cajoling, neutralizing greed with greed, patient at waiting, quick at striking, Metternich presided over the deliberations of the Congress of Vienna, and wrote the treaty there proclaimed as the new charter of Europe. Waterloo swept from the scene the only rival whom he feared.

Metternich's political creed was simple: he believed in absolute monarchy, privileged aristocracy, and a multitude of obedient subjects. It was for the interest of crown and court to treat these last well, to give them as sheep good pasturage and shelter; but if they were neglected, or abused, or even killed, there was no redress; no society for the prevention of cruelty to animals had as yet been organized. Metternich saw that the French Revolution attacked this social system,— that its promoters would have substituted representative for autocratic government; and he was shrewd enough to see that the rulers who would thus be chosen would rarely be those who owed their position to birth or privilege. If he perceived with equal clearness the rising spirit of nationality and its tendency, he acted as if unaware that it must be reckoned with. Yet this spirit had already given tremendous strength to France in her repulse of the first European coalition; it had been one of the secrets of Napoleon's success, in that he took care to identify his glory with that of the French people; it had been used by him to incite Italy, Poland, and Hungary, and then spurned when he thought it had served his purpose; it had kindled Prussia, nay all Germany, to such a fever of indignation that the Germans rose as one man in 1813 to throw off Napoleon's yoke. But Metternich ignored this principle, — at the most he laughed at it as a silly enthusiasm, an effervescence of political idealism, not to be encouraged. In reconstructing Europe, he attended only to dynastic interests. When it was necessary to cut a race into several slices, and to give these to different monarchs, he did so without scruple: for peace depended upon keeping, as nearly as possible, the equilibrium among the greeds of the various gluttons. His cardinal mistake was in supposing that by ridding Europe of Napoleon he had destroyed the Revolution. Napoleon was not the true embodiment of the Revolution; he was a despot who differed only in his genius and methods from the hereditary despots, — a man of force so herculean that he could bridle the vast energy liberated in 1789, and drive it along the road of his personal ambition. In thus confounding Napoleon's cause with that of the Revolution, Metternich made a blunder common to the politicians of his time, and often repeated by later historians, especially in England.

In 1815 much contributed to justify this error. Europe was thoroughly exhausted; the wars of twenty years had been waged for ambition and not for principle; Europe now asked for peace at any terms. The Arch-disturber being finally crushed, Metternich proposed to restore the good old times when the Corsican Ogre and the Reign of Terror were as yet undreamt of, and the divine right of kings was as yet inviolate. To accomplish this, it was only necessary to prevent any of the legitimate sovereigns from getting more than his share of the plunder; and then to agree that the division should be irrevocable. There were five great monarchs and a score of princelings, each of whom, like the Do-nothing Kings of yore, had his Mayor of the Palace, or Chancellor, or Minister, to take counsel with and to be guided by. It is a strange fact that God should have intrusted the government of the world to a few sovereigns, but it is stranger that, this being His pleasure, He neglected to endow them with ability to govern. The humor of this paradox escaped the notice of mankind until very recently; the sovereigns themselves have not yet perceived it, and they are certain never to be enlightened by their masters, the Ministers. Metternich himself enjoyed too well the reality of power to fret because a mediocrity wore the trappings of power. He valued things, not names. If his cynic eyes saw many absurdities, he repressed his smile and gravely performed them; for he knew that they too were essentials in the system from which his influence sprang. Dutifully he walked through his figure in the court quadrille, and stickled for the observance of the minutest punctilio. Perhaps he wished to believe that there was some occult virtue in these things themselves, — as a half-skeptic might wish to be benefited by touching holy relics, — at any rate, he held them to be indispensable for maintaining that form of society in which he was supreme. His almanac plainly read 1815, but he covenanted with his wit to humor the oligarchy which believed itself living in 1770; so a physician humors the follies of his mildly insane patients. He had in Emperor Francis a perfect master, a sovereign with just enough force to seem to act of his own motion, but not keen enough to see that his thoughts and will merely echoed Metternich's suggestions. As an Athenian actor spoke through a mask in order that his voice might carry farther, so Metternich's utterances gained in volume and authority in passing through the Emperor's lips.

Europe being thus at the disposal of a few monarchs and their counselors, diplomacy, — the art of ruling by chicane, — was brought to its highest pitch, and the control of Europe must needs pass to the diplomat who excelled in craft. A pretense of virtue was of course made; for even arrant villains do not publish themselves by that name, and in diplomacy as in other arts, perfection consists in hiding art. At the instigation of the Czar, the Emperor of Austria and the King of Prussia joined in forming at Paris (September 14, 1815) what is known as the Holy Alliance, a compact in which those three monarchs solemnly declare "that the present act has for its object to manifest in the face of the universe their immovable determination to take for the rule of their conduct, whether in the administration of their respective States, or in their political relations with any other government, only the precepts of this holy (Christian) religion, — precepts of justice, of charity, and of peace, which, far from being applicable to private life alone, should on the contrary directly influence the resolutions of princes and guide their actions, as being the only means in order to consolidate human institutions and to remedy their imperfections." The tender-hearted monarchs added that they would be as brothers to each other, and "as fathers of a family toward their subjects and armies."[1] Metternich, the worldly-wise, smiled at this manifesto as "nothing more than a philanthropic aspiration clothed in a religious garb." He suspected that the evil-minded would misinterpret and that the jokers would ridicule it, but none knew better than he the flimsiness of diplomatic agreements, and accordingly he consented to it. Christianity has had many crimes committed in its name; the Holy Alliance made Christianity the cloak under which the kings of Europe conspired to perpetuate the helotage of their subjects. Metternich found it all the easier to direct kings whose common interest it was to uphold the paternal system therein approved. He exerted his influence over each of them separately: if the monarch were obdurate, he wheedled his minister; if the minister were wary, he prejudiced the monarch against him.[2] Now by flattery, and now by specious argument, he won his advantage. When the Czar or the Prussian king grew restive at Austria's adroitly-concealed domination over them, Metternich frightened them by hinting that he had information of revolutionary plots about to explode in their realms. He made secret combinations between Austria and each of the Powers, so that, should one of them encroach, he could overwhelm it by an unexpected coalition. Like a trickster at cards, he marked every card in the pack and could always play the ace. He judged characters as he found them plastic or rigid in his

---

[1] Flassan, iii.
[2] Thus he tried to prejudice Alexander against Capo d' Istria, and Frederick William against Stein.

hands: George the Fourth was a noble prince and an uncorrupted gentleman; Castlereagh was a wise and just statesman; but Canning was a "maleficent meteor," Stein a dangerous visionary, and Capo d' Istria a fool. "Why is it," he asks in a tone of condescending pity, "that so many fools are thoroughly good men?"[1] He wrote in one vein to the king, in another to the king's adviser.[2] He would find justification for his claims in some treaty or custom centuries old, or he would unblushingly ignore any clause of a treaty which he himself had signed.[3] He told the truth when he knew it would not be believed; he prevaricated when he intended his falsehood should pass for truth. This was diplomacy, these the "Christian precepts" by which one hundred and fifty millions of Europeans were governed. In a society where every one lies, falsehoods of equal cunning nullify each other. Metternich took care that his should excel in verisimilitude and in subtlety. It was an open battle of craft; but his craft was as superior to that of his competitors as a slow, undetectable poison is more often fatal than the hasty stab of a bravo. He fished both with hooks and nets; if one broke, the other held. The chief falsehood, still potent to deceive, was to persuade nations that their interests coincided with the ambitions of dynasties and cabinets. When the Czar quarrels with the Austrian emperor, for instance, he persuades his Russians that they have a personal grievance against the peoples of Austria; and an army of Muscovite peasants set forth to slaughter an army of Austrian peasants: a wonderful delusion, which kings and chancellors will profit by, until the populations of Europe rise above the level of sheep! Metternich, who cared nothing for national sentiments,

---

[1] *Memoirs*, iii, 364.

[2] As in the case of Louis Philippe and Guizot; see Mazade: *Un Chancellier d'Ancien Régime*, chap. 6.

[3] As when, at Carlsbad, he ignored § 13 of the Treaty of Vienna.

nevertheless used them, as a chemist uses chemicals, to neutralize each other, by setting antipathy against antipathy, or by creating artificial combinations.

He was, we may affirm, sincerely insincere; strongly attached to the Hapsburg dynasty, and patriotic in so far as the aggrandizement of that House corresponded with the interests of the Austrian State. But the central figure in his perspective was always himself, whom he regarded as the savior of a social order whose preservation held back the world from chaos. When he stood off from himself and contemplated the responsibility heaped upon him, he was almost overcome by a mystic awe of himself; he felt as Atlas must have felt when, in gloomy moments, he reflected that he was mortal, and that when he died the heavens would fall and crush the earth. He spoke of his mission as an "apostolate." He was gratified by observing the sudden "moral improvement" which attended his visit, however short, to a recalcitrant sovereign, or to a hot-bed of conspirators. He testifies that the "pure and just" always hailed him as a deliverer, and he rejoiced in the hatred and fear he inspired in the "bad." Yet he cherished no delusions, except that primal delusion that the Old Régime could be permanently anchored in the swift-flowing, bottomless stream of time. He had every boat out, and every man tugging at the oars, to keep the prow of the old galleon headed against the current; but he saw her slipping down, decade by decade, and he knew that the rowers must at the end flag and fail. "They will last our time; after us, the Deluge," was a saying he liked to quote.

To resist all change, — that was his policy; to keep the surface smooth, — that was his peace. Mankind are mostly the dupes of appearances, and he had the art of draping Europe in what appearances he chose. After a paroxysm of fever, she lay in a stupor; he drew tight the curtains round her bed, pretty chintz curtains with

Watteau patterns; and if you asked to see the patient, he said, "She sleeps," and extolled the grace of those ladies in damask and gentlemen in satin, so artfully woven in the chintz. Yet with the facts on the surface he dealt quickly, decisively, outwitting his rivals in diplomacy because he knew exactly what he wanted and how to get it. Like Napoleon, he had a contempt for ideologues. "Phrases ruin the world, but save nobody;" "people only conspire profitably against things, not against theories," are two maxims of this adroit phrase-maker, who was sparkling-Gallic rather than opaque-German in his temperament. He likened himself to a spider, spinning a vast web. "I begin to know the world well," he said, "and I believe that the flies are eaten by the spiders only because they die naturally so young that they have no time to gain experience, and do not know what is the nature of a spider's web."[1] How many flies he caught during his forty years' spinning! but his success, he admitted, was due quite as much to their blindness as to his cunning. "I have never worn a mask, and those who have mistaken me must have very bad eyes."[2] The very ease and inevitableness of his capture cloyed him; he longed for worthier antagonists to increase his fame and call out his reserves. He regretted that there were no more great actors on the stage, after "the only genius the eighteenth century had produced" had been driven from it. He seemed to delight in royal conferences in order that he might have the excitement of manipulating Alexander and Frederick William; for his own Emperor, Francis, was as pliable as putty in his hands.

Such was Metternich, "the most worldly, the most dexterous, the most fortunate of politicians," the embodiment of that Old Régime strangely interpolated in the nineteenth century. Knowing him, we shall know the nature

---

[1] *Memoirs*, iii, 307. [2] *Ibid*, 326.

of the resistance which checked every patriotic impulse,
every effort towards progress in Italy, between 1815 and
1848. Few names have been hated as his was hated, or
feared as his was feared. The Italians pictured to themselves a monster, a worse than Herod, who gloated over
human suffering, and spent his time in inventing new
tortures for his victims. He regarded them, and all liberals, as natural enemies to the order in which he flourished; and he had no more mercy for them than the
Spanish Inquisitors had for heretics. One thing he knew,
they could not both thrive: and he having the superior
power used it. "All your cry for liberty and reform,"
he said, "means simply, *Otez-vous de là, que je m'y place*,
'You step down, that I may step up.'" Doubtless his
victims would have been surprised could they have seen
this "monster" in his daily life, where he appeared only
a polished man-of-the-world, too self-possessed to be a
dandy, and yet affecting a lightness not always becoming
in a statesman. Affable and never dull, few could remember to have seen angry flashes in those imperturbable
eyes, or any but a deliberate smile on those self-complacent lips. He cowered some men by a certain haughtiness; he captivated others by counterfeit frankness, or
by flattery; and he could even turn on the fountain of
tears, when the heats of diplomacy could be quenched
in no other way. Women of the highest rank were
proud to submit to his gallantry. After the fashion of
an amateur, he amused himself with painting and science,
and took satisfaction in having it appear that were the
cares of State ten times heavier, they could not exceed
his strength, nor interrupt his pleasures. He had the
dangerous privilege of believing that he was infallible,
that all his deeds were perfect, and in his old age, when
the hurricane of another revolution had swept his web
away forever, he declared that, were he to live his career
again, he would not alter a single act.

These, then, were the principles which dominated Europe after the downfall of Napoleon, and this was the man who signed the doom of tyranny against the Italians in the year 1815. The Era of the Lion was succeeded by the Era of the Fox, Force by Craft: but the Fox was too wily to trust wholly to diplomatic chicane; he had the Catholic Church as an ally, and when both diplomatic and clerical deceit failed, he had the armies of the Holy Alliance ready to compel obedience.

CHAPTER II.

THE RETURN OF THE DESPOTS, 1814–15.

THE Treaty of Vienna only confirmed the doom of tyranny which the Italians had seen to be impending for nearly a year. Early in 1814, when the Allies were tightening their coil round Napoleon, they made fine promises of liberty to the Italians, as they made also to the Germans. They enticed the fickle Murat, King of Naples, into their league, and they paralyzed the effort of Eugene Beauharnais, Napoleon's Viceroy in the North, by appealing to his troops to join Europe in her crusade against the colossal tyrant. Lord Bentinck, the abettor in behalf of England of Bourbon intrigues in Italy, landed at Leghorn, and issued a manifesto in which he called upon the Italians to rise and shake off the cruel yoke of Bonaparte. "Let Portugal, let Spain, let Sicily, let Holland tell you how England acts only from generosity and cares nothing for selfish interest. We do not ask you to come over to us: only let our voices admonish you to avenge your rights, and to regain your liberty."[1] Then proceeding to Genoa, Bentinck easily conquered the French garrison and set up a provisional government. Even earlier than this General Nugent, an Englishman who had long served Austria, proclaimed at Ravenna: "A new order of things is born, for the purpose of leading back to you and of consolidating public happiness. You are to become an independent nation. Show yourselves zealous for the public weal and keep faith with him who loves and protects you, and you will be happy.

[1] E. Poggi: *Storia d' Italia dal 1814 al 1846* (Florence, 1883), i. 12.

Very soon your lot will be envied and your state admired." Marshal Bellegarde, commander of the Austrian forces in Italy, was not less generous in his appeal.[1] "Behold in us your liberators," he said. "We come to protect your legitimate rights, and to set up that which force and pride threw down." Nugent, in a manifesto at Modena, February 25, 1814, repeated his siren song. "Soldiers! Let your servitude cease, let the Italian cease to shed his blood to serve the voracious ambition of foreigners. Do not fear lest in the new order of things, under different masters, you have at last to fall back into a state of weakness and subjection. No, Italians! this is not the scope of the Allied Powers. Among the many most just causes which brought about the actual war, there is that of your independence, conciliating your political and civil existence with the rights of the legitimate sovereigns of Italy, so that you may present in the circle of peoples a single body, a single nation, worthy of the respect of its neighbors, and free from the influence of any foreigners. Therefore, let every one of you kindle the desire of uniting under a banner which is that of the honor, of the happiness, of the regeneration of Italy."[2] Keen eyes might have detected dubious meanings in these artful appeals, but the Italians were blinded by their desire to rid themselves of their actual master, Napoleon; that accomplished, they looked to a brighter future.

The duplicity of the English and Austrians succeeded famously: with little resistance, Northern Italy was taken from the French. Had it been otherwise, had Murat and Beauharnhais joined their forces, they might have long held the Austrians in check, perhaps even have made a descent on Vienna; and although this might not have hindered the ultimate overthrow of Napoleon, yet it must have compelled the Allies, at the day of settlement, to respect the wishes of the Italians. But disunited, and

---

[1] Poggi, i. 14. [2] Ibid, 15.

deluded into the belief that they were partners in a war of liberation, the Italians woke up to find that they had escaped from the talons of the French eagle, only to be caught in the clutch of the two-headed monstrosity of Austria. They were to be used, in the language of Joseph De Maistre, like coins wherewith the Allies paid their debts. This was plain enough when the people of the just-destroyed Kingdom of Italy prepared to choose a ruler for themselves: one party favored Beauharnais, another wished an Austrian prince, a third an Italian, but all agreed in demanding independence. Austria quickly informed them that they were her subjects, and that their affairs would be decided at Vienna.[1] Thus, almost without striking a blow, and without a suspicion of the lot awaiting them, the Northern Italians fell back under the domination of Austria.

In the spring and early summer of 1814 the exiled princelings returned: Victor Emanuel I from his savage refuge in Sardinia to Turin; Ferdinand III from Würzburg to Florence; Pius VII from his confinement at Fontainebleau and Savona to Rome; Francis IV to Modena. Other aspirants anxiously waited for the Congress of Vienna to bestow upon them the remaining provinces. The Congress, as we have seen, dragged on into the spring of the following year; the self-styled brothers growled and quarreled over the spoils after the brotherly fashion of Cain, and they might not have concluded their settlement without another general war had not Napoleon's sudden return to Paris forced them to postpone their lesser differences. The Italians, already chafing under the restoration, were lighted by a momentary gleam of hope, when they learned that the Conqueror was once more master of France; they appealed to him to come and atone for his past duplicity by making Italy free, united, and independent. And Murat, who had by

[1] F. Confalonieri: *Memorie e Lettere* (Milan, 1890), ii, 5-10.

this time repented him of his desertion of Napoleon, and who began to fear that the intriguers at Vienna intended to deprive him of his Neapolitan Kingdom, proclaimed himself the champion of oppressed Italy, and marched northward to expel the Austrians. Brave but rash, he forgot Napoleon's counsel to remain on the defensive and wait for developments in France. After two engagements his army was dispersed. The Italians failed to rise at his exhortations, either because recent treachery had made them suspicious of everybody, or because the restored governments had already perfected their system of repression. Beaten, deserted by his troops and his friends, and in danger of capture by the Austrians, Murat escaped on a small ship to France. His unsuccessful exploit relieved Metternich of all embarrassment in finishing the reconstruction of Italy: on June 7, 1815, Ferdinand IV entered Naples under the protection of the Austrian army of occupation.

And here actually begins the complete restoration of the Old Régime, and the riveting of old fetters: a period of anachronism and conflict. Under the most favorable circumstances, crabbed age and youth cannot live together. How, therefore, in this case, when Youth, already advanced to middle life, beheld Crabbed Age, buried twenty-five years before, stalk back from the tomb and resume his hateful authority? Strive to realize what this word restoration meant in 1815; you will hardly succeed, even if you help your endeavor with imaginary parallels. And for this reason: that quarter of a century between the death and resurrection of the Old Régime is precisely the most prolific of changes that Europe has seen; not merely changes in the boundaries of kingdoms and in the names of kings, — that was but a surface ripple, — but changes in the views men held concerning the entire constitution of society, the right of individuals, the privileges of classes, the object and form of government.

These views spread, in spite of Napoleon's apparent contravention of them; they sprang up, wherever he planted his administration; they were borne by that irresistible but unobstreperous trade-wind, the *Zeitgeist*, into all lands. Men saw but dimly what the fruits would be; but they saw most clearly that the world's aspect had altered, that the current of events set strongly forward, and that some of the conditions which had prevailed in their youth were now as antiquated as the Crusades. But kings and ministers had "learned nothing and forgotten nothing." They believed that they could set back the horologe of time and by their simple fiat erase from men's minds the results of five-and-twenty years of momentous experience. It was as if you should take the blind creatures from the gloom and slime of the Mammoth Cave, and bring them into the light, where in the course of generations they might acquire eyes and new faculties: and then you should restore these more highly-endowed creatures to the darkness and the stagnant pool which had sufficed for their ancestors. Nature makes these changes, whether of advance or retrocession, so slowly, through the gradual adjustment of organs to environment, that there is little pain. But Bourbons never take lessons from Nature; they follow neither Reason nor Justice which is the supreme expression of Reason; but instead of these, take their own passions and interests for guides. And when Nature and Human Nature rise up and resist them, they apply their will yet more stubbornly and accuse the universe of being wrong. They had learned nothing of the needs required for directing by sane and just methods the new world to a higher goal: but they had learned through exile to be more bitter and more cruel: they had learned through the Revolution that changes must come, and therefore to dread change, and dreading, to hate it, and hating, to believe that the sole means of preventing it was to restore immediately and most rigidly the system which had obtained before the Revolution. They were logical, they were sincere; and in lieu of wisdom they obeyed instinct, which warned them that there could be no compromise between the old and the new. To surrender a part of their prerogatives meant inevitably to lose all at last: it was a death-grapple between the eighteenth century and the nineteenth, and for a long time the eighteenth believed that it had won.

With these purposes and doctrines in their heads, the champions of the Old Régime remounted their thrones in Italy. The course before them was not doubtful. They took the old fashions, customs, and dresses out of the wardrobes where they had lain in camphor during the long interregnum, and proceeded to attire themselves and their subjects in them. But here they were confronted by an aggravating obstacle: of their old subjects many had died, and those who survived had grown too broad of girth and stout of thigh to wear the apparel of their slender youth; while the new generation, trained in a later fashion, felt as uncomfortable and mistimed in ruffles, knee-breeches, and buckles as it would have felt in a Roman toga or an Athenian chlamys. Absolutism, perplexed but not beaten, decreed that the old clothes were a perfect fit, and that any one who thought otherwise should atone for his bad taste by imprisonment, banishment, or death: a simple expedient, which silenced for a time all open grumbling. A man might tell his wife, if he had full confidence in her discretion, that his sleeves pinched, or that his legs shivered in silk stockings, but woe unto him if he made these revelations in public. Let us now examine in detail the cut of some of this antique apparel in which the restored Absolutists dressed their Italians subjects.

The condition of the Kingdom of Naples was peculiarly confused. During the eighteenth century some necessary reforms had been promulgated by Charles of

Bourbon. The feudal system flourished; barons had their own courts and were exempt from many civil responsibilities. The Crown strove to get what contributions it could from the nobles, using force when it was strong, granting larger privileges in return for money when it was weak. The clergy, too, were almost free from royal authority; they had their own courts, and their pensions from the government in addition to the revenue they drew from their vast possessions, from the oblations of the poor and the gifts of the rich. Even in the courts controlled by the government there was little justice: the Crown prosecutor paid for proofs against the accused, and where the pay was in proportion to the amount of evidence, accusers were many and unscrupulous. The law being uncertain, both from the multitude of codes and the venality of judges, crimes abounded; women used poisons, men the dagger or other violent means, and punishment was rare, although the judges, whether civil or ecclesiastical, resorted to torture as well as to paid informers, to discover the guilty. Charles strove in some measure to abolish these abuses; but by passing special laws he added a twelfth to the eleven codes already in operation, and his reforms, from lacking uniformity, lacked permanence. He encouraged commerce, and somewhat curtailed the aggressions of the nobility and clergy, but since his purpose was to strengthen the Crown by autocratic methods, rather than to build up the welfare of the people on a constitutional basis, the perpetuation of his reforms depended on the whim of his successors.

Nevertheless, Naples had surely improved, when the French Revolution came to check the progressive tendency of every Absolutist ruler. Ferdinand IV, now King of Naples, willingly turned his face backward. Through the aid of England, he recovered his throne after the first storm of revolution. His Austrian wife, Queen Caroline, played the procuress between Lady Hamilton, wife of the British Ambassador, and Lord Nelson, commander of the British fleet. His minion, Cardinal Ruffo, punished rebels with an atrocity which, had it been exercised in a larger field, would have made the name of Ruffo as eternally detestable as that of Attila; and whatever Ruffo did, that Nelson tacitly approved by his presence at the Neapolitan court and council. But in 1806 the long-dreaded French could no longer be resisted. Ferdinand fled to Sicily, and the kingdom on the mainland was assigned by Napoleon to his brother Joseph, who two years later was succeeded by Murat. The French broom swept clean. The civil code, which had filled a hundred volumes, was replaced by the Code Napoléon; the feudal system was abolished; monasteries were suppressed; the army was replenished by a regular conscription; Murat's court repeated in miniature the grandiosity of Napoleon's; and he too, though revolutionary and though shrewd enough to perceive the benefits to be derived from an administration more in harmony with the new ideas of the century, was arbitrary in executing the laws. Nevertheless, Naples advanced under his rule. Liberal opinions circulated freely, acting as raw wine acts on men who have fasted too long. The masses, the most superstitious and turbulent of any in Italy, held religion in slight repute, now that a power stronger than the priests was in the ascendant. Murat, deeming himself strong, imitated Napoleon by drawing to him as many of the old aristocracy as had not followed Ferdinand into Sicily, and by filling the gaps with newly-created nobles from among his generals and friends. He coquetted with the nobles when he wished to coerce the people, and with the people when he wished to repress the nobles; and when misfortune fell upon him in 1815, both classes rejoiced at his departure.

The position of a restored monarch must always be difficult. If he be wise, he will forget the past and endeavor to treat with equal justice those who were loyal to him during his exile and those who upheld his rival. But Ferdinand was neither wise nor just. He had shocked even the English by his acts in Sicily, where he had showed that his only qualifications for governing were the perfidy and craft, without the resoluteness, which should belong to a Machiavellian despot. He began his new reign, however, with fair promises, issuing from Messina five decrees (May 20–24, 1815) in which he bespoke "peace, concord, and oblivion of the past;" proposed fundamental laws and political liberty, with formal guarantees for the State; hinted at a Constitution; pledged himself to confirm the existing civil and military appointees, to deal impartially with Muratists and Bourbons, Neapolitans and Sicilians, and to maintain the reforms introduced by the French.[1] Of similar import was the treaty of Casalanza (May 20, 1815) between the Austrian general and the defeated Neapolitan commander. The Emperor of Austria, through his agent, personally guaranteed that "nobody shall be persecuted for opinions or conduct previous to the establishment of Ferdinand IV on the throne of Naples;" "full and entire amnesty, without any exceptions or restriction;" that "the sale of property is irrevocably preserved;" that "the public debt will be guaranteed;" that "any Neapolitan shall be eligible to civil and military offices and employments;" that "the ancient and the new nobility shall be preserved;" that "every soldier in the service of Naples, who shall take the oath to King Ferdinand, shall be maintained in his grade, honors, and stipends."[2] To these promises the Bourbon king and the Hapsburg emperor pledged their solemn faith as sovereigns and as devout Catholics. On June 7 Ferdinand on horseback entered Naples amid the acclamations of a people easily cajoled.

---

[1] Colletta: *History of Naples* (English translation by S. Horner, Edinburgh, 1858), ii, 248.

[2] Full text in Turotti

The King chose ministers against whom the public had at first little to object; but they soon proved themselves easy tools of reaction and persecution. No more was heard of the Constitution: the French codes were in part abolished and in part continued, pending the compilation of others more agreeable to the Bourbon autocrat. His subjects learned erelong, says Colletta, "that the offices they held, the property they owned, and their very lives, were no longer theirs by right, but were to be considered as gifts conferred by the clemency of the King."[1] Immediate measures had to be taken to collect funds for the ordinary expenses of government and for discharging debts recently contracted by Ferdinand. He had agreed to pay the Austrians twenty-six million francs for reconquering his kingdom; he had spent nine millions more as a lobbying fund among the most influential members of the Congress; he owed Beauharnais five millions; and he had, besides, the Austrian army and his own troops to provide for. Tommasi, Minister of Finance, met the emergency by peculiar means: he proposed that national property should be sold, and that the Exchequer should issue *rentes* with which the public might buy in the property, but he took care to secure much of it for himself at a low figure, before the public sales. He also deprived hospitals, savings institutions, and other corporations of their patrimony, giving them *rentes* of uncertain value in exchange. Under this administration of dishonesty and incompetence the public debt was soon doubled.

The King was further perplexed in dealing with his army, chiefly composed of men who had favored Murat. In spite of his pledges, and disregarding the rule of seniority, he promoted Sicilians above Muratists, and assigned smaller pay to the latter, even when they held the same rank as the former. He reëstablished commissions of military judicature. Nugent, the Austrian general, was

[1] Colletta, ii, 249.

appointed commander-in-chief of all the forces, — an act of partiality which offended the native officers of either clique, as they were all jealous of being commanded by a foreigner. The King also abolished the conscription, which being a French method was hateful to him: in its stead he called for voluntary recruits, but he was obliged soon to return in fact, but not in name, to the conscription. These changes were unpopular. Under the French, conscripts had been well-treated and decently clad; now they had poor food and shabby uniforms. The old militia, eighty thousand strong, had been divided into twenty-one regiments, one for each province; now it was made exclusive, only landholders being eligible to it, and its numbers were reduced.

Still more unsatisfactory was the Bourbon administration of justice. After long waiting, the new codes, six in number, appeared. — imperfect, disorderly schemes, combining eighteenth century revivals and new defects with what had been least desirable in the French code. Divorce and civil marriage were prohibited. There were no juries. Trials were conducted by benches of three or five judges, who, having already taken part in the preliminary examination of the accused, could not be unbiased in their judgment. Arrests could be made promiscuously, and as there was no law of *habeas corpus*, the prisoner, whether guilty or innocent, might insist in vain for trial. Thus, arrest was often as burdensome as conviction. The power of the Court of Appeal was limited; the old abuse of fines and remissions was restored. This enabled the rich to buy themselves off; but what escape had the poor, who lacked both money and influence? Judges were removed for no other cause than that they had been appointed by Murat, and their successors, owing their offices to the pleasure of the Crown, took care to render verdicts satisfactory to the Crown. A spy dogged each judge, and reported all his acts to the Ministry. Open confiscation was not permitted, nor was torture at present revived; but in place of these former outrages, capital punishment of a most brutal kind was adopted. According to his offense, the condemned criminal, clad in yellow or in black, with feet shod or bare, with eyes bandaged or free, and with a placard stating his crime tied round his neck, was publicly executed, and after death his body was often mutilated. These spectacles stimulated the brutal instincts of a populace always excitable. Blasphemy was punished by confinement in a lunatic asylum, because, it was argued, no sane person would blaspheme. The commercial laws were mediæval and oppressive; the Court of Chancery was despotic. Merchants complained at the unwise tariff restrictions which enabled foreign ships to carry on all the commerce between Naples and other lands.

The Council of State, whose deliberations were secret and irresponsible, was a sort of Star Chamber; its members found their advantage in proposing measures which would be agreeable to the King. The Cabinet, composed of eight ministers and the Director of the Police, was likewise irresponsible. Tenure of office depended on the sovereign's whim; therefore, the ministers made a business of concealing from him any information concerning the state of the country that might turn him against them. A despot's advisers easily persuade him that his rule is just and popular. Ferdinand, who cared not a fig for justice or popularity, only demanded of his servants that, whatever they did, they would make his despotism secure. The man after his own heart was the Prince of Canosa, Director of Police, and an able imitator of Cardinal Ruffo. He had served Ferdinand during Murat's time, by instigating rebellion in the kingdom of Naples, collecting a band of ruffians from the galleys of Ponza and Pantelleria, and unloading them on the mainland. Now, he employed the vilest agents to carry out his orders. His ferocity was rather that of a merciless conqueror than that of an authorized minister, and since the police was the most valid support of despotism, Canosa had an unlimited field for his cruelty and deceit. His persecutions were so ruthless that they called out the remonstrance of the representatives of the foreign Powers at Naples; but it was only after repeated importuning that Ferdinand was induced to dismiss an officer who had fulfilled the royal wishes with more zeal than discretion. Canosa retired, but not in disgrace, for the King bestowed upon him new titles and an annual pension of sixty thousand crowns.

Upon the Neapolitans, a people which had been systematically corrupted by its Aragonese and Bourbon masters, and which had come to regard law as persecution and industry as the foolish amassing of wealth for the royal tax-gatherer to seize, Ferdinand's arbitrary and incompetent administration naturally produced evil results. Whatever was vicious or brutal in their temperament was aroused. The weak trusted to hypocrisy; the strong protected themselves by open violence. Crimes of the barbarous type were common. Respect for law, reverence for justice would have seemed foolish to men who knew that the judicial system arrayed against them was but a machine for punishing those who were suspected of political heresy or those who were too poor to buy an acquittal. This is the inevitable dire effect of a tyranny which bases its scheme of right and wrong, not on morality but on fictitious criminality. When a person suspected of liberal opinions is put to death, while a miscreant guilty of many murders is lightly punished, popular notions concerning virtue and vice must be perverted. How shall a community estimate crimes, when judges punish offenders whom the king hates, and pardon those whom he favors, though the guilt of both be identical? Italy's many masters had all taught one lesson, — deceit;

and the Italians, quick and subtle by instinct, had learned that to simulate and to dissimulate, to lie and to betray, are not evil in themselves, but evil only when they fail. And the police, who in a justly governed country are regarded as the protectors of law-abiding citizens, become odious when, as in Naples, they are employed to hunt down and persecute those whom the government proscribes.

Such a distortion of justice encouraged violent criminals in all parts of Ferdinand's kingdom. The burglars, thieves, and assassins who thronged the cities, the brigands and highwaymen who infested the country, committed their crimes in scorn, and often with the connivance of the police. Grant that an officer was honest, his very honesty might bring him a reprimand: for he could not tell but that the ruffian he arrested might be on friendly terms with the Crown or Cabinet. As an instance of this, we are told that some of the inhabitants of Piagine, a village near Salerno, seized and burnt alive a family which had been loyal to Murat. The brutes were arrested, but an advocate hurried to Naples to inform the King that they had in times gone by done him good service as brigands. The King at once pardoned them; but before the advocate could bear the news to them, they had been summarily condemned and executed by the local tribunal, which the King did not fail to punish.[1] Again, we might quote the case of Ronca, a brigand guilty of countless murders. Irritated by the crying of his babe, he snatched it from its mother and battered out its brains against a tree; and when the poor woman remonstrated, he turned and slew her. He was arrested, but the King, in view of the past fidelity of this devil, released him without any punishment.

Brigandage had been an instrument regularly employed by Ferdinand to harass Murat. He had kept

[1] Colletta, ii, 260.

Ronca, Guariglia, Fra Diavolo, and others only less infamous than these chiefs in his pay. He had even appointed Fra Diavolo a brigadier-general and Duke of Bassano. Romance has succeeded in throwing a glamour of respectability round these law-breakers, but their exploits, when shorn to the stature of truth, appear simply as crimes, vulgar or base or bloodthirsty. The prevalence of brigandage indicated the corruption of the government and the lawlessness of the people. Murat, through the sternness of his lieutenant Manhès, had, indeed, suppressed the brigands, in spite of the encouragement they received from the Bourbons; but when Ferdinand was restored to Naples, they sprang up again, and were as annoying to the Bourbons as they had formerly been helpful. Everything conspired to make brigandage popular and profitable. The administration was so slack that it was easier to steal than to earn one's livelihood. Besides the veteran bands temporarily dissolved by Manhès, there were many discharged soldiers who had now no occupation, and who preferred banditry to toil. There were also many criminals who, escaping arrest, took to the mountains, and preyed upon the peasantry. Some adopted the wild life from a love of adventure, others because they were in temporary need of money. Many of the communities sympathized with the brigands, but more frequently they were terrorized into paying tribute to them.[1] The situation grew so serious that even the Bourbon government felt ashamed, and took measures to check the disgrace. In each province a Junta was appointed composed of the intendant, the local commander of the troops, and the judge of the criminal court. They drew up a list of outlaws, set a price on every outlaw's head, and when one was captured, they had only to identify him with a name on the list. Identification

[1] A good account of the principal brigands will be found in D. Hilton's *Brigandage in Italy* (2 vols., London, 1864).

being established, he was executed without trial. This Draconic method might have served the ends of justice had the lists been honestly compiled; but among the names upon it were often those of persons whom the government wished to be rid of for political reasons, and sometimes those of private enemies of members of the Junta. As there was no appeal from injustice, so there was no preventive of carelessness, and victims perished whose names were inscribed through a mistake. Such blunders and such arbitrariness made the Juntas more hateful to the peaceable citizens than to the brigands themselves; and the repressive measures came to be regarded as ingenious masks for political persecution.

The Bourbons, though they wished to act uprightly, could not; their inveterate duplicity spoiled, in its execution, every just law they framed. There was a villain named Gaetano Vardarelli, who had deserted from Murat's army, turned brigand and fled to Sicily, where he had been welcomed by Ferdinand and made a sergeant in the Guards. In 1815 he deserted again, and soon had under his command a band of about forty highwaymen, some kindred in blood, all akin in villainy. These Vardarelli ravaged the Capitanata, plundering the rich but sparing the poor, and so winning popular esteem. Like Bedouins, they almost lived on horseback; their organization was strict, and the word of the chief was supreme. Neapolitan troops were sent against them, — the Vardarelli, on their swift steeds, vanished unharmed; Austrian troops pursued them, — the Vardarelli laughed at their pursuers. It was whispered that they were in league with the Carbonari. The government — even that government — felt annoyed and ashamed. Forty bandits on the one hand, a government with forty thousand soldiers on the other, yet unable to capture the forty. So the Cabinet resorted to deceit; it treated with the Vardarelli as a belligerent Power on equal terms.

The treaty, signed at Naples, July 6, 1817, is as follows: "1. The Vardarelli and their followers shall be granted pardon and oblivion of their past misdeeds. 2. Their band shall be converted into a squadron of gendarmes. 3. The pay of their chief, Gaetano Vardarelli, shall be ninety ducats a month, and of each of the three subordinate officers, forty ducats, and of every gendarme, thirty ducats. They shall be paid every month in advance. 4. The squadron shall take the oath to the king before the royal commissary; they shall be subject to the general in command of the province, and shall be employed to pursue the public malefactors in every part of the kingdom."[1] Thus the outlaws of yesterday became king's servants to-day. We are told that they fulfilled their agreement against the other bandits in the Capitanata, but although in the King's pay, they did not trust the King. They avoided cities, posted sentinels to guard their sleep, and continued in their nomad life. But one day, in the village of Ururi, in Apulia, where they expected to meet only friends, a volley was fired upon them by men concealed in buildings facing the little public square. Gaetano, his two brothers, and six comrades fell dead; the rest leapt on their horses and escaped. The government caused the assassins to be arrested and prosecuted with so great a semblance of sincerity that the Vardarelli were soon enticed into another trap. General Armato, commander of Apulia, invited them to come to Foggia to a military review, and to elect new officers. All but eight accepted the invitation, and rode gayly into the square at Foggia, shouting, "Long live the King." Then they dismounted, and were ranged in line for the review. Armato, from a balcony, smiled and applauded. Meanwhile, Neapolitan troops stealthily surrounded the square, and when Armato gave the signal by raising his cap, they advanced with muskets leveled and called on

[1] Colletta, ii. 292.

the Vardarelli to surrender. The ex-brigands mounted in haste and made as if to break through the ranks, whereupon the soldiers fired. Nine of the Vardarelli were killed, only two escaped in the confusion; the others, unhorsed, fled to the cellar of an old building near by. The troops lighted a fire at the entrance of this refuge, and would have suffocated them. Two shot themselves, one was burned to death, the rest, seventeen in number, surrendered. A court-martial found them guilty of having broken the treaty of July 6, and they were executed that same day. The eight who had kept away from ambush, and the two who had ridden off, were soon afterwards killed. Thus the government triumphed, but by such means that the people were inclined to regard the Vardarelli as heroes, and to pity them as martyrs to the treachery of the King.[1]

Such was the lawlessness on the surface, and such were the Bourbon methods of quelling it. We shall hereafter explore the burrows in which the secret societies plotted still more formidable rebellion. Other calamities beset Ferdinand's government. A virulent plague broke out which the superstitious regarded as a judgment of God on the execution of Murat. Insufficient harvests in two successive years caused a famine. The price of grain rose to a ducat for ten pounds. The Minister of Finance decreed laws intended to relieve the distress, but in reality they created a monopoly of cereals and enriched the monopolists. The Austrian army of occupation, which helped to exhaust the resources of the country, was at length withdrawn, in August, 1817, leaving behind it a "fair name for discipline and good conduct." But the general sickness and distress were not relieved until nature bore a good harvest in the following year. The government, through ignorance or perversity, failed in its efforts to reclaim waste districts to fertility; and it im-

[1] Colletta, ii, 291-5; Turotti, i, 527; Poggi, i, 178-81.

poverished others by restoring pre-revolutionary laws which reduced the peasantry to serfdom. The body politic was sick of a chronic disease, and the court physicians had only remedies as obsolete as those of an Iroquois medicine man.

In his relations with foreign governments, Ferdinand neither showed firmness nor commanded respect. He joined the Holy Alliance, and was the only ruler in Italy who submitted completely to Metternich's dictation. His most serious trouble was with the Pope. In old times, the King of Naples had done homage to the Pope for his kingdom, and had sent every year the offering of the *chinea*, as a recognition of his vassalage. This *chinea* was a white horse which, together with a purse of seven thousand gold ducats, the Neapolitan ambassador presented to his Holiness, amid much ceremony, every 29th of June. But in 1776 there had been a quarrel, and the tribute was discontinued. Pius VII now pressed the claim, not because he needed another horse in his well-stocked stables, but because he was jealous of preserving and increasing the temporal power of the Papacy. Ferdinand at first struck an independent attitude. In a letter to the Pope, he politely declined to renew the ancient custom, and advised that the Church should "conform herself in temporal matters to the century, and to the condition of the times."[1] There was bickering and finally negotiation, which ended in the signing of a Concordat between Naples and the Vatican. By the terms of this Concordat, signed at Terracina, February 16, 1818, by Cardinal Consalvi for the Pope and De' Medici for the King, Rome recovered her power in the Two Sicilies. The former dioceses, to the number of 109, were to be reinstated; they had been reduced from 132 to 43 by Murat. Compensation was to be paid by the State for Church property which the French had sold. As many

---

[1] Full text in Turotti, i, 517; Colletta, ii, 300.

monasteries as possible were to be restored. The Crown could not henceforth alienate ecclesiastical property. Rome was to receive an annual tribute of 12,000 ducats. Ecclesiastical tribunals were to be reopened. Bishops were empowered to censure all persons who transgressed ecclesiastical laws. Intercourse between the bishops and the Pope was to be unimpeded, and every one was to have the right of appealing to Rome. Bishops might suppress any publications contrary to the doctrines of the Church. The King was to nominate bishops, the Pope to confirm or reject them. Bishops must swear allegiance to the King.

By this Concordat, Rome regained an authority which caused dissatisfaction among the Neapolitans. Laymen complained because it virtually handed over education in the universities, colleges, and public and private schools to ecclesiastics; they complained, also, because it increased their taxes, since every bishop and priest received an annual subsidy from the State; they complained against an ecclesiastical censorship, and against turning the confessional into an instrument for revealing political secrets to the government. The disclosures made in the confessional were, in theory, inviolable; but the Neapolitans knew the untrustworthiness of their clergy, and moreover, every bishop, in taking the oath of allegiance, promised to inform the King of "anything which might tend to the injury of the State."[1] The clergy, on their side, also grumbled. Under the loose condition of the past twelve years, priests had enjoyed unusual independence; now they were held again to a strict episcopal discipline; and monks who, since the suppression of the convents, had lived like any other worldling, had to return to their gowns and their cloisters. The populace, ever skeptical of clerical virtue, laughed to see many of these fat-paunched, sensual fellows, after their long holi-

[1] Article 12 of the Concordat.

day of open libertinism, now reproved and driven to be more discreet, if not more chaste.

The grumbling availed not; for king and pope had agreed, and all must obey. Ferdinand paid a visit to Rome, did homage to Pius, and the reconciliation was marked by festivities. The Pope showed his good-will by canonizing Alfonso Maria de' Liguori, a Neapolitan by birth, and one of the ablest polemical writers among the Jesuits. The King tried to amuse his host and the Romans by the sallies of his buffoon, Casacciello, — the last court buffoon in Europe, — but the Romans found the poor fool's jests insipid, and ridiculed Ferdinand for finding them funny.

Ferdinand was of that common type of monarchs whom the accident of birth places in an eminent position to which their mediocre talents could never lift them. Kingship meant to him the chance of gratifying his carnal appetites and his whims without scruple or rebuke; government meant to him, first, the keeping of his subjects in such a condition that he could extort from them the largest revenues with the least resistance, and second, the intriguing with foreign Powers to insure the preservation of his throne. Although he had pledged himself to treat all parties alike, it was only natural that he should favor the Bourbons, who had been faithful to him, and should slight the Muratists, who had supported his rival. Towards these he did not conceal his rancor: for he decreed that the town of Pizzo, where Murat had been taken and shot, should have the title of "the most faithful city, that its civic imposts should be abolished, and that salt should be distributed to it every year free."[1] He founded the Bourbon Museum, with the collection made by the Farnese, and although he at first discontinued the excavations at Pompei, — because that work had been pushed by the French, — he subsequently ordered the digging to

[1] Turotti, i. 367 s.

go on. He was superstitious, but not religious, selfish, and without affection. When his brother, Charles IV, ex-King of Spain, lay on his deathbed, Ferdinand was amusing himself with the chase, and, in order not to be interrupted, he left unopened the bulletins from Charles's physicians. Even after the latter's death, while his body lay in state awaiting burial, the King did not give up his sport. But he was soon smitten with remorse and alarm. He remembered that none of his family had lived beyond the age of seventy, and he was now sixty-nine; so he vowed to build a Capuchin hermitage in the royal park of Capodimonte, in order to atone for his unnatural behavior and to persuade the angel of death to spare him yet a while. He, too, fell ill, it was thought fatally: but he recovered, and there were popular rejoicings; for it was whispered that he had promised to accord "something pleasing to Liberals," and that he had cut off his queue. How a monarch wears his hair might seem a matter of no concern; but under a paternal government that, too, had political significance. To cut off one's queue meant Jacobinism, and a decade or two earlier it was sufficient proof of political heresy to hang a man. That Ferdinand should adopt this fashion, what did it portend but that he was become a Liberal? His subsequent actions showed, however, that a man may change the cut or color of his wig without changing his heart.

In the States of the Church the restoration of mediæval conditions was more sudden and more nearly complete. Pius VII, and the cardinals who had shared with him Napoleon's severity, came back clothed in the attractive robes of martyrdom. Their reception was enthusiastic. Clericals of every order felt as the Jews felt when they reëntered Jerusalem after their long captivity; laymen hoped that the change would bring them benefits, — such is the temperament of restless, irresolute men. At first the Pope's firmness was hailed as a good omen; he reproached the arbiters at Vienna for depriving him of a part of his possessions; he asserted his ancient ecclesiastical rights in Naples, Piedmont, and France; he quarreled with Austria for occupying Ferrara with her garrison. The Holy Father evidently intended not to be Austria's lackey, — that was a hopeful sign: was it possible that he could have survived the radical revolutions of the past twenty years without perceiving that the old methods were worn out? But those cheerful hopers were soon grievously mistaken; for they learned that just as Robinson Crusoe, returning home after his long isolation, spoke the language of his youth, so the Roman hierarchy, having regained its capital, revived speech believed to be obsolete.

One of the Pope's early acts was to restore the Company of Jesus, suppressed since 1776; another was to encourage the Congregation of the Propaganda, whose purpose it was to spread Catholicism in all quarters of the earth. Civil and judicial posts, which the French had filled with competent civilians, were handed over to ecclesiastics. Each of the Legations was presided by a cardinal. Outside of Rome each of the nineteen delegations into which the provinces were divided was topped by a prelate; each delegation was further subdivided into governments and communes, and although laymen were admitted into the direction of local affairs, their power was only consultative; at best, they were but the shadows of the black-gowned churchmen. In the courts likewise, appeals and final sentences were always heard and given by priests. Feudal privileges sprang up again: baronial courts were established, and they only fell into disuse when the nobles found that they cost more than they were worth. Indeed, since the interests of the nobility coincided with those of the Curia, the ecclesiastical court could be relied upon to render satisfactory verdicts; and since all trials were secret, the public could not know whose gold or whose influence weighed down the scales of justice. Was it on this account that Justice from olden times was represented with bandaged eyes?

Measures, but not the wisest, were taken to consolidate and diminish the public debt, which had amounted in 1801 to seventy-two million crowns and had been wiped out by the French. But centuries of experience had shown prelates to be incapable financiers; skilful enough they were to gather the oblations and Peter's pence which flowed into the Vatican from every Catholic diocese, but inexpert and irregular, when not actually dishonest, in laying and collecting taxes. They now retained the French customs system, but revived the old papal system of internal taxation, with "monstrous and complicated" results. The police, in spite of their arbitrary powers, failed to protect decent citizens. Rome itself swarmed with ruffians who committed murders and other crimes, almost without fear of detection; in the provinces, where capture was more difficult, highwaymen and criminals abounded. Mendicity, which had been sternly prohibited by the French, was now tolerated, if not encouraged. Why wonder that the lazy preferred to live by alms rather than by work, when they saw thousands of authorized beggars in monasteries and convents?

The conscription was abandoned as being a French abomination, but a Civic Guard was established to prevent tumults in the city of Rome. Its members were exempt from duty outside of the capital; they were paid from the tax on wine and salt, and one fifth of the lottery prizes were given to their wives, daughters, or nearest female relatives. The Pope had his Pontifical Guard, in which young Catholic nobles from different countries enlisted. Theocratic was the government, and it was a bad government. The incompetence of prelates in performing judicial functions, for instance, was tacitly acknowledged, by the employment of lawyers to study the cases brought before the monsignori of the Segnatura and the Ruota, the courts of appeal in criminal and civil cases. These counsel were called "secret," because they swore not to reveal their relations with the courts. The real ruler was the Secretary of State and not the Pope, and while there was some supervision of underlings, the high officials gave no account of their stewardships. In the Legations, the mildness or severity, the justice or tyranny of the rule depended on the personal character of each cardinal. Education, except that of youths destined for the priesthood, was not encouraged, and was soon controlled by the Jesuits. There are mineral springs whose waters slowly petrify any object immersed in them; similar was the effect of the papal government on the minds and consciences of its subjects.

Of all the Italian States, Tuscany had the fewest grievances. The policy of the Grand Duke, strictly carried out by his chief minister, Fossombroni, was to restrain his people as little as possible in their daily affairs, so long as they did not meddle with politics. He preserved the reform laws of Peter Leopold as the basis of his administration, but he modified these so as to lessen the scope of municipal and communal liberty. This centralizing process had been perfected by Napoleon, and it was one of the few products of the Revolution which the Reactionist princes eagerly adopted. Centralization as a temporary means of breaking up local and provincial traditions, and of impressing a uniform government on an entire country, is commendable, and under Napoleon it was surely Italianizing Italy; but after the Restoration, the Peninsula being again cut up in small provinces, each of which was ruled by an irresponsible tyrant, the centralizing process took away from towns and communes traditional privileges and local autonomy, which might have acted as partial checks to tyranny. The Grand Duke allowed members of the local boards to be chosen by lot, but he himself appointed the gonfalonière and syndics, and since he doubled the property qualifications of those who were eligible to the boards, and required that twice as many names should be chosen as there were places to be filled, he insured even in local matters servile obedience to his wishes. For Tuscany was preëminently the land of a well-to-do bourgeoisie, who prospered by a wise system of agriculture and by commercial thrift, and who would submit to political dependence so long as their material interests were not interfered with. Ferdinand flattered this commercial spirit by reviving the Order of St. Stephen, admission to which was determined by the wealth of the candidates; and thus, as in England, the glamour of knighthood was cast round men successful in trade. He encouraged education; refused to patronize the Jesuits; permitted justice to have a deciding voice in the ordinary cases in the tribunals; maintained an army merely large enough to garrison the few fortresses, and to add dignity to his pompous celebrations; and he was satisfied with a lenient censorship. He himself took pride in mingling rather familiarly with his people, as a father with his family. By day you might see him, in straw hat and gaiters, walking unattended in the streets; by night, in State costume, he held his levees at the Pitti Palace; to which besides the Court any one distinguished in art or literature was invited. Thus Tuscany was regarded as an oasis amid the wilderness of despotism in Italy. Refugees fled thither from the less fortunate States, to enjoy freedom from persecution. Real liberty no more existed there than elsewhere, but the Tuscans were grateful for the Grand Duke's mild exercise of his autocratic power. Those who nursed patriotic sentiments knew well that this good-natured paternalism was a poor substitute for independence and self-government, but when they contrasted their condition with that of their neighbors, they were less eager to hazard a revolution which might deprive them of their actual privileges.

Very different was the rule of Francis IV, Duke of Modena. Upon his restoration in 1814 he refrained, indeed, from extreme retrograde measures, as if he thought that his subjects would of their own free-will put on the yoke of Absolutism; but the next year, Murat's ephemeral expedition, and the evident repugnance of the northern Italians towards their new taskmaster, taught him that, being unable to win the affection, he must compel the obedience of his people. He was dominated by two passions, — the determination to be absolute master of his present possessions, and the ambition to extend his power. He deemed himself endowed with faculties fit to govern a large kingdom instead of the toy duchy of Modena. He had married his niece, the daughter of the King of Piedmont, in the hope of falling heir to the Sardinian monarchy; he connived with Metternich in so far as Metternich encouraged his pretensions, but hated him when he perceived that the Austrian chancellor had no intention of allowing the rest of northern Italy to be united under Francis's sceptre. Secretly cherishing this ambition, he devoted himself to the task of converting his duchy into so perfect a model of an autocratic State that the most exacting champions of Absolutism should acknowledge his worthiness to be intrusted with a wider dominion. He, therefore, concentrated the government in his own hands. The three ministers of Public Economy and Instruction, of Finance, and of Foreign Affairs and Police, were mere servants. The Council of State, composed of sixteen of the high nobility never held a session. The public revenue he regarded as his private income, of which he set aside as much as he pleased to pay the current expenses of government. He recalled the Jesuits and gave them the charge of the universities of Modena and Reggio. He reopened the monasteries and convents and forced back into them the confraternities and sisterhoods which had been dispersed by the French. He made a show of patronizing art and science, but his protection was spasmodic and arbitrary. The decisions of the courts were set aside at his pleasure, so that the judges were tempted to pass verdicts of which he would approve. He suppressed the National Guard, maintained only a small army, organized "urban" guards to preserve order in the cities in case of emergency, and a military academy where young nobles were trained in the duties of court pages. Hating the very name of liberty, he was inexorable in his pursuit of the Carbonari. He allied himself with the opposing sect of Sanfedists and with the most reactionary party at the Vatican. A strict censorship was, of course, one of his usual weapons. Nevertheless, he had not yet displayed that cruelty which earned for him the nicknames "headsman" and "butcher." At the time of the famine he bought grain abroad, and sold it at low rates to his subjects. His administration was economical, and if he delighted in the erection of costly buildings, he paid for them, in part at least, out of his private fortune, which was large. Almost parsimonious in his ordinary style of living, on State occasions he entertained with an emperor's magnificence. He was believed to be zealous to the verge of fanaticism in his reverence for the Catholic Church, but his religion seems to have been based on calculation rather than on faith: there was a chance that the Church possessed the secret of salvation, and, like a prudent man, he invested in that chance; at any rate, it could not harm his prospects hereafter, while the coöperation of the Church was of very real practical aid to him in battling with the conspirators of this world.[1]

[1] Poggi, i, 106–8; Bosellini: *Francesco IV e V di Modena* (Turin, 1861), 14–31.

At Parma and Lucca, the return to the Old Régime was rapid but not violent. The presence of Austrian regiments discouraged resistance, and it was expected that the rule of the two women to whom those duchies had been assigned would prove mild. Nor were these expectations wholly disappointed. Maria Louisa, ex-Empress of the French and now mistress of Parma, cared for the interminable ceremonial to which she had been wonted at Vienna, rather than for the annoyance of politics. To be despotic in her court, with its thirteen ladies-in-waiting and its twelve chamberlains, to be arbitress in points of etiquette, and to amuse herself with Count Neipperg, her favorite, and, after Napoleon's death, her husband, sufficed for her ambition. Although she was under Austria's tutelage in politics, nevertheless she showed more respect for justice than the Austrians commonly showed, and she took a certain pride in having among her subjects a few literary men, as other rulers had rare animals or bric-à-brac. The Spanish Maria Louisa at Lucca was given to a life of pleasure. She, too, relied upon Austria for counsel and protection, but she permitted the French codes to remain generally in vigor, except that she abolished divorce. We need hardly remark that more depends upon the integrity and wisdom of judges than upon the wording of codes.

In Lombardy and Venetia, Metternich soon organized a thoroughly Austrian administration. The government of the two provinces was separate, that of Lombardy being centred at Milan, that of Venetia at Venice; but over all was placed an Austrian archduke as Viceroy. Each district had its civil and military tribunals, but the men who composed these being appointees of the viceroy or his deputies, their subservience could usually be reckoned upon. The trials were secret, a provision which, especially in political cases, made convictions easy. The pillory, flogging, and other barbarous punishments were revived. Feudal privileges, which had been abolished by the French, could be recovered by doing homage to the Emperor and by paying specific taxes. In some respects there was an improvement in the general administration, but in others the deterioration was manifest. Lombardy and Venetia had to bear a share of the Austrian public debt proportioned to their population; thus they were taxed not only for the support of their internal government, but also to replenish the imperial coffers at Vienna. They were crippled by tariff laws which excluded the introduction of muslin, cotton, silks, woolen, cutlery, and other foreign manufactures, — an economical blunder which deprived them of foreign markets for their own products, and which encouraged smuggling to such a degree that insurance companies were formed to pay smugglers the value of contraband goods if these were seized by the police.[1] The method of collecting taxes was monstrous and costly; and the means of transportation were so inadequate, and the imposts so numerous, that internal trade between neighboring districts could not thrive. Shipbuilding languished at Venice, where several large vessels which were on the stocks at the time of the Austrian restoration were sold for kindling wood. The government also endeavored to fix prices by publishing each week a list of rates which dealers must abide by; but the economic laws of supply and demand had no respect for autocratic Metternich, and in spite of his interference, articles fetched what they were worth. Fluctuations in the local currency caused further uncertainty; when the government wished to put silver coins in circulation, it arbitrarily depreciated the base-metal coins, thereby weighing most heavily on the poorest class; but it required that taxes and the public debt should be paid in French gold.[2] On the other hand, primary and

---

[1] Rose: *Letters from the North of Italy* (London, 1819), i, 224–5.
[2] *Ibid*, i, 149.

secondary education was encouraged by the State, which published the text-books and supplied them at slight expense to the scholars; but these books, generally translated from the German, were carefully edited so as to inculcate reverence for Austrian principles, and a political catechism was compiled in which servile submission to tyranny was skilfully set forth as a religious duty.[1] A remark of Emperor Francis to the professors at the University of Pavia revealed his real disposition towards education. "I want," said he, "not learned men, but obedient subjects."[2]

In dealing with the Church, Metternich insisted upon the independence of the State. Prelates were appointed by the Emperor and confirmed by the Pope. A German archbishop was brought to Milan and another to Venice. Very few of the religious orders had permission to reopen their convents. Civil marriage and divorce were abolished. The State maintained in part the hospitals and institutions of charity, and at the time of the famine it took extraordinary measures to relieve the sufferers. Upon the chief highways, upon bridges and canals, upon the reclamation of swampy districts, and upon the construction of public buildings it spent considerable sums.[3] A stranger who traveled over Lombardy and did not look below the surface, saw many indications to justify him in asserting that here was one of the most prosperous and best-governed countries in Europe. But the prosperity was at best material, due to the bounties of nature, which only the utter neglect of man could render fruitless. The chief and incurable objection to the Austrians was that they were conquerors and treated their subjects as helots. The Italian must obey laws imposed upon him by a foreigner, laws which had been framed

---

[1] Poggi, i, 229. [2] Ibid, i, 187.
[3] Cantù: Cronistoria della Indipendenza Italiana (Turin, 1873), ii, chap. 32.

without his voice, for the benefit of a master who dwelt at Vienna. Were a law good, he hated it because it was a cog in the great wheel of tyranny; were it bad, he hated it because it threatened directly his property, his freedom, or his life. Napoleon's rule had been despotic, but it had been despotic on a grand scale; he had conquered by force; he had opened avenues to glory; he had awakened a virile spirit, and shed round him large and stirring ideas: but these Austrians had sneaked into their supremacy; they were arrogant and conceited; their emperor was bigoted, petty, and unyielding; a man who depended upon eavesdroppers and tricksters for his information; a man who had not a single heroic attribute, nor uttered, during the course of a long life, a single thought whereby mankind was made stronger or wiser; a martinet, only fitted to be the superintendent of a small reformatory school for juvenile criminals. So to the Italians the contrast between the recent French rule and the present Austrian was typified by the contrast between Napoleon and Francis; but the incompatibility between the two peoples had the deepest source, — it sprang from racial antipathy.

Nevertheless, Metternich did not omit provisions for touching the vanity, if not the affection, of a part at least of Austria's Italian subjects. The vice-regal court, with its levees, its routs, its elaborate ceremonials, was a field where the Lombard aristocracy could display itself, forgetful of higher concerns. Crosses and cordons artfully distributed among the nobles were also helpful in winning the allegiance of their recipients. It was assumed that the upper classes did not sympathize with the subversive schemes of the revolutionists, and that being by instinct conservative, they would approve of any government which respected their privileges, enforced tranquillity, and gave them scope to spend their time and money in elegant leisure and dissipation. Nor was this assumption ill-founded; many of the aristocrats of Lombardy and Venetia felt no shame in playing the courtier to the Austrian viceroy and in disguising their servitude in pompous robes. Art, science, and literature were patronized, and they throve as potted plants thrive under the care of a gardener who cuts off every new shoot at a certain height. The hope of scanty pensions let loose the eloquence of flatterers both poetic and prosaic; Monti outeringing them all in his ode on "The Return of Astraea." Theatres were subsidized and the galleries of paintings maintained. In brief, the semblance of gayety was there, but at heart there was neither joy nor content.

We may liken the people of the Austro-Italian provinces to those Florentine revelers who, at the time of the plague, tried to drive away their terror by telling each other the merry stories reported by Boccaccio. The plague which penetrated every corner of Lombardy and Venetia was the Austrian police. Stealthy, but sure, its unseen presence was dreaded in palace and hovel, in church, tribunal, and closet. It was visible in the forms of countless gendarmes and constables, who patrolled the streets and watched the public squares; but it was even more terrible through the work of its secret agents, its spies and informers, who wore no badge and gave no sign of their duplicitous occupation. No one knew whom to trust, nor what eavesdropper might overhear and misinterpret the most innocent remark. Every police-office was crammed with records of the daily habits of each citizen, of his visitors, his relatives, his casual conversations, — even his style of dress and diet were set down. Their screen of secrecy allowed spies to vent their malice on a personal enemy by registering mere suspicions or downright calumnies; and the accused, having no chance to confront his accusers, was trebly embarrassed in attempting to clear himself. Had this Metternichian army of sneaks which, for five-and-thirty years, plied their trade in every town and hamlet, been put to some useful task, such as the reclamation of the malarious districts, they might have left a monument of permanent benefit behind them; instead of the heaps of folios, duly labeled and catalogued, and filled with tittle-tattle and innuendoes. As it was, notwithstanding their ubiquity and alertness, they hardly ever discovered information of great importance. The post-office was, of course, a recognized channel for spies, who opened letters and read, and then forwarded or kept them according as they seemed harmless or suspicious. The press being gagged, only such statements appeared in the meagre official gazettes as were authorized by the government. And when not an iota of evidence could be found against some person whom the police wished to discredit, reports were circulated that he was a spy. Let a single example of this reptilian process suffice. The Austrian minister, Sedlintzky, gave orders to search the house and rummage and examine the papers of Cæsar Cantù, a writer of wide renown. Torresani, Director of Police, replied that Cantù was much too clever to let papers be found that might incriminate him; all the more because he was used to domiciliary visits, through the political inquiries he had previously suffered; and he added, "once before I reverently suggested that the best way to ruin Cantù and to abate his unmeasured vanity is to slander him as a bought political emissary, who dogs persons in the dark so as to sell them; and thus to put him in the pillory. To attain this end, Torresani sent to the minister a notice to be published in the *Gazzetta di Augusta*, and the minister, approving the plan, ordered similar articles to be published in the Italian journals outside of the Lombardo-Venetian kingdom. And if I mistake not, it was at that time that the Emperor of Austria presented to Cantù a very valuable ring, as if in reward for his literary works, but certainly with the intent of making him suspected by the Italians, it being the nature, not only of tyrants but of slaves, to suspect for slight causes."[1]

Such was the Metternichian system of police and espionage that counteracted every mild law and every attempt to lessen the repugnance of the Italians. They were not to be deceived by blandishments: Lombardy was a prison, Venetia was a prison, and they were all captives, although they seemed to move about unshackled to their work or pleasure. But to them the consciousness of being watched and the dread of being betrayed were omnipresent. And there, too, were the garrisons of white-coated Austrian troops ready to shoot down any murmurers whom the police could not smother. Under Beauharnais, the army of Northern Italy had been composed of Italians, many of whom won honors in the great wars. But Austria, fearing lest the military spirit should become too patriotic, dissolved the native regiments, dismissed the Italian officers, and sent the recruits whom she levied in Italy to waste their lives in barracks beyond the Alps. Her civil and judicial offices she filled with Germans, many of whom did not understand the language of the people they were called to govern. She did, indeed, make a show of appointing in each province a Central Congregation, composed of native land-holders, but these might only suggest how the taxes should be apportioned, and they were so careful to suggest only what their masters wished, that their congregations were nicknamed "asylums for the dumb." Every matter, however trivial, was reported to the Aulic Council at Vienna, whose deliberations were as slow and ponderous as the old-time etiquette of the Spanish Court. Thus when General Rapp, then the Minister of Police, being very ill, sent to Vienna for permission to visit some neighboring baths, the reply came two months after his death;[2] and

---

[1] La Farina: *Storia d' Italia* (Turin, 1851), ii. 249-50; Cantù: *Cronistoria*, ii. 394.

[2] Lady Morgan: *Italy* (London, 1821), i. 156.

thus when the fire-engines at Venice fell out of repair, the governor could not mend them without authorization from the Aulic Council, and in the interval the Cornaro Palace was burned for want of the apparatus.[1] The Viceroy, Archduke Rainier, dismissed every petitioner with the words, "I will tell my master, the Emperor." In this wise were nearly five millions of Lombards and Venetians reduced, through the application of Metternich's system, to the condition of marionettes, whose speech, whose gestures, whose actions were controlled by those who pulled the strings at the Austrian capital.

Petty and irritating in detail and deadening in mass as was the Austrian tyranny, it yet seemed somewhat less reactionary than that which overwhelmed Piedmont[2] after the restoration of her legitimate king. But there was this great difference in the situation of the Lombardo-Venetians and of the Piedmontese: the former were oppressed by a foreigner and conqueror who could never hope to win the affection of his subjects, however just and enlightened might be his rule; the latter were oppressed by a native king, descendant of an illustrious line which had for more than two centuries been associated with the welfare and expansion of Piedmont. And, therefore, when Victor Emanuel drove into Turin in the gilt coach borrowed from Marquis d' Azeglio, May 24, 1814, and a paternal smile lighted up his commonplace features, he was greeted by the effusive and genuine enthusiasm of his people. True, they thought his pigtail and his chapeau of the time of Frederick the Great a little old-fashioned, but these were trifles compared with the great joy of welcoming the long-expected sovereign of

---

[1] Rose, ii, 149.

[2] For the sake of uniformity, I shall use "Piedmont" to denote the entire kingdom ruled by Victor Emanuel and his successors, who bore, however, the official title, "King of Sardinia." For the same reason I use "Austria" and "Austrian," though the Italians, remembering their mediæval history, often referred to them as "Germany" and "Germans."

their own race. Moreover, he came to them for the first time as king, as he had succeeded to the throne in 1802 on the abdication of his brother, Charles Emanuel IV, during the French occupation of Piedmont. He had spent his exile in Sardinia, holding a petty but punctilious court at Cagliari, reviewing his few battalions of soldiers, discussing schemes for future military glory, and imagining himself a personage of vast importance to a world which swept on forgetful of him. "I and Napoleon" was his favorite phrase, and to hate Napoleon with unquenchable hatred was his strongest passion. He was by nature neither cruel nor unreasonable, but his early education had been narrow and his exile had embittered him. Believing absolutely in the divine institution of kingship, he held that as king he was responsible for the welfare of his subjects, and that commands emanating from himself, the divinely-ordained, ought to be religiously obeyed. His attitude towards his subjects, therefore, was that of a Puritan father towards his children; it was admitted that he loved them, but he expressed his love by constant and unflinching chastisement.

His subjects were disposed at first to smile at the ludicrousness of some of his measures. He removed at once all the officials and employees of French appointment, and ordered that they should be replaced by those whose names were registered in the *Palmaverde* (or Court Almanac) for 1798. Alas, many had died in the intervening sixteen years! He called out the soldiers and subalterns of 1800; among them, too, death had made many gaps! Dismissing the higher officers, who had earned their rank in the Napoleonic wars, he substituted for them the aged aristocrats who had been loyal to him during the inactive years at Cagliari, or their callow sons, who knew no more about tactics and discipline than what they had read in their old-fashioned history books. For his courtiers, he prescribed a costume in the style of his youth, and though the Piedmontese nobles felt guyed in those old perukes, they were loyal and wore their annoyances gravely.

But the tragic was mingled with the comic in the King's "reforms." Of a very pious nature, he gave the Jesuits so cordial a welcome that they had erelong control of the schools and a preponderating influence in other temporal affairs. The French code was swept away and the musty Constitution of 1770 resuscitated. The law of primogeniture reappeared. Civil marriage and divorce were prohibited; it was even proposed to declare bastards all the children whose parents had been married by the mayor and not by the priest. Religious toleration was denied, and thus the steadfast Waldenses and other non-Catholics were in danger of persecution. Confusion prevailed in the judiciary; there were ecclesiastical courts, military courts, and courts of royal domain. Contracts and titles in property were thrown into chaos through ordinances which annulled transactions and leases made during the French occupation. The law of banality, one of the most oppressive products of feudalism, was revived for the advantage of the nobility. Benefices were again held *in commendam*. The French had purged the cloisters and convents and turned them to better uses; now the swarms of friars and nuns flew back. The King, resolved that outward forms of religion should be rigidly observed, established a kitchen inquisition to find out which of his subjects ate meat of a Friday. He granted monopolies and exemptions to private individuals; he set aside verdicts, already delivered in the courts. Prisoners might be tortured, and capital punishment was attended with shocking cruelty. The Jews once more fell under the ban of Christian injustice. In such a system individual liberty had of course no part. "The governor, the commandant, the director of the police, the fiscal advocate, the justice of the peace, the mayor, the carabineers, down to the lowest agent or spy of the police, each had the right to arrest. But if it was easy to get into prison, it was terribly difficult to get out again. A prisoner might be set at liberty to-day by order of the magistrate, and to-morrow an order from the governor, the director of police, the commandant, would send him back to confinement."[1] The provincial and communal councils had very limited jurisdiction, — often their power was merely nominal, — being checked and dominated by the ubiquitous police.

Fortunately the generally honest character of the people kept them in many cases from resorting to the unjust means which this monstrous system held out to them. The King himself was inclined to be fair according to his lights, but his good intentions were often thwarted by the influence of his Austrian wife, Maria Theresa, by his confessor, Botta, and by his reactionary ministers. He was generous to all who had been loyal, but implacable towards those who had acknowledged Napoleon's usurpation. So intense was his aversion for all things French, which to him meant Jacobin and revolutionary, that he dismissed clerks who wrote the letter *R* in the French instead of in the Piedmontese fashion. Hemmed in by counselors as sincerely retrograde as himself, he could not hear the protests of those of his subjects who believed that the paternal government of the seventeenth century was an abomination in the nineteenth. A king's court is, after all, only an echoing-gallery, which always gives back his own words, and the court of Victor Emanuel was beyond any other in Italy prim, punctilious, and obedient. In it "no one who loved his king and his God spoke otherwise than through his nose, the nasal twang being, we know not on what ground, taken as an evidence of loyal zeal and religious unction."[2]

[1] Ruffini: *Lorenzo Benoni* (New York, 1853), 187.
[2] Gallenga: *History of Piedmont* (London, 1855), iii, 315; see also Poggi, i. 198-218; Turotti, i, 387-410; M. D'Azeglio: *I Miei Ricordi*, i, chap. 9.

Thus did the Old Régime reintrench itself in Italy. Everywhere the government was Absolutist and paternal, differing in its rigor according to the personal character of the local despot, but everywhere based on the same theories and traditions. The restored monarchs kept what was least admirable in Napoleon's system, the tendency to centralization, and they revived what was most pernicious in the old system, craft, deceit, neglect of education, and encouragement of superstition. Jesuits and the police were their chief agents. Having declared war against opinions, their entire energy was directed to the suppression and punishment of political heretics, and the Church stultified herself by construing as religious heresies those political opinions to which she was hostile. In this arbitrary and factitious scheme, true morality and common decency were neglected. Obscene vices and violent crimes went unpunished: a man might do murder, but not eat flesh on Friday; the common highwayman, guilty of countless robberies and a score of assassinations, was pensioned by his king, while the patriotic citizen, who asserted that representative government was preferable to despotism, was sent to the galleys or the scaffold. Truly it was well said of the Bourbons and their fellows who came back to power in 1814, that they had learnt nothing and forgotten nothing. After a quarter of a century of the most terrific political convulsion in history, they returned to their old ways, and would fain believe that that convulsion had been but a bad dream. That wicked and stiff-necked people, who, in the ancient Hebrew myth, laughed at Noah building the ark, were not less blind than these princes of the Old Régime who disregarded all warnings of their own destruction. But the day of their calamity was still far off, and the conflict between the Old and the New seemed still but a quarrel between a host of policemen and a few noisy peace-breakers.

CHAPTER III.

FOREIGN INTRIGUES.

Thus the old rulers flew back into their last year's nests. Each princeling would have it appear that he was indebted solely to the "principle of legitimacy," but in reality he was the creature of the Congress of Vienna. In order that none might be strong enough to menace his neighbors, each had received but a small domain. Sectionalism among the people was thus provided for, and it was hoped that the recollection of common calamities in the past and of common dangers in the present would draw the rulers together. Mutual jealousy would prevent them from combining to rid the Peninsula of its foreign master.

Metternich, disregarding, when he chose, his sacred "principle of legitimacy," had annexed Lombardy and Venetia to Austria. He would have taken more, had not Russia, Prussia, France, and England been envious. But what he dared not to seize openly, he plotted to secure by intrigue. He attempted to Austrianize Italy, and, in so far as he was successful, he delayed Italy's emancipation for fifty years. His position along the north bank of the Po, and his garrisons at Ferrara and Comacchio already gave him a formidable advantage. The rulers of Parma, Modena, and Tuscany belonged to the House of Hapsburg; the other sovereigns had floated back on the tide of reaction which Austria, moonlike, directed. Kinship, therefore, or gratitude, or interest were the strings he could pull; these failing, he had brute force.

His first negotiations were with the King of Naples. Ferdinand had entered his capital under the escort of Austrian troops, and he knew better than any one else how the nine million francs, which his agents had slipped into the hands of the lobbyists at Vienna, had helped to persuade Austria to insist upon his restoration. Very readily, therefore, he complied with Metternich's request to form a secret alliance. He promised not to introduce into the Kingdom of the Two Sicilies any changes which might conflict either with the ancient monarchical institutions of his realm, or with the measures adopted by Austria in her Italian possessions. He bound himself, in case Austria were attacked, to furnish 25,000 troops, and in return he was to count upon 80,000 Austrians. Without the consent of the Emperor, he could make neither peace nor war, and he pledged himself to support the Austrian army of occupation until it should be withdrawn.[1] Four years later, he asked that the contingent to be equipped by him might be reduced from 25,000 to 12,000 men, and Metternich consented; for, the smaller the standing army in Naples, the greater the dependence of Ferdinand on Austria.

In the reorganization of Sicily, Metternich tightened his grip on Ferdinand. That island had had a most strange and interesting history. From time immemorial it had been the battlefield of races. There Phœnicians had planted settlements, and there Greeks had colonized. Under the brow of Ætna, Dorians and Ionians fought, and the power of Athens — and with the power, the splendor and the beauty — was irremediably stricken. In Sicily, already the cornfield of the Mediterranean, Romans and Carthaginians began that duel for the control of the Midland Sea that culminated at Cannæ and Zama and closed with the destruction of Carthage itself. In

[1] N. Bianchi: *Storia Documentata della Diplomazia Europea in Italia*, 1814–61 (Turin, 1865), i, 207–8.

the groves above Syracuse, Theocritus sang the last songs of the Hellenic genius, some plaintive, all sweet, like the warblings of the thrush at twilight. The roses of Girgenti, the orange-orchards of Messina, flowered perennially, but the owners of Sicily changed with each historic season. Roman governor reluctantly gave way to Gothic count, and he in turn to Byzantine prætor. Then came the Saracens out of the hot Orient, to make the garden of Trinacria theirs, and to keep it, until out of the misty north descended the Normans, and subdued the Saracens, and set up a kingdom more prosperous and more enlightened than that other island kingdom they had just wrested from the Saxons. In Norman Sicily there was religious toleration for the first time in Christendom. Greek and Latin Christian, Mahometan and Jew, worshiped God, each after his conviction. Then the Sicilian sceptre, as restless as Fortune's wheel, passed to the Germans, and under Frederick of Hohenstaufen, the first monarch of modern pattern, Sicily was still the best-governed land in Europe. And just as the latest strains of Greek poetry had been uttered there, so there the earliest strains of Italian poetry were uttered. But dynasties pursued each other like ghosts through the halls of the royal palace of Palermo. The House of Hohenstaufen vanished before that of Anjou, and after the Frenchman came the Spaniard. Like some precious Hindoo jewel, Sicily, much coveted, did not remain long in any family, but brought misfortune on all; till at last she dropped from the hands of Aragon into the hands of Bourbon. Nevertheless, amid these vicissitudes, she cherished the traditions of her mediæval independence and forwardness, and from the beginning of the fourteenth century she had curbed the despotism of her kings by a sort of parliamentary government, which neither the feudal innovation of the Spaniard, nor the autocratic encroachments and the perfidy of the Bourbons had been able wholly to destroy.

During the Napoleonic trouble Ferdinand had taken refuge in Sicily, where, thanks to English protection, he had weathered the storm. But his administration was so bad that the English agent, Lord Bentinck, threatened to withdraw his support unless the King should desist from his corrupt policy and the Queen from her interference. Ferdinand acquiesced, and Bentinck, in 1812, proclaimed a constitution which restored to the Sicilians many of their ancient privileges. As soon, however, as the fall of Murat and the consent of the Congress of Vienna opened the way for Ferdinand's return to the mainland, he found himself in an embarrassing plight. In Naples he ruled, despite his Liberal promises, as an absolute monarch; in Sicily he was hampered by a constitution which he had already violated so far as to stir up the wrath of the Sicilians. The rivalry between them and the Neapolitans was further intensified by the King's blunders and insincerity. The Sicilians, boasting of their loyalty whilst the Neapolitans were submissive to Murat, sulked when officials were dispatched from Naples to govern them: the Neapolitans grumbled to see their civil and military offices filled by courtiers whom Ferdinand had brought with him from Palermo. The King levied what taxes he chose in Naples; in Sicily he had to accept what taxes the Parliament voted to him. Evidently he must be annoyed as long as different systems existed side by side in the two halves of his kingdom, so he resolved to bring both under the same régime. But should he level Naples up to Sicily, or level Sicily down to Naples? He leveled down, depriving the Sicilians of their poor shred of a constitution, and he sealed this act of uniformity by assuming the title of King of the Two Sicilies, December 12, 1816.[1]

Metternich connived at this reactionary change, which

---

[1] Hitherto his title was Ferdinand IV of Naples, and III of Sicily; henceforth, it was Ferdinand I of the Two Sicilies.

erased the word "Constitution" from Italian politics. "It suited our interest," he wrote, "to enter into the designs of the Neapolitan Court, and thus prevent Sicily from serving as an example to the Kingdom of Naples subsequently, and also to prevent the numerous constitutionalists of this kingdom (supported by this example), from seeking to induce the ministry to give them also a representative government."[1] And he persuaded England — the sponsor of the Constitution of 1812, and the supposed exemplar of the blessings of a nation governed by a parliament — to consent to the strangling of her god-child. When Marquis Grimaldi, secretary to the Piedmontese embassy at London, remarked to Lord Melville that England allowed her daughters to die at nurse, the latter smiled and replied that it was not certain that a wholly English constitution would suit Sicily. Two days later Grimaldi, who had some irony, said to another Tory minister, "It seems to me that the constitutions of English manufacture which you ship abroad are of very light texture." To which Hamilton answered, "It was needed in Sicily when we planted it there: if they have now altered the cut, I believe it will adapt itself better to the different parts of the kingdom. When such goods are needed, it is better to make them at home than to import them from abroad."[2] The "principle of legitimacy" exacted the lopping off of all the offshoots of the Revolution, and Bentinck's Constitution was one of these; but the parliamentary rights which the Sicilians demanded had been acknowledged long before the Revolution, in that age which legitimists fondly extolled as golden.

Having thus bound Naples, Metternich passed on to Tuscany. The Grand Duke, Ferdinand III, was the Emperor's brother, and he had been induced, at the close of the Congress of Vienna, to sign a treaty of alliance with

[1] Metternich, iii, 91.   [2] Bianchi, i, 214-5.

Austria; the terms being that Ferdinand should furnish 6,000 troops in case Austria were attacked; that he should not conclude peace without her consent; and that he should communicate to Austria any information which might affect the tranquillity of Austria's Italian provinces. For economy's sake, Tuscany's relations with foreign Powers were chiefly conducted through Austria's diplomatic agents. Notwithstanding this apparent submission, the Grand Duke strove to be master at home, where the influence of the reform laws of Peter Leopold was still showing itself in the more peaceable disposition of the Tuscans. It was Ferdinand's rule to plead the littleness of Tuscany as an excuse for not meddling abroad, and when Metternich, not satisfied with the formal alliance, urged that Tuscany take the initiative in making a league of Italian States to be consigned to Austrian protection, she replied that, while she was touched by the honor, her modesty forbade her presuming to move before her big neighbors: let him consult them first, and then come to her. Again, when he invited her to intrust her postal service to Austria's superintendence, — a proposition too transparent to deceive anybody who knew Metternich's habit of lifting seals and reading letters not addressed to himself, — she declined; and she again asserted her dignity when Austrian regiments, on their way home from Naples, wished to cross her territory. It was doubtless this refusal to surrender wholly her independent action that led Metternich to speak somewhat gloomily of her "sadly altered feeling," of the weakness of her ministry and of the discontent of all classes of her people, and to regret, like the philanthropist he was, "that a land so highly favored by nature should have lost even the hope of a happier existence."[1]

In Parma he met with no resistance. Maria Louisa

[1] Metternich, iii, 94.

preferred the title of Austrian archduchess to that of
Napoleon's empress, and she willingly allowed her polity
to be directed from Vienna, so long as she was allowed to
direct the punctilio of her little court. In Modena, the
Duke treated Austria as a spoiled child treats a forbearing
nurse; sure of her protection when he needed it, he had
his own wilful way in his daily affairs. It was said that
he organized a gang of smugglers to introduce contraband
goods into the Austrian provinces by night; it is certain
that his subservience to the Vatican, and his selfishness,
displeased the Austrian chancellor, to whom he seemed
to behave more like a prudent land-owner than like a
sovereign. But Metternich shrewdly refrained from
saying downright, "I forbid;" he knew Francis's bull-dog
nature; he knew, too, that he could be whipped into
obedience if he became too unruly.

At Rome Metternich encountered greater opposition.
Cardinal Consalvi, the Secretary of State, had studied
the Metternichian wiles at the Congress, and was himself
passing clever in intrigue. Pope Pius was of a kindly
disposition but obstinate in certain matters, and his ob-
stinacy was none the less effective from being expressed
with a mildness more characteristic of compliance than of
refusal. He had not forgiven the Austrians for garrison-
ing Ferrara; he suspected their designs on the Legations;
he had evidence that Metternich's agents were coquetting
with the Carbonari. Metternich early saw the value of
this last ruse and often resorted to it. By instructing his
minions to insinuate themselves into the secret societies,
he could not only discover the schemes of the would-be
revolutionists, but also frighten rulers into accepting his
dictation. Sometimes he pretended to have warning of
an impending outbreak; sometimes he provoked a little
riot, and by quelling it immediately he awed rioters and
princes alike. But the Pope was too old a fly to be caught
in that web. He declined to league himself with Austria

because, he said, his duty as Christ's Vicar restricted him to a peaceful policy, and forbade him, the Father of the Catholic Church, from preferring one son before the others. Metternich protested that the story of his dealings with the Carbonari was a lie invented by them to injure him in the eyes of the Holy Father: in vain, even he could not bind the protean politicians of the Vatican, who, like the Homeric heroes, when hard pressed in their fight for temporal advantage, suddenly became invisible and invulnerable in a spiritual mist. Those petticoated old men wrangled manfully until the moment when a foe made as if to strike them; then they pointed to their feminine garb and exclaimed tauntingly, "What! you, a man, would strike defenseless women!" Metternich, who had more at stake than a coveted strip of papal territory, who knew that those epicene old creatures could foment trouble in every diocese and parish ruled over by Emperor Francis, wisely refrained his hand. But while he failed to get an open avowal of his mastery, he could content himself by reflecting that his influence was greater at Rome than the Pope admitted, and that at the first alarm the petticoated schemers of the Vatican would send post-haste for his help.

In Piedmont, however, his artifices ended neither in victory nor drawn battle, but in defeat. The little Kingdom of Piedmont lay in the bended elbow of the Alps; beyond them, on the west, was France, on the north, Switzerland; eastward the Ticino River separated from Lombardy, now Austrian; on the south, murmured the tideless waters of the Midland Sea. The Piedmontese were in character the most independent and robust of the Italians. Less than any of their brothers had they been inspired by the Renaissance, or enervated by its decay. In religion they were bigoted Catholics, as strict and intolerant and sincere as John Knox's Scotchmen or John Calvin's Genevans. They had been ruled by a line of remarkable princes, who believed literally in the divine right of kings, and who made soldiers of all those subjects who had not been made priests or monks. Thus little Piedmont was, among the emasculate States of Italy, what little Brandenburg was among the German States, — a drilling-field and barracks. During the eighteenth century it lay "between the hammer and the anvil," France threatening on the west, Austria threatening on the east. In 1814, when he recovered his throne, Victor Emanuel set about reorganizing his army and administration according to the traditional policy of his family. He was autocratic and exacting; but he was honest, and he haughtily resented foreign interference. Metternich saw that Piedmont, which the brief domination of the French had not debased, might become an eyrie whence patriotic Italians could pounce down upon and harry his slave-drivers in Lombardy. An independent Italian State, ruled by a native Italian prince, was a dangerous neighbor. His first endeavor, therefore, was to catch Victor Emanuel in an offensive-defensive alliance. Failing in this, he schemed to cripple Piedmont by acquiring the Upper Novarese district, which commanded the highway into Switzerland over the Simplon Pass. He pictured the ease with which the French could invade Italy by that route, and urged that, since Piedmont was already burdened with the defense of the Mt. Cenis and the St. Bernard, Austria be allowed to guard the other approach. Victor Emanuel replied that he owed nothing to anybody, that he was fully able to defend himself, and that he would not cede an inch of his soil. Metternich, foiled in front, next made a flank attack, and through his obedient tool, Castlereagh, he caused England to appear as the fautor of his plans. The English minister argued that as Austria had assumed responsibility for peace in Italy, — on which peace depended the European equilibrium, — it was only just that she should hold the positions which she deemed necessary for fulfilling her task. But the King of Prussia advised Victor Emanuel to stand firm, and the Czar informed the Austrian chancellor that he deceived himself if he thought Russia would acquiesce in despoiling Piedmont of the Upper Novarese.[1]

Renewing the attack on the other flank, Metternich again proposed the league; upon which Victor Emanuel wrote Emperor Francis that "inasmuch as my ancestors and myself have negotiated as equals with equals, whether with France or Austria, I cannot surrender this equality and cease to be an independent sovereign, in a confederation in which you would be such."[2] Again Castlereagh urged Piedmont to comply, adding as an inducement, that if she did comply, Austria would doubtless drop the question of ceding the Upper Novarese and would withdraw her troops from Alessandria. The Emperor, in an autograph letter to the King, hinted at these very favors, and covered his hook with tempting bait: his own position in the league, he said, would not be that of Austrian Emperor, but simply that of the Sovereign of Lombardy and Venice; hence there could be no inequality between himself and the sovereigns of the other Italian States. But Victor Emanuel would not nibble at this bait; and again the Czar encouraged him.

So Metternich was compelled for the present to desist from his scheme. Unable to coax or coerce Piedmont, he vented his spite in teasing and petty persecutions. The Austrian garrison which had lingered without excuse for more than a year in Alessandria was withdrawn, but it destroyed the outer fortifications before going. Not long after these events Victor Emanuel wrote to his brother Charles Felix: "Austria, left to her own resources, is not stronger in Italy than we are. I made this calculation some months ago when they were unwilling to restore

[1] Bianchi, i, 226.   [2] *Ibid*, 227.

Alessandria, and were asking for the Upper Novarese, and I made it in the presence of Stackelberg, Bubna, Bianchi, and other Austrian generals, showing that the Emperor could not employ more than 120,000 soldiers against us, whereas I can dispose of 100,000 soldiers in an offensive war against him, and in a defensive I can very far surpass him, having 80,000 men in the organized militia, besides the reserves, which, with the rest, form an army of 400,000 soldiers."[1] The King adds, not without humor, that the Austrian generals were so thoroughly convinced by his demonstration that the demand for territory soon ceased and Alessandria was evacuated.

[1] Bianchi, i, 234.

CHAPTER IV.

CONSPIRACIES.

By the end of the year 1815 despotism was thus restored in Italy, the obsolete became once more current, and the Golden Age of Paternalism was everywhere proclaimed. Each petty tyrant busied himself in securing the throne which the Holy Alliance had assigned to him, and Metternich labored without pause to bring all the princelings, either through intimidation or chicane, under the control of Austria. But to every government there are two parties, the governors and the governed; and the rulers who had imposed the Old Régime on Italy found that the submissive and nonchalant subjects of the eighteenth century had disappeared. Formerly the people had borne oppression as a patient bears an incurable disease, murmuring at times, and at times writhing to ease their bed-ridden backs, but not hoping for a recovery; the Revolution, however, had taught them that their ills were not irremediable, that despotism itself was not eternally fixed in the laws of nature, that there were hope and freedom for brave hearts. They had seen the rigid system of Absolutist kings and privileged nobles melt away like frost before the fires of revolution; they had seen monarchs scamper under cover, and the Pope himself led hither and thither, a mere feeble old man, whose protests were unheeded and whose sacred office was unrespected. Napoleon's achievements made that ancient superstition, — "the divine right of kings," — a mockery forever, and the force behind Napoleon spread the conviction that rulers should be the servants, not the masters of a people.

Moreover, the Italians had been roused into activity. In the wars, many had won distinction; in civil offices, others had risen to prominence. The conscription had helped to dim local jealousies and to infuse a spirit of discipline in the lower classes; education had been let down to thousands who had never before known their alphabet. This activity implied the use of powers long dormant; and from the consciousness of power came self-respect, — the recognition by men that they are of some value in the world, — and from this a national self-respect slowly unfolded. Fifty years before, the Italians had taken their servitude indifferently or with that fatalistic acquiescence which deadens effort; now they were ashamed of it, and were resolved to prove themselves worthy of the comradeship of freemen. You can trace the budding of this regenerative influence in their very dissatisfaction with their greatly improved material condition under Napoleon; they had better codes of justice, a more equal system of taxation, and a fair chance to rise high in the army or the State, and yet they were not satisfied. Bonaparte was a splendid master compared with the Bourbons, but he was still a master, to whom they submitted unwillingly. They could not hope to overthrow him; but they looked forward to his death as the signal for the assertion of their independence. When Napoleon succumbed in 1814, they thought the hour of their deliverance at hand, but they were unprepared; like sparrows they were limed by the cajoleries and insincerity of the English and Austrians. When a deputation of Lombards, headed by Confalonieri, went to Paris to plead for self-government in Northern Italy, the Emperor of Austria bluntly informed them, "You belong to me by right of cession and by right of conquest." Castlereagh, the English minister, to whom they appealed, entertained them with praises of their new master: "Austria," said he, "is a government against which subjects have less need to be on their guard than any other: in the history of that House down to our time there are no traces of abuse of power or violence; it never errs through excess, but sometimes rather through defect of these." The Czar, to whom they were admitted after many delays, cut off discussion of politics by saying that he hoped the Northern Italians would be content, as arrangements had been made to assure their happiness, and he dismissed the envoys by expressing his pleasure at having made their personal acquaintance.[1] Conscious at last that they had been betrayed and that the favorable moment had slipped by them, the Italians now resorted to plots. They had secret negotiations with Napoleon at Elba, whom they exhorted to appear among them, to unify Italy under his sceptre, and to crown his marvelous career by becoming Emperor, with Rome for his capital. But Napoleon trusted to the devotion and power of the French, rather than to them, in his last duel with Fortune, and after Waterloo the Italians were left without protection against their despots.

But when kings are tyrants, citizens conspire. The seeds of Liberalism had been sown in Italy, and the paternal governments could not exterminate them. Discontent, forbidden to utter itself, rankled in secret and exhaled contagion from town to town and from class to class. Officers, angry at being displaced by foreigners or by court favorites; soldiers, mustered out of the service; judges, magistrates, and a horde of bureaucratic underlings, dismissed because they had been appointed by the French; civilians, disgusted by uncertain taxes and restricted trade; priests and monks, reluctant at being forced back into a life of dependence; brigands and criminals, always hostile to the existing government: these, and all others who had a grievance, were drawn into the ranks of the Opposition. But discontent is a vague and sterile sentiment which soon wears itself out in

[1] Confalonieri: *Memorie e Lettere* (Milan, 1890), ii, 10, 19, 25.

vain fretfulness and grumbling unless it be centred on an attainable object: the object which now united the multitudes of malecontents in Italy was the abolition of despotism and the establishment of a representative government. Opinion differed as to what means should be used and what form of popular government was the best, but all agreed that the first attack must be directed against the tyrants. This was the nucleus round which all plans, however discordant, clung, the patriotic leaven which raised motives often selfish and base.

The Metternichian system allowed no discussion of politics. You might be a priest or a merchant, a doctor, lawyer, beggarman, or thief, but you could not be a citizen; because being a citizen implied having certain acknowledged interests and rights in the government of your city and State, — and this was an unpardonable heresy in the eyes of the Holy Alliance. Instead of being grateful that your ruler relieved you of the drudgery and worry of public affairs, you presumed to know better than he knew what was good for you. You cried for representation and liberty as a child cries for sweetmeats and dangerous playthings, and when these were denied you, how you stormed and sulked at your prudent tutors! As if you, forsooth, were as much interested as Prince Metternich, or the Duke of Modena, or the King of Naples, in your own welfare! This was the attitude logically taken by the upholders of the Old Régime towards the champions of political freedom, an attitude similar to that long since taken by the Catholic Church towards the advocates of liberty of conscience in religious matters. But the Italians insisted in believing that they ought to have civic rights, and since it was criminal to discuss politics openly, they were driven to deliberate and conspire in secret. In a short time, the Peninsula was honeycombed with plots.

For most men, generally in their youth, secret societies

have a strong fascination: the mystery which gives a fictitious dignity, the exclusiveness which seems to give distinction, attract not less than the social or benevolent purposes for which such fraternities are usually formed. In Italy the secret political sects were the only vessels in which the must of patriotism could gather and ferment. Secrecy was doubly imperative, because on it depended not only the existence of the organization, but also the very lives of the members. The revolutionary period had been prolific in clubs, and it was natural that the Italians should turn to these as the fittest agencies for undermining the fortress of Absolutism. Had not the despised Jacobins in France dominated the revolution which overthrew Louis XVI? Had not the Tugendbund in Germany aroused a patriotic fury which avenged at Leipzig the humiliation at Jena? The historian knows that there were mighty forces behind the Jacobins, and that Stein was behind the Tugendbund, but the Italians saw only the visible workers, and concluded that in the clubs themselves lay the victorious means. Long experience with crafty rulers and an innate aptitude for diplomacy — which is only a dignified and official kind of cunning — made them peculiarly expert conspirators. The intolerable political situation furnished them with an excuse, had any been sought, for embarking in their perilous secret enterprise against the restored governments. The majority of the conspirators, at least at first, had doubtless a sufficient motive in their vague but real desire for national independence and in their determination to escape from actual burdens; others conspired because they had failed of an office, or had lost their occupation, or merely because they loved the excitement of plotting; others, again, wished to avenge private insults; and many were drawn into the mysterious circles through curiosity or through the example of friends or through fear.

The most famous, the most widely disseminated, and the most powerful of all the secret societies which sprang up in Italy was that of the Carbonari, or Charcoal-makers. It multiplied so rapidly that after a few years its members hoped to clothe it with additional awe by inventing legends which linked its origin to a remote past. They affirmed that the Persian worshipers of Mithras, the adepts of the Eleusinian mysteries, the Knights of St. John, and the Rosicrucians had all been earlier Carbonari. A mediæval hermit, who spent his days in making prayers and charcoal in the forests of Germany, was the patron of the sect; a king of France, who lost his way while hunting, and was hospitably received by charcoal-burners, had, so the story ran, bestowed honors upon them and ennobled their guild. These were the legends, bred by that myth-loving instinct which cradles the infancy of sects and parties in the supernatural or the ancient. But Clio smiles incredulously at these fictions, and though she cannot, in the case of the Carbonari, tell just when and where that society originated, still she can discard fearlessly those reports of the hermit St. Theobald and the strayed monarch. The Carbonari first began to attract attention in the Kingdom of Naples about the year 1808. A Genoese named Maghella, who burned with hatred of the French, is said to have initiated several Neapolitans into a secret order whose purpose it was to goad their countrymen into rebellion. They quitted Naples, where Murat's vigilant policy kept too strict a watch on conspirators, and retired to the Abruzzi, where in order to disarm suspicion they pretended to be engaged in charcoal-burning. As their numbers increased, agents were sent to establish lodges in the principal towns. The Bourbon king, shut up in Sicily, soon heard of them, and as he had not hesitated at letting loose with English aid galley-prisoners, or at encouraging brigands, to harass Murat, so he eagerly connived with these conspirators in the hope of recovering his throne. Murat, having striven for several years to suppress the Carbonari, at last, when he found his power slipping from him, reversed his policy towards them, and strove to conciliate them. But it was too late: neither he nor they could prevent the restoration of the Bourbons under the protection of Austria. The sectaries who had hitherto foolishly expected that, if the French could be expelled, Ferdinand would grant them a Liberal government, were soon cured of their delusion, and they now plotted against him as sedulously as they had plotted against his predecessor. Their membership increased to myriads; their lodges, starting up in every village in the Kingdom of Naples, had relations with branch-societies in all parts of the Peninsula: to the anxious ears of European despots the name Carbonaro soon meant all that was lawless and terrible; it meant anarchy, chaos, assassination.

But when we read the catechism, or confession of faith, of the Carbonari we are surprised by the reasonableness of their aims and tenets. The duties of the individual Carbonaro were, "to render to the Almighty the worship due to Him; to serve the fatherland with zeal; to reverence religion and laws; to fulfil the obligations of nature and friendship; to be faithful to promises; to observe silence, discretion, and charity; to cause harmony and good morals to prevail; to conquer the passions and submit the will; and to abhor the seven deadly sins." The scope of the Society was to disseminate instruction: to unite the different classes of society under the bond of love; to impress a national character on the people, and to interest them in the preservation and defense of the fatherland and of religion; to destroy by moral culture the source of crimes due to the general depravity of mankind; to protect the weak and to raise up the unfortunate.[1]

---

[1] *Istruzioni per Maestri Carbonari, compilate dal B. C. G. M. Lanzellotti, ad uso della R. V. Partenope Rinascente* (Naples, 1820).

These were worthy aims, but, we ask, why did the Church, which had for centuries pretended that the regeneration of mankind had been intrusted to her by God's command, — why did she leave to conspirators, met in secret at the peril of their lives, the execution of her holy mission? Ah, her mission had ceased to be holy! By her league with Mammon, by her intolerance in matters spiritual, by her compact with tyranny in matters temporal, by the pride and hypocrisy of her prelates, by the sensuality and selfishness of her priests, by the ignorance and sensuality of her monks, she had lost her divine birthright, she had ceased to spiritualize the souls of her children. That Carbonaro catechism announced, what many men had long felt, that the observances and prescriptions of the Catholic Church were unnecessary to the leading of a pious, humane life. It went still farther and asserted the un-Catholic doctrine of liberty of conscience: "to every Carbonaro," so reads one of its articles, "belongs the natural and unalterable right to worship the Almighty according to his own intuition and understanding."

We must not be misled, however, by these enlightened professions, into a wrong notion of the real purposes of Carbonarism. Politics, in spite of a rule forbidding political discussion, were the main business, and ethics but the incidental concern of the conspirators. They organized their Order under republican forms as if to prefigure the ideal towards which they aspired. The Republic was subdivided into provinces, each of which was controlled by a grand lodge, that of Salerno being the "parent." There were also four "Tribes," each having a council and holding an annual diet. Each tribe had a Senate, which advised a House of Representatives, and this framed the laws which a magistracy executed. There were courts of the first instance, of appeal, and of cassation, and no Carbonaro might bring suit in the civil courts against a fellow member, unless he had first failed to get redress in one of these. If strictly followed, this complicated scheme must have given the Good Cousins some experience in living on terms of mutual equality and some notion of popular government, within the limits of the sect; but fictitious charcoal-makers were not less sensitive than other mortals to the distinctions between ability and dulness; and they fell under the dictatorship of a few leaders in whose election they had only a nominal part, and into whose proceedings they were not admitted.

The Carbonari borrowed some of their rites from the Freemasons, with whom indeed they were commonly reported to be in such close relations that Freemasons who joined the "Carbonic Republic" were spared the formality of initiation; other parts of their ceremonial they copied from the New Testament, with such additions as the special objects of the order called for. To many persons who do not understand the power which symbols and arbitrary ceremonials exert over nine tenths of mankind, those of the Charcoal-makers may seem puerile, but to the Charcoal-makers they were solemn enough, being the signs of life and death. The house where the meeting was held was called the "*baracca*," or hut, the lodge itself was the "*vendita*," or place of sale; members saluted each other as "*Buoni Cugini*," or "Good Cousins," and stigmatized the uninitiated as "pagans." God was honored with the title of Grand Master of the Universe. Christ, an Honorary Grand Master, was known as the Lamb, and every Good Cousin pledged himself to rescue the Lamb from the jaws of the Wolf,—tyranny, that is,—which had long persecuted him. St. Theobald was the special patron of the society. There were commonly two degrees, that of the Apprentices and that of the Masters, but there were sometimes others,—in Sicily we hear of eleven,—lifted above the vulgar level and

adorned with interminable titles. Having been elected
by an unanimous vote, the candidate for apprenticeship
was conducted to the barrack by his Master, and left
awhile in the "closet of reflection," where, we may suppose, excitement and suspense pitched his nerves on a
high key. Then he was brought, always bandaged, to
the door of the lodge, in which was a slide, whereby certain questions were put to him from within. Having
answered these satisfactorily, he was admitted into the
hall itself, where the Grand Master, seated before a huge
tree-trunk, thus addressed him; "Profane one! the first
qualities we seek are sincerity of heart and a heroic
constancy in scorning perils. Have you these?" The
neophyte replied, "Yes," and was then dismissed to take
his "first journey." On his return, he was asked what
he had observed: "Noises and obstacles," was his answer, which the Grand Master expounded in this wise:
"This first journey is the emblem of human life: the
noise of the leaves and the obstacles indicate that, being
of frail flesh, as we swim in this vale of tears, we cannot
arrive at virtue unless we be guided by reason and
assisted by good works." After that the neophyte must
take a "second journey," in which he passed through a
fire and beheld a trunkless human head, — the former
symbolized charity, which purges the heart, the latter
was a warning of the doom of traitors. Having been
brought back to the lodge, he was made to kneel before
the Grand Master's block, and to repeat the following
oath, "I swear and promise on the institution of this
order in general, and on this steel (the axe which served
the Grand Master as a gavel), the punisher of perjurers,
to keep scrupulously the secrets of the Carbonic Republic:
not to write, grave, nor paint anything, without having
received written permission. I swear that I will succor
my fellowmen, and especially the Good Cousins Carbonari, in case of their needs, and in so far as my means per-

mit, and likewise not to attaint the honor of their families. If I prove forsworn, I consent that my body be hewn in pieces, then burnt, and my ashes scattered to the winds, that my name be held in execration by all Good Cousins on earth. And so God help me!" Then he demanded light, and was unbandaged in the middle of the room, where the members surrounded him, and brandished axes. "These weapons," the Grand Master explained to him, "will serve to slay you if you perjure yourself; but they will fly to your aid if you prove faithful." Then the badge, countersign, and grip were given, and the meeting was concluded with regular business proceedings.[1] Sometimes the Apprentice was sworn in by a single Carbonaro, or again, he was received by members in masks so that he could not recognize them. He must pass a year's probation, during which, though ignorant of the secrets of the Order, he was liable to be called upon to show his obedience and courage before he was advanced to the Master's degree.

The ordeal prescribed for this occasion was more awful, to correspond to the greater responsibility imposed on Masters Carbonari, and consisted of an imitation, — shall we say a travesty? — of the Passion of Christ. The lodge assembled "when the cock crew at the appearance of the morning star." "Who is this rash Apprentice who dares to disturb our sublime labors?" asked the Terrible One; upon which the sponsors led the Apprentice out to the "Garden of Olives," where he repeated Christ's prayer. On their return, the Terrible One said, "The man is thirsty," and an Expert reached him a cup. Then he was bound, and led before other Experts who impersonated Pontius Pilate, Caiphas, Herod, and the Captain of the Centurions. "Art thou the son of God?" quoth Herod. "Thou sayest it," the Apprentice replied. Then

---

[1] *Nuovo Statuto organico della Carboneria della R. Lucana Occidentale*, 1818.

the Good Cousins mocked him, and clamored for his death. He was crowned with thorns, stripped, bound to a column and given 6,666 stripes, — not, we infer, by actual count, — and then he was stretched on the Cross. But the multitude relented, and cried out that mercy be shown to him. So his bandage was taken off and he stood among his fellows, a Master Carbonaro.[1]

The scheme of symbolism spun by the fantastic brains of the Carbonari would have delighted the quibbling students of the Zohar or the Kabbala. Thus when the neophyte was asked, "Who is your father?" he was to raise his eyes towards heaven; when asked, "Who is your mother?" he lowered them toward earth; and when asked "Where are your brothers?" he looked round on the members of the lodge. The Carbonaro colors were black, red, and blue: black signified first charcoal, and then faith; red was fire and charity; blue was smoke and hope. The Grand Master's block represented the surface of the earth; the tree from which it was cut reminded the Carbonari of the heavens which are spread impartially over all persons; its roots meant stability; its foliage suggested perpetual greenness, and that "as our progenitors, having lost their innocence, covered their shame with leaves, so we, amid the same universal depravity, ought to hide our brother's faults, and particularly our own." The linen sheet, in which the Apprentice was wrapped, taught that "just as the plant from which it was made by toil and maceration had become wings, so we should become pure and clean by continuous and unwearied effort." Water purified. Salt kept from corruption. The crown of thorns reminds us, says the Carbonaro chaplain, "that wearing it on our head, we must be motionless and cautious in order to avoid its pricks; likewise wearing it on our wills we must not be restive under the dominion of intellect and reason, but

[1] *Istruzioni per Maestri Carbonari, compilate dal B. C. G. M. Lanzelletti.*

ever removed from vice, and attached to virtue only." The cross, plainly enough the emblem of travail, persecution, and death, "teaches us to persevere in our efforts without fear, in imitation of Jesus Christ, who voluntarily suffered death that he might lead us on so sublime a road." The earth, which hides the body in oblivion, typifies the secrecy in which the mysteries of the Order must be hidden. The ladder was a sign that virtue can be attained toilfully, step by step. The bundle of fagots meant union: "it is also the material for the sublime furnace of our works," continues the expositor, "wherein, reunited by the same spirit, we love mutually to kindle our hearts with the fervid heat of charity, which makes us perfect and renews us, like the fagots in the fire, changing their quality into another; thus our hearts being kindled by the fragrance of our labors are sublimed in hope." [1]

But we need delve no farther into the mystic imaginings of the Charcoal-makers. The passion for symbols and allegory soars to the sublime or sinks to the ridiculous, as the poetry and creeds of the world and the pedantries of theology show; but even symbols which to the uninitiated seem commonplace or bizarre, may have vital significance to believers. Your national flag, for instance, what is it to the African savage but a strip of party-colored cloth; but to your countrymen in battle it means all that is dearer than life. And so that mummery and crude symbolism of the Carbonari may have touched their imagination and hallowed their resolves.

More practical were the penalties which they decreed for offenders. Treachery they punished by death, the execution to be secret, whether the culprit were brought to trial or not. Lighter offenses had lighter chastisement. Suspension from the lodge for a given time, general imprecation, burning in effigy, and the interdiction

[1] *Istruzioni per Apprendenti Carbonari* (Naples, 1820).

of fire, water, and all intercourse, were the usual punishments in a rising scale of severity. It was naturally deemed more heinous to injure a Good Cousin than a Pagan and there were curious discriminations in judging the importance of crimes. Thus a Good Cousin might be suspended from six months to a year for drunkenness, or from six months to two years for gambling or adultery, but the latter crime was more venial when the woman happened to be a Pagan, and not the wife or daughter of a Carbonaro.[1]

The Carbonari flourished in the Kingdom of Naples, but the ramifications of their order spread out into all parts of Italy, and where there was no Charcoal-makers' *rendita* there were sure to be other sects devoted to the same cause. Like the literary societies of the previous century, they delighted in grotesque or absurd titles, such as the Unshirted, the Hermits, the White Pilgrims, the Sleepers, the Adelphi, the Oppressed not Conquered. At Ravenna there were the American Hunters, to which Byron belonged; at Padua, the University students had a club called the Savages, and were accused of preferring blood as a beverage; in Romagna, there were the Sons of Mars, all soldiers past or present; at Modena, the Spilla Nera Society plotted in behalf of the Bonapartists; at Leghorn, the Bucatori were popularly believed to commit at least one murder a day; the Decisi, who infested Calabria and the Abruzzi, had among their officers a "registrar of the dead" and a "director of funerals," and they used blood as well as ink on their diplomas. Even the women caught the general infection; at Naples we hear of a society of "Gardeneresses" in whose ritual flower-pots and sprinklers rose to mystic significance. Carbonarism itself was carefully organized in

[1] *Carbonarismus* (Weimar, 1822), a German translation by H. Doering of a book published in London in 1821, entitled *Memoirs of the Secret Societies of the South of Italy, particularly the Carbonari.*

France, where, before long, Lafayette, Louis Philippe, and other prominent politicians were known to be Good Cousins. Of the Hetairia, a league formed with the intent of freeing Greece from the Turks, and having a branch at Milan, or of the plotters in Germany, we need not speak. Whoever has visited the slumbering crater of Solfatara near Naples will remember how he was first impressed by the supernal stillness and desolation: the whitish sandy surface of the crater seemed to be strewn with human ashes; but if he scraped a little hole in the sand he found the earth beneath too hot to touch; and if he but put his ear to the ground, he heard portentous rumblings; and now and then he saw jets of sulphurous steam puff and rise from crannies along the margin of the crater. After 1815, Italy was a political Solfatara — outwardly a dry, dead crust, but inwardly molten with suppressed passions and seething with pent-up desires.

Metternich and his pupils in government were not ignorant of their danger, but their maxim was, "Keep the surface quiet," and their wisdom lay in closing all the safety-valves. They saw no more in these symptoms of popular discontent with tyranny than the purpose of a minority of bad men to overthrow the legitimate order and to profit by the anarchy that must ensue. So Leo the Tenth saw only a "monkish squabble" in Luther's protest. Metternich himself, and those who like him imagined that they took a philosophic view of history, held the theory that the European body politic had recently been suffering from a virulent disease, Jacobinism, — a sort of political black measles, — which had been most fatal in France, and which was now wearing itself out under a milder form in Italy. As State physicians it was their duty to administer opiates, or even to clap the patient in a strait-jacket, until the delirium should be quelled. But we can see that those old practitioners were woefully mistaken. What they thought poison in the blood, was the fever of rejuvenescence; the spirit of Liberty, denied utterance and activity in the open, was secretly quickening the hearts of conspirators. God works not by whims and spurts but slowly, lawfully, without stay or afterthought: when He discerns that a species or a system has fulfilled its mission, He does not at once blot it out, He does not annihilate it, but He replaces it by another, and the process of substitution is gradual. He is the Great Joiner, who wastes no material, but fashions the new out of the old. Since Creation's dawn He has needed to make not a single atom; what then was, has sufficed for the infinite variety of His handiwork. When creeds or politics, having served their time, become materialized and obstructive, fearful of the Present and wholly relying on the Past, He discloses to a few souls the better Ideal which is to conquer and transform the world. And as if to teach us His omnipotence, He intrusts His message not to the world's *élite*, but often to menial and despised agents. As out of the catacombs of old Rome there issued a new spirit, so out of the burrows where the Carbonari plotted, the Ideal of Freedom was to issue and to pervade Italy, — an Ideal not soon to be realized, owing to the perverseness and frailty and blunders of those to whom it was revealed, and to the huge bulk of that other Ideal, of the Old Régime which it must slowly dissolve.

The safety of the clubs of conspirators depended upon secrecy, and we have seen by what terrible threats they sought to deter informers: but it was inevitable that the existence of an organization which had off-shoots in every district, and whose membership soon numbered a quarter of a million, should be known to the ever anxious, ever watchful myrmidons of tyranny. Carbonarism, as any one could see, set up a State within the State, a tentative Republic amid an Autocracy, and it proposed to abolish autocracy altogether. No government, however feeble or incompetent it may be, can tolerate such an enemy, which aims at its destruction. The Bourbons at Naples had a strong instinct of self-preservation and a strong love of power, both of which warned them that strenuous measures were needed. But how to seize the skulking Briarean monster? Hercules slew Hydra, but the many-headed Carbonaria was invisible. Nevertheless, Prince Canosa, the Neapolitan Director of Police, was not daunted. He set his spies and detectives on the track of the conspirators; with money in hand he waited to buy the revelations of traitors; he commanded his agents to join the Order that they might not only learn the secrets of the Good Cousins but also instigate discord among them. He knew the efficacy of fighting fire with fire, and so he organized a rival secret society to serve as a counterpoise to Carbonaro influence. The Calderari or Tinkers were his protégés, who had their mystic cauldron and fire, their ritual and buffoonery, and who were pledged to support the Bourbons. Thus when rats infest your house you send a ferret through the wainscoting to drive them out: but the Bourbon ferrets had dull teeth and little pluck, and the Charcoal-makers throve in spite of the Tinkers, and in spite of the eaves-dropping police.

Canosa himself was scarcely surprised that his cunning measures could only keep the surface calm, without checking the ferment beneath, for he looked deeper than did many of his colleagues, and he was wise in Machiavellian wisdom. *Divide et impera*, was his warning to the "Kings of the Earth:" "You have forgotten this maxim, carved on the foundations of thrones: you would have ruled the world with a single rein, and this has broken in your hands. *Divide et impera*. Divide people from people, province from province, city from city, leaving to each its interests, its statutes, its privileges, its rights and liberties. Let the citizens persuade themselves that they are of some account at home, —

allow the people to amuse themselves with the innocent playthings of municipal wire-pullings, ambitions and contests, — cause public spirit to revive by the emancipation of the communes, — and the phantom of national spirit will no longer be the maddening demon of all minds." Here, indeed, Canosa put his finger on that policy of centralization which Napoleon had adopted, and which the restored despots had retained in the belief that it would strengthen their power; but the wily Prince saw that they were throwing away the substance for the shadow. "Another chief cause of the overturn of the world is," he continued, "the too great diffusion of letters and of that itch for literature that has penetrated even the bones of fishmongers and hostlers. In the world are needed not so much learned and literary men as cobblers, tailors, smiths, agriculturalists, and artisans of all kinds, and there is needed a great mass of well-behaved and docile people who content themselves to live on the faith of others, and who let the world be guided by the light of others, without pretending to guide it by their own. For all such people literature is harmful, because it stirs up those intellects which Nature has destined to work in a restricted sphere; it promotes doubts which the mediocrity of its enlightenment is insufficient to solve; it incites to spiritual pleasures which make insupportable the monotonous and tedious toil of the body; it awakens desires disproportionate to the humbleness of their condition; and by rendering the people discontented with their lot, it disposes them to try to pursue a different lot. Wherefore, instead of unmeasuredly favoring instruction and civilization, you ought prudently to set some limit to them; and to consider that if there existed a master who in a single lesson could make them all as learned as Aristotle, and as polished as the major-domo of the King of France, it would be necessary to kill that master immediately, in order not to see society destroyed. Leave books and studies to the distinguished classes, and to some extraordinary genius who makes a road for himself through the obscurity of his grade, but cause the shoemaker to be contented with his awl, the rustic with his mattock, without going to spoil his heart and mind in the primary school." [1]

I have quoted this passage because it proves that some at least of the supporters of the Old Régime divined the depth at which the new spirit they dreaded was working, and that they dared with brutal frankness to prescribe a brutal remedy. To encourage ignorance would seem to be an easy task for a minister, since ignorance, like a fissiparous parasite, propagates itself by rapid subdivisions, each of which is in turn the parent of new swarms. No advocate of enlightenment could have accused a Bourbon ruler of being its patron, nor could the oldest inhabitant remember any master who went about making the peasants as wise as Aristotle and as elegant as the French king's major-domo. By intrusting education to priests and Jesuits, and by gagging the press, the princes of Italy followed part of Canosa's advice: but they were too dull or too rapacious to heed the rest and give up those centralizing measures which by allaying local jealousies fostered discontent and made men all the more ready to hearken to the "demon" of patriotism.

The order of the Carbonari grew, notwithstanding Canosa's vigilance, and shed what light it could through the darkened windows of its lodges. It attracted whosoever desired his country's emancipation and believed that plotting would lead to that goal. At its *vendite* men met as peers who were separated by class barriers in the world outside. They had a common purpose, a common judiciary, and they were bound together by the sense of a common danger. But what they lacked — and the defect

[1] Canosa: *Esperienza ai Re della Terra*, quoted by Cantù: *Cronistoria*, ii, 136, note 11.

was vital — was a resolute and prudent head. No great movement has ever triumphed which has been guided only by a committee: men must see their cause personified in one leader, round whom they can rally and for whom, if need be, they can die. Abstractions must be made flesh before men will fight for them. But the Carbonari and the other Italian conspirators had no commander-in-chief. The rank and file were expected to obey unreservedly whatever orders came to them from above. Often they did not know the names of their leaders, who shrouded themselves in mystery. Sometimes it was hinted that certain very distinguished personages were at the helm, but that they would reveal themselves only after the conspiracy should succeed.

While the sect was thus governed by an anonymous corporation, it was also the prey of local differences. Lodge vied with lodge in audacious proposals, and in each lodge the most daring or the most vehement Good Cousins naturally acquired the greatest influence. If the prudent demurred, they might be written down in the Black Book as cowards or traitors. If the Salernitans deemed the moment ripe for a revolt, the Neapolitans might insist on a delay. We wonder how, in that flux of plot and counterplot, any trust or sincerity remained in men; for the conspirators were not only aware that they were spied upon by the police, but they were also vexed by doubts and jealousies among themselves. Brother could not be sure of brother, nor father of son. Judge distrusted judge of espial, friend distrusted friend. Even from his wife a man was not safe: his confidences might be frightened from her at the confessional and pass up from the bishop to the director of police. The strongest oaths seemed weak, the most terrible threats seemed mild to conspirators who knew that their lives hung on the honor of their associates.

Many of these defects were inseparable from any widespread political conspiracy; others were traceable to that heirloom of local feuds peculiar to the Italians; while others arose from inexperience in self-control and from an imperfect estimate of the amount of education that would be necessary to fit the great mass of the Italian people to govern themselves. The political dusk swarmed with the glittering maxims of the French Revolution about the "rights of man," "liberty," "equality," and "fraternity," as a June night swarms with fireflies: and it was still the fashion to believe that a race could be regenerated by manifesto and voted into independence by a show of hands. But there were Italians of Liberal cast who held aloof from the sects, either because they preferred to sail by the Pole-star rather than by fireflies, — and the Pole-star was still wrapt in clouds; or because they scrupled to become accomplices in violent deeds which they felt could not advance the patriotic cause. This sense of futility or dread of criminality withheld many; others, made languid by the turmoil of the past twenty-five years, craved repose. They would have chosen liberty, but they were too dispirited, or too weary, to fight for it. "And what, after all, has fighting profited us?" they asked. "Torment us no worse with bright but unrealizable dreams. We can at least end our days unmolested if we do not meddle with the forbidden topics." Against this inertia of fatalism also, the conspirators had to contend.

Whilst they were making proselytes in large numbers and revolving terrific plans, Metternich was cautiously dredging for information. Not content with the news supplied him by the local ministers of police, he sent his own agents into Italy. They reported that the dissatisfaction was due partly to natural causes, — a failure of crops in 1816 having been followed by an epidemic of typhus fever, — and partly "to the results of the conquest, which by overthrowing political order had shattered the foundations of the public welfare."[1] The Chancellor himself made a triumphal journey through the Peninsula in 1817, where he divided his time between courtly entertainments and secret investigations, and was able to assure his Emperor that, although the existence of the sects could not be denied, and although their purpose conflicted with Austrian principles, yet they had failed "to enlist leaders of name and character," and lacked "central guidance and all other means of organizing revolutionary action." "In design and principle divided among themselves, these sects change every day," he added, "and on the morrow they may be ready to fight against one another. The surest method of preventing any one of them from becoming too powerful is to leave these sects to themselves. Yet we must not look with indifference on such a mass of individuals, who, more or less adversaries of the existing order of things, may easily be led to disturb the public peace, especially if it is ever united by the alluring pretext of Italian independence. England has for the moment relinquished these chimeras, and since she gave her consent to the union of Genoa with Piedmont, and the withdrawal of the Bentinck Constitution in Sicily, she has almost entirely lost the confidence of the Independents."[2] Nevertheless, Metternich thought he discerned signs of foreign connivance in the activity of the plotters. He suspected that Russian emissaries were fanning discontent against Austria, and were encouraging Liberal dreams, in the hope that Russia might secure, were the revolution successful, one of the Italian ports for her navy. But whatever he suspected, Metternich was not alarmed; he believed that neither from within nor from without could any force there be massed strong enough to endanger Austria's position in Italy; and with a confident and self-satisfied heart he went to direct the family gathering of the European monarchs at Aix-la-Chapelle.

[1] Metternich, iii, 89.   [2] Ibid, iii, 99.

The best justification of Metternich's confidence was furnished by the conspirators themselves. That they were very numerous, that they were "men of action," every one knew; but what had they accomplished between 1815 and 1820? Nothing that the eye could estimate. Sporadic assassinations and incendiary fires were imputed to them, but not an exploit indicative either of courage or of foresight. An occasional street-brawl, hardly worthy to be called a political demonstration, served to show the weakness of the plotters and the rigor of the police.

There was a little affair at Macerata, for instance, over which the Papal authorities might well chuckle. It was the spring of 1817. The aged Pope lay very ill, not expected to recover. The Carbonari believed that in the confusion at his death they would find their opportunity. They agreed upon a general revolt, took every precaution, and laid their mines in all directions. The outbreak was to begin at Macerata; Bologna, always a restless city, was ready to respond. So carefully had every detail been arranged that four buckets of pitch had been carried by stealth into the belfry of the Macerata cathedral to be lighted at the appointed time as a signal to watchers on the hills that the revolt prospered; and these watchers were to flash the news, by beacons and rockets, over all the land. A free government was to be set up, with Count Gallo, the chief conspirator, as consul. Other offices had been allotted to his accomplices, and — mark the minuteness of the preparation — it was agreed that as soon as the revolutionists had Macerata in their power, they should assemble in the cathedral for a ceremony of thanksgiving at which St. Ambrose's Hymn was to be sung. The roster of two regiments, one of cavalry and one of infantry, was made out, the pay of each soldier being fixed at five pauls a day. A proclamation, not lacking exhortatory eloquence, was printed. "People of the Pontifical States:" it began, "When it is God's will to punish a people, He gives them over to an ignorant government. When He sees them aware of their error, He pours courage into them, and bids them to shake off the barbarous yoke. . . . To arms! to arms. Let your war-cry be love of country and charity towards your children. To overthrow tyrants, to tax the rich, and to rush to the assistance of the needy, — be that your aim. Already is History busy preparing a place for you among her heroes." Thus was every spring set: but the Pope would not die, and the conspirators, becoming impatient, resolved to strike at all hazards. On the night of June 24, just as they were collecting for action, a squad of carabineers happened to bear down upon them. Believing that they were betrayed, they scampered hither and thither for their lives. The watchers on the hilltops saw no beacon, till the great torch of day rose again out of the Adriatic and announced that the plot had failed. The Hymn of St. Ambrose was not sung that morning in the minster, but four suspicious buckets of pitch were found in the belfry. Count Gallo and seven of his principal confederates made good their escape. A few accessories were arrested and sentenced, after a tedious trial, to the galleys; the ringleaders were condemned to death in contumacy. From the witnesses examined, the judge learned that the rebellious sects were all scions of Freemasonry and that their purpose was to secure "independence, or at least a constitutional government!"[1]

This revolt at Macerata, so ignominiously stifled, is a specimen of all the ineffectual splutterings of conspiracy during those five years. There were arrests at a ball at Rovigo, arrests after a feverish spasm at Rimini; the conspirators at Ravenna concerted a rising with Romagnoles, but at the last moment the Romagnoles wavered. In the Neapolitan provinces an explosion seemed always imminent, but the fuse always smouldered and went out.

[1] *Carbonarismus*, II, 138 seq.; Poggi, i, 157-8.

Oftentimes we cannot distinguish between the Neapolitan conspirators and brigands. Those ferocious Decisi, for example, who sent death-warrants underscored with blood to their proposed victims, had not patriotism but plunder in view, if we are to believe their enemies. They ravaged the provinces of Bari and Otranto until put down by General Church, who executed above a hundred of them and stuck their heads on the gates of the towns they had despoiled.[1] The conspirators grew more wary, the police more alert. Ferdinand issued a proclamation prohibiting all secret sects, and threatening their chiefs with death.[2] The Pope launched a bull of similar import, in which he especially charged the Carbonari with irreligion, on account of their assertion of freedom of conscience in matters of belief; but the Carbonari treated this fulmination as they had treated an earlier one in 1814, when they asked: "Was not the Christian Church from its origin until Constantine's victory over Maxentius a secret society?" They waxed numerous in spite of failures and repression, so that by 1820 their membership was reckoned at nearly three quarters of a million.[3] If their achievements were indeed trivial, it must be remembered that they had to contend against the inevitable defects of their organism, not less than against their outward foes. They hesitated and postponed; they began to wait on Chance, — the death of king or pope, the embarrassment of a cabinet, the sudden exasperation of the populace, or the prospect of a foreign war, — before firing their train. But they did not abandon their determination; on the contrary, time and delays only rooted it deeper in their hearts. Five years had almost elapsed since the restoration of the Old Régime, when sparks blown over sea from Spain dropped among the powder-kegs of Italy, and set off the long-expected revolution.

[1] *Carbonarismus*, 120. [2] Aug. 8, 1816; text in Turotti, i. 464-6.
[3] In 1818 the minor sects — Decisi, Filantropi, and Filadelfi — were said to number 20,000 members.

CHAPTER V.

NAPLES IN REVOLUTION, 1820.

We are wrapt about with an æther more wonderful than the atmosphere in whose depths we live; a spiritual æther which communicates messages from times and places most remote, and makes of the world a whispering gallery; which has its trade-winds and its tornadoes, its lightnings and its auroral calms. No cry of distress breathed upon this subtler element is lost, but it circles earth till it finds a listener; deeds good or evil are sown in it, and are borne like pollen up and down the fallow field of years, till at last they fructify and bring forth harvests of wheat or tares, each after its kind. This æther it is which binds men and nations together in a solidarity, invisible and subtle, but broad as earth and durable as time.

But for this mysterious transmitter it would concern us but little to know that in the year 1819 the *guachos* of the River Plata were struggling to free themselves from Spain, and that the Spanish government had collected troops to ship to the insurgent colony. But on New Year's Day, 1820, Raphael Riego, who commanded a battalion in the village of Las Cabezas de San Juan, having revolved in his mind the injustice of helping an Absolutist king to crush Americans struggling for freedom, and having listened to the voice of his own patriotism, drew up his troops, and proclaimed to them the Spanish Constitution of 1812. In an instant enthusiasm seized the soldiers: there was no more talk of embarking, for the battalion, which others soon joined, pressed on to capture Cadiz.

The news of the mutiny spread from province to province, gaining volume, as it flew: when it reached Madrid, the cowardly and treacherous King, bent only on saving his throne, granted the Constitution. Europe was surprised at the suddenness and success of the revolt. The Absolute monarchs and the oligarchy of ministers who then farmed the Continent for their personal benefit were frightened; for the preservation of their tyranny depended on the fidelity of the army, and here was an army which had been the first to rebel, and which had forced its sovereign to yield. Where might not another Riego spring up? What troops could be trusted?

To the people of Europe these tidings brought hopes as great as the alarm of their rulers. To the Neapolitans it seemed that the hour of their redemption had struck. Their King, as Infanta of Spain, must swear to the Constitution adopted in Spain; having sworn, how could he object to the promulgation of the same Constitution in his own dominions? The hour had indeed struck, but the man was wanting; Liberals and Carbonari discussed a thousand plans, as if out of the Babel of sound a strong sane deed would emerge. The government, aware of the growing agitation, but not yet terrified, proposed a few mild reforms by way of sedative. The membership of the Chancellory was to be increased to sixty, thirty to be elected by provincial councils, and thirty to be appointed by the King: they to pass votes on legislative matters, and to hold public sessions. It happened, also, that about this time the King held a review of the army in the plain of Sessa, — he was preparing, it was said, to join Austria in seizing the Legations and the Marches on the death of the Pope,[1] — and the agitators looked to this as a fitting occasion for a military mutiny. But the review passed off undisturbed, although it afforded the Carbonari the best opportunity to make converts and to circu-

[1] Colletta, ii, 324.

late their doctrines from regiment to regiment. The camp broke up about the middle of May, and almost immediately the revolutionary symptoms became acute in the province of Avellino, where the regular troops were commanded by General William Pepe, and where many Carbonari from Salerno and other districts had assembled. Pepe was a Liberal and a Carbonaro, but he hesitated to proclaim himself. So an humbler hand fired the train.

There was stationed at Nola the Bourbon regiment of cavalry, lax in discipline, owing to the neglect of its colonel, who passed his time in dissipation at Naples. On June 20 he was superseded by a commander of sterner type, who forbade his subordinates to quit the barracks after nightfall. The officers grumbled, and talked over their grievance with some Carbonari of the town, among others with one Menichini, a priest. He advised them to gather the malecontents of the regiment, to proclaim the Constitution, and to march to Avellino, where the sectaries would welcome them. His advice hit true. At daybreak on the 2d of July two sub-lieutenants, Morelli and Silvati, with 127 mutineers, including soldiers and subalterns, deserted from their quarters and took the road eastward. On they went, shouting, "For God, the King, and the Constitution," on the still morning air, as thoughtless and jubilant as boys broken loose from school. They wakened the villages as they passed, and peasants just going afield and townspeople half-dressed thronged after them and shouted, "For God, the King, and the Constitution." At Mercogliano, about a league from Avellino, Morelli halted and dispatched a note to Colonel De Concili, who commanded the regular troops in Pepe's absence. Would he join the patriotic cause, and free his country? De Concili's heart was with the revolutionists, but he was restrained by prudence; he must wait for Pepe's orders before giving his decision.

Meanwhile, news of the mutiny had startled Naples. The King was out in the bay on his royal barge, and when a messenger reached him, his first impulse was to put to sea and stay there till the trouble should be quelled;[1] but on second thoughts he decided to return to the palace. Before he came the ministers met to concert instant measures. General Nugent in a council of war proposed to send Pepe to pacify the insurgent province. Pepe accepted the commission, but he had not had time to set out from the capital before his orders were countermanded: the King and his councilors suspected his loyalty and disliked him for having been a Muratist. Finally, they gave the charge to General Carrascosa. Through these delays a day was lost during which the insurrection swept on. By nightfall not only the province of Principato Ultra, but parts of Principato Citra and Capitanata were in commotion, and De Concili, no longer doubtful, cast in his lot with the revolters. Amid acclamations and brotherly greetings, Morelli with his band of original mutineers entered Avellino, and in the cathedral, with the blessing of the bishop and the huzzas of the multitude, he resigned his authority into the hands of De Concili. The stars that night looked upon sleepless villages and noisy towns; black, red, and blue banners were unfurled, tricolored ribbons and cockades were hastily sewn on coats and hats, there were many harangues, many huzzas for God, King, and Constitution, but no serious disorder, no bloodshed.

Fate pays the suspicious and deceitful in their own coin. Ferdinand, whose whole life had been perfidious, was now in his desperate need perplexed in whom to confide. He no longer could distinguish between loyalty and deceit. His ministers had hidden from him the dangerous condition of the kingdom; now that he knew the truth, how could he trust them? What general could

---

[1] Colletta, ii, 329.

he believe in? Nevertheless, something must be done, and done at once. On July 3 Carrascosa appeared in Nola only to find there too few troops to justify him in attacking the insurgents, who had taken up a strong position at Monteforte, near Avellino. In lieu of fighting, he proposed to buy off the leaders of the revolt, offering to give them, besides a large sum in cash, a safe conduct out of the kingdom, — truly, a Bourbon expedient. But he could get no one to conduct the negotiation. So he lay idle in Nola, waiting for reinforcements, whilst the enemy's camp was being hourly swelled. Yet within easy marching distance were General Nunziante at Nocera and General Campana at Salerno. Why did not the three unite their forces, and strike the rebels while there was still time? Because the King would not give the order: he feared that if they united they would desert. On the 4th Campana marched towards Avellino, met a body of insurgents midway, indulged in an inconclusive skirmish, and then retreated. On the 5th Nunziante, likewise unsupported, set out; but before ever they came in sight of the enemy, his soldiers deserted in such numbers that he returned hastily to Nocera with the few that remained loyal. That evening he dispatched a note to the King; "Sire, your people desire the Constitution; opposition is vain. I entreat your majesty to yield."

This appeal but confirmed the fears which the reports of the last few days had heaped upon Ferdinand and his ministers. At Foggia a regiment had mutinied; Apulia and Molise had risen; Terra di Lavoro was seething. It was too soon for couriers to arrive from the remoter Abruzzi and Calabria, but there could be no doubt that those provinces also were up in arms. This very night (July 5) Pepe, fearful of arrest, had ridden out of Naples, followed by a regiment of cavalry and several companies of infantry, all bound for Monteforte. If the

King cherished any delusions as to the situation, they were soon dispelled. Five Carbonari pressed into the palace, declaring that they came as ambassadors from the people to speak with the King. The Duke of Ascoli heard their business, went to Ferdinand's apartment, and quickly brought back this reply: "His Majesty, having learned the wishes of his subjects, and having already decided to grant a constitution, is now consulting with his ministers upon its just limits." "When will it be published?" asked one of the delegates. "In two hours," replied the Duke. The delegate pulled the Duke's watch from his pocket. "It is now one o'clock," he said insolently; "at three the Constitution must be published." Then the interview ended.[1]

By daybreak (July 6) the following edict was issued by Ferdinand: "The general desire of the Kingdom of the Two Sicilies being manifested in favor of a constitutional government, of our own free will we consent, and we promise to publish the bases thereof within eight days. Until the publication of the Constitution the existing laws will be in force. Having thus satisfied the public desire, we order the troops to return to their corps, and every other subject to his ordinary occupations."[2]

Whilst the Neapolitans that morning gave themselves up to jubilation, messengers were hurrying eastward with copies of the edict for the rival camps commanded by Carrascosa and Pepe. The latter, on reaching Monteforte, had himself drawn up a proclamation in which he exhorted the insurgents to persist in their revolt until they secured a constitution for their country, and he promised to resign his command as soon as that victory should be won. The joyful tidings put a stop to impending hostilities. Both armies fraternized, and congratulated each other on a revolt equally dear to each, and when Carrascosa led his troops back to Naples that evening he found

[1] Colletta, ii. 336. [2] Turotti, i, 587.

the streets illuminated and festooned, and the populace singing patriotic hymns and shouting patriotic watchwords. Thus in four days had the Neapolitan people, so excitable, so little acquainted with self-control or public law, achieved a bloodless revolution. A wiser people would have been distrustful of the ease and suddenness of their success, but the Neapolitans, unversed in the difficulties of self-government and unaware that the best constitution is but printer's ink and paper unless a nation is fitted to abide by it, supposed that they had passed their ordeal, and could count upon a future of endless felicity. Prince People having wedded Princess Constitution, of course they would live happily ever after — as all fairy tales announce.

The King on that same day (July 6), as a handsel of his good intentions, appointed a new ministry, but he also issued a suspicious decree in which he nominated his son Francis, Duke of Calabria, regent with full power; assigning as a reason his own infirmity, which he feared might prevent him from performing his duties "in a manner acceptable to God." At this the populace took alarm. Bands of Carbonari went up and down the streets shouting for the Spanish Constitution; others guarded the ships in the harbor lest Ferdinand should sneak away. The Regent, to allay suspicions, put forth a decree (July 7), in which he pledged that the Spanish Constitution, only amended in so far as the different conditions of Spain and Naples might make emendation necessary, should be granted; but the people were still suspicious, because this decree was not signed by the King. Then appeared a proclamation from Ferdinand himself, ratifying all his son's acts; and the popular murmurs evaporated in cheers. The ordinary business of the capital was resumed, and, amid rejoicings and hopefulness, the publication of the Constitution was awaited.

Pepe in his camp at Monteforte now deemed the time

ripe for a demonstration of the strength of the Constitutionalists, who but last week had been called by harsher names. He proposed that with all his forces he should make a triumphal entry into Naples, as a sign of the patriotic and peaceful intentions of the late insurgents, and as evidence of the prevailing concord. King and Regent demurred; they loved their dear subjects, but at a distance; they feared some subterfuge; they disliked to see Pepe in the position of acknowledged leader of thousands of armed men, who, at a wink from him, might seize the reins of power. What if he should be overcome by ambition, and play Cromwell's part? But, on the other hand, how could he be kept out of the city, if in spite of royal refusal he persisted in entering it? To close the gates upon him would precipitate a civil war, in which the King could rely upon neither his soldiers nor his citizens. Discretion and fear argued that there was less risk in consenting than in forbidding; accordingly, the 9th of July was fixed for the triumphal entry. Wild rumors and gloomy apprehension flew about. It was said that the lawless classes would seize this opportunity for plunder, — that the Royalists were concocting a treacherous scheme, — that the Carbonari would imprison the royal family and proclaim the Republic. No suggestion was too extravagant to gain credence at a time when all classes were uncertain of themselves, and when many feared the worst results. To inspire a little confidence, a Junta of fifteen members, chosen in the camp and approved by the Regent, was provisionally organized to help in preserving order until the convocation of Parliament.

Amid this excitement the dreaded day broke. Into the city the Constitutionalist forces poured, and long before the head of the column marched into the square in front of the palace, the Regent was warned of its approach by the cheers of the crowds. Morelli and Silvati, with the original company of deserters (now glorified as "the Sacred Squadron"), led the van; then on horseback between Generals Napoletano and De Concili rode Pepe, his jaunty elegance reminding some of the bystanders of his former chief, Murat; then followed regiments of regulars, a little sheepish, despite the bravado with which they wished to have their late mutiny forgotten. When the militia appeared, the shouts grew louder and heartier. Finally a promiscuous band of Carbonari brought up the rear; Menichini, the priest, was at their head, his scholar's face, wide-rimmed spectacles, and clerical garb, comporting strangely with the Carbonaro flag he waved and with the Carbonaro emblems which dangled against the cross on his breast. But that day was a feast of paradoxes. Did not the Regent on the palace balcony, surrounded by his ministers and his Junta, pin the Carbonaro ribbons upon his coat, and applaud the Constitutionalists, as they passed in review beneath him? And later in the day, when the soldiers had retired to their quarters and the throngs had dispersed to the tap-rooms and cafés, did he not graciously receive Pepe and his generals?

A strange audience that, in which Pepe, who but four days since stood in danger of arrest, was thanked by the Regent for his patriotism, and was promoted to be commander-in-chief of the army. Pepe explained that his work had been not to foment the revolution but to lead it along guiltless paths, and to prevent acts which might harm both the throne and the country. Mutual compliments having been passed, the new hero was conducted into the King's bed-chamber, where Ferdinand lay in bed, — sick or shamming. Pepe knelt, and kissed the wrinkled perfidious hand. "You have done good service to me and the nation," said the monarch: "therefore, I doubly thank you and yours. Assume supreme command of the army to complete this enterprise of holy peace, which will so honor the Neapolitans. I would have given the Constitution earlier, if the utility or the general desire had been made known to me. I thank Almighty God that He has granted to my old age to do a great good to my realm."[1] Thus honored by the esteem of his sovereign, Pepe retired, the foremost subject in the kingdom. But his elevation made him a target for envy. The older generals, over whom he had been promoted, were piqued; Bourbonists muttered, as was their habit, against the advancement of an ex-Muratist; the more audacious conspirators, who had forced the crisis, were nettled to see him made the hero who had hesitated to join them until success was certain; many predicted that he would henceforth be a partisan of the King rather than of the people. These suspicions were for the most part unjust: if Pepe nursed a secret ambition, he lacked the dauntlessness and judgment to gratify it; his acts, so far as we know them, were centred in the support of the Constitution. That he was so soon stung by envious or calumnious tongues, indicated the fatal fickleness and the disunion of the revolutionary party. They paid allegiance to no single leader, but to a hundred. Each clique had its pet scheme, its loudest haranguer, and it suspected all the rest. The irremediable defects in the Carbonaro organization — the lack of a head and of a general definite policy — were now manifest; and it would soon be proved that no secret society can fit a people to maintain a popular government.

But the Neapolitans did not yet surmise whither back-biting and dissension were leading them. They had not yet recovered from their astonishment at the ease with which they had won their first battle, and their very ebullitions seemed to them to prove their strength. On July 13 they believed that their victory was complete, for the news came to them that the King had just ratified the Constitution. In the royal chapel he heard mass, and then in the presence of his Court, the Junta, and the

[1] Turotti, i, 601.

generals, he approached the altar, and laying his hand on the Bible, he solemnly swore: "I, Ferdinand of Bourbon, by the grace of God and by the Constitution of the Neapolitan monarchy, King of the Two Sicilies, with the name of Ferdinand I, swear in the name of God and on the Holy Evangelists that I will defend and preserve the Constitution. Should I act contrary to my oath and contrary to any article in this Constitution, I ought not to be obeyed; and every act by which I contravened it would be null and void. Thus doing, may God aid and protect me, otherwise may He call me to account." Then, uplifting his eyes he uttered this brief prayer: "Omnipotent God, who with Thine infinite gaze readest the soul and the future, — if I lie or intend to break this oath, do Thou at this instant hurl on my head the lightnings of Thy vengeance." Again he kissed the Holy Book, and, turning to Pepe, who stood near, he said meekly: "General, believe me, this time I have sworn from the bottom of my heart."[1] The Regent and his brother, the Prince of Salerno, next took the oath, and were embraced and blessed by their father, while tears of emotion ran down their cheeks. The faculty of simulation, transmitted and perfected through many generations, made these Bourbons the best royal actors in the world.

Popular enthusiasm exulted over this impressive act. All were willing to believe in the King's sincerity, because all hoped that the King would be sincere; and even those who had no reverence for the Bible thought it was sacred enough to bind his oath. The Carbonari openly enjoyed the prestige of having emancipated the nation. Their guard in uniform paraded the streets; their orators thrilled eager crowds in the public squares. Everybody made haste to enroll himself in an order so powerful and so popular. Every messroom, every magistracy, every convent, had its *rendita;* nobles and beggars exchanged

---

[1] Poggi. i. 262–3.

the secret grip and mystic watchwords. And when the Order asked permission to celebrate its triumph, the government dared not refuse. Priests with rosaries and poniards at their belts and tricolor banners in their hands led the procession; and another priest blessed the concourse when it assembled in church. In a time so unsettled there were of course evilly-disposed persons who tried to mask their criminal plans under the shadow of the Order; there were also sectaries who conspired to overthrow the government and set up a republic; but the designs of both fell short. A few sporadic cases of turbulence were quickly checked in the provinces, while in the capital even the lazzaroni, that large body of habitual loafers and potential law-breakers, remained docile. There was, indeed, much cackling from newly-hatched journalists, but it is the silent swooping old birds and not the unfledged that are to be feared. It seemed as if the nation had given bonds for good behavior until the Parliament should convene on the first of October; and credit is undoubtedly due to the Carbonari for the generally tranquil condition. It is a hostile critic, and not a Carbonaro, who is forced to admit that through the exertions of the Order "malefactors disappeared from the country, and that the public service" received a great impulsion "from the same source."[1]

While the revolution was thus spreading without violence over the mainland, far different scenes were enacting in Sicily. The islanders hated the Act of Union of 1816; they hated the stamp tax and the autocratic laws; they hated the presence of Neapolitan garrisons; they hated to see Sicily the subject instead of the peer of Naples. Each class, each province, had its grievance. The old nobility, the barons, chafed at their loss of power; Palermo resented being degraded to an equality with the other six capitals of the *valli* or districts into which the

[1] Carrascosa, quoted by Pepe: *Memorie* (Paris, 1847), ii, 26.

island had been divided. The aristocrats clamored for the Constitution of 1812, which established an Upper House; the populace, saturated with Carbonarism, preferred a democratic statute; both parties agreed in desiring Home Rule for Sicily.

It happened that two Sicilian nobles, Prince di Villafranca and Prince di Cassero, were in Naples when the Spanish Constitution was granted. They immediately protested that it would never satisfy the people beyond the Faro. The King and his partisans secretly chuckled at this portent of a quarrel in which they foresaw an advantage for themselves. The Regent, in receiving the protest, slyly remarked that he regretted that the Neapolitans had not chosen the Sicilian Constitution of 1812.

Messina was the first town to hear of the revolution, and the plebs, to whom the Spanish Constitution was agreeable, seized control of the government there. The news did not reach Palermo until July 14, when the populace were celebrating the Feast of Santa Rosalia. They quickly turned to discuss the startling change. The more prudent citizens were for sending a petition to the King to grant Sicily her former Constitution, when their deliberations were broken in upon by the soldiery, who as Neapolitans and Carbonari upheld the Spanish system, and threatened to burn the houses of all who opposed it. The populace, inveterately hostile to the upper classes, sided for the moment with the soldiers. That night Palermo was noisy with multitudes wearing the tricolor cockade, to which they added the yellow ribbon of Sicily. On the morrow Naselli, Lieutenant-General of the island, issued a proclamation stating that the King had granted a constitution, but he left in doubt whether it was the Sicilian or the Spanish. This suspense heightened the excitement, and that same evening soldiers and officers in large numbers swarmed to and fro in Via del Cassero, the main avenue of the city, shouting for the Spanish

Constitution and for Independence. General Church, a military adventurer who slashed his way to notoriety during the Napoleonic wars, and who now commanded the army in Sicily, odious as an enemy of the Carbonari and as the agent of conscription, appeared among the boisterous soldiery and ordered them to their quarters. Thereupon the populace fell upon him, and but for the succor of some of his officers would have killed him. He lost no time in stealing out of the city to take refuge at Trapani, whence he fled at the first opportunity to Naples, leaving his house burnt behind him. Another night passed and still Naselli wavered. He promised to send envoys to acquaint the King with the wishes of the Sicilians; but no vessel made sail out of the port, and the populace demanded that the fortress of Castellamare, which juts seaward midway in the crescent of Palermo's harbor, should be surrendered to them. Naselli consented, on condition that the garrison should remain there undisturbed. Still unappeased, they wrecked the Stamp Office, the Bureau of Registry, and other offices associated with the detested Neapolitan government. Deep in the night of July 17 the troops expelled the rabble from Castellamare, and when day came all classes were seething with wrath which must soon find vent.

There is in every large modern city a forlorn, desperate mass, little heeded in tranquil times, when the police are vigilant and the courts severe. It is composed of the wretches who have failed in reaching even the lowest plane of independence, or who more often have never tried to rise; of the wicked and reprobate, whose crimes have driven them like rats into foul places. Among them are the beggars, loafers, and swindlers, the burglars and cutthroats, the ex-convicts and the panders to vice. The women are slatterns and harlots, womanly only in sex, but as gross and brutal in their speech and acts as the men. The children, bred in corruption and

nurtured with blows and curses, instead of the innocence
of childhood display a precocious cunning, an infantile
depravity, saddest of all evidences of human degeneracy.
This human cesspool is kept at the flood by the creatures
spawned in its depths, and by in-pourings from the social
levels above it. There it reeks from decade to decade,
little affected by the changes which improve the rest of
the city, — a pestilent hopeless Malebolge, hidden just
below the surface of respectable society. The outcasts
who welter therein know no more of life than its squalors
and disgusts. They have the primal brutish instincts of
savages, but they have not those compensating instincts
which enable even savages to form a primitive community.
Hunger and thirst, heat and cold and goatish lust, are
the grim demons which in turn possess them. To appease
the appetite of the hour and never to be appeased, is
their impulse, their experience. Those desires and wants
which spur other men to endeavor, which evoke a fortitude greater than the hardship, a self-control stronger
than the desire, and which in noble minds are vanquished
by a stoical disdain, overwhelm these wretches and make
them baser than slaves. Ties of family, they know them
not: how should they know them, stived as they are, a
score of men, women, and children together in a single
room? Brother would slay brother for the possession of
a woman; the mother begrudges her child the garbage he
has snatched from the gutter. Laws they respect not:
are not the laws barriers set up by the rich and fortunate
to keep these abject ones from the loaf and flagon they
covet? Religion they understand not: at most they are
conscious of a dumb foreboding lest To-morrow be more
horrible than To-day. This mass, whose health is rottenness, lies inert but ominous at the very core of our proud
capitals: the Arts flourish round it, Commerce thrives,
Philosophies are published, Politics are discussed; but it
remains unaffected, the depository of the aboriginal bes-

tial instincts of mankind. It is a monster whose survival from a preglacial period mocks our civilization and condemns our religion. Missionaries hasten to Papua and Ashantee to expound the doctrines of predestination and purgatory to astonished savages; but at home, a few streets away from the churches, lie Papuas and Ashantees far more needing regeneration.

In times when respectability prevails, this monster is held in check; its members, like the wolfish mongrels of Stamboul, prowl the streets at night in search of refuse, and snarl among themselves; but you can cower them easily with a menacing gesture. But suppose all the butchers were suddenly called away, leaving their shambles unguarded, do you think those currish scavengers, for all their long diet of offal, have lost their craving for meat? Let Paris tell you how her outcasts behave when their keepers sleep. Presently you shall hear how the many-headed beast glutted itself at Palermo: but first you must reflect that the rulers of Italy, whether by their perfidy, oppression, or incompetence, had helped in every city to swell the numbers of the desperate class and to whet their brutal instincts.

When the third day broke on Palermo (July 17) there were signs of imminent danger. All classes were sullen, ready to fly at each other's throats at the least provocation. The nobles who had first raised the cry of independence had been out-shouted by the populace, who in their turn were exasperated by the soldiery. More than sixty hours of excitement, little sleep, much wine, and many harangues would unfit the soberest legislators for deliberation; far more did they unfit these passionate Palermitans, whose brains reeled with wild impulses, whose tongues uttered delirious hopes, whose hearts were festering with old grievances and wrath long repressed. The continued suspense, due to the evident incapacity of the Lieutenant-General, and his duplicity in ordering the garrison to drive the militia from the fortress, intensified that impulse, common to human nature in critical moments, to do something, if it be only to do amiss. Troops of cavalry and infantry, commanded by a General O'Faris, blustered through the streets, and by their taunts invited a quarrel. Some of the more temperate citizens, being unable to placate them, sought Naselli, who had quitted the city, and as they were returning from him with a written order for the troops to withdraw to their quarters, the soldiers opened fire, and shot down two of the peacemakers. That volley was the signal for the long-awaited tumult. The soldiers, now beyond restraint, fired at the windows and balconies of the houses, and killed women and children drawn thither by curiosity. The populace, lashed to fury, seizing one a musket, another a knife, a third a bludgeon, set upon their assailants. Each street echoed with the fusilade and the shouts of the fighters, and the groans of the wounded; each square was a battlefield. The nobles and bourgeois held aloof, but they were not missed; for plebs have always the majority: and to honest plebs were soon added the dishonest and desperate who glided out of their hiding-places at the sound of war. The prisons being unlocked, the convicts rushed thence to aid the artisans, who were disposed in squads according to their guild, and led by a priest, Joachim Vaglica. It was a struggle for life or death: the populace fought madly to wreak vengeance upon the instruments of their past injuries; the soldiers knew that they could expect no mercy from the foes whom they had infuriated by their insolence and brutality. The bells had tolled nine when the first blood was shed; they tolled noon amid the unslackened roar of the conflict. Hour by hour the insurgents gained, gradually driving the troops to bay in the piazza before the Royal Palace. There both sides had cannon, but the populace by pouring into the piazza from its tributary streets were able to attack the troops in many points simultaneously. The cavalry charged to drive them back, when an unexpected cannonade swept through their squadrons: they wavered, they fell back, they took to flight. Then the infantry broke and followed pell-mell through those streets which were unblocked by the mob. Sixty of the populace had been killed; the military losses were five hundred in killed and wounded, and many more made prisoners, including O'Faris and two other generals, whose lives were barely saved. Naselli, as soon as defeat threatened, had taken refuge on shipboard and then sailed for Naples.[1]

Palermo was now in the hands of its populace. The provisional Junta which Naselli had appointed was as powerless to restrain the victorious mob, as it had been to prevent the riot. The day closed with the sack of the Royal Palace. Among the guilds, each of which was nominally commanded by a consul, the Tanners took the lead by their vehemence. The torrent of lawlessness was swelled and darkened by the streams drained into it from the prisons and galleys and by the inpourings from the social cesspool I have described. For several days terror reigned. Dwellings were gutted and burnt, shops and warehouses were plundered, suspected persons were cast into prison or slain. Prince della Cattolica, supposed to have been in collusion with Naselli, was hunted down in his retreat in the country, was killed without mercy, and his body was left for days to rot by the roadside. Prince d'Aci, hated for his past severity when prætor, was dragged from the palace of Cardinal Gravina, whither he had sought asylum, and murdered; and then the mob

---

[1] Poggi, i, 273-5; Turotti, i, 617-24. Some historians, among whom is Turotti, affirm that Naselli was underhand rather than incompetent, and that all his acts during these critical days were planned by him to instigate an insurrection which should afford the Bourbon government an excuse for withholding the Constitution from Sicily, and for punishing the island by a more oppressive tyranny.

bore his head on a pole through the streets. Fury is as contagious as panic fear among crowds; and many of these Palermitans, crazed by the general frenzy, committed crimes without deliberation; others were bent on revenge, others again on booty. The soberer citizens seconded the effort of the consuls to form a Junta of ten cavaliers and ten jurisprudents, and they were careful to select men supposed to favor Sicilian independence, and to be acceptable to the populace. But the Junta had no force wherewith to make itself obeyed. At its first meeting, a band of marauders gathered ominously before the palace of Cardinal Gravina, the President of the Junta, and cried out for absolution for their crimes, till he deemed it wise to appear on the balcony and make the sign of pardon over them. When the proceedings of the Junta were too slow to satisfy the impetuous, it was whispered that Gravina was a traitor, and but for the protection of the priest Vaglica, who still retained the confidence of the mob, he too would have been dispatched.

We need not rehearse the details of the atrocities committed during that summer in Sicily, when the sun blazed with unusual fierceness, yet not so hotly as the passions of the islanders. We need not follow the precarious fortunes of the Junta, nor of the leaders who, lacking power to dam the flood, resigned in quick succession from their dangerous, hopeless post. We need not tell how bands of guerrillas sprang up in all parts of the island, to fight each other and to harass the peaceful; how towns were sacked, farms devastated, women ravished; how province wrangled with province, city with city; how the partisans of the Spanish Constitution smote the partisans of the Sicilian Constitution, and all parties made their political disagreement an excuse for murder, pillage, and rapine; how the desperate classes crawled everywhere out of their burrows, and the prisons were voided of their criminals;

the ten weeks' orgie but proved how much of the tiger still survived in the Sicilian nature, and how near that tiger crouched to the surface. The government at Naples, we surmise, might have tamed the monster by a quick display of energy; but energy was not a characteristic of the Bourbons. Possibly, too, the King and Regent were not unwilling that the Sicilian discord should become so intense that they might have an easy victory by playing off one faction against the other. At any rate, when envoys from Palermo reached Naples, instead of being listened to, they were locked up. At last, however, the government took alarm and dispatched Florestan Pepe, brother of William, with a considerable force to subdue the island. Landing on the northern coast he advanced towards Palermo, and having driven back small forces of insurgents began to invest the city. The Palermitans were in no condition to undergo a long siege: the chaos of more than two months had wasted their provisions; the neighboring country, exhausted by depredation, could have furnished no new supplies, even had the means of communication not been closed. When a few days of famine had dashed the bravado of the besieged, Prince di Paternò, one of the nobles who was still popular with the masses, by a shrewd policy brought them to think of surrender. Haranguing the multitude, he bade them to brand as a deserter whoever talked of peace: he offered money to all who would then and there join him in an attempt to break through the enemy's lines. When no one moved, he chid them for their cowardice and laughed at their sham pugnacity. Having thus gained their confidence and proved their weakness, he was chosen to negotiate with Pepe. A general amnesty was agreed upon, Sicily consented to accept the Spanish Constitution, but the question of a separate Sicilian parliament was left to be decided later. The day on which these terms were made (October 5), the Neapolitan troops marched silent and sullen into Palermo and occupied the forts. It was estimated that four thousand of the islanders had been killed during the civil war; the damage to property was enormous; and who can compute the harm done to the Sicilian character by that long delirium of carnage and brutality?

On the mainland the summer waned without witnessing grave disorders. The Carbonari were the heroes, and in all but name they were the rulers of the country. They had a central assembly hall in the capital, and no longer kept up a show of secrecy. Beards sprouted on all male chins, and bushy locks waved over all male necks, because such was the Carbonaro fashion. Samson should have been the patron saint of modern revolutionists, who have attached more importance to the length of hair outside their skulls than to the strength of the thoughts within. The relations among all parties were delicate, but each side knew that forbearance was necessary, and, strange to say, they forbore. The Regent, as the King lurked in shadow, gave no cause for the suspicion that he would not fulfil his pledges to the people. William Pepe and the chief Constitutionalists ostentatiously protested their loyalty to the monarchy; the extremists, who had a republic and universal happiness on the tips of their tongues, contented themselves with exercising that organ and no other. So the weeks wore on, and by the time the first grapes had begun to ripen, and Naples was bristling with Carbonari beards, the deputies had been chosen without disturbance and were come up to the capital for the opening of the Parliament.

On October 1, that Parliament, the first representative body of modern Italians constitutionally elected, convened in the church of Santo Spirito. There were the King and Regent, the members of the royal family and Court, the dignitaries of the Church and generals of the army, the two and seventy deputies, and as large a concourse of citizens as the church would hold. The King, placing one hand on the Bible, again took the oath to defend the Constitution. Galdi, President of the Chamber, delivered an address, temperate in tone but not in length, to which Ferdinand made approving gestures. Then Pepe resigned his commission of commander-in-chief of the army, was complimented by the King, and thanked by the Regent for his devotion to the royal family and to the public welfare. The King then rose, and having declared the Parliament opened, he and his cortége quitted the church. The superstitious remarked that the weather, which had been cloudy at his arrival, poured down rain at his departure.

On the next day Parliament opened its regular sessions in the hall of St. Sebastian. Worthy, and earnest, and willing were those three-score and twelve deputies, but they lacked experience. Imagine, in a country without physicians, a troop of novices called in to prescribe for a sick man; what disputes, what blunders must ensue! Happy the patient if he escape alive. Yet the body politic of Naples, wasted by a complication of chronic diseases, was now left to the mercy of politicians without a diploma. Some advised an opiate, some an emetic, others were for heroic treatment and itched to ply the knife. As always happens, the assembly soon split up into three sections, composed of the Moderates, the Waverers, and the Radicals. And besides this legally convened parliament, there were numberless other unofficial and irresponsible parliaments, whose meeting-place was on the sidewalk or in the public square and in every lodge of Carbonari; and they all showered suggestions and demands upon the poor bewildered deputies. These, with a fine disregard of separating the important from the trivial, began their work by changing the names of the Neapolitan provinces: jumping the Christian era, they revived the names of the Samnites, Hirpini, and Marsi. One deputy endangered the

tranquillity of the Parliament by throwing into it the
question, "Is this assembly constituent or constituted?"
The prudent and fearful, remembering whither a similar
question had brought the French Assembly, trembled lest
discussion should lead to an explosion, but fortunately
news came of the surrender of Palermo, to turn attention
away from that dangerous topic. The Neapolitans were
angry at the terms Florestan Pepe had made with the
rebels, who, they said, had virtually gained from him the
recognition of their right to Home Rule. Parliament
echoed the anger of the populace, annulled the compact,
ordered the Sicilians to elect and send deputies to Naples, and replaced Pepe by Colletta. The latter, a stern
soldier, resolved on doing right as he saw it through Carbonaro glasses, succeeded in preventing another outbreak
in Sicily; but the order he maintained was due to his vigorous application of martial law, and not to the healthy
removal of grievances. So determined were the Neapolitans not to recognize the separatist claims of the Sicilians, that they decreed that the Straits of Messina should
be known as the river of the Pharos. Whilst they were
thus engaged in amending geographical nomenclature,
and in disputing over internal affairs, there was brewing
in the skies to the north of them, — of which they
seemed as oblivious as if they had been dwellers on Pit-
cairn's Island, — a great tempest whose rumblings they
could already hear in the intervals between their own
debates.

The Jupiter who rode this storm and hurled its thunder-
bolts was clean-shaven, blandly-smiling Prince Metternich, clad not in Olympian nudity, but in ruffled muslin
shirt, in embroidered brocade coat sparkling with many
orders, in satin waistcoat, in silk knee-breeches and stockings, and in shining pumps with silver buckles; a sort of
Beau-Brummel-Jupiter, equally at home in the boudoirs of
demi-goddesses and the councils of kings. The mundane

events of this year, 1820, had more than once wrinkled his Jovial brow and dropped bitterness into his cup of nectar; for it was less than five years since he, in his supernal wisdom, had decreed a government for Europe, and here were the Europeans up in rebellion declaring that his government was not good. The military mutiny at Cadiz and subsequent revolution in Spain, the assassination of the Duke of Berri, the revolutions in Portugal and Naples, what were all these but signs of the naughtiness and ingratitude of mortal men, whom the bounty of even a Brummel-Jupiter could not satisfy? They spurned his smiles, let them beware his frowns: let them not think that he who but a little while ago had helped to bind the Prometheus of the Revolution on St. Helena's rock, would see Olympus stormed by a horde of revolutionary pygmies.

Metternich surveyed the danger, and prepared to crush it. He might leave the rebels in the Spanish peninsula to wear themselves out, but the revolution in Naples called for his immediate interference. If the Neapolitans were allowed a constitutional government, how could the other Italians be denied? And how would the Lombards and Venetians suffer Austria's paternal tyranny, if they saw their brothers across the Po living in liberty? Evidently Austria would have to redouble her garrisons in Venice and Lombardy if that calamity befell. To Metternich, on his Olympian peak, those efforts of oppressed people to win their freedom looked but like the work of tramps setting fire to hayricks. "The revolt breaks out," he writes; "it is indubitable and evident: it is the beginning of a conflagration; if they are in good order, take your fire-engines there; ask no questions: do not hesitate; extinguish the fire: success will be certain. . . . Our fire-engines were not full in July, otherwise we should have set to work immediately."[1] But although

---

[1] *Memoirs.* iii, 448.

taken by surprise, he did not regret that the conflagration at Naples had been allowed to burn brightly enough for him to see the faces of the incendiaries. And when he recognized them as Carbonari, as members of those secret societies which deposit "everywhere the seeds of a moral gangrene which is not slow to develop and increase,"[1] he exulted; because he preferred "to take in hand Carbonarism rather than Liberalism."[2] The Liberal he deemed a half-hearted fellow, but the Carbonaro was one who never qualified his demands through fear or bashfulness or policy; and as "the man who desires the whole is very strong in comparison with him who desires only the half,"[3] Metternich believed that if he played his engines on Carbonarism, the half-ignited embers of Liberalism would fizzle out of themselves.

Had his troops been ready, he would have marched them immediately to Naples without asking leave, and he felt sure that Europe would have applauded his prompt success: but since he could not do this, he planned that Austria should receive from the chief Powers the mandate to put down the revolution. He could count upon Prussia's consent, and England, through Castlereagh, he soon cajoled. England had scruples, indeed, as to the justice of interfering in the internal affairs of an independent State, but those internal affairs became of international concern when they menaced the peace of neighboring States; viewed from this point they justified foreign intervention; and, since Austria was chiefly affected, England was willing to allow her to take what measures seemed proper to her.[4] France, ambitious to regain the influence which she had lost since Waterloo, was inclined to look less harshly on the Neapolitan Constitutionalists: "at least," she urged, "let us sanction what is moderate and beneficial in their reforms, although we condemn the

[1] *Memoirs*, iii. 164.   [2] *Ibid.* 151.   [3] *Ibid.* 150.
[4] Bianchi, ii. 10–12.

military sedition out of which they sprang."[1] But Metternich's chief opponent was the Czar. Alexander was mercurial and enthusiastic in temperament, easily caught by high-sounding phrases, and ruled by favorites who flattered his vanity to be considered a monarch of large ideas and generous purposes. At the downfall of Napoleon he aspired to play the part of the Good Genius of Europe; he coquetted with liberal doctrines, but never imagined that, because they pleased his fancy, he was under obligation to put them into practice. Genuinely solicitous of the welfare of his people, he never dreamt that that welfare could be promoted by any methods of which he did not approve. As Russian autocrat he was opposed to the aggrandizement of his rival, the Austrian autocrat, and he had, as we have seen, interfered more than once to block Austrian machinations in Italy. It was believed, and probably with reason, that he had encouraged his agents in their friendly intercourse with Italian Liberals. He was even suspected of having a secret understanding with the Carbonari. He coveted a seaport on the Mediterranean, and he hoped perhaps that, in certain contingencies, the Russian flag might fly over Ancona or Spezzia. In 1820 he and his chief minister, Capo d' Istria, were still amusing themselves with their pretty doll Liberalism, of Parisian make. Metternich, who had no high opinion of grown-up monarchs and ministers who delight in childish toys, wished to arrange a private conference between the Czar and Emperor Francis; but to this Alexander would not agree. Then it was arranged that the sovereigns of the Five Powers should meet and confer at Troppau.

To Troppau, therefore, Alexander, Frederick William, and Francis went at the end of October; England sent Lord Stewart, Castlereagh's brother, and France was represented by La Ferronays and Caraman. To discredit

[1] Bianchi, ii, 6-7.

Càpo d' Istria before the Czar was Metternich's first move. Pretending that Alexander's generous impulses were in the abstract worthy of so intelligent and noble a monarch, he shrewdly proceeded to show how different, how dangerous Liberalism appeared, when it took its natural concrete form. Did his majesty regard with satisfaction the recent mutiny of his troops at St. Petersburg? Had he forgotten his ambition to guarantee the peace of Europe against political incendiaries? Had he not, only two years before, declared that resistance to the legitimate authority in any country would justify the Allied Powers in armed interference?[1] To reinforce these oral arguments, Metternich submitted to the Czar a written "Confession of Political Faith," a long document, in which he set forth his political maxims, dogmatically supporting them by historical examples, and deducing from them corollaries so cogent and predictions so plausible that they could not fail to convince a monarch who prided himself upon being a philosopher.[2] Metternich's reasons prevailed, and he could soon write, "The Neapolitan revolt and all its charms have been put in quarantine." The Powers agreed that they "would never recognize anything which is the work of the rebellion," but that "before resorting to extreme measures, they desire to exhaust every means of reconciliation, not between the rebellion and lawful power, but between the real interests of the Neapolitan Kingdom and those of Italy and Europe." The three monarchs, therefore, invited the King of Naples to visit them, and to lay before them the condition of his subjects and his plan of restoring order. The King, being free, as the Neapolitans persisted in affirming, "he should feel it his duty to take upon himself this great work." If he refused, the Neapolitans ought to surrender him; but if he acquiesced, and they prevented his going,

---

[1] Fyffe: *History of Modern Europe* (New York, 1887), ii, 195.
[2] Full text in his *Memoirs*, iii, 153-76.

every Neapolitan should be held responsible for his safety. This action being taken, the Congress at Troppau dissolved,[1] to convene forthwith at Laybach; couriers sped southward with the invitation to Ferdinand, and Metternich at least had no doubt that Ferdinand would accept it; for he had in his portfolio a letter in which the King intimated his wish to flee from Naples and begged Austria to send an army to reconquer his kingdom for him.[2]

To the Neapolitan deputies the report of these proceedings came as a warning that they had foes more formidable than the Bourbons. On December 7 the Regent read a message before the Parliament, announcing the receipt of the invitation and of the King's willingness to accept it, in order that he might be the peacemaker between his people and the sovereigns of Europe, and that he might secure a constitution establishing national representation, personal liberty, freedom of the press, and immunity for the July insurrectionists. The discussion of the message was postponed till the following day, and meanwhile the city fell a prey to rumors and suspicions. On the morrow, when the deputies went to the hall of Congress, they were accompanied by crowds of angry sectaries, who shouted for "The Spanish Constitution or Death!" and flourished daggers to emphasize their meaning. Borelli, an able speaker, sought to dissipate the doubts as to the King's loyalty: it would be monstrous, he said, to suspect the descendant of St. Louis and Henri Quatre of treachery.[3] So it was voted that he be allowed to depart on a mission which could not harm and might help the country. The deputies little knew that in the Royal Palace it had been resolved that, should the Parliament refuse, an attempt would be made "to overthrow

---

[1] Metternich, iii, 449-50; Bianchi, ii, 22-3.

[2] Bianchi, ii, 23. It is also asserted that Ferdinand asked the monarchs to invite him to Laybach: Colletta, ii, 385.

[3] Colletta, ii, 389.

the anarchists, by another 9th Thermidor," — as if by the trimmers and poltroons cowering round the King, much less by the King himself, a downright bold deed could be done![1] But the Court took precautions to redouble the guards at the palace, — a sign of distrust which had exasperated the populace, and had led the Central Assembly of the Carbonari to remain in session until the crisis should pass. The only condition exacted from the King by Parliament was that, before setting out on his journey, he should renew his oath to the Constitution. Ferdinand, who was thoroughly alarmed lest escape should at the last moment be cut off, complied in a written message, in which he promised that if he were unable to persuade the monarchs at Laybach to respect the wishes of his subjects, he would return in time to draw his sword in their defense. He also requested that four deputies accompany him, to give him advice and to bear witness to his veracity.[2] Parliament and populace accepted this last asseveration of sincerity and deemed it unnecessary to send the four deputies with the King, whose honor and patriotism, they were glad to believe, needed no guardians nor advisers. Ferdinand embarked (December 14) on an English ship, which was delayed for a short time by an accident near Baja: whereupon a delegation of deputies and officers visited him to express their regret at the mishap. When the frigate at last got under way, they saw the Carbonari ribbons still fluttering on the royal bosom, and they went home filled with proud hopes for the royal mission to Laybach.[3]

Metternich reached Laybach early. He came with the buoyant heart of a man about to consummate business

---

[1] Carrascosa, 237, quoted by Pepe, ii, 35.

[2] The text of this message is in Pepe's *Relation des Evénemens Politiques et Militaires* (Paris, 1822), 116-17.

[3] On being asked at Laybach why he had worn the Carbonari colors on this occasion, Ferdinand replied that he had observed that his ship was within range of two cannon on the fort at Baja: Pepe, *Memorie*, ii, 41.

of benefit to the race and to his own renown. He had, to be sure, still a few formalities to arrange, but as he was a master of formalities, this work was his recreation. He had the advantage over his diplomatic rivals in that he coddled no delusions concerning the propriety of Absolute monarchs flirting with Liberty. Months before (August 10) he had written to his political valet, Gentz: "In Naples no one, not even the first leaders, know where they are going, where they can go, or even where they want to go. There the revolution has really dropped from the clouds; it lies like a spectre on the land. Those who have summoned it have gained their end so quickly that they are quite astonished to be suddenly obliged to rule."[1] Metternich had increased their astonishment by refusing to receive the Neapolitan envoy. He had arrayed all the other Italian princes against the constitutional government except the Pope, who felt it his duty to remain neutral, and the Grand Duke of Tuscany, who trusted so fully in the good-will of his subjects that he did not need Austria's protection. Conscious of his well-laid preparation, Metternich breathed the balmier air of Laybach, and his spirits rose. His only concern was to hold the volatile impulses of the Czar long enough to make him an accomplice in the Austrian policy; so he employed his leisure before the arrival of the sovereigns in conferring with the Czar's chief councilors, Nesselrode and Capo d'Istria. The former he likened to a trout, which nature fitted to disport itself in a clear running brook, but which chance had penned up in a stagnant pool. "Since I have let a little fresh water in upon him he has astonishingly revived," writes Metternich. "He has become lively, and longs for the harder but healthier medium. He will certainly not remain so, for what is a glass of pure water in such a swamp?"[2] Capo d'Istria, however, was not so easily wrought upon by a draught

---

[1] Metternich, iii. 441.   [2] Ibid, 478.

from the pure Metternichian spring. The Austrian chancellor came from his interview with Alexander's Greek favorite in disgust, almost in anger. "A tyrant does not alarm me," he says: "I should know how to avoid his attacks, or bear them with honor. But the Radical maniac, the sentimental Boudoir-Philanthropist, makes me uncomfortable. I like iron and gold, but I hate tin and copper. This childish feeling is so decided in me that I never can endure plated things."[1]

The monarchs arrived, and with their ministers made up a family party, which seemed more bent on pleasure than business, and from which all strangers and uninvited guests were excluded. Metternich devoted himself to the Czar, upon whom, over a samovar of caravan tea, he brought to bear all his charms, and diplomatic expedients. He was witty, he flattered, he argued, he entreated, he suggested dangers, and all so plausibly that on January 10 he was able to write: "To-day, if the earth does not break up or the heavens fall down, or the commonest and vilest ruffians destroy all good people with right and strong wills, we have won the cause. Capo d' Istria twists about like a devil in holy water; but he is in holy water and can do nothing. The chief cause of our activity to-day arises from my thorough agreement with the Emperor Alexander. Here, again, the tea makes its astonishing power felt."[2] Sure of the Czar, Metternich had little difficulty with the other Powers. England took the ground that the Neapolitan revolution touched Austria more closely than the rest of Europe, and that Austria ought therefore to be allowed to interfere; for the sake of formality, Austria might act as the mandatary of Europe.[3] Pasquier, the French Minister of For-

---

[1] Metternich, iii, 479. [2] Ibid, 480.
[3] Castlereagh's course was ambiguous. In his official dispatches in December, 1820, he protested against the doctrine that a change of government in any State justified the Allied Powers in interfering; but he seems, in his private instructions to his agents, to have abetted Austria.

eign Affairs, resisted the assertion of the right of foreign intervention and of military occupation as contrary to the laws of nations, but his opinion was overruled by the reactionary advisers of Louis XVIII, and France therefore sided with Austria. But what of the Neapolitan king who had come to plead the cause of his people before the Laybach Congress?

Ferdinand announced to his brother monarchs that he had taken the oath to the Constitution under compulsion,[1] — that he was as unconverted as themselves to the heresies of Liberalism, — that he left it to them to chastise his rebellious subjects. But what of the honor of a king? what of the oath twice sworn on the Holy Bible? The descendant of St. Louis was so base that he would not have understood how men could look upon his perjury as shameful. And whilst the Congress was deciding the fate of his kingdom, he amused himself at the chase, or with the Russian bears which the Czar presented to him. Metternich felt contempt for Ferdinand, not because he was a liar, not because he was a sneak, but because he did not lie and deceive successfully. "For the second time," Metternich wrote, "the task devolved

Fyffe (*Modern Europe*, ii, 197) takes the former view; Bianchi (ii, 38) takes the latter.

[1] Turotti (i, 177) reports a conversation between Ferdinand and his confessor from which I quote a part. "*King.* Does n't the oath I made on that book of yours bind me to my promise? *Confessor.* You did not make the oath with the intention of keeping it, and it was a mere formality; where there is not a precise act of the will to do wrong, there is no sin. *King.* Then I am free, for my intention was not to fulfil by my act what I promised in my words; 't was a violence of those Carbonari rascals, who constrained me by force; I was like a Christian amid Turks, who, to save himself from the stake, promises to become a Mussulman. *Confessor.* I tell you the crown is yours, and that a people may exact no terms from its king. God gave it to your race, and you may use every means to preserve it. They deceived us by their secret tricks, let them equally be deceived." Where Turotti got this interview, I know not, but, as the Italian proverb says, *Se non è vero, è ben trovato;* it contains nothing unfair to what we know of Ferdinand's character or to the moral standard of the Neapolitan clergy.

on me of picking him up, — for he has the unfortunate
habit of always throwing himself down. Many kings
fancy that the throne is only an armchair, in which one
can sleep quite comfortably. In the year 1821, however,
a seat of this kind is inconvenient to sleep in, and badly
stuffed."[1] "Picking Ferdinand up" meant sending an
Austrian army to subdue and occupy Naples; it meant a
warning to Liberals throughout Europe, that any attempt
of theirs to wrest concessions from their despotic rulers
would be punished by the combined forces of the Holy
Alliance; further, it established the precedent of foreign
interference in the internal affairs of an independent
State, and it familiarized Europe with the idea that when
anything went amiss in Italy, Austria was naturally the
Power to step in and set it right. While, therefore, he
despised Ferdinand, Metternich must have felt grateful to
his incompetence for furnishing an excuse for Austria's
encroachment. The Congress speedily accepted Metternich's view that it could have no dealings with the "product of a revolution;" it refused to listen to any partisans
of the Constitutionalists; and it empowered Austria to
dispatch forces to restore the legitimate sovereign, — if
more were needed the Czar would send an army. Even
Capo d'Istria, finding that Metternich had converted the
Czar, changed his course and proposed to spin a web of
respectability over Ferdinand's perfidy by forging a correspondence in which it should appear that Ferdinand
protested against the violation of the government he had
sworn to uphold, and that the monarchs would not listen
to him.[2] But this trick was deemed futile; the Congress
decided that its acts needed no defense. On February 6
Metternich wrote, "To-day sixty thousand men will
cross the Po. In less than thirty days they will sit in the
curule chairs of the Parthenopean lawgiver as a proof
that there is no procrastination with me. My enemies

[1] Metternich, iii, 479. [2] Fyffe, ii, 200.

must find me very inconvenient."[1] Thus did our Brummel-Jupiter gather the storm, and grasp the thunder-bolts firmly in his kid-gloved hand.

In Naples, after the King's departure, men began to realize that should the King's mission fail, they might have to defend themselves against an invasion. By insisting on "the Spanish Constitution or death," they had left no scope for negotiations. But they were still intoxicated with their good fortune and still prone to mistake their tumultuous energy for enduring strength. Whilst Parliament discussed reforms in the judicial system and then adjourned, public order became more unruly, and violent sectaries resorted to violent deeds. Giampietro, odious to many as Director of Police, was dragged from his house and stabbed forty times by a band of Carbonari, who pinned on his body a list of twenty-six persons marked for assassination; opposite his name being written the words, "Number One."[2] The ministry was reorganized, but stability was still lacking. From time to time the Regent communicated to Parliament the letters he received from his father, but the King did not refer to the vital issues under discussion in the Congress, and had nothing more important to relate than that his hunting dogs were better than the Czar's. Letters from Duke del Gallo, who had been prevented by Metternich from appearing at Laybach to speak in behalf of the Constitutionalists, renewed the apprehensions of danger, and the Regent called a council of generals to draw up a plan of defense. Here, too, the lack of firmness and leadership was ominous. Personal discords and military jealousies, the old feud between the Bourbonists and Muratists, and the new hostility between Carbonari and non-sectaries, boded ill for the national cause. More than eighty thousand conscripts were levied, but they mustered less than fifty thousand soldiers, undrilled and

[1] Metternich, iii, 483-4.   [2] Colletta, ii, 305-6.

ill-equipped. Nevertheless, the Carbonari kept up popular enthusiasm, even at the risk of encouraging delusive hopes. They drew succor from history and recalled how the French people, roused to a frenzy of patriotism, had, with far inferior forces, defeated the veterans of Prussia and Austria in 1792. What might not a people, united and fighting for freedom, accomplish against the minions of tyranny?

At last the suspense was broken by the arrival of Duke del Gallo, who had been permitted to enter Laybach after Metternich had dictated the policy of the Congress. He brought a letter from the King to the Regent, which the latter laid before Parliament, reconvened for that purpose. Ferdinand wrote that he found the Great Powers "irrevocably determined not to permit a continuation of the present state of things;" that they would use force, if persuasion were not enough; but that, if their conditions were accepted, the measures to be adopted should be guided wholly by Ferdinand; otherwise, he intimated, the sovereigns would themselves impose measures on Naples to insure the tranquillity of that kingdom and the peace of the neighboring States.[1] The Regent, after reading this letter and promising to remain loyal, exhorted the deputies "to be prudent, cautious, and firm;" but "it was observed that when reminding them of the danger and repeating his oath, his voice faltered, as if choked by some sudden emotion."[2] Joseph Poerio, one of the most intelligent of the Moderates, spoke in defense of the King. It was incredible, he said, that Ferdinand had sanctioned this perfidy, for he had freely granted the Constitution in July and freely ratified it in October: the presumption must be, therefore, that the sovereigns having him in their power at Laybach had frightened him into this recantation of his principles; his honor, not less than that of his kingdom, demanded

[1] Text in Colletta, ii. 399-400.   [2] Ibid. 401.

that the Neapolitans should take up the challenge of war. And war, clamored for in the streets, was declared in the Chamber and sanctioned by the Regent.

Then was there much bustle of preparation and little results. The men in the bureaux at Naples had no experience in mobilizing and provisioning an army; the men in the camps were ill-clad and undisciplined. A considerable part of the regular troops was still in Sicily, preserving order by martial law. The populace, confronted with the grim certainty of war, shrank from the death-grapple. Most of the recruits came from the Carbonari, who showed in this that they were not afraid to fight; but the rank a Carbonaro held in his lodge, if superior to his rank in the regiment, produced a conflict of authority; a private or subaltern who was a Grand Master chafed at the commands of a captain who was not a Carbonaro at all. Nevertheless, an imposing campaign of defense was sketched on paper. The first army corps, under Colletta, was to guard the frontier along the Liris; the second, under William Pepe, was to be stationed in the Abruzzi, by which it was expected the enemy would invade the kingdom. Pepe spared no effort to prepare his raw troops for the encounter; he drilled them, he talked to them of glory and of duty; he assured them that they would be more than a match for the whitecoated veterans of Austria. But day by day passed, and no supplies or reinforcements came from Naples, and day by day General Frimont, with that Austrian army sixty thousand strong, was drawing near. At length its vanguard appeared near Rieti. Pepe's troops began to desert; he perceived that the suspense was melting their courage, and therefore, though he would have preferred to await an attack, he was forced to give the order to advance. His troops engaged the Austrians between Antrodoco and Rieti (March 7), and fought with considerable valor, but when he found that they were gaining no ground, he signaled them to fall back. The undisciplined soldiers construed a retreat to mean a rout, and many threw away their arms and fled; nor could Pepe rally a remnant sufficiently large to enable him to make another stand against the enemy in the mountain passes.[1]

Desperate, he hurried to Naples to collect a fresh force, and to urge the Regent and Parliament to take refuge in Sicily; the war had but just begun, he said, and it would not be decided by a single skirmish; let the nation rise in mass and dispute every inch of soil, and the Austrians must surely be repelled. His entreaties fell on ears in which the booming of Austrian cannon struck terror. The few who listened to him whispered rumors that but for incompetence or treachery he would not have been defeated; but the greater part of the Neapolitans were busy concocting excuses by which they hoped to save themselves from the retribution which previous restorations had taught them to expect. Ferdinand, lurking well out of danger in the rear of the Austrian army, emitted manifestoes in which he called upon his faithful subjects to receive the forces of his august allies not as enemies, but as friends come to protect them. General Frimont exhorted them to listen to the royal and paternal voice of their King, whose interests were inseparable from theirs. Parliament, still plucky, addressed a letter to Ferdinand, begging him to remember that it had merely exercised functions which he himself had granted it, and requesting him to return to his people and express his wishes to them, without interposing a foreign force between him and them. When the Austrians were within a short march of the capital, the deputies adopted a formal protest, drawn up by Poerio, stating that the presence of a foreign army obliged them to suspend their business and that, according to the report of the Regent, the latest reverses made it impossible to transfer the Parliament to a place of safety. General Carrascosa had already been

[1] Pepe: *Relation*, 52-75.

commanded to negotiate with General Frimont, and on March 23 the Austrian troops entered Naples by the Capuan gate. Some of the leading revolutionists, including Pepe, had fled when they found that to remain was hopeless.[1] Besides the foreign invaders and the Bourbons, the only creatures in Naples who rejoiced that day were the barbers, who were kept busy cropping the telltale locks and beards of frightened Carbonari.

The revolution which thus failed had, like many human undertakings of larger note, a comic aspect. The gods who favor the strong may well have smiled at the presumption of four or five million Neapolitans who dared to assert their manhood against the menaces of tyrants, holding one hundred million Europeans in subjection; they may have smiled at the self-confidence of men who, without education or experience, believed themselves able to conduct a constitutional government, and to reform by legislative fiat the character of a people debased by centuries of corruption; they may have smiled to see discord instead of harmony, factional zeal mistaken for patriotism, private envy weakening arms raised for the public good. But there are other gods who look with kindlier eyes upon the failures and mistakes of men; true gods, who "sigh for the cost and pain" when the worthy hopes of mortals are disappointed; whose hearts are touched with sympathy when they behold men abandon ease and fortune and life itself to pursue a noble ideal, without measuring obstacles, or dreaming of defeat, gods who wove crowns of glory for Leonidas and his three hundred dead, and scorned Xerxes and his victorious myriads at Thermopylæ. To them, the tragedy of human life is ever present: doubt not that they sorrowed at the disaster in Naples; doubt not that their sympathy was with those misguided, beaten enthusiasts, rather than the cynical Metternich and the perfidious King.

---

[1] The best account of the fall of the constitutional government is in Pepe's *Relation;* other authorities corroborate his statements.

CHAPTER VI.

THE REVOLUTION IN PIEDMONT, 1821.

THE excitement of the year 1820 sped northward from Naples, and found in almost all parts of Italy smouldering embers which might easily have been fanned into a blaze, had not the firemen of the Absolutist princes been on hand with their engines. In the Papal States small fires did, indeed, break out, and at Parma and Modena incendiaries were on the alert. But although the year passed without a general conflagration, the successes of the Neapolitans emboldened patriots everywhere. The sects plotted more busily and less vaguely, for they had now a definite scheme.

In Lombardy the best men were in the movement. They had founded at Milan a literary newspaper called *Il Conciliatore*, which, though devoted to literature and criticism, appealed, so far as the strict censorship permitted, to patriotic sentiments. Manzoni, Confalonieri, Porro, Silvio Pellico, and others whose social position or intellectual ability made them respected, and who were known for their Liberal aspirations, conducted this journal, and some of them, notably Confalonieri, promoted reforms for enlightening the masses and improving their material condition. They organized night schools and societies for mutual support; they formed a company to light Milan by gas and to introduce steamboats on the Po. The Austrians watched these efforts suspiciously, but as yet they espied no treasonable intent upon which tyranny might pounce. Still, it was probable that these philanthropic gentlemen had secret relations with the conspirators; education leads so easily to Liberalism, and philanthropy to patriotism. And the sects were, indeed, active in Lombardy. Under the Napoleonic régime that had been the most flourishing province of the Kingdom of Italy; its ablest men had been employed in the army or in the government, and they chafed under the rusting idleness into which they had been forced by the restoration. But, as they had had more experience than the other Italian plotters, so they were more prudent. Estimating the chances in favor of a rising against Austria, they found that, themselves unaided, the struggle would go against them. To secure allies was therefore their purpose, and they dispatched emissaries to sound the intentions and to gauge the strength of the sects beyond the Ticino.

In Piedmont the situation was peculiar. As at Milan the leaders of the Liberals belonged to the most intelligent and aristocratic classes; they were as eager as any other Italians for independence, but, unlike the other Italians, they were attached to their King. They inherited a loyalty to the House of Savoy that had been strengthened by the courage and fair dealing of the princes of that dynasty for more than two hundred years. When Victor Emanuel came back from exile in 1814, they had rejoiced as at the return of a father, and now they had no wish to dethrone him. Nevertheless, his paternal despotism was intolerable: the Jesuits had control of public worship and of education; the civil offices were in the hands of inflexible reactionaries; the army and the Court were petrified by Pre-Napoleonic methods. Officers who had won renown at Austerlitz or Borodino grumbled to see themselves displaced by men who had slumbered through fourteen years of exile in Sardinia; scarred veterans laughed at being officered by young graduates from the military school, whose only recommendation was that they were aristocrats "by the grace of God."

The bourgeoisie complained at the revival of obsolete customs which made business precarious, and at arbitrary interference with the tenure of property. Only the peasantry, the long-suffering peasantry, obedient and still inarticulate, uttered no murmurs as they sowed their rice in the swamps and garnered their maize in the plains.

This, then, was the problem before the Piedmontese Liberals, how to secure a constitutional government without removing their autocratic King. The abuses were there, the desire for freedom was there; and there was Victor Emanuel, a sovereign as deeply imbued as any in Europe with the old notions about kingship. The conspirators hit upon a strange solution, they would make the King their accomplice! Assuming that the misdeeds under which the country groaned were due to his ministers and not to himself, they counted upon his benevolent disposition to grant the petition of his subjects so soon as their desires should be unmistakably expressed. Hitherto the ministry had acted as a dead-wall beyond which no appeals could penetrate to the sovereign; but now these patriotic zealots would raise so loud a cry that the sovereign must hear it. And they proposed, moreover, to strengthen their cause by including the territorial aggrandizement of the House of Savoy in their scheme. Long had the Piedmontese princes bided their time there, in the northwestern corner of Italy: France had swept down upon them from the west, Austria from the east; yet resolutely and unchanged had they waited. Theirs was now the only native dynasty in Italy, the only dynasty which could rely upon the devotion of its people. And now fortune approached, holding the long-coveted prize towards them. Had Victor Emanuel forgotten that maxim of his ancestor, Emanuel Philibert, "Italy is an artichoke, to be eaten leaf by leaf"? Had he renounced the hereditary ambition of his family? Would he refuse to add Lombardy to his kingdom, when he knew that the Lombards were ready, at a sign from Piedmont, to rise and expel their Austrian enslavers? And if Lombardy, why not Venice? Why should not the flag of an independent and Liberal Italy fly over every town from the Alps to the Adriatic?

To patriots who saw the Promised Land thus in mirage, the way seemed short. Not, indeed, that they had no differences of opinion. There were Lombards who insisted that Lombardy should be an independent State; there were Federatists who proposed a league, without even a nominal sovereign, for the Northern Italians, including the Tuscans; there were Radicals whom only a republic could satisfy. As beggars discuss what they will do with a fortune, they even discussed which city should be the future capital: the Piedmontese could not consent to have Turin relegated to second place; the Lombards argued that Milan would be central, and they remembered her glory under Viceroy Beauharnais; and there were partisans for both Genoa and Venice. Meanwhile, the most urgent need was to oust the Austrians and to convince Victor Emanuel that his revolutionary subjects were conspiring in his behalf.

The reliance felt by the conspirators in their ability to arouse the dynastic ambition of the House of Savoy was not so Quixotic as it at first seems; their error lay in misjudging Victor Emanuel's character and in being ignorant of his diplomatic engagements. Many of his predecessors had dreamed that the King of Piedmont would some day rule over a larger Italy. In 1804 Joseph de Maistre, one of the acutest political observers of his time, had written that the chief reason why Austria must hate the House of Savoy "is its tendency to increase its dominions, and its being called to greater Italian possessions by universal good sense and by regard for the safety of the Peninsula and of all Europe. This is the great crime of the House of Savoy, that its powerful neighbor has never forgiven."[1] In 1814 Valesia, Piedmontese Minister of Foreign Affairs, urged Victor Emanuel not to let slip the opportunity to act; above all, he said, "let the Italian national spirit be cherished."[2] Later, the King himself, as we have seen, firmly resisted both the threats and the blandishments of Austria in her attempt to secure the Upper Novarese and to coerce Piedmont into a league. But when the Spanish and Neapolitan revolutions broke out, Metternich stampeded the King and his ministers by prophesying ruin to those legitimate monarchs who lived at the mercy of rebellious subjects, instead of accepting the protection of the Holy Alliance. Piedmont unwittingly fell into the ambush of her hereditary enemy, and made terms with the sovereigns at Troppau, but she wished so far as she might to reserve independence of action in her own concerns.[3]

The conspirators knew of these negotiations, but not precisely, and they made their knowledge help the patriotic cause. Was it not their duty, they asked, to rescue their noble King from the bondage to Austria into which he had been delivered through the perfidy or incompetence of his advisers? Let him but see that his devoted people were bent on restoring him to the liberty his race had most highly valued, and he must approve. So loyal were the motives, so plausible the arguments of these unselfish conspirators!

The year 1820 was touching its end without witnessing any attempt to effectuate these plans. A new ministry, composed of abler and milder men, had been formed, but the autocratic principle had in nowise been renounced by the King. The plotters dreamed and talked and conspired, and after every consultation they believed more earnestly that their project was so rational that it had only to be revealed in order to convince everybody. The Carbonari fraternized with the Federatists, and both were

[1] Bianchi, i. 45.   [2] Ibid, 47.   [3] Ibid, ii, 16-18.

busy enrolling converts. Even those Liberals who would not associate themselves with any sect, knew of the general scheme and gave it an abstract encouragement. The ringleaders were, with but a few exceptions, officers of distinction; therefore, they naturally determined that the army should be the immediate agent of the revolution. If the army demanded the Constitution, how could Victor Emanuel resist? For he, like his fathers, was a military king and must accept the preferences of his troops as indicative of the will of his people. Many subalterns and battalions having been won over, it only remained to find a general whose reputation would give dignity and whose ability would give a successful direction to the movement. The man for the place was unquestionably Gifflenga, who, of all the Piedmontese officers, had most distinguished himself in the Napoleonic wars; but Gifflenga declined the honor, deeming the time unpropitious and the hazards too great. Then the conspirators turned to Charles Albert, Prince of Carignano, and they thought that they had in him a leader whose name would be irresistible.

This singular man was then only twenty-two years old, but he had already outlived many vicissitudes. Born in 1798, just on the eve of the French invasion, his infancy had the roll of drums and the tramp of regiments for lullabies. His father, Charles, was head of the younger branch of the House of Savoy; his mother, Charlotte Albertina of Saxe-Courland, coming when still in her teens to Turin, startled its prim Court by her free-and-easy yet not ungracious manners. When King and Court fled to Sardinia and Piedmont became a province of the French Republic, Charles of Carignano turned Republican, donned a liberty cap, and styled himself Citizen. Citizeness Charlotte, unconventional always, visited her husband on duty at barracks, discoursed vehemently in the dialect of Jacobinism, and even, it is said, danced the Carmagnole to the delectation of the French officers.[1] The good Citizen and Citizeness were nevertheless suspected, and summoned to Paris, where they dwelt under surveillance. In 1800 Charles died, and for several years his widow with her boy, Charles Albert, and a younger sister, Elizabeth, lived precariously. Then Napoleon suddenly relented and showered favors upon them, being attracted, gossips whispered, by the personal charms of Madame de Carignan. She, however, married an obscure gentleman, M. de Montléart, by whom she bore several children, leaving her son Charles Albert to the care of boarding-school masters, first in France and then in Switzerland. The boy was naturally of an affectionate but melancholy temper; he craved tenderness which no one showed him; he was homesick for a home he had never seen. His jumbled experience puzzled his youthful will; from his earliest days he had heard the conflicting doctrines of Republicanism and Imperialism, and though nominally a Catholic, he was now confided to a Swiss Protestant. Another change, and he found himself at Bourges with a lieutenant's commission in a regiment of French dragoons.

When Napoleon's downfall permitted the King of Piedmont to return to Turin, Charles Albert also returned thither. With what suspicion the lad of sixteen was received by the rigid Victor Emanuel we can easily imagine; still, the youth was not wholly to blame for his career among Jacobins and Bonapartists, and, moreover, he was heir to the throne of Piedmont. Victor Emanuel had only daughters, whom the Salic law cut off from the succession; his brother, Charles Felix, was childless; therefore, at the death of Victor Emanuel and Charles Felix the crown would pass to the young Prince of Carignano. Charles Albert had already been the subject of many

---

[1] Beauregard de Costa: *Prologue d'un Règne* (Paris, 1889), 10; Gallenga: *Hist. of Piedmont* (London, 1855), iii, 320.

diplomatic wiles, for Metternich knew his royal pedigrees as a parson knows his catechism, and he hoped to lop off the Carignano branch of the family-tree of Savoy, and to engraft an Austrian scion in its stead. Accordingly, he persuaded Victor Emanuel to give his eldest daughter in marriage to her uncle the Duke of Modena; then he left no artifice untried in attempting to have the Salic law revoked. Failing in this, he requested that Charles Albert should be sent to the camp of the Allies, just then celebrating their entry into Paris; but both the King and his brother suspected a foul design. "Prince Carignano's affair is not less disagreeable," wrote the latter. "I have expected it for a long time. If I may give you my advice frankly, it is for you to get him married as soon as possible. Otherwise, either they will kill him, or they will debauch him so that he cannot beget an heir, or they will entangle him in some bad marriage. He would be quite as badly off at Wellington's headquarters for religious reasons, as with the Germans for the other consideration. 'T is a great trick, open your eyes! They have treated us so well only to enjoy our spoils later, and to make an end of the House of Savoy."[1] These were serious charges to be made against Prince Metternich and his imperial master, who always professed to act from pure Christian motives; but Victor Emanuel saw the danger, and guarded the scapegrace youth in whose safety the perpetuation of the Piedmontese dynasty was bound up. The order of succession was formally declared by the Congress of Vienna to appertain to the Carignano branch.

The young Prince was therefore established at Turin as the heir presumptive to the throne, but his position was not agreeable. He was taken in hand by the King, who strove to eradicate in "him the bad impressions of the Liberal education" he had received. The Queen,

[1] Charles Felix to Victor Emanuel, July 17, 1814; Bianchi, i, 306.

Maria Theresa, hated him because, true Austrian that she was, she wished the succession to go to her daughter, the Duchess of Modena. Charles Felix felt a personal antipathy for him, mingled with distrust. The restored nobles of the Old Régime looked upon him with wonder and suspicion, as if a wild cygnet had alighted amid a flock of dodos. Yet by his youth, his tact, and his submission to the King's process of disinfection, Charles Albert won general respect. He acquiesced when the King warned him that it would be well to marry as soon as possible for the sake of an heir, and accepted Maria Theresa, daughter of the Archduke of Tuscany, who was chosen for him. "Mathematically speaking, I ought to be happy," he wrote, after having been introduced to her. Sombre shadows already flitted through his mind. Yet he had his enthusiasms — who has them not at twenty? — his gallantries, his love of horses, his fitful hours of study. Deepest in his heart lay patriotism, still a vague but sweet sentiment, not yet a duty calling for sacrifices and leading to danger. The petrified manners, the prim, servile conversation of the Court must, we imagine, have chilled one whose youthful imagination had been fired by the Napoleonic world, and who felt that his life was a reality and not a reminiscence. No wonder, therefore, that his boon companions were men of the younger generation, most of whom had great hopes of their country's future and came to associate him with the fulfilling of their hopes. Whether they whispered it to him or not, he could not fail to perceive that he would, in the course of things, be in the position to check or to encourage the aspirations of the Piedmontese, perhaps of all their brother Italians. He hated Austria, he loved liberty, but his love was of the Platonic kind. Making no secret of his relations with men of Liberal views, whom he received cordially at his palace, he shocked the harsh Charles Felix and gave rumor many tasks. The more temperate critics contented themselves by the thought that many follies and much sowing of wild oats, political or other, must be expected of a lusty young prince. Nevertheless, we would not predict evil for a young man who thus confessed himself to his stanchest friend: "I read much, I study, I draw. When one has the misfortune to be a prince, especially at this time, one must know everything, more than mediocrely, and learn to suffice unto oneself, for now the veil has fallen. Princes are judged severely. It were well if being judged were all, but, through calumny, our estate as prince is only tenable for those who do not understand it, or for those who have enough vigor of soul to follow the path of honor through all imaginable vexations. Unhappy indeed is he who at all distrusts himself."[1] That a prince so earnest in the main, worthily ambitious and having kingship in prospect, should welcome the most intelligent and progressive of his future subjects is no more wonderful than that they should have spared no persuasiveness, even to the point of flattery, to make him feel that destiny had marked him out to be the glorious instrument of his country's welfare. He and they were mutually deceived, but their deception was born of good intentions. They believed that when the moment came to strike he would lead them, and he in his glow of enthusiasm believed this too.[2] Neither as yet saw how incongruous it was that the heir to an Absolutist monarchy should conspire to force the actual King, his cousin, towards whom he felt most loyal, to grant a constitution.

Relying upon the coöperation of Charles Albert, the Liberals set about priming their guns. Further delay might ruin the plot. Happily the news came that Austria intended to dispatch an army to subdue the Neapolitans. Here was the occasion that patriotic Italians had

[1] Beauregard, 88.
[2] Cf. B. Manzone : *Il Conte Moffa di Lisio* (Turin, 1882), 45-6.

long awaited. The invasion of Naples would draw off many regiments from Lombardy and Venetia, and encourage the conspirators in those provinces to rise. The revolt would spread through the Legations and the Duchies, the Austrian army would be hemmed in on all sides, and the issue could not be doubtful. One thing was indispensable: Piedmont must give the signal by declaring a constitution and marching her army across the Ticino. The gates of Milan would fly open to welcome it, and nothing could stay its triumphal progress to Mantua and Verona, perhaps even to Venice.

Whilst this general revolt was ripening, an event unexpectedly occurred in Turin which showed the state of popular opinion and served to exasperate the temper of the various partisans. One evening a company of university students appeared at the D'Angennes Theatre with Phrygian caps on their heads (January 11, 1821). The police, making grave of what was probably mere youthful deviltry, tried to arrest them. A tussle ensued, in which the police succeeded in carrying off several prisoners. Their companions flamed with indignation, and declared, what was true, that the delinquents ought to be tried by the magistracy of the University, and not by the criminal court. The carabineers surrounded the University; the students within barricaded the entrance and prepared for a siege. Count Prospero Balbo, Cabinet Minister and President of the University, strove to pacify the students, and went to lay their grievance before the King. But presently four companies of grenadiers marched to reinforce the police, and the contest broke out. The soldiers of course won, but not without receiving many hard knocks. Twenty-seven wounded students were taken to the hospital; the rest were rusticated to the provinces. It was found that most of the wounds had been given by the officers' sabres and not by the soldiers' bayonets; and this increased the popular hatred of

Thaon di Revel, governor of the city, who led the attack, and his officers; but the outraged citizens, lacking force to retaliate, had to content themselves by dubbing the aggressors *sabrers*. At the first news of the broil Charles Albert had hastened to the King for orders; but he let his sympathy be seen by sending money and delicacies to the wounded students.[1]

An ominous calm followed this accidental outburst. The government knew that the conspirators were active, but waited for these to show their hand; the conspirators, inferring that the government hesitated through indifference or fear, began to count on winning an easy game. Had they been less confident, they would have been more troubled at the arrest of Prince della Cisterna, Marquis di Prierio, and Chevalier Perrone, three conspicuous personages, upon whom were found incriminating papers. But there is reason to believe that they were only amateur conspirators uninvolved in the great plot, which now approached maturity.[2] The main course had been laid down, and the discussion waxed hot over details. What sort of constitution should be demanded? — that was the question. One party advocated the Spanish, another the English or French. The Spanish was more democratic, establishing only one chamber; the others established two chambers, an upper and a lower. In a country like Piedmont, having a strong aristocracy, and among conspirators who were themselves aristocrats, a house of peers ought to have found favor; but the majority voted for the democratic scheme. For the Spanish Constitution was the fashion that year, and the conspirators wished to propitiate the middle and lower classes, even at the expense of their own aristocratic traditions. And now all was ready; instruction had been sent to

---

[1] Poggi, i, 326-8; Santarosa: *Rivoluzione Piemontese del* 1821 (Turin, 1850), 38-44; Beauregard, 145-6.

[2] Santarosa, 46.

every accomplice in the army; each lodge of Carbonari or Federatists had its work marked out; it was believed that the necessary arrangements with the Lombards had been concerted.

On the evening of March 6 the four principal conspirators were ushered by a secret staircase into Charles Albert's library. They were Lieutenant-Colonel Marquis Charles Asinari di San Marzano, of the Queen's Dragoons, and son of the then Minister of Foreign Affairs; Count Santorre di Santarosa, major of infantry; Count Moffa di Lisio, captain in the regiment of the King's Light Horse; and Chevalier Collegno, major of artillery. Santarosa thus describes the interview: "Charles di San Marzano spoke first: his words were those of a man profoundly convinced. There was no obstacle, no difficulty that his ardent imagination did not clear away; he described them as they had been foreseen by him, but all-powerless before the ascendency of a firm and resolute will. The others explained to the Prince that they had Italy and posterity in view, that the Piedmontese revolution would mark the most glorious epoch of the House of Savoy. They added, and the future justified their words, that in the movement prepared, nothing sinister to the King and his family was to be feared, to whom our breasts would be a shield on every occasion. Count Santarosa unfolded one by one the means to be adopted the moment the revolution occurred, in order to assure internal liberty and the independence of the fatherland. Nothing was concealed from him, and these memorable words were addressed to him: 'Prince, everything is ready, only your consent is wanting; our friends assembled await at our return either the signal to save the country, or the fatal announcement that their hopes are vain.' And the consent was given by Charles Albert."[1]

[1] Santarosa, 53.

The Prince, writing of this interview a few weeks later, told a different story. These gentlemen, he says, after a long dissertation on Liberalism, concluded by expressing the hope, "that I would put myself at their head to obtain some slight concessions from the King. I replied to them that the only course open to me was that marked out by religion and honor; that nothing in the world would make me abandon my duty. I then sought to reason with them and to prove to them the folly of their enterprise; but they replied that my words were futile, as they were bound by the strongest of oaths. Then I let them understand point-blank that, if I could not prevent them from acting, I would take stand against them: I discovered with amazement that the greater part of my artillery officers were involved. I then threatened these gentlemen that I would go to the King. They departed, saying that they counted on the secret; that they hoped I would change my view, and finally, that the revolution would break out the very day the King went to Moncalieri."[1] This was the explanation given by Charles Albert, when, having been branded as a traitor both by his former friends and enemies, he strove to make his peace with triumphant Absolutism. Did his memory fail? Did he intentionally falsify? Did he impute to himself in the retrospect a decision which he had not shown at the crisis? Or were the four conspirators so bent on having him accept, that they misinterpreted his words? Let who can fasten upon the truth among these contradictions: history can assert at least one fact, — to wit, that though the Prince's treachery was unintentional, it had the effects of wilful betrayal. Weakness is often as baneful as downright wickedness.

Santarosa and his companions quitted the Prince, firmly persuaded that he had given his consent. Thus they reported to their eager accomplices, and boundless

[1] Beauregard, 110-11.

was their exultation. The word was passed to begin the revolt on the morning of March 8. The intervening day dragged for those men, who, after years of hoping and plotting, saw success at hand. Great was their consternation when, towards evening on March 7, they heard that Charles Albert had drawn back. Reflection had painted all the risks of the undertaking before his wavering imagination; the patriotic enthusiasm engendered by contact with the persuasive conspirators gave way to doubt; loyalty to the King outweighed his pledge to the patriots: he bowed to what he believed to be his duty, and went to inform the Minister of War that he had intimations of an imminent outbreak, which must be prevented. He sought counsel of Cesare Balbo and General Gifflenga, who, though Liberals, agreed that the revolution would be untimely, and that the proposed war against Austria for the liberation of Lombardy must fail. Collegno and San Marzano, at the first tidings of the Prince's defection, hurried to brace his courage. "They protested," he wrote, "that I would ruin them, and dishonor myself in the eyes of Europe. I dismissed my tempters, adding that I had done my duty, and saved them from themselves. Then they sent counter-orders everywhere, and I had thus the satisfaction of hindering the execution of the first plot."[1] The orders were indeed countermanded, but only to enable the desperate leaders to make a last effort to win back the Prince. On March 8 San Marzano, Santarosa, and San Michele, colonel of the Light Horse, had a final interview with him. They assured him that they would strike the blow, with or without his consent; but mistrusting his interference, they concealed the hour from him. Charles Albert, disingenuously, it appears, probed in vain to discover their secret. He told them that he could take no active part in the enterprise, but that he sympathized in their wish to secure

[1] Beauregard, 112.

a more Liberal régime. Santarosa construed this to mean that the Prince was at heart with them, and if they were bold they might fix his fickle resolution. But the following morning (March 9), after another consultation in which Charles Albert again attempted to unmask their designs, and after there could be no doubt that as commander of the artillery he had taken measures to frustrate them, Santarosa with grieving soul admitted that the movement must be abandoned. Messengers were sent to Alessandria, Fossano, and Vercelli to communicate this decision to the leaders in those places.

But the rescindment came too late. Early on March 10 Turin was startled to learn that the garrison of Fossano had marched out under Collegno, whither no one knew, and that the garrison of Turin was under marching orders. Santarosa, Lisio, and San Marzano, who a few hours before had regarded their plot as abortive, now felt in honor bound to support their reckless or misinformed comrades, and accordingly they set out post-haste for Alessandria.[1] There the Carbonari, assembling in the citadel, had quickly been joined by the troops in acclamations for the Spanish Constitution and for the King, and a Junta had been organized to take control of the city.

Victor Emanuel, returning from his country-seat at Moncalieri, found the capital excited by the report of these events, and by rumors that the revolt had been caused by the threat of an Austrian intervention. The King at once published an edict in which he denied the rumors, and stated that the intervention of foreign troops in Piedmont would only happen in case of an unauthorized movement on the part of his subjects.[2] This failed to calm the feverish Turinese, for the sectaries were busy haranguing and exhorting, and each hour brought news of further disaffection among the troops. The whole country seemed, to judge by the gossip, to be up in arms,

[1] B. Manzone, 57.   [2] Text in Santarosa, 251-2.

regiments marching hither and thither, but to what purpose none could tell. The King and his courtiers were in consternation. "There is here," writes Charles Albert's equerry, Costa, "the astonishment of Jonah on awakening suddenly in the whale's belly, and the prophet doubtless showed himself more daring and inventive than our poor King in seeking an outlet. They content themselves here with groaning and losing their heads."[1] Yet there was something pathetic in the fidelity of the old nobles to their sovereign in his emergency. Many of them seventy years old and some eighty, they put on their uniform of a bygone generation, and hastened to the King, and they had their horses led within the palace inclosure in order that, were it decided to charge the threatening crowd, they might be lifted into the saddle by their squires; outside they feared they would be too stiff to mount unattended. Charles Albert was among the earliest to offer his services, he having already visited the barracks in the city in the hope that his example and appeals might prevent the sedition from spreading. At the citadel he was not listened to. A great crowd, in which were many aristocratic women, surged round him as he returned to the Palace. They flaunted a tricolor flag before him, shouted "Liberty and the Constitution," and those who were nearest besought him to prevail upon the King to make concessions. Thus up to the very gates of the Palace they swarmed, where the guards alone hindered them from pressing into the royal presence-chamber.

There among his venerable and devoted vassals the King was hesitating. He would have got on his horse and rebuked the insurgents, but the governor of the city and the Minister of War assured him that this would be a useless exposure; personal courage he had, it was hereditary in the House of Savoy, and the risk did not

[1] Beauregard, 111.

frighten him, but he recognized the futility and remained in his palace. What was to be done? The insurrection would not subside of itself, yet where was the force to quell it? The King and his faithful nobles deliberated, conflicting suggestions flew out against each other, the indecision increased. Charles Albert, Count Prospero Balbo, and Count Valese urged that, things having gone so far, it would be expedient to promise some reforms. Marquis Brignole and Count Saluzzo said nothing. The stubborner councilors exhorted the King not to budge, and he agreed with them.

Thus two days passed; in the Palace, irresolution; outside, the flood of agitation rising. Once an officer, bleeding from a stone-cut in the face, entered the King's cabinet and exclaimed: "Sire, give me leave, and with my single company I will settle this matter before I have my wound dressed." Doubtless a dose of lead would have quieted those feverish spirits; doubtless any show of firmness would have checked the turbulence; but Victor Emanuel was humane, the thought of shedding blood displeased him, and he would not give the word. The return at this juncture of San Marzano, Minister of Foreign Affairs, from the Congress at Laybach, silenced the advocates of conciliation, for he reported that the Allied Sovereigns were in no mood to permit Liberal concessions, and that they would interfere in Piedmont as certainly as they were interfering in Naples. The Minister of Police aggravated the alarm by repeating an unfounded rumor that thirty thousand mutinous troops were marching on the capital, and that the militia could not be relied upon.[1] Distracted and weary, Victor Emanuel came at last to a decision — he would abdicate. Abdication is the back-door by which rulers who fail to defend themselves in front hope to escape the humiliation of formal surrender.

[1] Poggi, i, 340.

On the evening of March 12 Victor Emanuel announced his purpose to his ministers and nobles in attendance. Not without tears they accepted the resolve as inevitable. The successor to the throne was the King's brother, Charles Felix, but as he was at that moment at Modena, it was necessary to choose a regent. Charles Albert was designated, but he refused, — how could he, already misunderstood and entangled, assume such a responsibility? The Queen, who had always favored the pretensions of her daughter, the Duchess of Modena, tried to turn the King against this suspected Prince of Carignano; but the King saw no other fit person. At the council Charles Albert spoke earnestly against abdication, saying that it would be the ruin of the country, and that he would never consent to serve as regent. But, he wrote afterwards, "the ministers pressed me. I told them that they knew that I had been for two years past at odds with the Duke of Genevese (Charles Felix) and that, if I accepted the regency, sinister results must follow. . . . But all the ministers then represented to me that this was the last order the King gave me, and that I owed it to my country to accept, to preserve it from greater ills. Then I deemed it my duty to obey."[1] The instrument of abdication was accordingly drawn up and signed, but in such haste that all mention of Charles Felix was omitted. It gave to Charles Albert full authority as regent, until the new king should take control of the government. Victor Emanuel stipulated, with that instinct for their material comfort which even falling rulers do not lose, that he should be paid an annual pension of one million *lire*, and should retain all the privileges of a king. Before dawn on the morning of March 13 he quitted the Palace with his Queen and daughters, on the way to Nice. He was touched by the tears and grief of his officers and courtiers, but the Queen, haughty and in-

[1] Beauregard, 122.

dignant, replied to the farewell homage of the Minister of Police, "We have paid very dear, sir, for a police which you managed very ill." And then the royal coach rumbled out of the courtyard and out through the city streets into the country, just as the first dimness of a new day glimmered along the heights of Superga.

That abdication was the one element the revolutionists had not foreseen. In their calculations, Victor Emanuel was to be made, willy-nilly, an accomplice; they were to save him from his obscurantist advisers, and he, having allowed free-play to his patriotic instinct, would some day forgive and thank those who had made him king of six million Italians. And now this was impossible. The Regent was a turn-coat, whom every patriot suspected; the new King was harsh, unpopular, stubborn, mediaeval in his hostility to reform, a supposed Jesuit in his religion. Well might Santarosa exclaim, "O night of March 13, 1821! Night fatal to my country, that didst plunge us all in squalor and hast shivered so many swords raised in defense of liberty and of the fatherland, and hast dissipated so many dear hopes like a dream. The fatherland did not fall with the King, but it was for us in the King, nay, incarnate in Victor Emanuel. Glory, successes, triumphs, all was for us summed up in that name, in that person."[1]

To Charles Albert, the Regent, the embarrassment was equally great. He saw that he was an involuntary sacrifice both to the monarchy and the revolution. Victor Emanuel had fled, rather than yield to the forcible demands of his people, and break his pledges, of which the people were ignorant, to Austria. Charles Felix would surely be quite as unyielding, and he, moreover, was at present in Modena, where every wind blew from Austria. What was the Regent to do? He would have preferred to remain inactive, merely checking disorder, until he

[1] Santarosa, 70.

could receive instructions from the new King. But the avalanche of revolution neither pauses, nor spares any unfortunates in its track, and Charles Albert was now swept along by the force he had been unable to stay a week before.

In the afternoon of March 13 a crowd thronged the little square in front of the Carignano palace and shouted for the Spanish Constitution. The sentinels at the gates were pushed into the courtyard, and several persons were roughly handled; but spokesmen of the people forced their way into the Regent's presence. They entreated him to publish the Constitution and thus to prevent bloodshed. He declared that he would give his life to maintain the authority of the King whom he represented. They spoke of liberty, of patriotism, of the great anguish of their fellow-Italians that a word from him could relieve. "I, too, am Italian," rejoined the distracted Prince. The municipal authorities and other dignitaries seconded the appeal, by depicting the alternative of refusal, — a massacre and the horrors of civil war. The Prince could withstand no longer; the troops, he was told, had deserted; the insurgents controlling the citadel were ready to bombard the city. He therefore signed a proclamation announcing that the Spanish Constitution would forthwith be promulgated. But in their flurry neither he, nor his councilors, nor the populace, had observed that the Spanish Constitution contained two obnoxious articles: first, it did not recognize the Salic law, so that the succession to the throne of Piedmont might have fallen, at the death of Charles Felix, to the wife of the Duke of Modena; and, second, by establishing the Catholic as the State religion, it excluded other forms of worship. When these radical defects were pointed out, there were cries of "Expunge them!" and they were expunged.

The next day (March 14) the Prince, his newly-formed Ministry, and a provisional Junta composed of temperate men, took oath to abide by the amended Constitution. The people now had their will, what would they do with it? The Regent cautioned them to preserve order; he commanded the seditious troops to return to their allegiance and to put away the Carbonaro tricolor flags which had everywhere replaced the royal banner of Savoy. He dispatched his equerry, Costa, to Modena, to bear a submissive letter to Charles Felix, and to bring back the new King's instructions. Meanwhile agents from the Lombard conspirators came and urged him that all was ready for a rising beyond the Ticino as soon as the Piedmontese army should enter Lombardy. He praised their patriotism, but at a second interview later in the day he said that for the present he must restrict himself to forming three camps, at Turin, Novara, and Alessandria. "Let us hope in the future," were his words at parting.[1] A few days later other messengers came from Milan to warn that it would be madness to count on an insurrection there.[2]

Too soon Costa posted back from Modena, where Charles Felix had received him angrily and had refused to write a word to the perplexed Regent. "Tell him," said the King, "that if there still flows one drop of our royal blood in his veins, he must set out for Novara and there await my orders."[3] To this message he added a proclamation, in which he declared all the acts of the Regent illegal and null, and hinted that his august Allies were ready to place their forces at his service to sustain the legitimacy of thrones, the fulness of the royal power, and the integrity of States.[4] This treatment confirmed Charles Albert's presentiments; but fearing to publish the proclamation, because of the crazed condition of the country, he issued instead a brief manifesto stating that "the King had replied in such a way as to make

---

[1] Poggi, i, 346. [2] Cantù: *Cronistoria*, ii, 186.
[3] Beauregard, 132. [4] Text in Santarosa, 263–5.

us believe that his Majesty is not fully informed of the situation of affairs in his royal dominions. We faithful subjects, I the first, are in duty bound to enlighten his Majesty as to the actual position and desires of his people."[1] This announcement failed to satisfy the public; the King's peremptory words echoed in Charles Albert's mind, and like the whisperings of an Evil Genius drove him to a decision: he, too, would abdicate. Lacking that audacity which quells insurrection by a "whiff of grape-shot," dreading a reign of terror which he was incompetent to grapple with, distrusted by Royalists and Liberals, censured by the King in whose name he acted, wounded in spirit to see himself the victim of a fatal misunderstanding, what else could he do but obey Charles Felix and retire? His enemies hinted afterwards that threats of assassination influenced his resolution, but we may well discredit this of a prince whom physical fear never swayed. His duty now bade him depart, and the entreaties of his advisers could not restrain him. Nevertheless, in order to escape possible detention, and to prevent a tumult, he concealed the hour of his departure. Late in the evening of March 22 he quitted the city, attended by the royal body-guard, the light artillery, and other troops. When he reached Novara, General Della Torre — commander of the Royalist forces — received him coldly. A few days later a curt letter came from Charles Felix bidding him to proceed at once to Tuscany: "by your action," the King concluded, "I shall know whether you are still, or have ceased to be, a prince of the House of Savoy." Charles Albert submitted, though submission meant exile and expiation. His melancholy journey took him through Milan, where he came not as a liberator but as a victim whom the Austrian general, Bubna, mockingly addressed as the "King of Italy;" and through Modena, where he hoped to vindicate himself

---

[1] Text in Santarosa, 265.

before the King, but Charles Felix refused to see him. On April 3 he entered Florence and had worse than a stranger's welcome.

Meanwhile the revolutionists outside of Turin had been fruitlessly active. At Vercelli and Alessandria were their strongholds, but in many other towns the seditious troops had raised the tricolor flag and shouted for the Constitution. They captured Genoa almost without bloodshed. They still talked confidently of the ease with which they would free Lombardy from the Austrians as soon as the word came to cross the Ticino. But it was obvious that the strength of the insurrection was not increasing: the middle classes held aloof from it; the peasantry had no enthusiasm for a cause they did not understand. To the end it remained a movement of a part of the army and of the professional conspirators. Every day that passed without a decisive blow chilled the lukewarm interest of the waverers and emboldened the Reactionists. The abdication of Victor Emanuel had shattered the pivot on which success turned; the retreat of Charles Albert took away the last semblance of legitimacy from the provisional government; the wrath and threats of Charles Felix left no doubt as to the punishment awaiting the rebels. But like men who, having burned their ship, are caught between the sea and an overwhelming foe, the leaders of the revolution resolved to die with honor, rather than ignobly to drown themselves in the impassable waters.

This resolve, the alternative of despair, was fixed chiefly through the urgency of Santarosa, the ablest of the insurgents, and as disinterested as any. From Alessandria, where he had been tirelessly organizing the troops for battle, he returned to Turin just before Charles Albert's withdrawal, was appointed Minister of War, and became thenceforth the centre of energy. The Junta was timid, but he did not flinch. He assumed that they acted legitimately because they had been appointed by Charles

Albert, the lawful representative of Victor Emanuel, and that they were not bound to obey Charles Felix so long as he was detained in an enemy's country. Whatever commands issued from Modena could not be the product of the new King's free-will; it was his duty to return to Piedmont, where he might learn what his people needed; if he were prevented in coming, it would be their duty to try to rescue him. This well-meant casuistry can hardly have comforted even its author; it does not seem to have deceived any one else. While Santarosa bravely provided munitions for the insurgent troops, and wrote orders-of-the-day full of patriotism and encouragement, the Junta strove to defend the country from anarchy and discussed reform laws. But now the news came that the Neapolitans had been routed, that the Austrians were marching unresisted to Naples, and that all hope of a popular rising in Central and Northern Italy had vanished. To keep this a secret for more than a day or two was impossible; to hope further was madness. Gladly, therefore, all the members of the Junta except Santarosa listened to proposals of mediation from the ministers of France and Russia. Charles Felix was to be besought to grant a full amnesty to all the Constitutionalists, to spare the country the shame of a foreign invasion, and to pledge himself to concede a statute adapted to the needs and wishes of his people. The insurgents, as a guarantee of good faith, were to deliver up the citadels of Turin and Alessandria to the Royalist General Della Torre. But when these terms were laid before Della Torre he refused them, demanding unconditional surrender.[1] Nothing remained for the insurgents but a trial of strength. Della Torre, whose forces had been increased by gradual accessions, prepared to march on Turin. Santarosa gave orders to prevent him by advancing on Novara. There was a disingenuous truce, which allowed time for the

---

[1] Bianchi, ii. 62-4.

Austrian vanguard to join the Royalists, and then on April 8, after a brief but not wholly inglorious conflict near Novara, the Constitutionalists were routed. Like the Neapolitans, they learned that patriotism, however brave, however worthy it may be, cannot of itself win battles; the God of War bestows victory not on the just but on the best equipped, and if patriots would conquer, they must have strength as well as justice on their side. The routed troops dispersed: some to Genoa, whence they embarked for foreign lands, and some to Switzerland; a few fled westward towards France, and brought the news of disaster to Turin. Santarosa would still have made a last effort, but he, too, was soon convinced that the delusion was played out; and heavy of heart he bade farewell to his country forever.

As the clouds clear away, as the parching sun of Absolutism shines again over Naples and Piedmont, we catch another glimpse of Metternich, serene and Jove-like, preparing to depart from Laybach. "While military operations are going on," he writes (April 13), "a minister takes his holidays. The Neapolitan war gave me eight days; the Piedmontese only four. Everybody must acknowledge that no time has been lost."[1] When the gods are thus satisfied with their work, why should mortals find fault? Can it be that men know better than the Olympians what is right and necessary?

[1] Metternich, iii, 494.

CHAPTER VII.

RETRIBUTION.

Thus failed the first organized attempt of the Italians to win their freedom. The failure, although complete, was not ignoble; the courage of many of the leaders, the very audacity of the undertaking, suffice to lift the revolutions in Naples and Piedmont above the reach of contempt. Viewed in themselves, those revolutions were calamities with scarcely a mitigating phase, for they proved how easily Patriotism could be defeated, and they made Tyranny more insolent than before: but viewed historically, as episodes in a deep and prolonged national movement, rather than as sudden and unsuccessful spurts, they appear salutary. For what were those disasters but lessons set by Adversity, the great teacher who dispels illusions, who will tolerate no compromises, who rewards only patience and courage and strength? Henceforth the issue could not be misunderstood. The conflict was not simply between the Neapolitans and their Bourbon king, or between the Piedmontese and Charles Felix, but between Italian Liberalism and European Absolutism. Santarosa and Pepe cried out in their disappointment that the just cause would have won had their timid colleagues been more daring, had promises but been kept; we, however, see clearly that though the struggle might have been prolonged, the result would have been unchanged. Piedmont and Naples, had each of their citizens been a hero, could not have overcome the Holy Alliance, which was their real antagonist.

The revolutionists had not directly attacked the Holy

Alliance; they had not thrown down the gauntlet to Austria; they had simply insisted that they had a right to constitutional government; and Austria, more keen-witted than they, had seen that to suffer a constitution at Naples or Turin would be to acknowledge the injustice of those principles by which the Holy Alliance had decreed that Europe should be repressed to the end of time. So when the Carbonari aimed at Ferdinand they struck Austria, and Austria struck back a deadly blow. They learned, what in their days of hope they had ignored, that they had to deal with Metternich at Vienna, and not alone with their local sovereign. And now, in defeat, they could learn many other matters which it behooved them to know. They could contrast the decisive harmony amongst the powers of despotism with their own fatal hesitation and dissensions. The secret societies which had promoted the insurrection never had the great majority of the people with them. The peasantry and artisans, who composed at least half of the population, were scarcely interested in the movement; like eel-grass, they were accustomed to be drawn to and fro by the fluctuating tides of government, but it made little difference to them whether the tide ran in or out; rooted to the soil, even their slight motions were not due to their own volition. The tradespeople were timid and conservative, — that is the characteristic of the well-to-do or rich. The privileged classes, the nobles and clericals, were for the most part upholders of the despotic system to which they owed their privileges. That the Carbonari, Federatists, and the score of smaller kindred sects, induced some nobles — and those among the most intelligent and energetic — to join them, and that their membership was considerably recruited from among professional men, are the best indications of the essential worthiness of those societies. But the lack of a responsible head, the cheap mysteries and vague purposes, the evident desire to get strength by numbers rather than by character, the excesses committed by the most unprincipled members, — all this tended to discredit conspiracy before it came into action, and hastened its dissolution as soon as it began to act. A political party, whose operations are public, must have leaders and principles known to all its adherents and presumably approved by them; the very publicity encourages loyalty; but a conspiracy, unless it be limited to a few men, must lose in efficacy in proportion as it gains in volume. Even in a conspiracy whose aim is patriotic, the instinct is often irresistible to aggrandize the sect at the expense of the country, because the welfare of the country is believed to depend upon the aggrandizement of the sect. Secrecy which binds conspirators together so far as they share a common danger, may, on the other hand, weaken their sense of a larger personal obligation; and it gives too much scope to schemes of the most audacious or the most unscrupulous. When the average member discovers that the forces of his lodge are being employed in the interest of an ambitious Grand Master, he becomes jealous, or at least lukewarm; when he finds that his own moderate views are outvoted by a majority of extremists, he becomes hostile, for no man would risk life and fortune to join in a plot to which he was opposed. Hence cliques within the sect, itself a clique; hence a babel of tongues and conflict of schemes, in which the loudest and the most turbulent prevail. History is a prolonged refutation of the proverb that "in a multitude of advisers there is safety." The Italian conspirators learned in disaster that many heads are not always better than one. It was Hydra, and not Athene, — the monster of discord, and not the goddess of wisdom, — whom the Greeks pictured as many-headed.

Besides these defects inherent in all extensive conspiracies, — especially where the object conspired for is not a person but an abstraction, — the Italian conspirators had to contend against special difficulties. The hereditary feuds between province and province, as old as the days when Guelf and Ghibelline were living watchwords, were not forgotten. The recent Napoleonic upheaval, causing allegiance and opinions to be quickly and often changed, threw strange elements together, and split up elements which had till lately been united. Above all, the distinctly military aspect of the revolution, both in Naples and Piedmont, gave it too much the appearance of a sedition, rather than that of a popular uprising.

What, then, was gained by the patriots in their unsuccessful endeavor? Nothing of immediate benefit, but much which, unrecognized at first, might afterwards advance their cause. They had gained experience, bitter indeed, but necessary. They had shown that Italians could and would fight for their independence. They had proved at Naples that they could govern honestly, if not strongly, and at Turin that they were not the wild anarchists which all revolutionists were supposed to be. They had, in a word, announced to Europe that Italians dared to protest against the shameful condition of their country. But their protest had not been listened to; their efforts had failed, and now their punishment was terrible. Through their failure Austria had become more powerful than ever in all parts of the Peninsula; the Allied Powers had conceded to her the right to interfere in every province; her army had again occupied Naples; she had at last won her way into Piedmont, so long her stubborn opponent.

But Austria and the Reactionists were not content with simple victory; treating the revolution as a crime, they at once proceeded to take vengeance. Logically they were justified; but this would be a poor world indeed had it no higher laws than those of partisan logic to direct it to truth and justice. Your syllogism is like a loaded gun, which will go off, whoever pulls the trigger; but it depends upon the aimer whether the shot hits the right mark. Most of the abominations of history — slavery, polygamy, sacerdotal celibacy, the Inquisition, tyranny, theological superstitions, standing armies, economical fallacies like protection — have had plenty of logic, of a certain kind, to defend them. In Italy in 1821, however, there was need of no more logic than that which prompts a cat to torment a mouse; instinct and superior strength sufficed to guide the avengers.

Ferdinand, the perjured Neapolitan king, tarried behind in Florence, whilst the Austrians went down into his kingdom and squelched the patriotic army. He was too prudent a monarch to risk himself among his subjects until they should be brought into a loyal frame of mind; and it is a king's privilege to fight by proxies and to reward them with titles and honors. But as soon as Ferdinand was assured that the Austrian regiments were masters of Naples, he sent for that Prince of Canosa whom he had been forced unwillingly to dismiss on account of his outrageous cruelty five years before, and deputed to him the task of restoring genuine Bourbon tyranny in the Kingdom of the Two Sicilies. A better agent of vindictive wrath than Canosa could not have been found; he was troubled by no humane compunctions, nor by doubts as to the justice of his fierce measures; to him, as to Torquemada, persecution was a compound of duty and pleasure.

Arriving at Naples, he learned that a Provisional Council, appointed by the King, had already begun the work of chastisement. Every act of the revolutionary Parliament was annulled: that "Sacred Squadron," which had led the revolt on the 2d of July and had been received with honor by the Viceroy, was attainted of treason; the right of assembling, no matter for what purpose, being denied, the universities, schools, and lyceums had to close; proscription lists were hurriedly drawn up, and they contained not only the names of those who had been prominent in the recent rising, but also of all who had incurred suspicion for any political acts as far back as 1793, — a direct violation of the Treaty of Casalanza, to which the king had sworn in 1815. In order to expedite punishment, special Juntas of Scrutiny were created to try accused civilians, and courts-martial to try officers and soldiers; but what hope of justice was there from these tribunals, composed, in part, of men who but a few months before had been engaged in the same enterprise as the victims over whom they sat in judgment? To purchase pardon by turning State's evidence has been from time immemorial the last resort of cowards; but it was a baseness reserved for the Bourbon government to raise renegades to the judicial bench, where they passed sentences upon their late confederates. There being no *habeas corpus* law, arrest might be followed by long imprisonment without trial; there being no court of appeal, perpetual imprisonment or summary execution depended upon the caprice or prejudice or ignorance of a single judge. As the accused was not allowed to confront his accusers, many vile wretches made a business of informing, either to earn a few crowns or to gratify a personal spite. Others became Iscariots through fear. But all these were mere skirmishers in advance of the army of police, carabineers, and paid spies that Canosa employed in his campaign of extermination. Houses were searched without warrant; seals were broken open; some of the revelations of the confessional were not sacred. The church-bells tolled incessantly for victims led to execution. To strike deeper terror, Canosa revived the barbarous torture of scourging in public. "At midday in the populous Toledo Street a large detachment of Austrian soldiers was seen, drawn up in military array; next to them stood the assistant of the executioner, who, at intervals, blew a trumpet, and a little behind him more Austrians, and several officers of police, who surrounded a man naked from the waist upwards, his feet bare, his wrists tightly bound, and with all the badges of the Carbonari hung round his neck; he wore a tricolor cap, on which was inscribed in large letters, 'Carbonaro.' This unhappy man was mounted on an ass, and followed by the executioner, who, at every blast of the trumpet, scourged his shoulders with a whip made of ropes and nails, until his flesh was stained with blood and his agony was shown by his pallor, while his head sank upon his breast. The mob followed this procession in silent horror. Respectable citizens fled, or prudently concealed their pity and disgust. If any asked the meaning of this punishment, they were told the person flogged was a Carbonaro, a gentleman from the provinces (and a gentleman he appeared to be both in face and person), who after being scourged, was to suffer the penalty of the galleys for fifteen years; and this not by the sentence of a magistrate, but by the order of the Prince of Canosa, Minister of Police, who had just arrived in the city."[1]

At the capital, where a large Austrian garrison made resistance impossible, the avengers worked methodically. To seize and punish the obscurer victims, who had neither rank nor wealth to plead for them, was but the prologue to the tragedy; Canosa and his minions soon brought those on the scene who had both wealth and rank, which only hastened their destruction. When he wrote to Ferdinand to ask if he might punish without discrimination, Ferdinand replied, "Punish." No one, however innocent he knew himself to be, could escape the dread of being accused and persecuted. Many of the most prominent of the revolutionists had fled before the collapse of the

---

[1] Colletta, ii, 440-1. I have substituted "Austrians" for "Germans." During the first half of the century the Italians called their Northern persecutors indiscriminately "Germans" or "Austrians;" the latter is of course the correct term.

constitutional government; many who had remained, trusting to their guiltlessness, now hesitated whether to flee or to remain. If they fled they would be declared guilty, their families would be maltreated, and their estates confiscated; if they stayed, they might at any moment be imprisoned on a false charge. Many hid themselves. In the provinces, anarchy and punishment went side by side. Brigandage, recruited from the multitudes, under the ban of the police, flourished again. Reckless Carbonari took swift vengeance on hated judges, or broke into the prisons and liberated their companions. Woe to the peaceful rustic, exposed alike to the extortions of the bandits and the suspicion of the police!

How many victims actually suffered during this reign of terror we cannot tell. Canosa's list of the proscribed had, it is said, more than four thousand names. The prisons were choked with persons begging for trial; the galleys of Pantelleria, Procida, and the Ponza Islands swarmed with victims condemned for life; the scaffolds, erected in the public squares of the chief towns, were daily occupied. And as if the political motives for persecution might fail, a religious motive was soon added. The Pope declared the Catechism in common use to be unorthodox. It had been compiled from the writings of Bossuet, and sanctioned in 1816; but its allusions to patriotism as a duty which citizens owe to their country were now pronounced dangerous. The book was publicly burnt, and whoever was caught with a copy of it in his possession was liable to be severely punished. Spies went about to ferret out this and other interdicted works; many persons voluntarily brought their prohibited literature to the Piazza Medina, to be burnt by the hangman; others destroyed their libraries in private.

At length, when his deputies had terrorized the country into apparent submission, and when the Austrian regiments made it safe for him to travel, Ferdinand quitted

Florence and returned to Naples. His entry was magnificent, being accompanied "by rejoicings prepared by flattery and fear." Perhaps to his perfidious soul these insincere expressions were as grateful as is honest approbation to the hearts of the sincere; but henceforth he took greater precautions than ever to surround his person with a strong guard; to whet the vigilance of the police; to employ spies to watch every official, and other spies to watch those spies; to forbid every act or practice which might be the germ of rebellion. He intrusted education to the clergy, honored the Jesuits, bestowed pensions on bishops, and was himself most assiduous in performing the mummery of worship. To Frimont, commander of the Austrian army, he gave the title of Duke of Antrodoco and a purse of two hundred thousand ducats; to Francis, his son and late accomplice in perfidy, he offered no reproaches. He was as barren in mercy as in honor. He spared not even those who had had no part in promoting the revolution and who had come forward only after he had himself ratified the Constitution. To commute sentence of death into confinement in the galleys for life — a sentence worse than death — was the limit of his mercy.

In the government Ferdinand adopted principles more Absolutist than at any earlier period of his reign. He appointed a council, composed of six councilors and six ministers, who were merely the instruments of his will. He separated the administration of Sicily from that of the mainland. He decreed that a Consulta, having eighteen members in Sicily and thirty in Naples, should discuss the ordinances for those two portions of the kingdom, but without power to amend or execute them; that provincial councils should assess taxes, and that communes should be less dependent on the central government. These were the new orders. The King, by reserving to himself the right to nominate or remove any official, held his subjects, high or low, in the hollow of his autocratic hand. The public debt, which had not increased under the honest administration of the Constitutionalists, now rose rapidly. The Austrian garrison had to be paid; the King must have money to lavish on foreign friends and to expend on his own ostentation, and on his gifts to the clergy. In Sicily the revolution smouldered and spluttered for years, in spite of remorseless efforts to stamp it out; on the mainland, robberies and brigandage, and outbreaks now political and now criminal, proved how delusive was a security based on oppression and lies. Amid these conditions Ferdinand passed the later years of his infamous reign: as if repudiated by the God and saints to whom he built churches, and as if even Orcus itself loathed to receive him. Despised by his parasites and by the princes whom he pompously entertained, and hated by his subjects, he strove to banish his terror of death by the follies of his buffoon, by the antics of his pet bears, and by the droning of his priests. Such was the king, and such the government, that the Allied Powers of Europe — Austria, Prussia, Russia, France, and England — imposed on Naples during the fifth lustre of the nineteenth century.

In Piedmont the retaliation was as effectual as in Naples, but less blood was shed there. Della Torre took command of the kingdom in the name of Charles Felix. Count Thaon de Revel displayed his loyalty by the rigor of his administration in Turin; armed with special authority from the King, he rivaled Canosa in his implacable baiting of the rebels. A special commission, composed of officers and magistrates, devoted itself exclusively to investigating "the crimes of rebellion, treason, and insubordination." Seventy-three officers were condemned to death, one hundred and five to the galleys; but as nearly all of them had escaped, they were hanged in effigy; only two, Lieutenant Lanari and Captain Garelli, were executed. The property of the condemned was sequestrated, their families were tormented, and the commission, not content with sentencing those who had taken an active part in the revolution, cashiered two hundred and twenty-one officers who, while holding aloof from Santarosa, had refused to join Della Torre at Novara and fight against their countrymen. A second commission examined the civil employees of the government, and removed many of them from office, while a third took the students in hand, rusticating some to distant villages, annulling diplomas which had been granted during the month of rebellion, and closing for a year the universities of Turin and Genoa. One prelate, the Bishop of Asti, who had spoken disparagingly of Absolutism, was shut up in a Capuchin convent until he publicly retracted his opinions. The prisons were crowded with suspects, and, as invariably happens after the collapse of an insurrection, many base spirits purchased pardon for themselves by denouncing their late colleagues or their private enemies. Few, indeed, were the families in the upper and middle classes which had not to tremble for the safety of one of their members under arrest, or to mourn him wandering in exile.

Charles Felix lingered meanwhile in Modena until his kingdom and army should be "absolutely purged."[1] As the work progressed, he sent approving letters to be published in the official *Gazette* at Turin, and he issued a manifesto calling upon his subjects to submit, and warning them that to murmur would be high treason. They could not refrain, however, from rebaptizing him Charles Ferox, but they took care to utter the nickname under their breath. The King himself had soon reason to learn the truth of a former epigram of his, "Austria is a bird-lime which you cannot wash off your fingers when you have once touched it;"[2] for Austria soon showed that

[1] Bianchi, ii. 341.   [2] Beauregard, 151.

her motive in bolstering falling monarchs on their shaky thrones was not simply philanthropic nor disinterested. General Bubna, on taking possession of Alessandria, sent the keys of that fortress to Emperor Francis, in order, he said, — and we wonder whether there was no sarcasm in his voice, — in order to give Charles Felix "the pleasure of receiving them back from the Emperor's hand." "Although I found this a very poor joke," wrote Charles Felix to his brother, "I dissembled."[1] How, indeed, could he do otherwise? The Austrian troops, on the pretext that there was danger of a counter-revolution, had occupied Casale, Alessandria, and Tortona; and by a convention signed by Bubna and the agents of the King, it was agreed that an Austrian army corps of twelve thousand men should remain in Piedmont at least until September, 1822, their rations and a monthly stipend of 300,000 francs to be supplied by the Piedmontese government.[2] Charles Felix had in truth become but the vassal of the hereditary enemy of his line, and that not by conquest, but by his own invitation.

So the summer wore away, and the King, having received news that the purging had proceeded so far as to make it desirable that he should return to Piedmont and be crowned, prepared to leave Modena. But first, as a mark of his paternal clemency, he issued an amnesty (October 4), in which he granted full pardon to his guilty subjects, only excluding "those who had been heads, authors, or promoters of the conspiracies and tumults; those in whose houses meetings had been held for revolutionary purposes; those who, with money, flattery, or promises, had shaken or attempted to shake the loyalty of the troops: those who, having charge of public education, had led the youth astray; those who by writings, whether printed or not, had promoted the revolution: or had been leaders, directors, or members of the Italian

---

[1] Bianchi, ii, 68. [2] Santarosa, 283-8.

Federation; or had assumed military command, whether to promote or maintain the sedition; or had been guilty of homicide, or of taking funds from the State or communal treasuries, or of arbitrary imposition on the communes or on private individuals."[1] Well might the Piedmontese ask if this amnesty was meant in jest, — royal humor being often unintelligible to the vulgar mind. As if to make his meaning clear, however, Charles Felix accompanied this edict by another in which he remitted or annulled the punishment of many common murderers and violent criminals as a sign of his sovereign benevolence. And then, triumphal arches having been erected and illuminations having been made ready, he entered Turin and listened to the perfunctory congratulations of his loyal officials and magistrates; but the populace, it was remarked, greeted him with unobsequious silence.

In spite of these severe measures, Charles Felix was not by nature bloodthirsty. His narrow mind was possessed by a single idea, — that it was the divine will that he should have absolute control over his subjects. For them to object was heresy; for him to yield would be to disregard the divine command. Alone of all his line, he lacked the soldier's instinct and territorial ambition which had raised the Counts of Savoy to the small but sturdy Kingdom of Piedmont. That ugly countenance of his, with its ever-gaping mouth, bespoke neither vigor of will nor dignity of character, but rather a bull-dog tenacity; and, like a bull-dog, he could be good-natured when he was not crossed. He adopted, therefore, the policy which seemed most likely to secure him the undisturbed play for his autocratic impulses. Though not particularly devout, he gave full range to the Jesuits in both education and public worship, because he recognized their ability in paralyzing Liberal sentiments and in hunting down the perverse. "I am not King to be bored," was

[1] Turotti. i, 803.

a favorite saying of his; to which we may add this other: "Austria holds half a million bayonets in her pay quite at my service, and I need no other troops." He spent his days in dabbling in diplomacy, or in gossip; his nights at the theatre; but he was not without a certain condescending kindliness towards those of his subjects who prostrated themselves to his authority. Under such a guardian, the cause of Absolutism seemed safe in Piedmont.[1]

In Central Italy, which had escaped an open revolution, sufficient evidence was collected to bring several batches of suspects to trial. The Tuscan Grand Duke, to whom the mildness of his reign had been a better protection than espionage and severity had been to his neighbors, was inclined to punish the offenders so lightly that Austria remonstrated. "Send me Metternich," he replied; and in the absence of the Chancellor he pursued his lenient policy.

Cardinal Consalvi and the Pope likewise chafed at Austria's charge that they encouraged conspiracies by not taking vengeance on the conspirators. That they should be so reproached was indeed strange! The Legate at Forlì, Cardinal Sanseverino, redeemed his own reputation for energy by making wholesale arrests, and by banishing many innocent persons without a hearing. Austria, under the pretense that the Papal States were in danger, left a garrison of two thousand troops at Ancona, despite the protests of Cardinal Consalvi.[2] The Pope, however, removed all doubts as to his agreement with the monarchs of the Holy Alliance by launching (September 13, 1821)

---

[1] Beauregard, 156; Gallenga, iii, 327-9. Gallenga adds some touches to the King's portrait: "Evening after evening he sat in his box, at Genoa or Nice, his favorite sojourns, leering at the dancing-girls, munching *grissini* — the famous Piedmontese crisp-baked bread — and napping. . . . By day he hid himself in his palace, enjoying the stale fun of obscene favorites."

[2] Bianchi, ii, 351.

a bull against all secret societies, especially against the Carbonari. He condemned their blasphemous ritual and their sacrilegious initiations. He warned the faithful against their discourses, which, he said, "seem smoother than oil, but are naught else but arrows which these perfidious men use to wound more surely those who are not on their guard. They come to you like sheep, but they are at heart only devouring wolves." He excommunicated not only the Carbonari themselves, but any one who, knowing a Carbonaro, did not denounce him, or who read or had in his possession any of their tracts.[1] With both the spiritual and temporal agencies of the Papacy thus directed against the sects, and with Austria's troops and Metternich's secret spies on the alert, the cause of Liberalism had a more desperate outlook than ever in the Roman State.

But the tyrant who most distinguished himself in these orgies of retaliation was Francis IV, Duke of Modena. He had, as we have seen, a restless ambition, justified in part by forcible qualities, which found his little duchy too small a stage on which to exhibit themselves. He coveted the throne of Piedmont, to which, could the Salic law be abrogated, his wife might succeed: but not content with this tantalizing possibility, he already dreamed of making himself master of Northern Italy. He accepted Austria's tutelage in so far as it shielded him from other interference, but he was of too imperious a nature not to fret at Metternich's dictatorial manner of giving advice. And now he resolved to show the autocrats of Europe that, since they made persecution the test of ability, he could out-Herod them all.

When Austrian troops had passed through Modenese territory on their way to suppress the revolution in Naples, incendiary tracts had been secretly circulated among the Hungarian soldiers, urging them to refuse, at the bidding

[1] This bull is entitled *Ecclesiam a Jesu Christo*.

of their Austrian masters, to crush the efforts for freedom of a people, like themselves, oppressed. The appeal failed to rouse the Hungarians; but it roused the Duke of Modena. He had flattered himself that no conspirators dared wink or whisper in his police-haunted duchy; yet here was proof positive of a conspiracy. Francis, therefore, ordered many arrests, and he converted the old fortress of Rubiera, midway between Reggio and Modena, into a political prison. Thither assembled a special sanguinary commission charged with prosecuting the accused. In no case was the trial to extend beyond eight days. "The hangman will hold himself in readiness," was the Duke's command, "and according to circumstances the scaffold may be erected beforehand, and it will be arranged to have the priest ready to attend those who are condemned." Notwithstanding these preparations for dispatch, some time elapsed without noteworthy results. Then it was announced that one of the prisoners had made a confession implicating other citizens. Suspense brooded over Modena, — suspense and wrath. At length, at dusk on May 14, 1822, Sesini, the Director of Police, hated as the right hand of the persecution, was stabbed by an unknown assassin. Sesini, though dying, deposed that while he had not recognized his assailant, he felt sure it was a certain Ponzoni, against whom he bore a grudge. Ponzoni was arrested, and although he established an alibi, and although the real assassin, Moranti, was known to have escaped, he was imprisoned for nine years. Then the bloody assizes began in earnest. The commission proceeded to examine the prisoners from whom Sesini, by barbarous means, had extorted confessions. One of the victims, Giovanni Mariotti, had been chained in an upright position for many days, and flogged daily until his mind gave way, and he subscribed to a deposition the very contents of which he did not understand; when the judges came to pass sentence, they found him a maniac.

Antonio Nizzoli, similarly tortured for forty days, had still mind enough left to tell the tribunal that the revelations which Sesini had wrung from him were false. "Conti was entrapped by a forged confession attributed to another prisoner; Alberici was gained by allurements and flatteries; Caronzi was persuaded by the prayers and tears of his wife, whose honor was said to have been the price of a fallacious promise of her husband's deliverance, he being sentenced to twenty years' penal servitude, a term reduced by the Duke to fifteen. Perretti, Maranesi, Farioli, and others testified to similar deceits and cruelties, ineffectually employed against themselves; some, unbeguiled by the inducement held out to them, remained silent."[1]

The Duke, whose vindictiveness could not be appeased by the punishment of his own subjects, reached over to Parma, and through Austria's agency compelled the Grand Duchess to surrender several Parmese suspects to be tried at Rubiera. The commission, which, although appointed by the Duke, had still a regard for justice, dared to report that none of the prisoners were guilty of misdemeanors deserving more than a year's imprisonment; but Francis reversed their decision and sentenced nine to death (some of whom had fled), seven to the galleys, and thirty-one to long imprisonment. Andreoli, a young priest, was the only one who suffered death; the charge against him was high treason as a Carbonaro, but it was proved that he had joined the Carbonari in the spring of 1820, whereas the ducal decree imputing high treason to any one who joined that sect had been issued on September 20, 1820. But to Francis a retroactive law was as valid as any other. The most distinguished of the fugitives who escaped execution was Panizzi, who afterwards rose to be Librarian of the British Museum.

By this remorseless ferocity, Francis introduced himself

[1] Fagan: *Life of Sir Anthony Panizzi* (London, 1881). i. 33.

to the autocrats of Europe as a man of action, not unworthy, in spite of the limited sphere of his activity, of a place among the fiercest of them. The Italians, who had sarcastically nicknamed him the "Dukeling," now showed respect for his ability by calling him the "Butcher" or the "Hangman." Henceforth he took no pains to conceal his ambition to exercise his powers in a larger field than his little duchy offered. When a proposition emanated from the cabinets of Turin and Vienna, that Europe should unite in shipping to America all the political plotters under arrest or suspicion, Francis was one of the few rulers who approved the monstrous plan.[1] He seconded Metternich's almost equally monstrous suggestion, that the princes of Italy should establish a sort of central police station, or criminal clearing-house, before which political offenders from any part of the Peninsula might be haled and summarily punished; and he hoped that Modena would be selected as the site of this police station, and himself as its chief jailer. He presented to the Congress of Verona a memorial in which he set forth distinctly the causes of the existing troubles. Among these he cited the lack of religion, the diminution of the clergy, the annihilation of the nobility, the subdivision of fortunes through the abolition of the law of primogeniture, the mercenaries of the army, corruption of manners, evil education, the abolition of religious corporations and of secular guilds, "which distinguish the classes of men, hold them in a necessary and helpful discipline, and serve to keep them busy." He inveighed against the too great increase in the number of government employees; but above all against "the excessive consideration given, without distinction of merits, to any literary man; and the excessive multiplication of all kinds of professors and the excessive power and right accorded to them; and the excessive facility established everywhere

[1] Bianchi, ii, 90.

for the youth to study, which makes so many unhappy and discontented, because they cannot all find an occupation; and the excessive education given to every one, so that he learns nothing thoroughly and becomes conceited." As further causes of the epidemic of Liberalism, the Duke specified laziness, intercourse with strangers, the slow administration of justice, the capricious levying of taxes, and the laws which hindered free traffic in provisions. He scoffed at the idea of uniting the diverse elements of Italy into a single national bond, and maintained that the way to preserve tranquillity was to foster sectionalism by giving to each district a government in harmony with its traditions and genius.[1] No doubt, when the diplomats at Verona listened to this utterance of thoughts they all were thinking, they congratulated themselves in having in the Duke of Modena an ally who could act fearlessly and reason clearly.

The presence of Austrian regiments and the vigilance of the Austrian police had thwarted the plans of the conspirators in Lombardy and Venetia; for there, also, many men, and among them many eminent in rank or culture, were secretly nursing patriotic hopes. At the time of the Neapolitan revolution, the Liberals had expected day by day the cropping out of some favorable incident which should be the signal for a rising; but a few precautionary arrests — among them, those of Silvio Pellico, an amiable young man already known as a lyric poet and successful playwright, and of Maroncelli, Ladeschi, and Count Porro — warned the plotters that the government was on the alert. Nevertheless, they did not lose heart, and when the insurrection broke out in Piedmont they dispatched messengers to Turin to urge the Piedmontese to march into Lombardy, where the Lombards would receive them as liberators. But at the last moment, as we have seen, Count Confalonieri had

[1] Bianchi, ii, 357-64.

been obliged to send word that the Milanese were not ready, and that an insurrection would be futile. So the months passed without witnessing any commotion; Metternich's "quiet on the surface" was as unruffled as the bosom of an ice-bound lake. But while the conspirators were congratulating themselves at having escaped the penalty of an unsuccessful attempt, or were, like Confalonieri, burning with shame for those who had let "I dare not stand upon I would," the Austrian police were noiselessly picking up evidence and here and there arresting suspects. In the autumn of 1821 they established an Inquisitorial Commission at Milan under the direction of Salvotti, a Tyrolese as relentless as Draco, and as cunning as he was relentless. Still, no very damaging facts had been discovered, until a certain Gaetano Castiglia was arrested on the suspicion of having been the bearer of the dispatches to the Piedmontese. Castiglia would doubtless have been released, through lack of sufficient testimony against him, had not his friend, Marquis Pallavicini, hoping to save him, appeared before the Commission, and announced: "Castiglia is innocent. He knew nothing about the dispatches. I took them myself." This generous act proved fatal. Salvotti, who had been angling for minnows, suddenly found himself in the way to land larger fish. Pallavicini, impetuous and unskilled in dissembling, revealed more than he was aware, and then, perceiving that he had not only ruined himself, but also endangered his friends, he feigned madness. But this ruse did not deceive the handsome, flashing eyes of Salvotti. "Give him some hen-food," he said sarcastically, when Pallavicini, flapping his arms and insisting that he was a bird, was brought before the tribunal.

Consternation and suspense reigned at Milan. No one knew what secrets were being extorted by the silent, imperturbable Commission. It was observed that larger prison quarters were preparing, that domiciliary visits were more frequent, that the police had cast their dragnet and taken in victims at Brescia, Venice, and Mantua. Rumors, almost as distracting as the truth would have been, flew from lip to lip, and made anxiety contagious. When friend bade friend good-night, neither knew which of them might be hurried to prison before morning. Consciousness of innocence was no safeguard against dread; for the innocent and the guilty were alike exposed to arrest, examination, and torture.

At last the thunderbolt fell. Milan, bewildered, heard that Count Frederic Confalonieri had been seized in his palace, and was now in one of the cells of the Inquisitorial Commission. This distinguished man, whose tragic doom soon rang throughout Europe, belonged to an old and noble family. His natural gifts had been enhanced by an education far superior to that which the Italian aristocrat ordinarily received. In his younger days he had traveled in France and England, studying the conditions of those countries and forming acquaintance with men of worth. His rare culture was directed by a character of simple dignity and uprightness. At the downfall of Napoleon he had headed a delegation of Lombards who went to Paris to plead before the Allied Sovereigns for an independent government. Failing in this, he had devoted himself to the improvement of his countrymen by establishing schools for mutual instruction, by introducing better machinery into the factories, by encouraging the adoption of gas in the streets of Milan, and of steamboats on the Po. He had been associated with the public-spirited men who conducted the *Conciliatore* newspaper. While he never concealed his patriotic aspirations, he accepted the rule of Austria as a temporary evil which must be cured through the gradual advance of the Italians in education and integrity. He was, in a word, such a citizen, enlightened and public-spirited, as any but a despotic government would have honored.[1] His rank and superior qualities made him the representative of the nobility; his efforts in their behalf gained for him the affectionate confidence of the masses; and when the Liberals laid plots for a rebellion, he was the leader to whom they turned for advice. His name was a warrant of the moderation and plausibility of their efforts. How far he allowed himself to be drawn into the formal proceedings of the sects we cannot say, but he was known to have had communications with Tuscan Liberals, and with Charles Albert, and to have dissuaded the Piedmontese from their invasion when he saw that it would be hopeless. At the time of the rising in Piedmont he had been confined to his bed at the point of death. Months passed, and he felt secure. Even the warning of Bubna, the Austrian general, to Countess Confalonieri, "It would be wise for your husband to travel abroad for his health," did not alarm him; either because he believed he had left no traces for the police to track him by, or because he feared that flight would be taken as proof of his guilt, and would subject his property to confiscation and his family to ruin. Nevertheless, he took care to cut a secret door in the wall of his palace by which to escape in case of need; but on that winter morning when the carabineers came to arrest him, the key to the door could not be found, and he was forced to give himself up.

Almost at the same time a young Frenchman named Andryane, who came into Italy as a secret agent of the Sublime Masters of the French Carbonari, was put under arrest, and among his effects the police found papers most damaging to the Italian conspirators. Other arrests followed, and then ensued a long and harrowing trial. The prosecution, conducted by Salvotti, spared no means which cunning could suggest, to wring from the prisoners

---

[1] In the *Life and Letters of George Ticknor* are several interesting references to Confalonieri.

a confession not only of their own guilt, but of the names
of their accomplices. Sometimes the dazed wretch was
seduced into a revelation by hearing the forged deposition
of one of his fellows; sometimes, after being left in his
dungeon for months, he was examined anew, and then
confronted by his former testimony; sometimes he was
promised pardon if he would tell what his accusers wished,
or his mother or wife was brought to him in the hope
that womanly tears and entreaties and the strong incite-
ments of affection would overcome his silence. The
Austrian code did not permit the accused to question or
even to know his accusers; it also denied him legal advisers. "We are both your counsel and your judges,"
was Salvotti's curt reply to Arrivabene, who had asked
for an attorney.[1] But Austria had still more violent
means for breaking the spirit of those who were too wary
or too steadfast to be disconcerted by cross-examination.
She added physical torture to the horrors of imprisonment and to the persecution before the tribunal; as many
as forty stripes were laid every other day on the backs
of stubborn prisoners. "I call to mind by dozens those
unfortunate wretches to whom this torture was applied
for months, both men and women," says Confalonieri.
"One counts 500, another 1,000, another 2,000 lashes
received with the interval prescribed in order to increase
their painfulness."[2] Nevertheless, in spite of all this
cruelty, few, indeed, of the prisoners gave way; in all
but a few cases, whatever indiscreet admission was made
slipped out through unwariness rather than through an
ignoble purpose to escape punishment by treachery.

We need not follow in detail the tedious trial of Confa-

[1] Arrivabene: *Memorie* (Florence, 1880), i, 64.
[2] Confalonieri: *Memorie e Lettere* (Milan, 1889), i, 42, note, where he adds: "Alcuni vi hanno interamente perdute le natiche, le quali dilaniate ed imputridite dovettersi amputare; altri ne rimasero sciancati e non più uomini per la vita; ed i qui giunti sono quelli che pure non soccombettero sotto il bastone!"

lonieri and his fellow-victims. From the first, conviction was certain, and the pretended adherence to legal forms but a mockery. Salvotti's intent was to implicate other conspirators, but in this he failed. December came, and it was known that the evidence against the prisoners had been forwarded to Vienna for the Emperor to pass sentence upon them. The guarded hints of Austrian officials left no doubt that the sentence would be death. Then Countess Confalonieri, accompanied by her aged father-in-law and her brother, secured passports in spite of Salvotti's hindrance, and posted to Vienna. Day and night that coach with its agonized occupants did not rest: on it sped over the Alps, on through bleak Carinthia, on through the valleys of Styria, till at last it reached the Austrian capital. The Countess first visited the Empress, whose heart was touched and who promised to intercede for her; then she had an audience of the Emperor himself. But how could she touch the heart of that frigid, self-complacent, little man, who bluntly replied to her supplication, "Madam, your husband is the most dangerous fellow in Italy. Were our positions reversed, how would he have treated me?" Still, the decree had not yet been signed, there might still be hope of turning the Emperor's decision towards mercy. She saw Prince Metternich, who was polite, but told her that he had no power to help her; she saw the Duchess of Parma, who gave her sympathy. But the days flew by, and she had no relief from suspense. Then she was summoned before the Emperor again. "Madam," he said, "as a special mark of my good-will towards yourself, I inform you that a courier has already been dispatched with a sentence of death for your husband. If you wish to see your husband still alive, I advise you to quit Vienna immediately." At these cruel words, Countess Theresa fell in a swoon.[1] When she was restored to con-

---

[1] Poggi (i. 407) says that the Countess had no audience with the Em-

sciousness, after a brief, sobbing interview with the Empress, she and her stricken relatives took coach again and posted back. On the second day of their journey the father, too ill to proceed, had to be left behind; the sister and brother went on, desperately, sleeplessly, traversing those snow-blocked roads, asking at each station news of the courier who had started many hours before them. And so they repassed the Alps, and galloped over the milder plains of Lombardy, and reached Milan. The courier had not yet arrived. Fortunately, he had been delayed by the breaking of his carriage, and before the sentence he bore could be executed a second messenger came, bringing a respite which Francis had granted at the entreaties of the Empress. A respite, — but for how long? No one knew. But hope revived, and again Casati, Theresa's brother, set out on that journey to Vienna, — that *Via Crucis*, — taking with him a petition signed by the Viceroy and the Archbishop, by the clergy and nobility, beseeching the Emperor to be merciful.

Such being the suspense, the agony of their friends outside, who shall tell the condition of the prisoners themselves, who had not even physical liberty, nor power of action, nor compassionate voices to direct or to comfort them? Judges and jailers gave them not a hint of what they might expect. The death-watch was stationed over them, — at last they need suffer no more suspense. At one o'clock on the morning of January 21, 1824, they were removed from their cells to the chapel in the Palace of Justice, where condemned prisoners passed the last few hours before execution. There several of these men who were involved in a single calamity spoke to each other

peror, and cites the Countess's brother as witness. I have followed the account which she herself gave Andryane's sister, immediately after returning from Vienna. (See Andryane: *Memoirs of a Prisoner of State*.) All accounts agree that the Emperor said substantially what I have quoted; but whether he said it to Theresa or to her father-in-law is the point in dispute.

for the first time. Confalonieri, who had been for months at the point of death from heart-disease, had to be helped in by gendarmes and laid fainting on a cot-bed. When he had recovered sufficiently, he held out his hand to his fellow-victims. Pallavicini, whose rashness had brought them all to this strait, asked and received forgiveness. Presently officers came and led them to another room, where the Inquisitorial Commission was assembled. Next to the President sat Salvotti, whose black hair and flashing eyes made his always pale face seem paler in the lamplight. The Secretary read the sentences. Confalonieri, guilty of high treason, was condemned to death; but, the Secretary added, after a pause, "the capital punishment, by the inexhaustible clemency of his majesty, has been commuted to imprisonment for life in the fortress of Spielberg." To Andryane a similar doom was allotted; Pallavicini, Borsieri, and Castiglia were condemned to twenty years' solitary confinement, and Torrelli to ten years'. But their ordeal was not yet ended for that day. Smiths came and riveted chains on their legs, and then they were led bareheaded out in the wintry air to the pillory erected against the walls of the palace. Confalonieri was so weak that he had to be supported; and all the time he dreaded lest the multitudes assembled in the square, and the Hungarian troops who hemmed them in, should mistake his physical weakness for cowardice. The sentence and commutation were read from a balcony, and then the victims were taken back to their cells, to await their departure for Spielberg.

On his way thither Confalonieri had a memorable interview with Metternich at Vienna. The Chancellor came out of breath into the room assigned to the prisoner, and chaffed him for lodging so high up. Then, assuming a more serious tone, he discussed at great length the Italian revolutions and their failure. The struggle between opposing and irreconcilable principles had been decided, "and decided," he said, "not only for ours, but for many, many generations." He spoke with that air of candor which he could so well simulate. He became confidential. He hinted that, now that the crisis had passed, Confalonieri could do no better than confess that he had been led astray into treasonable acts through miscalculating the resources of Liberalism. Let them talk freely, as gentlemen who knew each other too well to wish to deceive each other. Any admission that Confalonieri might make could not possibly harm him; it might, on the contrary, help to melt the Emperor's sternness. As a hawk, which has soared high, turns earthward in contracting spires before swooping on his prey, so the astute Chancellor circled a long time round the real purpose of his inteview, which was to secure proofs of Charles Albert's complicity in the revolution. He was too wily to put the question point-blank. "We have examined more than a hundred and fifty persons and spent more than a million and a half, and with what results? We have only convicted yourself, and three unimportant conspirators. Of members without a head there are examples, but a head without members is an absurdity. When we come to you and to all those who are nearest to you, everything is dark, and but for the ingenuousness of an inexpert youth, who was certainly not in your secret, all would perhaps have remained dark forever." But Confalonieri protested that he had nothing more to disclose than he had already told at his trial. Then Metternich touched another chord: "Your conduct has been by your own evidence confused and irrational; yet we know that you are a man of high intelligence, — that you do not act without deliberation and clear motives. Surely you will not consent to remain before the world in this absurd posture, which detracts from your reputation of reasonableness!" Still Confalonieri resisted; even this appeal to his vanity could not move him. It was suggested that he might prefer to make his revelations to a more August Personage, but he replied that, as he could only repeat to the Emperor what he had said to the Chancellor himself, the interview would be unnecessary. Then Metternich, having exhausted his arts, looked at his watch, found that more than three hours had been spent in his fruitless visit, remembered that he had an engagement at a ball, "and took his leave with that amiable urbanity which he had shown throughout the whole conversation."[1]

Two days later Confalonieri set out for the fortress of Spielberg, which frowns over the city of Brünn, the capital of Moravia. Infamous Prison of Spielberg, your name shall still be loathsome among men long after the Austrian State shall have been dissolved forever! Nature may hide with wild-flowers your crumbled foundations; children may play among your ruins; yet shall the memory of the crimes against humanity committed within your walls come back to plague the conscience of Europe! In history you shall loom up as a monument to the tyranny of Metternich and his Hapsburg master, as the Bastille looms up in condemnation of the wickedness of the Bourbons.

It is not because many Italian prisoners suffered on the Spielberg, — they numbered but a few score altogether, — nor because Austria was not justified from her standpoint in punishing political agitators; it is because she employed means that were base, torments as inhuman as they were needless, that we condemn her. She sullied her hand in persecutions so foul that all the perfumes of Arabia could not sweeten it. She played with her victims as a cat with a mouse, biting, harrying, but not killing. If there must be, let there be capital punishment; have off the head by guillotine, or break the neck by hanging; and then say justice has been appeased with as little inhumanity as possible; but, after having

[1] Confalonieri, i, 155-77.

shackled your enemy to the wall of a filthy, cramped dungeon, to starve him by inches, to corrupt his soul by lying confessors and spies, to reduce his mind to idiocy, — this is not justice, but the malicious cruelty of the coward and the brute. And of all this, Emperor Francis, your pettifogging soul was guilty; this was your "inexhaustible clemency," this was your sanctimonious regard for the spiritual welfare of even your erring subjects!

For, in truth, the Emperor took the treatment of the political prisoners under his especial charge. In his writing-desk he kept a plan of their cells, and received minute reports of their condition. Not so much as a coarse coverlid could be given to one of them unless the permission were granted by him. He canceled their names, and referred to them only by numbers; so that the superintendent of the Spielberg received from his imperial master such messages as these: "Diminish Number Ten's ration of beans," or "Allow Number Seven coffee once a month." He denied them books, even their prayer-books. "You have sinned by your intellect; by your intellect you shall suffer," was his decree. But when he found that several of them were being driven to insanity through this enforced idleness, he commanded that rags from the hospital be furnished them to pick. Later, as a sign of his favor, they were given yarn and needles, and bidden to knit stockings or mittens, which were sent to him. In looking them over, if a heel were not well rounded or a thumb well joined, he took it as proof that the knitter was still refractory, and had him threatened with severer punishment. This man was not a poor loutish turnkey, but his Apostolic Majesty, Francis the First, by the grace of God, Emperor of Austria, King of Hungary and Bohemia, the monarch upon whose wisdom the fate of thirty millions subjects depended, the arbiter of Europe! Poor Europe!

To rehearse the story of the misery undergone by the

prisoners of the Spielberg, it is not here required. That story, written in their blood, has been told by several of the survivors. In the pages of Pellico, Maroncelli, Andryane, and Confalonieri, whoever so wills can read how some of the noblest men of Italy were subjected by the Austrian emperor to torments which he deemed too cruel for common murderers; how their bodies, fed only on nauseating slops, wasted; how their reason tottered, worn out by sleeplessness and lack of mental food; how the priest Paulovich was sent to entice revelations from them at the confessional; how they learned to communicate with each other by tapping on the walls of their cells; how they strained their ingenuity to devise means for writing; how decoy prisoners were stationed with them to draw their confidence in unguarded moments; how Confalonieri was twice on the point of escaping, and twice frustrated; how Maroncelli, after months of suffering, had his leg amputated; how a man like Pellico, whose literary work was already the delight of thousands, was reduced to watch spiders spinning their web; how in spite of outrages worse than death, in spite of the terrible temptations to purchase liberty by betrayal, their honor and fortitude stood firm to the end. These things man recorded, and Nemesis did not forget. Little could those passive sufferers foresee that their very captivity would contribute to the liberation of their country. Little did the sleek Metternich imagine that for every day's agony of each prisoner in the Spielberg, he was raising up in Italy a score of irreconcilable patriots, whom all the blandishments of Austria could not seduce, nor all her menaces terrify.

But as yet the day of reckoning was still distant, and only believed in by those who do not lose faith in Nemesis when its reprisal is not immediate. Metternich and the European sovereigns had met in Congress at Verona late in 1822, and after congratulating themselves on the ease with which the "genius of evil" had been suppressed in Naples and Piedmont, they gave their tacit approval to Austria's interference in Italy. One of the important matters they had to settle was the succession to the throne of Piedmont. Charles Albert, the heir presumptive, had, through his implication in the late revolt, roused the violent hatred of the actual king, Charles Felix, and revived Metternich's hope of transferring the crown to the Duchess of Modena. The unfortunate prince, condemned by the Absolutists as a Liberal and despised by the Liberals as a renegade, dwelt in disgrace at Florence, trying to show, by his submissive conduct and quiet life, — broken only by occasional gallant escapades, — how deeply he repented him of having given any cause for misunderstanding. But Charles Felix was one of those who mistake their prejudices for manifestations of the moral law, and it was hard to convince him that his resentment was out of all proportion to the young man's faults. "I do my utmost," he wrote, "to keep him safe, until such time as it may please the Divine Goodness to operate in him a miracle, which will certainly be very great and very difficult to prove: for even if he should undergo the penance of an anchorite and even draw blood, it would not be certain that his conversion were sincere." Although only good reports came of the penitent, still the King was unmoved. "I think," said he, "that the Prince of Carignano's big moustaches indicate the Carbonaro rather than the Convert. God alone sees the heart. He may have wrought the miracle of his conversion, but He has not yet wrought in me that of being convinced of it."[1] There was, nevertheless, one thing more repugnant than Charles Albert's Liberalism to Charles Felix; and that was the prospect of Piedmont's passing out of the control of the House of Savoy. At the most, he would have provided for a regency to govern at his death until Charles Al-

[1] Bianchi, ii, 113.

bert's infant son, Victor Emanuel, should grow up. But the views of the Grand Duke of Tuscany, of the French king, and the Czar, at length prevailed with him; he agreed that the young prince should be forgiven and acknowledged as heir to the throne. Metternich, when he saw that he could not carry through his scheme in behalf of the Duchess of Modena, did not press it, but he exacted that Charles Albert should secretly pledge himself in no wise to alter the form of government in Piedmont if he ever became king. Alone among the ambassadors at the Congress, Wellington deemed it unfair thus to foreclose the future of a possible sovereign.[1]

Shortly afterwards the French Bourbons, to win a little of that military glory which keeps Frenchmen talkative and manageable, organized an expedition to Spain, to restore to the Spanish king that autocratic power of which he had been deprived by the Constitutionalists. Austria had stifled Liberalism in Italy; France could do no less in Spain. Charles Albert had permission granted him to join the French staff, and by a campaign against rebellious Spaniards to expiate his own unlucky connections with a rebellion. He distinguished himself at the storming of the Trocadero, — the only serious skirmish of the war, — which effected the release of King Ferdinand, who, while shut up in Cadiz by the Constitutionalists, had spent his time in flying kites, and who now made a triumphal progress back to his capital, accompanied by thirty-eight cooks and the French heroes. The glory achieved was tawdry enough, — the rescue of Ferdinand, with his kites and his cooks, seems but an Aristophanic joke; but the French Bourbons took care to advertise themselves as mighty men of war, and they hoped that the capture of the Trocadero would dim the troublesome splendor of Marengo and Austerlitz. Let Bonapartists cease to boast of their Napoleon, — the

[1] Wellington to Canning, Nov. 29, 1822.

Bourbon Duke of Angoulême was a very God of War. The chief interest of this campaign lies for us in the fact that it served to rehabilitate Charles Albert in the eyes of the European oligarchy. Although some of them still distrusted him, they could no longer give a decent excuse for excluding him from the Piedmontese throne; that he was not excluded had, as we shall see, a tremendous influence upon the destiny of Italy.

Such was the vengeance taken by the despots on the unsuccessful Italian revolutionists of 1820–21. The issue was now plain: the Liberals had not only their respective princes against them, but also all the might of Austria, behind whom loomed the other partners to the Holy Alliance. The odds were as desperate as the collapse had been complete, and they might well teach caution if they did not justify despondence. But this very baptism of suffering was to prove regenerative. Only after men have learned to prize their ideal more highly than their comfort, or than life itself, are they equipped to win their ideal. In those days of sorrow, the Italians began to realize that the precious liberty and independence for which they yearned must be paid for in sacrifices and heroism equivalent to the full value of those blessings.

CHAPTER VIII.

UNDERCURRENTS, 1820-30.

WE have thus witnessed the first conflict between the New Spirit and the Old Spirit: the former proclaiming, *Italy shall be;* the latter replying, *Italy shall never be.* The two ideas, having seethed a long time in many heads, have got into the hands, have met, have clashed, and the Old Idea has conquered. The thought first, then the act, — that is the invariable sequence; and as acts are outward, they express themselves by material forces. Cherish what aspirations you will, they remain aspirations, — mere pretty dreams and sterile fancies, — unless you realize them by mastering the physical forces which would prevent them. Is it a statue your imagination has conceived? You must make your hand harder than the marble. Is it a bridge or building? It will lie *perdu* in your brain until you have overcome the hostility of gravitation. Is it a law? It will be a dead-letter in the statute book unless you have convinced a majority of your countrymen that they ought to abide by it. Or have you beheld, as in a vision, a great reform in government or church? You must vanquish the dulness, the conservatism, the greed, the timidity of society, or these will destroy you. This is the elemental tragedy of life, — the Ideal striving to utter itself, to realize itself, in the material world, where Force seems often hopelessly against it. And Force unguided by the higher Reason, — how brutal, how pitiless it is! In mankind, as in nature, we see its tempests and volcanic outbursts, its seasons of long drought, its blight and mildew, — as then in Italy. But from Force there is no appeal, except to greater Force, for the gods will not allow that an ounce outweigh a pound, either in the physical or the moral world: they demand deeds, not intentions.

The Italians, massing what power they could, had been overmatched. Had it been only a duel between them and the King of Naples, or the King of Piedmont, they would have had an easy victory; but it was more than that, — it was a duel between them and Austria, and Austria had twenty units of force, better drilled, better armed, and better captained, to every one of theirs. And behind Austria was the organized Old Régime throughout Europe.

Evidently, in order that Italy's independence should be attained, two things must come to pass: first, a majority of the Italians themselves must will it, and be strong enough to use it; second, Europe must consent to it. The former requisite, which must precede, could be brought about only by patriotic education; the latter depended upon a happy combination of the ever-turning cogs of diplomacy. Thus far we have watched the men of action, who hoped through conspiracy and a sudden show of force to free Italy. But their strength was inadequate, and they failed as much in persuading many of their soberer countrymen to join them as in ousting their despotic monarchs. Now we have to examine the work of the thinkers, whose influence, though indirect and less easily gauged, was far-reaching and indispensable.

If we analyze the thought of the eighteenth century, we shall find that it had two distinct phases, — the one skeptical and destructive, the other affirmative and constructive. Locke and Hume had hurried on philosophy to its last negation. Voltaire and the Encyclopædists had peered with sarcastic eyes into the institutions, beliefs, and customs of society, and had shown them to be abusive or absurd. Those philosophic critics spared nothing, —

revealed religion, the pomp and ignorance of the Church, the absolutism of kings, the insolence and injustice of the privileged classes, — all were stripped of their gala costume. Feudalism stood there naked and ridiculous. Satires are successful only when the evil they attack has begun to wane: chivalry had become an affectation before Cervantes wrote "Don Quixote;" the search for the Philosopher's Stone was abandoned by all but quacks when Ben Jonson wrote "The Alchemist;" and so Feudalism must have been far gone in decay, ere even Voltairean sarcasm could have affected it. The very centre of that tottering system, Louis XV saw that it was doomed, but he consoled himself with the reflection that it would at least endure for his lifetime. But decay presupposed a new growth; and just as philosophy and satire seemed to have destroyed everything wherein mankind trusted, — leaving the world barren of faith in God and reverence for man, a waste where the nettles of persiflage flourished, but neither flowers budded nor fruits ripened, — there sprang up a new growth of regenerating ideas. In philosophy this new spirit embodied itself in the works of Kant. Briefly stated, his message was this: Each individual soul emanates from the Universal Soul; whatever hampers its free intercourse with and expansion into the Universal Soul, weakens it and leads it astray. Crystallize this doctrine to its ultimate meaning and you have the single word *Liberty;* liberty of conscience for the worshiper, liberty of person for the citizen, liberty of utterance for the thinker. But these were heresies against that Feudal System in which churches interposed their creeds between the worshiper and God, in which kings might do their will with their subjects, and in which inquisitors and censors decided what might be uttered.

Kant wrote the philosophy of this new era, but long before his thoughts were generally understood, the Spirit of Liberty had announced itself through the deeds of

men; and first of all in government, which, touching
society in its daily practical life, seemed most to require
readjustment. Rousseau felt the presence of the new
spirit and bore witness to it in words full of emotion; the
American colonists obeyed it, and from their obedience
was born a mighty republic; then the French, made delirious by the vision of freedom, would have cut themselves off forever from the tyrannical Past by one stroke
of revolution. The modern political doctrines of civil
equality and a representative franchise were thundered
over Europe from the cannon's mouth; once proclaimed,
they could not be silenced.

Less noisy, but not less momentous, was the change
which slowly permeated Religion. The ancient arks of
faith, launched when the sea was placid, were now waterlogged and barnacled to the point of foundering; but if
any one suggested that to save the ships they must jettison the cargo of dogmas and traditions, each stubborn
commander replied, "Throw over every passenger that
talks of Reason." So the wise took to the life-boats,
leaving that fleet of orthodoxy where we still see it, the
pennons of worn-out creeds dangling at the masthead,
the sails torn, the water rising in spite of the men at the
pumps; sodden, battered hulks, they are driven by winds
and tides, in mutual danger of collision. A strange spectacle to all: bewildering and terrible to any who believe
that when those leaky vessels sink, as sink they must,
they will carry to the bottom with them that without which
there can be neither religion nor virtue, neither hope nor
love among men! As if spiritual truth could be kept
afloat only by the doctrinal life-preservers of Calvin's or
Aquinas's patent!

In Italy the new Spirit of Liberty manifested itself, as
we have seen, in the frustrated revolutions; it also vainly
strove to penetrate the thick crust of theology,— the
Church insisting that reason meant treason; but it found

literature more plastic, and through literature it began to unfold itself. The writers who were the mouthpiece of this new influence were but half conscious of their mission; they would have said that they simply followed nature and common sense, and they would have pointed to the recent examples which Germany, England, and France had furnished, as evidence that they were in first-rate company.

The struggle between Romanticism and Classicism which was the result of the clashing of the Old and the New Spirit belongs, in so far as it was a literary quarrel, to the history of literature; but in Italy it was so bound up with the general cause of Liberalism that it needs to be mentioned here. The Italian mind had to be liberated from the tyranny of ancient and mechanical literary dogmas, not less than the Italian body had to be freed from political fetters. The conventionality of centuries had reduced Italian literature till it had become soulless, but pompous, like the popular religion. Even the most conspicuous of its recent contributors, Alfieri, had cast his tragedies in the old classic matrix, which was like the bed of Procrustes; he read Shakespeare often with admiration, he tells us, but not without "distinguishing most clearly all of Shakespeare's defects," which he took care to avoid by obeying Aristotle's formula about the Unities.

It was in the drama that the intellectual war of independence was first waged. Niccolini and Pellico in their early plays broke away, although with some hesitation, from rigid Classicism; then Manzoni brought the strength of his genius to the cause of Romanticism. The older generation of writers, led by the facile Monti, fought bitterly. They abused, they ridiculed the innovators; they indicted them as heretics, for the three Unities laid down by Aristotle were as sacred as the sacraments invented by the Church. To put in a plea for nature, to cite the unexampled richness of the Elizabethan drama, to appeal to the recent achievements of Schiller and Goethe, only exasperated the upholders of the antique school. Nevertheless the Romanticists gradually prevailed.

But while they were emancipated in the form, they were still hampered in the substance of their dramas. In Italy, as in France, the theatre was not merely a place in which to while away a tedious evening; the stage was a platform on which the public issues of the hour might be artfully presented; it was a substitute for the hustings, and for an ungagged press, in free countries. Therefore it was strictly watched by the censors and the police. The playwright, if he had a patriotic idea, must disguise it so that it might escape the eyes and scissors of the expurgators. And if the author sometimes outwitted his critic and excited an audience by some forbidden sentiment, more frequently the censors construed his harmless lines as treason, and suppressed them. In spite of these checks, a dramatic literature sprang up, and, what is more, it was saturated with Liberalism. Niccolini, Pellico, Manzoni, and others, while keeping within the letter of the law, infused their patriotic spirit — they could not help infusing it — through all their plays. They chose episodes in the past history of Italy, and so treated them as to make them serve as indirect commentaries on the existing political situation, and especially as strengtheners of the budding national spirit. Romanticism everywhere sought the unusual and the picturesque, by which it might express that new passion which rebelled against the commonplace and prosaic by which life was actually hemmed in. It studied history with a zest hitherto unknown, and among all the historic periods the mediæval was its favorite, because that offered the striking contrasts, the glow of legend, the large play of passion, and the richness of costume, wherewith the imagination could work unrestrained. Hence the seeming paradox that a literary movement which marked the dissolution of Feudalism should have devoted itself to the glorification of the feudal world. The European oligarchs smiled on the Romanticists so long as these, by poem or romance or history, invested with fascination the rugged fighters and robber barons from whom the royalties and aristocracies of Europe were descended. Absolutism had nothing to fear from antiquarian squabbles over the origin of the Italian language and the propriety of using any word which had not the sanction of a fifteenth century writer. Lamartine called Italy "the Land of the Dead," and if the purists could have had their way, they would have made the Italian a dead language. But Romanticism wrought its own cure; a deeper study of mediaeval society, by dissipating the halo of romance, laid bare the very unpoetic methods by which kings had come to assert their divine right, the Church had grasped its worldly possession, and the privileged classes had heaped up their wealth.

The first conscious purpose of the Italian Romanticists, however, was to recall to their countrymen great scenes and striking personages from the past of Italy, with the inevitable result of stimulating the spirit of nationality. Indirectly, their dramas served, as I have said, as political allegories. Niccolini (1782–1861) began his career with the Classicists, and after their fashion he remodeled the stories of "Medea," of "Agamemnon," of the "Seven at Thebes," and of "Polyxena;" but, while he held aloof from the literary quarrel which soon raged, he became in practice a Romanticist, as in politics he was a Republican. In his later and stronger tragedies, "Antonio Foscarini," "John of Procida," and "Arnold of Brescia," he was thoroughly Italian, using the themes which his historical study supplied him as texts by which to illustrate the iniquity of church and tyrants, and the surpassing beauty of patriotism and liberty; he preached so elo-

quently that even in Tuscany the censors frowned upon
his plays. Silvio Pellico (1789–1854), in genius less
robust, became through misfortune more famous than
Niccolini, and he had already won reputation by his romantic
play, "Francesca da Rimini," before he was seized
by the Austrians and immured in the prison of Spielberg.
But greater than these, and greater than any other contemporary
Italian author, was Alexander Manzoni (1785–
1873), one of the few masters in the world-literature of
the nineteenth century.

At first sight Manzoni's literary product seems singularly
small; the best — a few lyrics, two dramas, and a
romance — is contained in two small volumes. Compare
that with the quantity produced by Scott, Dickens,
Thackeray, and George Eliot; and by Balzac, Sand, and
Hugo; or with the complete editions of the works of the
foremost poets who were his contemporaries, and you perceive
that Manzoni, of all the men of genius in our voluble
and diffuse century was the most reticent. In his
restraint, compactness, and sense of proportion, he resembled
the Greeks, but in spirit he was a modern, and in
his method a Romanticist. He was perhaps the only
man of first-rate ability in his time who believed devoutly
the dogmas of the Catholic Church, yet his belief did not
prevent him from approving the abolition of the temporal
Papacy. He was never a conspirator, never any other
than the modest, retiring, but steadfast poet; and yet few
of the men of action contributed so largely as he to the
liberation of Italy. What was the secret of his power
amid these apparent contradictions? It was his character:
he represented that intelligence and integrity,
that earnestness not to be misled by fitful passions, that
patriotic self-control and self-abnegation, without which
liberty, whether of the individual or of the State, is a
dangerous gift. Though he submitted to Austrian rule
in his native Lombardy, and though Austrian spies could

never find cause for prosecuting him, he never suppressed an opinion through fear or self-interest, and there was none whose Italianism was more widely known. A little while ago Monti, the turncoat and sycophant, stood at the head of Italian letters: from him to Manzoni, what a contrast, what an advance! The sons of fathers who had excused Monti's baseness for the sake of his brilliance, had a master whose life was not less venerable than his works were noble.

Manzoni expressed his piety in a series of "Sacred Hymns" which are probably as excellent as any modern paraphrase can be of the simple and beautiful narrative in the Evangelists of Christ's birth, passion, and resurrection. He then gave wider scope to his imagination in two tragedies, "Adelchi," and "Il Carmagnola," in which he flung down a challenge to the Classicists, and hid many a patriotic appeal. The choruses in those dramas, and above all the splendid "Ode on the Death of Napoleon," showed the high lyric quality, the fervor, and clearness, of Manzoni's poetic genius; but it was by his romance, "The Betrothed," that he won instant popularity, captivating alike the humblest reader and the most fastidious critic. Here at last was a genuine book, woven of the simplest elemental passions. Mark with what naturalness the love-story of a peasant youth and girl comes to concern far other than peasants, till at last Cardinal Borromeo himself is touched by it, so that the whole social fabric is unfolded, with its interrelation of class with class, and its varied but perpetually interesting human colors. Mark the humor which, like gold thread shot through damask, plays over it from end to end. Mark the exquisite precision, the unerring lifelikeness, pervaded everywhere by a rich, poetic atmosphere, like the shores of Lake Como itself. This is the true realism, because it is the ideal. Only in those passages where, as Goethe said, Manzoni "throws off the poet's mantle and stands as a naked historian," does our interest slacken; and yet, make what deductions we will for this defect, "The Betrothed" remains the most beautiful of romances.

Not as a literary masterpiece, however, does this work of Manzoni's concern us, so much as a landmark in the progress of Italian regeneration. It gave the Italians an object worthy of their admiration; it settled forever that pedantic question as to what words a writer might use; deeper still, it was an indictment of foreign tyranny, and of the oppression of the people by the nobles. The tyrants in the story were Spaniards, but every Italian as he read substituted the word *Austrian* for *Spaniard*, and the book became a Bible of patriotism. Its influence, like the personal influence of Manzoni himself, was thus very wide and permanent, but so quiet and reasonable and pervasive that we have no means of measuring it accurately. All that we can say is that from about the year 1825 Manzoni stood among his countrymen as the embodiment of a pure and dignified patriotism, which based its hopes on no mere outward political upheaval, but on moral regeneration.

Fame, and the love of multitudes and their trust, — which are better than fame, — came to Manzoni early in his career, and increased throughout his long life: painfully different was the fate of James Leopardi (1798–1837), the only other Italian poet of this century whose genius, transcending the limits of his time and country, has an international significance and bids fair to command the attention of generations yet unborn. The story of his life, aside from the quality of his work, would suffice to make him one of the most interesting figures in modern literary history. His very existence was a tragedy so cruel and so inexplicable that we can only wonder and pity and be silent: for in him a genius of all but the highest capacity was united to a feeble frame, a sickly spine, and tattered nerves, as if Destiny, in a sardonic mood, sought entertainment in witnessing the unequal combat between this soul and body. Nor was this all: Leopardi's lot fell to be born in the torpid, cheerless Adriatic town of Recanati, among a bigoted and uncongenial people. And yet, though thus stinted in health and sympathy, and though harassed by poverty, he raised himself by the might of his intellect to one of the loftiest reputations of his epoch. At an age when other boys had not left their marbles and kites he was mastering Hebrew, Greek, and Latin; at fourteen he was proficient, probably none more so in Italy, in patristic lore; at eighteen he had written two *canzoni* which had had no peers since Petrarch wrote; and then, through twenty years of physical anguish, sometimes nearly blind for months, or plunged in nervous torments, he produced works, whether in poetry or in prose, which have long been esteemed classics by his countrymen, and which, so profoundly do they express one of the dominant characteristics of human nature, have merited the attention of thinkers everywhere.

For Leopardi represents that spectre of pessimism which continually dogs the footsteps of humanity, and at one time or another whispers its terrific questions to every earnest soul. He cannot, like the Stoic, satisfy himself by saying, "Though Fate be grim, I can bear it:" for to what end would you resist for a little hour the omnipotent monster? He cannot, like the Mystic, trust that, in spite of the evils of life on earth, there will be heaven hereafter: for he would ask how an alleged beneficent Creator could look unmoved upon such sufferings as mortals endure between the dawn and twilight of a single day. Leopardi is honest with himself: he will not call evil good; he does not, — as so many do when they feel the supports of dogma slipping away. — he does not try to convince himself that they are still firm; he takes no moral opiates, but dares to know the worst, let the pain be what it may. Religion, love, hope, progress, patriotism, seem to him but delusions, — iridescent films hung over the mouth of the abyss, — to prevent mankind from realizing too early the vanity and nothingness from which they and all things spring and to which all return. And yet Leopardi's despair is not selfish, like that of the cynic; he may indulge in sarcasm when he contrasts the arrogance of some men with the insignificance of their power as compared to the universe which grinds them, but he feels even more deeply the pity, the pathos of it all, that creatures so frail should be teased by desires so noble. "Ennui," he says, "is in some fashion the most sublime of human sentiments. Not that I believe that from the examination of this sentiment those consequences are begotten which many philosophers thought were deducible from it; but, nevertheless, the impossibility of being satisfied by anything on earth, or, so to speak, by the earth entire: to consider the measureless amplitude of space, the number and wonderful magnitude of worlds, and to find that all is little and petty compared with the capacity of the mind itself; to imagine the number of worlds as infinite and the infinite universe, and to feel that our mind and our desire would be still larger than such a universe; and forever to accuse things of insufficiency and nullity, and to suffer a loss and void, and therefore ennui, seems to me the chief sign of grandeur and nobility that can be seen in human nature. For ennui is little known to men of no worth, and very little or not at all to the other animals."[1]

It is because Leopardi uttered with force and beauty and with unfaltering courage the last secrets of despair, that he has come to be regarded as one of the significantly typical poets of the century. Psychologists may perhaps be able to determine how far his pessimism was

[1] *Pensieri*, lxviii.

due to his diseased body; he himself believed that his physical infirmities had not warped his mind. . "Before dying," he wrote to a friend, "I am going to protest against this invention of feebleness and vulgarity, and to beg my readers to set about destroying my observations and reasoning, rather than to accuse my maladies."[1] The enigma of so inadequate a constitution as Leopardi's should make even the most buoyant optimists sober. His poetry, like impassioned mournful music, does not lift us by inspiring hope, but soothes us by giving utterance to the regrets and sorrows which, if unuttered, would stifle the heart. And as there will always be death and partings, and the wistful looking back to vanished youth, Leopardi's lyrics might still be read long after the golden age of Utopia had transformed the earth, and optimism were the only philosophy.

Leopardi's direct influence on the Italian cause was wrought by the patriotic odes written in his youth, when he felt bitterly the degradation of his country, and before he had formulated his philosophy of despair. His work was never popular in his lifetime, but it moved a small circle of the elect by whom it was transmitted to the many. The Italians, who were gradually being vitalized by a great idea, were thereby rising above pessimism, and they drew from Leopardi an incentive for improving rather than for accepting their wretched lot. It is characteristic of the conflicting aspects of our epoch, that Manzoni and Leopardi should represent Italy in the modern world-literature. Like two ships borne in opposite directions by the same trade-wind, one had a smooth voyage, and cast anchor in a pleasant haven; the other, buffeted and distressed, sailed along dangerous shores, and disappeared amid Antarctic ice and fog.

These are the chief names in that post-Napoleonic literature in which Romanticism was expressing itself and

---

[1] Letter to De Sinner, May 24, 1832.

the new ideas of liberty in Italy. Of many other men, some of whom enjoyed a wide contemporary reputation, and all of whom were swayed by a similar purpose, it is not necessary to give a detailed account. The short-lived *Conciliatore* newspaper at Milan, the more fortunate *Antologia* at Florence, the stirring verse of Berchet, the revived study of Dante,[1] and of the history of Italy during the Middle Age and the Renaissance, — all these were symptoms of the intellectual awakening, and evidence that there was gathering a body of temperate patriotic men who by example and precept should prepare their country to deserve freedom. They held aloof from plots; they seemed lukewarm to the men of action; but they insisted upon character and intelligence as prerequisites without which national unity could not be permanent nor independence beneficial; and their influence, though gradual and indirect, went far and sank deep.

These being some of the forces active at home, what was the attitude abroad? How was foreign public opinion disposed towards the resurrection of Italy? We have seen how, since the Congress of Vienna, foreign nations treated the desires of Italians; but we must distinguish between the diplomatic interference and official injustice of governments, and the attitude of individual foreigners. The oligarchic cabal which, under Metternich, had striven to bind tyranny upon Europe, could not wholly stifle the expression of Liberal thoughts. Byron's elemental vigor, for instance, had swept his poems over the world, and they carried with them a passionate plea for down-trodden Greece and Italy. At a time when Europe had sunk back into feudal reaction, he boldly protested that neither Holy Alliances nor Metternichs nor Castlereaghs could postpone forever the day of reckoning between the gov-

---

[1] In the fifteenth century 15 editions of the *Divine Comedy* were issued; in the sixteenth, 42; in the seventeenth, 4; in the eighteenth, 40; in the first half of the nineteenth more than 150 editions. See preface to Dr. Carlyle's translation of the *Inferno*.

ernors and the governed, and that no treaty nor diplomatist had the right to perpetuate the slavery of a people. Many Englishmen shared Byron's enthusiasm, though with reservations. They blushed in private to think that England, which had been for generations the abode of liberty, was now officially leagued with Continental despots in oppressing races which asked for self-government; they blushed at the recollection of the perfidy by which English agents had, in 1814, deceived the Italians; but while they sympathized in the abstract, they were not prepared to give material aid. They were tired of wars abroad, for which they were now paying the cost in increased taxation; they were involved at home in a great political struggle, the beginning of the end of aristocratic domination; they were just entering on that vast commercial expansion which threatened to choke spirituality through a surfeit of gold. At best, therefore, the Italians could as yet hope for no more than passive sympathy from the more kindly-disposed English. The average Briton — the typical John Bull, with his mixture of cant and Philistinism, of worldly wisdom and shopkeeper's integrity — was too insular to understand, and consequently to pity, a race so different from his own. He was reticent and gruff, they were emotional; he gloried in his strength and wealth, they were weak and poor; he was practical, they, he supposed, were visionary. He had come to look upon them as good pastry-cooks and dancing masters, a degenerate race which had ages ago written poetry that his daughters read, and had painted pictures which he was dragged to see when he made the grand tour. In Italy, he admitted, the beggars eating their macaroni were picturesque but dirty; in London, the Italian opera-singers sang divinely, but they were immoral and expensive. What business had a people whose mission it was to go round the world with a barrel-organ and a monkey to talk about self-government? If they wanted

their freedom, why did they not fight for it, nay, why
had they ever lost it, unless they were unworthy of being
free? John Bull has always been quick to discern the
retributive hand of God in the afflictions of his neighbors,
felt it his duty to say, like Bildad the Shuhite, "If thou
wert pure and upright, surely now He would awake for
thee, and make the habitation of thy righteousness prosperous." Therefore, if Italy was wretched as a punishment for her past sins, might it not be meddling with the
decrees of Providence to interfere in her behalf? Moreover, John Bull, impregnable in his "sea-girt isle," took
not into account the geographical conditions which exposed other countries to foreign conquest. His hereditary
hatred of papists had become an instinct; but these Italians, were they not papist idolaters? He despised civil
broils and dreaded violence, or whatever smacked of Jacobinism, for Jacobinism had begotten a Napoleon; who
could be sure that the Italian agitators, for all their glib
talk of liberty, were not another brood of Jacobins? Still,
he had an instinctive love of fair play, and if he could be
brought to understand that Italy was really bent on making a fight against great odds, he might possibly see to it
that her antagonist should take no mean advantage, —
always provided British commercial interests were not
involved in the dispute.

With British public opinion at this stage, there came
a change in political leadership which affected the relations of Great Britain with the Allied Powers. Castlereagh killed himself in a fit of melancholy, and Canning
succeeded him as Foreign Minister. Canning belonged
to that noble order of English statesmen who, because
they have had faith in liberty, have made the Anglo-Saxon
race the pioneer of liberty throughout the modern world.
He cut adrift from Castlereagh's servile obedience to Metternich; he encouraged the Greeks in their struggle with
the Turks; by recognizing the South American republics

which had freed themselves through the heroism of Bolivar and other patriots, he frustrated the purpose of the Continental despots to restore the Spanish tyranny in South America. Although he could not hinder the expedition of the French Bourbons into Spain, he gave warning that England disapproved the Metternichian policy of interfering in the domestic affairs of small States, and he hinted in a memorable speech, that if such encroachments were pushed, England would ally herself with the revolutionary elements on the Continent, and see justice done.[1] Probably, had a crisis arisen, even Canning would have been unable to urge the British nation to engage in a general war for the sake of peoples that were not large buyers of British manufactures; nevertheless, his achievement in withdrawing England from the influence of the Holy Alliance, and in checking Metternich, must not be too lightly rated. He died prematurely, but not before he had given back to his country her honorable reputation as friend of the oppressed, and had banished from the Foreign Office the precedent by which a British minister acted as the menial of a Continental chancellor.

In France the eddies and counter-currents of politics were more perplexing. It seemed as if Louis XVIII and Charles X were prospering in their restoration of Bourbonism. Their policy had these two ends: to stamp out Liberalism at home, and to recover that ascendency abroad which France had lost at Waterloo. The French ministers respected the Holy Alliance so far as it helped the first aim; but where it tended to keep France in a subordinate position, they wished to evade it, and secretly reached out for new diplomatic combinations. Frenchmen, ever thirsty for glory, must be slaked by such insipid draughts as the Spanish campaign and the Algerian expedition. In Italy they intrigued to undermine Aus-

---

[1] Speech delivered Dec. 12, 1826. See Stapleton: *Political Life of George Canning* (London, 1831), iii, 223.

tria's predominance, and to hasten the time when France might openly contest with Austria the enjoyment of Italian spoils. The general course of France during these years was therefore away from the Holy Alliance and towards England, so that there slowly grew up a new division of the Great Powers, — a division not sanctioned by treaty but tacitly recognized, in which the "Western Powers" (France and England) represented the progressive tendency, and the "Northern Powers" (Austria, Prussia, and Russia) represented the stationary or retrograde tendency of the century. But officially, between 1815 and 1830, France seemed the enemy of every Liberal hope.

It was in unofficial France, among the professed Republicans and the discontented Imperialists, that the deeper purposes of the nation were germinating. There, conspiracies and revolutionary preparations gave the lie to the superficial firmness of Bourbonism, which was but as a thin crust hardened over a stream of molten lava. The French Liberals sympathized with the Italians as comrades in misfortune, and French writers echoed that romantic sentiment towards afflicted Italy that Byron had uttered with a force unknown to French poetry. Nor did official France lack the means of learning the truth about those Italian agitations that were stigmatized by Metternich and the clique of despots as the efforts of anarchists to destroy civilization. Chateaubriand, then ambassador at Rome, gave the following clear statement concerning Italy, in 1829, to a member of the French Cabinet: "Read with caution what may be sent to you from Naples, and elsewhere. They deem conspiracy the universal discontent, the fruit of the times, the clash of the old with the new society, of decrepit institutions against the young generations, the confronting of that which is with that which might be. The great spectacle of France, — powerful, peaceful, happy, — striking the eyes of nations which have remained, or fallen back, under the yoke, excites laments and nourishes hopes. Representative governments and absolute governments cannot endure together: perforce one or the other must perish, and the political system become everywhere uniform. Can custom-house lines any longer separate liberty from servitude? Or a man be executed on this side of a brook for principles which are reputed sacred on the other? This, and this alone, is conspiracy in Italy, that in this sense may be called French. But from the day when she shall enter upon the enjoyment of rights pointed out to her by her intelligence and brought by the times, she will be tranquil and purely Italian. It is not obscure Carbonari, goaded on by the manœuvres of the police and hanged without mercy, that will overturn this country. Governments are given very false ideas about the true state of the world; they are hindered from doing what they should for their own safety, by being induced to regard the effect of a permanent and general cause as the conspiracy of a few Jacobins. These conditions obtain throughout Italy; but each State, besides the common troubles, is tormented by some special malady: Piedmont, the prey of a fanatical faction; the Milanese, devoured by the Austrians; the Papal domain, undermined by a bad financial administration, — for the imposts amount to nearly fifty millions, and do not leave to the proprietor one per cent. of his revenue; the custom house produces almost nothing, and smuggling is general. The Prince of Modena, in his duchy, — a spot where ancient abuses have full play, — sets up storehouses for contraband goods, which he introduces into the Legation of Bologna by night. The government of the Two Sicilies has fallen into the lowest depths of contempt, — the Court, living amid its guards, ever under the incubus of fear, offering no other spectacle than ruinously expensive hunting-parties and executions, makes monarchy more and more detestable in the eyes of the people, and the weakness of the government is protected only by the baseness of the multitude. The lack of military qualities will prolong Italy's agony. Bonaparte had not time to revive this virtue; the habits of an indolent life and the enticements of the climate contribute to take from the Italians of the South the desire to rouse themselves for improvement. The feuds bred by territorial divisions increase the difficulties of the internal movements; but if some impulse should come from outside, or if any prince among the Alps should grant a statute to his subjects, there would ensue a revolution, for which everything is ripe. More fortunate than we, and taught by our experience, these peoples will be sparing of crimes, of which we were so lavish." [1]

We see from this that official France had cognizance of the facts: individually some of her politicians may have felt as Chateaubriand felt; but officially she gave Italy no encouragement. And yet, Italians looked to France for guidance; they waited for her to take the initiative. Since 1789 Continental Europe had come to have a superstitious belief that France alone could give the signal for a successful political movement. The collapse of the revolutions in Naples and Piedmont had introduced a new element in Italian conspiracies: for the thousands of Liberals who then fled, or were banished from Italy, settled abroad and dedicated their lives to the redemption of their country. In Switzerland, at Marseilles, at Paris, at Brussels, at London, they had their refuges, and formed relations with the exiles and the malecontents of other lands. So much of their time as was not taken up with bread-winning, they gave to discussion of the Past and to plotting for the Future. Through emissaries and clandestine correspondence they communicated with the sects at home, urging them to be bold,

[1] *Mémoires d'Outre-Tombe*, v, 121-2.

promising them aid, chiding them for half-heartedness, and always holding out to them the prospect of speedy and easy success. They had suffered so much, that they were impatient at the hesitation of their fellow-countrymen. They deemed prudence cowardice; and in their homesick zeal they both exaggerated the chances of victory and underrated the probability of defeat. They were the victims of those delusions which tease all who look backward upon failure; it seemed to them that but for this trifle, or that accident, the judgment of Fate would have been reversed, and their cause would have prospered. So they were eager to make another trial, confident that they could not repeat their previous blunders.

Sad was the lot of the political exile, — sad, and calculated to unfit the sanest intellect for dealing with his country's affairs. He lived among strangers, he tasted the salt bread of strangers, and felt that their charity was but sufferance. Every child he met reminded him of his children, who were growing up without his care, perhaps forgetful of him or corrupted by the men he hated. In his sorrow he thought of his parents sorrowing for him; in his loneliness he felt again the sweet embraces of his wife, and wept at the cruel vividness of his imagination. His heart ached for news that never came from friends shut up in prison. As he groped through the fogs of London, he thought of the sapphire skies of Naples; as he shivered in a foreign garret, he remembered the warm South and his youth. His existence was a living death, in which all the sweetness and joy of his past life were become as wormwood to his soul. When Death takes our beloved from us, we submit as best we may, for we cannot strike at Death; the exile had to bear not only the pangs of bereavement, but also the thought that he was the victim of unjust men and not of the irrevocable sternness of Providence. And as he had sacrificed happiness for his patriotic ideal, so he was goaded by the desire to strive, and strive again, to free his country from those who oppressed her and injured him. The tyrant was not, like Death, intangible; he was mortal, he could be assailed; and both patriotism and his personal grievance drove the exile to strike at this embodiment of public wrongs, this cause of private sufferings. No wonder that a tincture of personal injury often gave to his deliberations a hue of vindictiveness.

The position of the exiles in their Continental asylums was never secure; for, although the plan of Metternich and the Duke of Modena to ship them all to America had not been followed, nevertheless they were everywhere watched by the police, and they might at any moment be arrested or conducted to the frontier of the State in which they had taken shelter. Only in England, to whom belongs the honor of being the first European nation to distinguish between civil and political criminals in her treatment of foreigners,[1] were they beyond the reach of Metternich's requisitions; but there, too, they were dogged by his spies.

The majority of the Italian refugees settled in Paris, eluding so far as they could the surveillance of the Bourbon government, and conniving with a host of French conspirators bent on overturning that government. They were not always united among themselves, for they carried their local prejudices with them, and they had mutual recriminations, charges of incompetence and cowardice, to thresh over. They were preyed upon by theories, and they sought remedies for the conditions which they had known before their exile, rather than for those actually existing in their country. No matter how close their correspondence might be with the Liberals at home, it was inevitable that they should be ignorant of many vital details concerning the men and the public sentiment that

[1] Stapleton: *Life of Canning,* iii, 140.

were to coöperate with them. Even when their information was most recent and exact, they were hindered by distance from profiting by it. Campaigns cannot be won by letter-writing; and the failure of the conspiracies of the Italian exiles during more than forty years proved that Theory is quite another thing from Reality.

Nevertheless, the existence of those bands of refugees abroad deeply affected the current of plotting in Italy, and contributed indirectly to swell the stream of Liberalism. Among the exiles were the men who had been most eminent in fomenting and guiding the revolutions, and to them those of their confederates who had escaped banishment still turned for leadership. In this way, as the Italian secret societies were drawn through their banished members into relations with the conspirators from all parts of Europe, they began to rely upon external aid, and to watch the train of events beyond the Alps for the signal for their own activity. This waiting for a foreign initiative revealed their lack of concerted energy not less than of a strong commander, but also it indicated that the Italians felt themselves bound by the ties of a common purpose to the revolutionists of Europe. The cause they were fighting for was international; it was the cause of Peoples against Despots; and the Peoples were awakening to the conviction that the artificial barriers set up by diplomacy must not separate themselves from their brothers in distress. From France — terrific mother of revolutions — they expected the initiative to issue.

In yet another way were those exiles helpful to their country's redemption: they were serving her as martyrs. Out of their love for her they had given up their hopes and happiness, to be living sacrifices to patriotism. Suffering is the holy water which purifies the heart of man; renunciation fortifies his will. When the Spirit reveals Truth to him, there comes with the revelation the sense of a higher duty to which he must consecrate his life. The moral progress of the race has been marked by the discovery of objects which it is nobler to die for than to live without. And now thousands of Italians were willing to endure exile or imprisonment in behalf of an ideal for which, a generation earlier, scarcely one Italian felt called upon to suffer. This example of devotion could not but make a deep impression on their countrymen, teaching them that the national cause had been sanctified by blood and tribulation, and imposing upon them also a patriotic duty. Only the partisans of tyranny, or those who were basely indifferent, could be unmoved when they reflected that many of their fellows were wandering in foreign lands or pining in loathsome prisons, because they had dared to assert that Italy must be free. From the fortress of Spielberg was flung a black shadow of mourning, — a constant reminder of the government which had sworn to keep Italy enslaved. Metternich in his shortsightedness believed that he could pluck out the heart of Italian Liberalism and cast it into his Moravian dungeon, there to rot; but every pang he caused, every drop of that blood he shed, multiplied an hundred fold the hatred of the Italians for their tormentors. That hatred, no tardy graciousness of his could soften; it became an instinct, a ruling passion, which must destroy its antagonist, or be itself destroyed.

The pitiless retribution which had been exacted from the revolutionists of 1820–21 did not quash conspiracy; on the contrary, the gaps made in the secret societies were filled with new members, whose wrath was heightened by the thought of their exiled and imprisoned brothers. But recent experience had taught the plotters caution, and many of the sects split up into new organizations or changed their names. They had a dangerous enemy in the Sanfedists, — literally the "Holy Faithists." — a sect founded and encouraged by the Roman Curia for the special object of neutralizing the subversive influence of the revolutionists.[1] The Sanfedists were more widely diffused, and they had more pertinacity, than Prince Canosa's Tinkers, and they were, therefore, more successful in following the trail of the Carbonari and their confederates; but neither they nor the ever-vigilant police, nor the severe punishment that was dealt out, deterred the conspirators, who made proselytes, and laid their plans against the day when France should signal, "Strike."

The despotic governments, having taken vengeance on the insurgents and plotters of 1820–21, did not relax their sternness. They reformed no abuses; they would not conciliate even the most moderate remonstrants by listening to them, but held stubbornly to their policy of treating every murmur as a crime. In Piedmont Charles Felix gave himself up to the Reactionists, even neglecting the army which had long been the particular pride of his dynasty and had served to gratify the ambition of the active Piedmontese. In Lombardy and Venetia the Austrians maintained their enervating rule, which seemed outwardly less oppressive than that of any Italian province except Tuscany, but which was inwardly unyielding and merciless. Towards the end of the decade, when Metternich judged that his police were sufficiently expert, and that the examples he had made of the victims in the Spielberg would frighten other conspirators from violence, he adopted different methods, hoping that, by allowing the upper classes to indulge freely in luxury and pleasure, he could divert them from political affairs and gradually render them too supine to raise even a protest against their master. Milan became again the gay capital, where balls, theatres, vice-regal entertainments, and aris-

[1] Cantù (*Cronistoria*, ii. 135) doubts the existence of the Sanfedists; but every history of that time refers to them, and it is improbable that an imaginary society could for more than twenty years have been treated as actually existing both by its supposed friends and by its avowed enemies.

tocratic dissipations of all kinds created fictitious merriment. It is an old trick of tyrants to make vice seductive. In Lucca the death of Maria Louisa (1824) and the succession of her son, Charles Louis, caused no change in the condition of that principality; nor was Tuscany disturbed when her easy-going Grand Duke Ferdinand died (1824); for his son, Leopold II, pursued, under the guidance of Fossombroni, the system of not interfering with his subjects so long as they refrained from meddling in politics. But Tuscany, with her commonplace prosperity and her unaspiring respectability, seemed a land of freedom compared with the neighboring States of the Church, where the material condition grew year by year more wretched, and the government of the priests became as intolerable to man as if devils were secretly directing it.

Pius VII, after several false alarms, died, to the satisfaction of the Cardinals eager to succeed him, in August, 1823. The Conclave chose Annibale della Genga in his place. Leo XII, for by that name the new pope wished to be called, was a reactionary, who construed reform to mean the restoration to the Cardinals and the higher prelates of those autocratic privileges which had been curtailed by Consalvi. His early days had not been without scandal, but he now lived austerely with his breviary and his pet cat, and meditated measures for enforcing a stricter observance of religious ceremonials. To protect the morals of his subjects, he ordered tin figleaves to be put on the antique statues; to show that he believed the human body is made in God's image, he forbade vaccination as a process whereby the "human form divine" was tainted by virus from an animal. He enforced savage ordinances against the Jews, revived the rule of primogeniture, and granted feudal immunities without stint. He degraded the judiciary more than ever; he showed his mediaevalism by requiring Latin to be spoken in the law courts and in the universities. In dealing with concerns of larger note, his administration oscillated between untimely cruelty and untimely compliance. Thus when brigands — the unerring products of bad government — became so audacious and insolent that the Pope was shamed into a display of energy, he dispatched Cardinal Pallotta with full powers against them. But Pallotta by indiscriminate executions only exasperated the evil, and had to be recalled. Then Cardinal Benvenuti was charged with the task; and he brought about a temporary cessation of brigandage by buying off the brigands, many of whom were promised pensions for life. Equally monstrous and blundering was Leo's policy towards his discontented subjects in Romagna and the Legations. By his harshness the Liberal sects were hounded into open turbulence. They had frequent conflicts with the Sanfedists, who were incited by priests and wandering friars. A revolution being imminent, Leo commissioned Cardinal Rivarola to restore tranquillity by any means. Rivarola was an ecclesiastic of the Torquemada stripe, — fanatical, merciless, shortsighted, — a physician who did not prescribe a cure, but only palliatives for the moment. He worked with such vigor that he had soon filled the prisons with actual or alleged conspirators upon whom he passed sentence, having scarcely deigned to observe the form of legality. Five hundred and eight victims were condemned by him, some to death, — the sentence was not carried out, — some to the galleys for longer or shorter terms, and some to daily registration at the police stations. Having sufficiently inspired terror, he published a specious amnesty; but the sectaries were not to be lured from their revenge. They hated him with an immitigable hatred, and at Ravenna they made an attempt on his life. Thereupon an extraordinary commission, presided by Monsignor Invernizzi, a man as much like Rivarola as wolf and wolf, was appointed to punish the supposed assassins. Many arrests, barbarous tortures, seven victims for the gibbet, another company for the galleys, and a multitude of suspects consigned to police surveillance, — these were the consequences of this new process, which caused Invernizzi to be detested, and the assassins to be pitied. Intermittent spurts of ferocity like this could not conceal the constitutional feebleness of the Papal government, and they only envenomed the sects which they were intended to dissolve. The key of heaven was rusty from disuse; with his other key, Leo seemed to have unlocked hell, whence demons issued to plague his realm. They laughed at excommunication, and feared not holy water; they assumed the shapes of cardinals not less than of conspirators; but they must be exorcised, if the Holy See was to retain its worldly power.

In the Kingdom of the Two Sicilies, where there was no cant pretense of governing by the inspiration of the Holy Ghost, the situation grew yearly worse. King Ferdinand was found one morning dead in his bed (1825): terror frozen on his countenance, his limbs stiffened in convulsed posture, just as he had unexpectedly been seized by Death, and striven to writhe himself free; no friend present to comfort him, no priest to absolve him from his mountainous burden of crimes. Though we excused his tyrannical methods as the product of his education and inheritance, yet there would remain against him a record of personal iniquity seldom equaled even by his Bourbon kindred; for he was a liar, a debauchee, a perjurer, alternately a bully or a coward, and an inveterate dissimulator. Nevertheless his son Francis, who succeeded to the throne, in some respects surpassed him in baseness; for Ferdinand, it was said, had made tyranny detestable, while Francis made it despicable. He it was who had acted as viceroy during the revolution, and the abject fear which then impelled him to feign loyalty to the Liberals haunted him to the end. He dared not drive through the streets of Naples without having first learned from the Minister of Police what route would be safe. He relied upon the Austrian garrisons to keep popular discontent from flaring up in another rebellion; and when the Austrians were withdrawn, he contracted with Switzerland to furnish him a guard of six thousand soldiers for thirty years. Under him the *Camorra*, a sort of Blackmailers' Coöperative Society and Thieves' Alliance, sprang up. Corruption rankled in every department of his administration. Through his valet, Vaglica, and a chambermaid, Catherine de Simone,— two illiterate and venal creatures whom he chose for his favorites, — he maintained a traffic in government appointments.[1] "Whoever buys an office," he used to say, "takes care not to lose it, and is faithful." So great was his dread of poison that he would allow only this woman to prepare his food, and she must first taste it in his presence before he would eat. Like his father, he had a passion for hunting, and spent more money on this sport than on public education throughout his kingdom. He, too, was annoyed by brigands and by conspirators; but the barbarity with which he persecuted the fractious who fell into his power aroused popular detestation against himself, and sympathy for them. Indeed, brigandage was often a protest, on the part of men who had still enough manliness to protect themselves, against the unjust, venal, and cruel government. The King's minion, Intonti, Minister of Police, and Delcarretto, commander of the gendarmerie and special military agent, earned by their bloodthirstiness and duplicity a reputation hardly less atrocious than that of Ruffo and Canosa. The Neapolitan State, with its prisons full, its offices, civil and ecclesiastical, possessed by bribers,

---

[1] Bishoprics sold for 4,000 ducats ; civil offices for a usurious percentage of the salary attached to them ; collectorships were bestowed upon infants, the father of the appointee taking the money. See N. Nisco : *Gli Ultimi Trentasei Anni del Reame di Napoli* (Naples, 1889), i, 71.

its towns swarming with sectaries and spies, and its
provinces infested by outlaws, must have burst asunder,
had not the Holy Alliance covenanted to preserve even
rottenness, so long as any trace of Legitimacy could be
discerned on the rotting carcass.

If, therefore, the Italian Liberals had grievances sufficient to justify their revolution in 1820, every year in the
decade that followed brought fresh aggravations upon
them, and urged them to hazard another effort. Their
governors waxed more despotic, manifesting a reckless
indifference to the wishes of their subjects, and a determination never to compromise; for the certainty of being
protected by Austria made rulers insolent who were by
nature cowards. The recollection of the persecution which
their friends had suffered after the defeats in Piedmont
and Naples quickened the anger of the conspirators; the
activity of the exiles seemed to be based on strength that
would prove invincible. The sects were busy, and if they
still lacked leadership and union they felt that they were
engaged in a movement not restricted to Italy, but em-
bracing the oppressed and discontented elements of society in Central and Western Europe. The conflict between the Italians and their tormentors might be delayed;
it could not be avoided; but the success of the patriots
would depend not only on their own energy and prudence,
but on favorable international contingencies. As the year
1830 approached, the hearts of the plotters grew buoyant, for the stars which ruled the political destinies of
Europe seemed to be nearing that position which por-
tended good fortune to Italy.

CHAPTER IX.

THE REVOLUTIONS OF 1831.

At the end of July, 1830, Paris blazed into revolution. For months previous every one had predicted an eruption, but when it came, and belched firebrands over France and Europe, many persons were taken by surprise. On the very eve of the calamity Charles X played whist at St. Cloud; the next day he was scampering across France to seek refuge in England. It does not concern us to unravel the intrigues which interrupted his card-playing, and set Louis Philippe, his Orleanist cousin, on the French throne. The details are not always clear, but it is clear that the most vigorous of the plotters had not worked for this result. They aimed at establishing a Republic, for they had no more illusions about monarchy, and they were disgusted with the Bourbons. The friends of Louis Philippe — a royal Micawber, who had for forty years been good-naturedly waiting for a crown to turn up — saw their opportunity, fraternized with the Republicans, and professed an unquenchable desire to exterminate the whole brood of European Absolutists. Therefore Republicans and Orleanists plotted along parallel lines; the Twenty-ninth of July came, and the government of France fell into their power. Which of them should keep it? The majority of the active conspirators still desired the Republic, but was the majority of the French people with them? The middle classes feared anarchy, and the Orleanists cunningly excited their fears. The Republic was a noble ideal, — none would deny that, — but what if it should sink into another Reign of Terror?

The country was not yet educated for an out-and-out democracy; why not, therefore, compromise? Why not agree upon the most Liberal form of constitutional monarchy? The decision had to be made quickly, for tumults were impending at home, and the Absolutist Powers abroad might at any moment interfere. Lafayette, who was only less facile than Talleyrand himself in moulting his plumage to suit the political season, commanded the National Guard at this crisis, was persuaded by the Orleanist arguments, and threw his great influence in favor of Louis Philippe. Thus, without an appeal to the nation, was set up a constitutional monarchy which broke the fall between autocracy and republicanism.

There are certain amphibious creatures which seem so well adapted to a life on land that you never suspect their aquatic nature; but let them by chance come down to the water, and they swim off, and adjust themselves to their new element as if they had known no other. Such a creature, in the political sense, was Louis Philippe; once on the throne, he forgot his past promises and confederates, and was only intent on making his dynasty firm. This double nature explains the insincerity of his attitude towards the European Liberals, — insincerity which, as we shall presently see, was disastrous to the Italians who had trusted in him. Although by adroitness he had glided into kingship, a considerable faction of the French felt that they had been swindled. To conciliate them, he sang a song of reform, and went about with an ostentatious simplicity which might persuade the stubbornest Radicals that, although he was called king, he was at heart as much a citizen as the best of them. To the autocrats of the Holy Alliance he had to play another tune. Since 1815 they had maintained the principle of Legitimacy, forbidding any change in dynasties that was not provided for by the Congress of Vienna: they had refused all transaction with the products of the revolution; they had stifled the efforts of Liberals in Naples, in Piedmont, and in Spain; they had made it the cardinal doctrine of their creed that no people had the right to alter their government against the wishes of their sovereign and the consent of his allies. How, then, could they admit to their exclusive circle this subverter of the principle of Legitimacy, this product of a revolution in France? Louis Philippe played to them a seductive air. Instead of spurning him as an incendiary, he said, they ought to be grateful to him for having put out a fire that threatened to ravage Europe. Duty alone had overcome his unwillingness to burden his shoulders with kingly responsibility at that dangerous crisis, when he alone had the power to save France from ruin and his neighbors from calamity. His intentions, he assured them, were conservative and peaceful, and he would endeavor to fulfil the international engagements of his predecessors in so far as he could do this without clashing with the moderate sentiments of the French.

The Great Powers were not fooled by these declarations: they saw that Louis Philippe's ill-concealed dynastic ambition was a better guarantee than all his protests that he would henceforth keep the peace and eschew the revolution. Metternich regretted that the Allies had not an army on the French frontier, to march double-quick to Paris and strangle the monster of Jacobinism once for all. He sounded the Allies as to their willingness to hold another Congress, but they were disinclined; England had already recognized the July monarchy, and Prussia soon imitated her. The Czar, indeed, was angry enough to go to war, had not his neighbors' reluctance and the internal affairs of his Empire restrained him; therefore, though he officially accepted Louis Philippe as King of the French, he allowed his irritation to appear through the insulting terms in which his consent was couched. Metternich, also, who had reduced snubbing to a fine art, expressed his contempt for the Orleanist usurper, but in a form so subtle that no stickler for courtesy could resent it. When General Bellard, the French envoy, discoursed to him of Louis Philippe's good intentions, and of his service to European tranquillity in checking the revolution, and of his ability thenceforth to keep France quiet, Metternich ironically replied that this was the old story which previous French ministers had told him: "but," he added, "after our recent experience, how can we ever put faith in such declarations?" Nevertheless, he realized that at present it would be more prudent to acquiesce in a disagreeable infringement of his principle of Legitimacy than to hazard a war: so Emperor Francis, at his dictation, wrote a chilly letter of recognition to the new French king.

Whilst Louis Philippe, by secretly disavowing any sympathy with revolutionists, was humbly seeking admittance to the clique of European sovereigns, he had to speak deferentially of the revolution to his French subjects; for to have denounced before them the methods of the Twenty-ninth of July would have been to admit that his elevation to the throne was illegal, and that the Allied Powers would be justified in restoring Charles X, as they had formerly restored Louis XVIII. He therefore proclaimed that each people has the right to manage its internal affairs, and that any attempt by a foreign government to restrict or to crush that right must be resisted. France was strong enough now to defy an invasion; or, say rather, the Allies were in an unfavorable position for invading her. They remembered how she had hurled back their armies in 1792, and for many years afterward; they knew, too, that the moment in which they ordered their troops to cross her frontier would be the signal for rebellion in their own lands; they dreaded a death-grapple with Liberalism; and so they allowed Louis Philippe and his ministers to babble about non-intervention. After all, had they not private assurances from himself that if they did not interfere with his schemes in France they would find him a very safe neighbor?

Such was the Revolution of July as it appeared to the actors behind the scenes; an unheroic performance, in which mean ambitions and diplomatic chicane were the web whereof the plot was woven; a solemn farce to any spectator who knew that all the bluster and patriotic affirmations were counterfeit, and that only the ill-humor was real. But the European public, as unsophisticated as children at their first play, were thrilled by it beyond measure, and, mimicry being instinctive in childhood, they set about rehearsing revolutions of their own. Erelong, Belgium had risen against the Dutch; the native troops in Russian Poland had mutinied and proclaimed the independence of their unhappy country, which had become enslaved through the sins of their forefathers; hope was throbbing in the hearts of stolid German Liberals; and the Italian conspirators were already discussing what to do after they had rid Italy of her tyrants.

To the Italians, indeed, the news of Louis Philippe's easy victory did not come as a surprise; they had been expecting the revolution for a long time past, and were only surprised that it had exploded so early. There was at Paris a Cosmopolitan Committee, composed of exiles and plotters from all parts of the Continent, which was not only in close relations with Lafayette, Dupont de l'Eure, and the other French Republicans, but also with the leaders of the revolutionary sects in their several countries. This Committee had planned that the uprising should take place simultaneously in France, Spain, and Italy, and that those three Latin peoples, once free, should unite in a league to defend each other against the probable attack of Austria and Russia. Charles the Tenth's mad wilfulness had forced the issue upon France

a little too soon for her confederates. Nevertheless, the
Italians were almost as exultant as if their own victory
had been secured; for they had the success of the French
to cheer them, and on the French throne they saw a king
who had been created by their friends, and whom the
Holy Alliance had not dared to assail. France was again
the Grand Nation, whose armies had thundered through
Europe a generation ago, and France was now with
them, and with all those who would break the chains of
the Old Régime. For, listen to the utterances of Louis
Philippe's ministers. "Whereas the Holy Alliance was
founded on the principle of interfering in the domestic
affairs of foreign countries," said Marshal Sébastiani,
in Parliament, — "a principle which destroys the independence of States, — France now hallows the opposite
principle, and will cause the independence of all to be respected." And Lafitte declared with equal resoluteness:
"France will not permit the principle of non-intervention
to be violated." What assurances more sure, what in-
citement more direct, could the Italians require? The
enemy which had thwarted their patriotic comrades since
1815, and had decreed perpetual serfdom for Italy, was
Austria, and now France had said that she would tolerate
no longer Austria's meddling in the concerns of weaker
States. So the Italians had no doubt of their ability to
deal with their local tyrants, and the last preparations
for the revolution were diligently pushed forward.

The area of expected disturbance included the Duchy
of Modena and the States of the Church, but the rest of
the Peninsula was in a feverish condition which predis-
posed it to catch the revolutionary epidemic. Never had
Italian conspiracy entered a phase so dramatic and interesting as the present. The sects at home were in touch
with their exiled colleagues at Paris, where, in the enthusiastic imagination of the plotters, there existed a maga-
zine or reservoir whence they might draw unlimited assist-

ance. The sects themselves had as usual their differences and rivalries: there were the Unitarians, who made the unification of the Italian provinces the chief object to be attained; there were the Federatists, who insisted that only a federal union would satisfy them; there were smaller factions, each with its peculiar hobby and panacea; but sufficient harmony ran through these discordant elements to cause each to waive for the present its pet design, and to join in the common struggle for independence. More strange even than their temporary unison was their belief that they had secured as their ally and leader the Italian tyrant who had hitherto been the most active and the most execrated enemy of Liberalism. Francis of Modena, whose cruelty after the revolt of 1821 had earned for him the nickname "Butcher," — he who had never slackened his oppressive government, and who had recently taken Prince Canosa into his confidence, — was now leagued with conspirators whom he once urged the Allied Powers to send like convicts beyond the sea. How had this singular truce between the wolf and sheep been compacted?

I am not one of those historians whose self-confidence suffices, in the lack of an authentic clue, to guide them through the labyrinth of dark and tortuous events. The supreme value of history depends upon the truthfulness with which it traces the great currents of human life, rather than upon its ability to explain why some particular eddy or ripple disturbed the surface of the stream at a given point. The individual man is often a mystery to himself and a paradox to others; and it is as rare in matters of State as in private matters that you can say with certainty, "This deed resulted from a single motive." As a tree has many roots, so actions usually spring from many motives: our volition has an ancestry whose pedigree is unknown to us. And yet, in spite of the eccentricity and contradictions of special acts, we discover, by comparing one act with another, that one law unifies them, and that in their sum, they reveal the character out of which they grew. The moral integrity of the universe will not be violated; each seed brings forth fruit after its kind. If we are deluded by external inconsistencies into a belief in luck, if we fall into that deepest of errors, — the only atheism, which pretends that we can sow Evil and somehow reap Good, — it is because we are still but as children in our knowledge of the laws of spiritual growth and compensation. The desire to be guiltless of this immoral worship of Chance, and to leave no nook for Chaos, prompts some historians to round out with theories of their own the gaps made by defective evidence; and this they do with no conscious purpose of falsifying, but with dread lest the mysterious paradoxes of human nature be charged to them. But the historian, I repeat, has no business to invent motives for the sake of clearness, nor to pass judgment on insufficient testimony, for the sake of showing his respect for justice. It is not he, but the poet, — a Sophocles or a Shakespeare, — whose duty it is to illustrate by the typical creatures of the imagination the unerring operations of the moral law, and to complete and classify what seems to our ignorance fragmentary and confused. Let us, therefore, frankly admit that in the transactions of the Duke of Modena with the conspiring Liberals there are dark places which have never been satisfactorily lighted, and inconsistent deeds for which we can only suggest the motives. The chief actors in this curious episode never spoke out, nor left a written confession; but the main facts, the external events, are known, and from this knowledge of the *how* we can conjecture with more or less plausibility concerning the *why*. Let us take care, however, not to mistake our conjectures for facts.

The Duke of Modena, we may remember, had so prodigious an ambition that three of its giant's strides in any

direction took him clean out of his little duchy. He was
not one of the languidly covetous, but one who, being
endowed with vigorous qualities, pursued steadfastly the
object he coveted. He had been baffled in his designs on
the Piedmontese succession, — baffled, but not yet beaten.
A believer in the Old Régime, he had forced the sovereigns
of the Holy Alliance to regard him as one who, on a small
scale, had approved himself a master in persecution; and
if they, or Fate, would but grant him a wider field, he
had both the will and the energy to outdo the most virulent of them in Herod-like atrocities. He constructed a
miniature model of a perfect engine of autocracy; he had
paid agents in all parts of Italy to inform him of the intrigues of diplomacy and the plots of conspirators. He
was closely linked with the extreme Reactionaries at Rome,
and he instigated the Sanfedists in their machinations
against the Liberals. But dearer to him than Sanfedism
or Reaction was his personal aggrandizement. Suddenly,
towards the close of 1830, it was whispered about that he
was secretly encouraging the Liberals in their designs for
a general revolution. Just when he turned a friendly ear
to them we do not know. It may be that his motive was
at first treacherous, — that he pretended friendliness, in
order the better to learn their plot and so to foil it: and
then having listened to their seductive projects, he seems
to have been fired by the idea that these very conspirators
might be the instruments of his ambition. They felt certain of success in the Legations and Piedmont; they had
a fighting chance in Lombardy and Tuscany: by collusion
with them, therefore, he might in a few months become
the sovereign of the larger part of Northern and Central
Italy. Once established in so important a kingdom, could
he not rule according to his favorite methods? The Absolutist Powers, especially Austria, would doubtless object, but he would persuade them that the system to which
they clung was safe in his hands, and that the peace of

Italy could be secured only by uniting under him the government of the several turbulent States.

That considerations such as these may have induced Francis to connive with the Liberals seems at least plausible; but it is more difficult to suggest why the Liberals accepted him as a confederate.[1] None knew better than they his tyrannical nature; none had more cause to suspect the sincerity of his conversion to Liberalism. One fact, however, is plain: a considerable body of the revolutionists still attached great weight, in spite of the defection of Charles Albert in 1821, to the prestige that would accrue to their movement from the coöperation of a legitimate prince. If they succeeded in their enterprise, they could disarm the indignation of the Holy Alliance by pointing to their leader as a sovereign whom the Alliance itself had deemed worthy to rule. It may be that they were far-sighted enough to perceive that the first step towards the complete independence of Italy must be the fusion of as many of the small provinces as possible under one government: that accomplished, should Francis prove ungrateful to the forces which had raised him, they could depose him and set up such an administration, whether monarchical or republican, as the majority preferred. Perhaps they meant to use him only as a decoy for drawing as many of the aristocracy as they could into their net. Perhaps they hoped to discredit all the Italian despots in the eyes of Europe, by showing that Francis, the most despotic of them all, could be lured into complicity with the rebels whom he professed to hate. Whatever may have been their motive, history teaches this general truth: ambitious rulers and zealous conspirators are never scrupulous in the choice of tools by which they expect to attain their end; no stone is too dirty to serve them in rising; no briar too thorny to be clutched to save them from falling.

[1] Bianchi in his *Ducati Estensi dal* Anno 1815 al 1850 (Turin, 1852), gives a detailed account of this whole affair.

Whatever the terms of their union, then, by the close of the year 1830 Francis and the revolutionists were known to be united. The Duke had taken Ciro Menotti, the leader of the Modenese conspirators, into his friendship, and those who were not in the secret could easily guess the purpose of Menotti's frequent visits to the Ducal Palace. One other actor in the drama deserves mention, a certain Misley, who seems even earlier than Menotti to have won the Duke's confidence, and who was now employed as intermediary between Modena and the Cosmopolitan Committee at Paris. He sent reports of the forwardness of the preparations there, and of the sympathy which Louis Philippe's ministers expressed for the Italian cause. Menotti went on missionary journeys into Tuscany and the Legations, inciting the Liberals to rise, and concerting the final details of the plot. He was most urgent, too, that the Piedmontese should revolt at the appointed day, and that they should decide to join the revolutionary union.[1] The Duke's sister, Maria Theresa, queen-dowager of Piedmont, was also busily renewing her endeavors to secure the Piedmontese throne for Francis, on the death, now imminent, of Charles Felix. In France, William Pepe, with the connivance of Lafayette, had enrolled a thousand volunteers, with whom he was to embark at Marseilles and make a descent on Sicily. Large stores of weapons and ammunition were to be shipped by way of Corsica to the Tuscan coast, where trusty agents would attend to their distribution.[2] Never before had Italian conspirators seemed so well justified in reckoning upon victory.

What, then, had been the cause of the change in Francis's attitude towards the great enterprise, as referred to in the following note from Menotti to Misley, dated at Modena, January 7, 1831? "I arrive in this moment from Bologna. I have to tell you that the Duke is a

[1] Poggi, ii, 6. [2] Cantù, ii, 269.

regular rascal. I have run serious peril of being killed. The Duke has spread reports through the Sanfedists that you and I are paid agents to form centres and then betray them. This was so strongly believed at Bologna, that I just missed being assassinated. The fact is, that in eight days the entire Romagna had turned against me, but it will come back. . . . Now that I know I am regarded as an agent of the Duke, I will act with such prudence that I shall attain my goal without breaking my promises."[1]

Mystery upon mystery! The Duke already plays a double game, in spite of which Menotti still hopes to bind both the slippery Duke and the suspicious conspirators! These are bad omens on the very eve of an enterprise for whose success harmony and mutual trust are indispensable. Prudence whispers to abandon the plot whose issue must be disastrous; but to Menotti such whisperings seem not prudent but cowardly. He is a man whose handsome face and commanding person bespeak a fearless, self-confident nature; and there is in him a dash of recklessness, as the stories about his desperate amours show; above all, he is only thirty-two, and burns with patriotic ambition. The Duke's defection, therefore, cannot frighten him.

More than five months had elapsed since Louis Philippe had been lifted by the wave of revolution into the French throne. He had placated the neighboring monarchs and repudiated in private to them the means of his elevation. Nevertheless, his ministers still parroted the Orleanist watchword of "non-intervention." It was high time that the Italians should rise, unless, indeed, they had realized that the lucky moment for rising had slipped by. They had delayed at first in order to perfect their arrangements at home; then they had waited for assurance that

---

[1] Poggi, ii, 6; see also Bianchi, Ducati Estensi, i, 50. Bianchi attributes the Duke's change of face to his discovery that Louis Philippe would not support the revolution.

the Spaniards were ready; now the news came from the Paris Committee that everything was prepared, and they might strike. The 5th of February was fixed upon as the fateful day. But the Duke of Modena's insinuations had sunk into the hearts of the Romagnoles, who bluntly informed Menotti that they distrusted him, and that each province must rebel on its own account. Menotti, still undismayed, gave the last directions to his Modenese confederates; yet a few days, and events would prove how unjust were the suspicions against him.

On February 3 the Duke ordered the arrest of Nicholas Fulvizi and the banishment of Generals Fontanelli and Zucchi, who were involved in the conspiracy; but, as if he still shrank from breaking irrevocably with the party which might fulfil his dream of kingship, he left Menotti, the chief conspirator, unmolested. The latter, believing that to wait longer might defeat their undertaking, hastily arranged that the signal for the insurrection should be given at midnight. That evening about fifteen conspirators assembled at his palace for the final instructions; while they were concerting, a traitor sneaked away and revealed the plot to the police. Presently a squad of gendarmes appeared at Menotti's palace and attempted to enter, but the conspirators defended themselves so hotly that their assailants withdrew. Then, after a brief quiet, during which hope ran high, the Duke himself, accompanied by a strong force of soldiers and one small cannon, marched into the square. From behind a pillar, he directed the bombardment of the conspirators' nest. They returned the fire, until their ammunition failed, when they had to surrender. Menotti, wounded in the skirmish, was carried off by the Duke, who a few hours later sent to the Governor of Reggio this famous dispatch: "To-night a terrible plot has burst against me. The conspirators are in my hands. *Send me the executioner.*" But before even so prompt an avenger as Francis could hurry his prisoners to the scaffold, the news reached him that the Pope's subjects were in revolt, and that the neighboring Bolognese were marching on Modena to rescue Menotti and his fellow-conspirators. Without waiting for the confirmation of this report, Francis, in alarm, on February 5, retired to Mantua, whence he sought protection from the Austrians. In his flight he took Menotti with him, some said to be a hostage to deter the Modenese rebels from wreaking vengeance on the ducal partisans who were left behind; others said to prevent Menotti from disclosing secrets which would have made the Duke as intolerable to Austria as he was now odious to the Italians.

The revolution had, in fact, broken out on February 4 in the Papal States. At Bologna, bands of excited citizens filled the air with shouts of "Liberty and Independence;" and when the police remonstrated, they showed a disposition to reinforce their shouts with violence. The Prolegate, being informed by the commander of the gendarmerie and the commander of the garrison that their men could not be relied upon to quell an outbreak, called a conference of nobles of reputed loyalty. They, too, advised against measures which would provoke a civil war at a crisis in which the government was evidently weaker than its opponents; but they were willing, if the Prolegate deemed it expedient to hasten to Rome for instructions, to undertake to preserve order in his absence. Accordingly, on the next day he appointed a Temporary Commission, and departed. There was no blood spilled, nor so much as a broken head.

As when, on a given day in early spring, all the almond orchards in the same belt of sunshine burst into blossom, so along the Adriatic coast town after town bedecked itself with the tricolor flags and joyous aspect of Freedom. Imola and Faenza freed themselves without a struggle; at Parma, Maria Louisa found that her subjects would fight rather than give up the holiday of independence on which they had set their hearts, so she quitted her little capital and left them to their merry-making; at Ferrara, the presence of the Austrian garrison did not hinder the formation of a Provisional Government composed of Liberals; at Forlì, as at Ravenna, there was a brief contest between the revolutionists and the ecclesiastical governor, and in both cases the prelate withdrew; at Pesaro, the National Guards, throwing away the papal banner and setting up the tricolor, elected Sercognani, a veteran of the Napoleonic wars, to command them, and under his leadership they marched gayly southward, till they had opened the gates of all the cities and towns as far as Spoleto to the harbingers of Liberty. It seemed as if the inhabitants of Emilia and the Roman State were celebrating some national festival, or had given themselves up to the sweet transports of a general joy, rather than that they were engaged in so grave and perilous a business as an attempt to shake off the yoke of immemorial tyranny. Success so instantaneous and so easy might well instil forebodings into sober hearts, if there were such, as they reflected that the blessings which the gods grant quickly they quickly recall.

But surely, we exclaim, even a blear-eyed and palsied government like that of the Vatican must have had inklings of the impending danger and must have made some effort to avert it. As with decrepit old men, so with decrepit rulers, — their tenacity of life often increases in proportion as their vitality wanes. Had those aged Papalists lost their passion for dominion, the primal instinct of the Papacy? Would they wrap their purple cloaks round them, and calmly await death, as ancient Romans had once awaited Brennus and his barbarians in the Senate House? Or did they think to exorcise the Demon of Revolution by droning masses and sprinkling holy water? No, none of these things was true of the

Roman hierarchy: it was weak, but not resigned; it was hard-pressed, but it would concede nothing.

The insurrection had beset it at an embarrassing crisis. On November 30, 1830, Pius VIII, a paralytic old gentleman, who had succeeded Leo XII in the previous year, died, and the interregnum which ensued had been seized upon by the conspirators as a heaven-sent occasion for achieving their plans. The Conclave dragged on through many weeks, to the satisfaction of the plotters, and to the disgust of the Roman shopkeepers and landlords, who were thereby deprived of the profits they always reaped during the Carnival season. The factions in the Sacred College fought stubbornly, for in these latter days the Conclave must select not only a pope agreeable to the Catholic Powers, but also a secretary of state, this dignitary having become a personage of greater influence than the Pope himself. Indeed, so jealously is the Holy Father guarded, he can only know what his chief minister chooses to report to him, and his official acts, therefore, are often merely echoes of the policy thrust upon him by his advisers. In the Conclave of 1830-31, Cardinal Albani, Austria's faithful minion, was bent on defeating every candidate who would not promise to appoint him to the secretaryship of State; and for nearly two months there was such a conflict of jealousies, wranglings, underhand intrigues and deceits as prevented an election. Finally, on February 1 the secrecy of the Conclave was violated by the clandestine introduction of a letter from the Duke of Modena, in which he informed the Cardinals that a revolution was about to explode, and he urged them, if they would save their country from destruction, to agree immediately upon a pope. Thus alarmed, on the following day they elected Cardinal Cappellari, who took the name Gregory XVI, and made Cardinal Bernetti his premier.[1]

[1] Bianchi, iii, 29-42.

Three days later the new Pope had tidings of the insurrection in Modena and the Legations. Every successive courier brought gloomier reports, and erelong the fugitive prolegates and ousted governors came panting and frightened into Rome, to spread panic among the ecclesiastics and joy among the Liberals. The Papal ministry saw that it could neither put down the rebellious provinces, nor defend the Holy City itself, should the insurgents attack it from without, or their confederates within rise in a body. Terror-stricken, Gregory secretly besought the King of Naples to lend him some Swiss regiments in order that the Vatican at least might be protected; but the young King, Ferdinand II, who had succeeded his father Francis on November 8, 1830, refused the demand, either because he feared an outbreak among his own subjects, or because he did not wish to give offense to his uncle, Louis Philippe. The Pope also wrote to the Austrian emperor, not officially asking aid, — for he trembled at the French shibboleth, "non-intervention," — but painting the situation of the Papal States in colors so lurid, that Austria might be moved of her own accord to hasten to his rescue.[1] If Austria took the hint, he could wash his hands of responsibility for any quarrel between her and France. To his "best beloved subjects" he addressed an edict, February 9, in which he assured them that he was only solicitous of their welfare; he chid them gently for allowing themselves to be led astray at a moment when the Holy See was vacant, but he promised them "pity and pardon," and to interpose his prayers between them and God's punishment if they showed their penitence by immediate submission.[2] As well might he have expected to dispel an epidemic of cholera by proclamation!

The insurgents, reveling in their easy victory and still

[1] Bianchi iii, 49; Poggi, ii, 18-20.
[2] Text in Gualterio: *Ultimi Rivolgimenti Italiani* (2d edit.). i, 309-12.

guiltless of bloody excesses, applied themselves without delay to the task of giving their provisional governments a permanent form. At Bologna, on February 8, it was decreed that the temporal dominion of the Pope over that city and province, having ceased in fact, should never more be recognized in law, and that a general election should be held to choose deputies.[1] The tribunals were remodeled after the French system, and a new tariff of taxes was drawn up. General Zucchi hurried to take command of the disaffected troops at Modena. In order not to excite the hostility of the Orleanist monarchy, Louis Bonaparte, the putative son of the ex-King of Holland, and his elder brother Charles, who had for months past furnished money for the revolution, and had personally contributed to its success, were induced to retire from Bologna to Forlì, where Charles died soon afterward.[2] The Bolognese also dispatched envoys into Tuscany, to assure the Grand Duke that they had no intention of molesting him, and incidentally to urge the Tuscan Liberals to strike for liberty. The manifestoes launched by the Papal Secretary of State, as a boy launches paper boats on a rippled pool, scarcely attracted the attention of the insurgents, although they, as partisans of "felony and irreligion," were therein threatened with excommunication. And when Cardinal Benvenuti, charged with plenary powers, risked himself in the rebellious provinces, he was taken prisoner and conveyed to Ancona. For a brief time there was unwonted blitheheartedness among the Italian revolutionists, for they put faith in the French doctrine of non-intervention, and they had no misgivings but that, if undisturbed by Austria, they could constitute and maintain a Liberal government in Central Italy.

Vain was their confidence! delusive were their hopes!

[1] Text in Gualterio, i, 312.
[2] Poggi, ii, 17-18.

Non-intervention might be declared by France, but would the other Powers respect it? Metternich could neither be fooled nor frightened by a mere phrase, and, even before the Italian revolt, he had penetrated the artifices of Louis Philippe and his ministers. To make France ridiculous by carrying out Austria's immemorial policy, in spite of French bravado, was henceforth his purpose. Therefore, on March 5, General Frimont, the Austrian commander in Northern Italy, began operations against Modena. Metternich was already sure of Russia's consent to his intervention, and he did not fear England, who limited herself to expressing the opinion that the outbreak in the Papal States was due to the evil government, and that she would have preferred that pacific negotiations had been exhausted before forcible repression was resorted to.[1] In his messages to the French Cabinet, the Austrian chancellor insisted that his only desire was to check anarchy, and he did not spare vague hints that, if the Orleanist king continued to cherish the revolutionary viper, he might discover, too late, that his nursling was of the Napoleonic brood. "We know that the movement in Italy is a Bonapartist one," said he. "We are resolved to resist it. The Emperor owes so much to his Empire, and to all that is yet left standing in Europe. By this determination we at the same time render the most signal service to King Louis Philippe. If, on the simplest showing, there was an incompatibility between his existence and that of a subordinate member of the Bonapartist family on a throne contiguous to weak and feeble France, how much more real does that incompatibility become in view of an Italy placed beneath the sceptre of Napoleon II? Yet this is the direct object of the party of anarchy against which we are still struggling."[2] The presence of Charles and Louis Bonaparte in the Romagna; the recent attempt to abduct Napoleon

[1] Bianchi, iii, 52-3.   [2] Memoirs, v, 104.

II from Vienna, with the view to proclaiming him king at Rome;[1] and the expected descent of Achille Murat upon the Kingdom of Naples,[2] naturally gave a semblance of truth to the assertion that the Italian movement was only an ill-disguised Bonapartist plot. Metternich went even so far as to intimate that Austria, if driven to bay, might release Napoleon II, and use him as a lever for overthrowing the July monarchy;[3] for the Napoleonist infatuation was growing stronger in France, and the presence of the son of the Great Emperor might suffice to render it irresistible. Louis Philippe needed not these disagreeable reminders that his throne was founded on quicksands; at heart, he had no other desire than to be allowed to establish his dynasty by exterminating Bonapartist and Bourbon enemies at home; but he was entangled in a dilemma, and he had neither the strength nor the sincerity to escape from it.

Meanwhile, into the midst of this whirl of wordy chaff Metternich had thrown his blunt, solid fact: Austria, flouting the principle of non-intervention, was actually stifling the rebellion in Central Italy. But French national dignity, always sensitive and quick to impute insult, and French glory, always insatiate and never squeamish about the food provided for it, — how would Louis Philippe reckon with them? To Casimir Périer, now President of the Ministry, fell the task of juggling with these inconvenient elements of French public opinion. "I do not believe," he said to the Chamber of Deputies, "that France should hold herself pledged to carry her arms whithersoever the principle of non-intervention may be violated. Where this were done, there would arise a new kind of intervention: the pretensions of the Holy Alliance would be resuscitated: we should fall a prey to the chimerical ambition of all those who wished to subject Europe to the yoke of a single idea and to

---

[1] Bianchi, iii, 333.   [2] Ibid, 334–42.   [3] Ibid, 345.

vitalize universal monarchy. Understood in that fashion, the principle of non-intervention would serve as a spur to the spirit of conquest. We shall uphold that principle everywhere by means of negotiation; but only the interest and dignity of France could induce us to draw our sword. We do not recognize in any people the right to lead us to fight for its cause; the blood of the French belongs to France alone."[1] This official elucidation of the meaning of the chief dogma of the July monarchy was unexpected, but being spoken with authority, it must be orthodox. Nevertheless, there were many French Radicals whom the interpretation dissatisfied, and who did not hesitate to accuse the government of allowing the honor of France to be smirched.

To appease these grumblers, Périer, at the very moment in which he was secretly informing Austria that "France would in no wise suffer the overturn of the temporal power of the Pope,"[2] dispatched Count Sainte-Aulaire on a special mission to Rome, to induce the Pope to get rid of the Austrian troops as soon as possible. Metternich, who had already secured his twofold aim of discrediting the principle of non-intervention and of making Austria for the third time the queller of Italian Liberalism, professed that as an evidence of his peaceful intention he would consent to the evacuation of all the provinces lately in revolt, leaving garrisons only in Ancona and Bologna until such time as the Papal government should declare itself strong enough to curb another outbreak. In Rome, Sainte-Aulaire consulted with representatives of Austria, Prussia, Russia, England, and Piedmont concerning the reforms which should be recommended to the Pope for the maintenance of order among his subjects. In participating in a conference whose object was to meddle with the internal administration of an independent sovereign, France thus violated her own

[1] Bianchi, iii, 60.   [2] Ibid, 64.

principle of non-intervention; but of what use was it to
charge her with another inconsistency? As well blame
a weather-cock for fickleness. The Papal government
cordially detested the officiousness of the Great Powers
in its behalf, but lacking material vigor to oppose, it
poured out assurances of its gratitude, and professed to
be willing to be guided by its troublesome friends. At
length a Memorandum was drawn up, and signed by all
the envoys, except the English, who had declared that
the only way to establish permanent reforms was to secu-
larize the papal administration, and who now declined to
guarantee the temporal power of the Papacy.[1] The Austrian garrisons had lingered on, in spite of the secret exhortations of Sainte-Aulaire, and the French ministers
at Paris had more and more difficulty in keeping up their
bombastic rôle. Only a little while ago they had put on
a fierce and martial scowl, and warned Austria that she
must immediately evacuate the States of the Church, or
take the consequences: now, with equal robustiousness,
they warned her that, if she dared to interfere in Piedmont, they would let slip the Gallic war-dogs upon her.
Since there was no reason for her to meddle in Piedmont,
however, the latter threat could have served no other
purpose than to make Metternich laugh. In his own
good time, about the middle of July, he ordered the
Austrian regiments out of the Legations: in so doing, he
announced that it was the determination of Emperor
Francis to respond to any future appeals for aid that the
Holy Father might send.[2]

Austria, having with impunity bedeviled the French
pet formula, and having given notice that she would do
so again, the international phase of the Italian revolt
seemed to be concluded: it only remained for the French
Cabinet to expound the transaction in such wise as to
commend it and themselves to their fellow-countrymen.

[1] Bianchi, iii, 89.   [2] Metternich, v, 119, 124.

M. Périer, as wizard-in-chief to Louis Philippe, was the first to conjure up for the edification of the French Chamber a phantom of victory from the dispatches and blue-books which contained full evidence of the snubs, rebuffs, and defeats which his diplomacy had suffered at the hands of Metternich. "Romagna has been pacified," Périer began. "That feeble insurrection which could not liberate her was not able to drag her down with itself in its oppression. Thanks to our negotiations, useful reforms have been in part assured. What more was there to do? When our government was formed, the Italian events were already under way. We found the Duchy of Modena already occupied by the Austrians; they were already on the road to Romagna. We then promised that, even though they penetrated, they should not occupy that province. The promise made has been maintained. Italy breathes again, and but for us she would by this time be the theatre of sanguinary reactions. These are facts, gentlemen, which attest that, but for France and but for what she did, the States of the Holy See would be now covered by a foreign soldiery, by proscriptions, by confiscations. France spared Italy the most grievous consequences of an abortive attempt, and universal peace is assured."[1] Marshal Sébastiani also tried to extract glory out of insult, like the philosophical gentleman who proposed to extract sunbeams out of cucumbers. "I appeal to your consciences, to your justice," said he to the deputies, "to know if we have not fulfilled all our duties, and if the honor of France has not remained intact in the negotiations concerning Italy?" Even the King, in his speech from the throne, expatiated on the noble achievements won by his diplomacy; but Cardinal Bernetti, in republishing the royal address, gave the lie to some of its falsehoods, nor would he retract, when requested to do so by the French ambassador.[2]

[1] Bianchi, iii, 91-2. [2] Ibid, 93.

This, then, was the humiliating collapse of the bubble of non-intervention which the Orleanist ministers blew skywards, proclaiming that it should henceforth be as a sun to illumine European diplomacy. The French had neither hindered Austria's armed interference in Central Italy, nor compelled her to withdraw a day earlier than she was willing: whether their strutting policy deterred her from annexing the Legations — a dream she was supposed to cherish — is doubtful, because there is no evidence that she then deemed the time ripe for that act of aggrandizement.

The Orleans monarchy, so shuffling and uncandid, as we have seen, could wriggle out of its humiliation, but the Italian Liberals, who had staked their lives on the assumption that the principle of non-intervention would be upheld, had no evasive phrase in which to disguise their defeat, nor noble memories to sweeten their regret and inspire fresh hope. They had simply over-trusted, and they had been duped. We have no need to follow the path of the Austrian invasion which swept down their provisional governments like card-houses. An occasional resistance, a skirmish at Rimini, a last stand at Ancona, proved that the Liberal recruits did not lack bravery; but could bravery without discipline avail, when one man was pitted against five or ten? The great body of revolutionists therefore submitted, while a few score of their leaders, fearing the Pope's vengeance, took ship for Corfu, but being captured by an Austrian man-of-war, they were conveyed to Venice, and confined there for several months.

And now was witnessed the usual retinue of persecutions which follow unsuccessful rebellion. In the States of the Church, indeed, the retaliation was less severe than it would have been had not the representatives of the Great Powers been still at Rome suggesting reforms which the Papal government promised to carry out.

Amnesty was granted to all but thirty-eight of the foremost rebels, but there were many ways by which the government could show its real temper towards amnestied insurgents without directly torturing them, and these ways it employed. The police pestered the suspects with exasperating restrictions, and the Sanfedists, sure of official sympathy, renewed their bullying irritation. Above all, the Pope refused to ratify the terms to which Cardinal Benvenuti, his legate, had agreed when the rebels capitulated; his excuse being, that since the Cardinal had previously been a prisoner, any compact that he made was vitiated by the suspicion that it had been forced upon him.

In Modena the Duke signalized his restoration by a repetition of cruelties which in 1822 had horrified Italy. Several of the conspirators were condemned to death, but the sentence was executed only upon Menotti and Borelli. As Menotti was the most conspicuous victim of the revolution of 1831, so he became in the imagination, not only of the Modenese but of all Italians, its martyr-hero. The mystery which surrounded his relations with the Duke, the paradox of a tyrant joining a conspiracy of Liberals, the perfidy of the Duke, and the manliness with which Menotti died, wove legendary veils about his memory, so that it is impossible even now for the historian always to separate myth and hearsay from fact. That Francis had Menotti executed in order to preclude him from revealing momentous secrets was generally believed by his friends, and still seems probable. Henceforth, the Duchy of Modena groaned under a tyranny which left no excuse for even the most confiding Liberal to imagine that the Duke could be enticed again into the patriotic camp. The uncontested succession of Charles Albert to the throne of Piedmont, April 2, 1831, dashed forever the Duke's hope of ruling there, whilst recent events could but teach him the folly of his other dreams of power.

Parma, after Maria Louisa's return, showed a happy contrast to Modena, no one being persecuted for his complicity in the late tumult. In Piedmont, Tuscany, and the Two Sicilies, the efforts of the agitators had failed to do more than increase the anxiety, and therefore the vigilance, of the governments. The proposed invasion of Savoy, the landing of troops and munitions on the Tuscan coast, the swoop of William Pepe and his legion on Sicily, the descent of Murat's son on Naples, — all those brave schemes of the Paris Committee had to be abandoned, owing to the deceitfulness of the French government.

Yet the inhabitants of the Papal States could not, in spite of the flogging Austria had given them, reconcile themselves to defeat. Their day-dream had been too delightful to be renounced, their chagrin and misery were too keen to be borne without murmurs. They grew desperate, reckless, and, like angry children, they cared not whether they were whipped again or not. The Austrian troops had hardly been withdrawn before it became evident that the Pope's government was still too weak to preserve order. He reorganized the pontifical army; he created a body of centurions; he appealed to loyal subjects to enroll themselves in a volunteer corps; he hired two regiments of mercenaries from Switzerland, — that stud of despicable freemen, — and yet he was unable to suppress the turbulents. During the autumn of 1831 Romagna was the scene of constant broils between the Papalists and the sectaries. A Civic Guard took possession of several of the towns, and under the plea of Liberty committed outrages, and kept decent citizens of whatever party in a state of trepidation. The sectaries squabbled among themselves and manifested that they were only strong in their capacity for doing harm. The Liberals who had led the previous revolution and who had given to it a worthy character if not victory, being now in exile, the leadership inevitably fell to more violent and less disinterested men: and we are not surprised to learn that when, at the request of Cardinal Albani, who had been sent to restore order and had failed, the Austrian troops marched back into Romagna and put down this second revolt, they were welcomed by all respectable Romagnoles as the extirpators of anarchy. Then Cardinal Albani, having the foreign army to support him, proceeded to purge the country by drastic measures which recalled the severity of Rivarola.[1]

This second intervention of the Austrians revived the diplomatic controversy of the preceding spring. The French ministry, by its shuffling and treachery, had incurred the detestation of the Italian Liberals, whom it had duped, and of the French Republicans and Imperialists, who still smarted at the thought that they had been the cat's-paw for Louis Philippe's ambition. Throughout the autumn of 1831 the French ministerial policy was aimed, therefore, at conciliating the Great Powers, by assuring them that France ceded to none in her desire to uphold the temporal administration of the Pope, and at conciliating the rebellious Romagnoles, by recognizing that they had just cause for complaining: only, before they could expect France to interfere in their behalf, they must lay down their arms and submit to the Pope's authority. To which hot-and-cold advice, one of the Liberals replied: "How can confidence and submission be engendered towards a government which, after fifteen years of intolerable abuses and errors, having scarcely recovered from the consternation of all but general revolution, returns to the same rut, and repeats the same errors."[2] As the situation in the Legations grew worse, and it became evident that something more than the moral disapproval of the Great Powers was needed to bring back quiet, the anxiety of the French Cabinet in-

[1] Farini, i, 57–62. [2] Bianchi, iii, 98.

creased. On one side Périer was confronted by the fact that Austria, Russia, and Prussia secretly hated the July monarchy as the product of a revolution; if he angered them, they might declare war; on the other side, he had to reckon with a large body of Frenchmen who were eager to overturn a government which they accused of double-dealing towards them and of cowardly subservience to the Northern autocrats. After long search, the bewildered premier found an expedient which he hoped would satisfy every one. Foreseeing that the Pope would be forced to call for aid from Austria, he acknowledged that such intervention would be both the most legitimate and expeditious method. "But, on the other hand," he continued, "we must not forget that, if France ought to respect that legitimate influence which Austria may exercise in Italy, she ought not, therefore, to allow that influence to become excessive. Should it happen, then, that the Imperial forces were again obliged to occupy the Papal States, French troops also will appear there, if only, so to speak, as a mere formality. A battalion or two of our soldiers would be sent to Ancona; they would suffice to attain the simple moral result we have in view. So small a corps could not arouse just fears of wars against any one."[1] When the Austrian ambassador pointed out that there was a radical difference between intervention when requested by the legitimate sovereign of the Papal States and such masked for intervention as the French minister proposed, Périer was unconvinced. "At any rate," said he, "we shall enter the Pope's dominions together with you. The honor of France demands it."

Sainte-Aulaire feigned surprise when the news reached Rome that the Austrians had reoccupied the Legations. He protested to Cardinal Bernetti, the Papal Secretary, but the latter threw the responsibility on Cardinal Albani, who, he said, had followed his own judgment in

[1] Bianchi, iii, 101.

calling in the Emperor's troops. Then ensued a clash of intrigues between the French and the Austrian agents at the Holy See. The former besought the Pope to make an official request for, or at least to sanction, the French occupation of Ancona, because, he said, it was not just that the head of the Catholic world should allow Austria alone the privilege of guaranteeing his inviolability. Metternich's man parried guile with guile: he told the Pope that the French were, at heart, revolutionists; that it was their collusion which had promoted the insurrection of 1831; and that, even granting that they were now sincere in their professions of friendship for the Holy See, their entrance into Ancona might kindle a general war, of which the Pope, the Vicar of the Prince of Peace, would thus be the indirect originator. In this diplomatic parry-and-thrust the Austrian fencer excelled his French rival, and the Pope stolidly refused to acknowledge the necessity of French interference.[1]

But the French Cabinet had ventured too far to retreat; its own existence, perhaps also that of the Orleanist monarchy, depended upon Périer's decision to risk the high-handed stroke he had long threatened. So he ordered a French squadron to proceed immediately from Toulon to Ancona. On February 22, 1832, the French vessels entered the latter port, and during the night disembarked eighteen hundred soldiers. The French captains, Gallois and Combès, called upon the Papal commander to allow them to occupy the citadel, as had been agreed, they declared, between their government and the Holy See. The commander replied that he had heard of no such agreement, but, being threatened with a cannonade, he yielded. Accordingly, on February 23. the Papal flag was lowered and the French tricolor hoisted, and Captain Gallois, whilst his soldiers mingled with the populace of the town and taught them how to sing the

---

[1] Bianchi, iii. 105–7; Gualterio, i. 106–8.

"Marseillaise" after the vehement fashion of '93, set about inditing a flamboyant proclamation. In the hands of men accustomed to use the sword the pen is seldom mightier than the sword; Gallois's manifesto bristled with indiscretions that might have stung Austria to declare war; but fortunately, Cubières, a political agent who had been dispatched by the French government, reached Ancona in time to prevent the placarding of the lively captain's effusion, although copies of it got abroad among the foreign ministers, to incense the Pope and Metternich, and to cause Périer additional embarrassment.[1]

As soon as the fact of the French occupation was known at Rome, the Papal Secretary protested against it. He informed the French ambassador that the only reparation possible was the immediate recall of an expedition which, in lawlessness and effrontery, had had no equal since the days of the Saracen corsairs. But Sainte-Aulaire had no authority to repudiate the display of vigor on which, as he well knew, the very life of his government hung, and he therefore apologized for the rudeness of Gallois and Combès, without offering to give up the positions they had seized. For a while he insisted that he had honestly believed that the Pope would consent to the intervention, but when Cardinal Bernetti, by referring to the minutes of the notes that had passed between them, proved that there was no ground for this belief, he allowed himself to be made the scapegoat of the Cabinet at Paris, and took upon himself the blame for the misunderstanding.[2]

Metternich, meanwhile, probed the intentions of the Great Powers in the hope of discovering them united for war. England, then in travail with her Reform Bill, declared that she sympathized with the French expedi-

[1] Bianchi, iii, 108-10; Poggi, ii, 16-7; Farini, i, 62; Gualterio, i, 110.
[2] Bianchi, iii, 117 seq.

tion, but it was evident that she would take no active part in a Continental quarrel; Prussia announced that, so long as the conflict was restricted to Italy, she would remain neutral, but if it spread North of the Alps, she would consult her interests before choosing her allies; only Russia was willing to follow immediately Austria's lead. In this absence of harmony, Metternich, mindful of the fact that a war with France would precipitate a mortal struggle between Autocracy and the revolutionary elements of all Europe, prudently decided to treat the Ancona affair as too trivial to warrant an appeal to arms. But he gave orders for the Austrian forces in Italy to be increased, and to be held on the alert against any attempt of the French to advance beyond Ancona, and he urged the Papal government not to retract a single jot of its protest, nor to pause in its demand that the French should withdraw forthwith.[1] Towards the French Cabinet he assumed a condescending attitude, as of an all-wise master of diplomacy, who criticises the blunders of a novice whom he might punish if he did not prefer to laugh at him. He knew that sarcasm will often dissolve obstacles which it would be dangerous to blow up with gunpowder. So he pointed out how easy it was for inexperienced diplomats to be tumbled headlong into a mire of inconsistencies, merely because they gave the rein to a hobby: only last year, for instance, the French had taken the world to witness that they would do battle in behalf of their chosen principle, non-intervention; and now they themselves are violating that principle by occupying Ancona. They excuse themselves for this folly, by declaring that they wish to hasten the evacuation of the Papal States by the Austrians; but the Austrians, who were just on the point of going, will now remain. M. Périer will find, Metternich said to Marshal Maison, the French ambassador at Vienna, that he has "lent his

[1] Bianchi. iii. 114 *sq*.

countenance to a farce; to go to Ancona merely to retreat from it immediately is an error, and if in order to shift the blame off his own shoulders he were ever to allow himself to make it appear that our departure was due to the appearance of a French expeditionary force, he would compel us to give his statements a public disclaimer. . . . You will have to avow yourselves the friends of revolt and the patrons of anarchy."[1]

M. Périer, however, who was working to save his own ministry, having long since dropped his pretense of being actuated by sympathy for the Italians, took Metternich's sarcasm without wincing, nay, almost with gratitude, as soon as he saw that there would be no war. Let diplomatic experts laugh at his comic-opera seizure of Ancona, his glory-loving countrymen had taken it seriously as an exploit worthy of the Grand Nation; and so long as the deed had dazzled the French, he could afford to make lavish apology to Metternich and the irate Pope. He refused to withdraw his troops, — that would have been fatal to his prospects at home, — but he recalled and reprimanded the over-zealous Gallois and Combès; he agreed that France should defray all the expenses of the garrison, that the Papal banner should again float over the citadel of Ancona, that the Papal authorities in the town itself should in no wise be disturbed, and that the garrison should return to France whenever the Austrian troops had evacuated the States of the Church. Pope Gregory made a virtue of necessity and consented that the French should temporarily remain; or, as he expressed it in pious verbiage, he wished to set the world an example of mildness, one of the noblest characteristics of divine religion, and to avert any wrangle which might plunge Europe in war.[2]

Thus ended the Ancona affair, which served Louis Philippe and his Cabinet as a ruse whereby they fooled a

[1] Metternich, v, 209. [2] Bianchi, iii, 128.

part of the French people, but which gave France no real influence in Italy and did not contribute to the improvement of the political lot of the Italians. During the first few weeks of the French occupation, the Italian Liberals and conspirators had, indeed, been encouraged to hope that their deliverance was at hand; for the French soldiers talked bravely of driving the Austrians out of their country, and French agents went about instigating rebellion: but as soon as Périer came to an agreement with the Papal government, the Italians discovered that these proceedings were unauthorized, and thereafter the garrison was forbidden to associate with the natives.

Our survey of this diplomatic intrigue would be incomplete, if we failed to note that it has been asserted that the French government, before dispatching the expedition to Ancona, secretly secured the Pope's consent, and that the indignation which the seizure of that town roused at Rome, and the protests of Cardinal Bernetti, had been preconcerted with the French prime minister, and therefore did not alarm him. There is no reason to suppose that the Roman hierarchs, devoted as they were to cunning and deceit, would shrink from such an artifice through any scruples of conscience, or that they would play their rôle clumsily; but we are skeptical of Périer's ability to carry through so delicate a sham without betraying himself; for we have seen how quickly all his other designs were penetrated and balked by Metternich. There was indeed a sufficient motive for the Pope's collusion in so subtle a stratagem: ever since the Congress of Vienna, the Roman Curia had suspected that Austria planned to annex the Legations, and if, being now in virtual possession of these provinces, and being emboldened by the timidity of the French the year before, she refused to give them up, what means had the Curia for expelling her? To implicate some other Powers — and France was the most convenient — in the defense of the integrity of the

Roman State, would be a shrewd policy; for even if France and Austria came to blows, the Papacy would have a good chance of keeping her provinces in any settlement after a war. This explanation does not lack plausibility, although perhaps it will never be established beyond question.[1] Whatever the wiles adopted, the outcome of them all was that Austria garrisoned the Legations, and France Ancona, until 1838, and that the burdens of Pope Gregory's subjects grew heavier as the years dragged on.

This third revolution marks the close of the first phase of Italy's long struggle for emancipation. The Italians had learned by their failures in 1820 and 1821 that their chief adversary was Austria, and not their local princes. These they had dislodged with but little effort, but Austria, the irresistible factor of the Holy Alliance, had come and replaced them. Evidently the Italians could not reasonably hope for freedom so long as Austria — whom they could not overwhelm by arms, nor persuade by arguments, nor soften by entreaties — guarded the Peninsula. "We make the maintenance of public tranquillity in Italy a question of our own existence,"[2] said Metternich, who meant by "tranquillity" a lethargy so deep that it precluded even dreams of political reforms. But through their exiled brethren, the Italian Liberals had contacts with the Liberals of the rest of Europe; they felt that their cause was no longer isolated, but international, and they were electrified when their French confederates, having overturned the Bourbons, set up a monarchy whose watchword was "non-intervention." With France eager, as they supposed, to enforce that principle, and with England in sympathy with France, the Italians deemed that they had a clear field in which to try conclusions with their local tyrants, and that Austria would not

[1] Poggi, ii. 17-8; Gualterio, i. 110-11.
[2] Metternich, v, 258.

dare to interfere. The ease with which they captured Parma, Modena, and the Papal States almost to the gates of Rome, proved that they had not underestimated the weakness of their rulers or the impotence of the governments against which they had so long protested. But then came the terrible disillusion: the Orleanist monarchy deserted them; Austria again fulfilled her abominable mission; and the revolution collapsed in the moment of victory. The Italian insurgents thus learned that, as they had no official recognition, so they could not bind a recognized government like that of France by any covenant which it would be ashamed to break. They were international outlaws, who had not the power to hold any lawful ministry to its agreement with them. Disappointed and duped, they could lay to heart that sober warning which Washington gave his countrymen in his Farewell Address: "There can be no greater error than to expect or calculate upon real favors from nation to nation."

But this revolution of 1831 taught the Italians not only how illusory and uncertain was their hope of foreign assistance; it taught them also the folly of seeking to make an accomplice of a native prince by flattering his ambition. The Duke of Modena, like Francis of Naples in 1820, and Charles Albert of Piedmont in 1821, had failed them: it was time to abandon the expectation that princes bred and nurtured by Autocracy would turn against their dam. You may tame a lion's cub and have him for your pet, but at the first smell of blood he will spring upon you; for instinct may long be checked, but cannot be destroyed. This revolution gave further evidence of the underlying weakness of the entire fabric of Italian conspiracy. The cause lacked a centre; it lacked a head: it still beat about ineffectually for a unifying ideal: it was still entangled in secret mummeries, and distracted by local feuds. These conditions, as I have often stated, belong to every large conspiracy whose aim is not summed up and personified in one leader to whose authority all defer; but the inherited divisions of the Italians only increased the difficulty of bringing harmony out of elements so discordant. We ought perhaps to be surprised that the plotters in Modena, Parma, and the Legations could so far sink their mutual differences as to exhibit, if but for a moment, a show of concord on the surface, rather than that they failed to make concord permanent.

Finally, these events of 1831-2 warned Europe that, after fifteen years of oppression, Italy's desire for freedom had not been crushed. There was no longer an excuse for attributing her periodic rebellions to the machinations of a few evil-minded or visionary men: the ills she suffered were intolerable, — they must be cured before Europe could expect to behold her tranquil. It was not against a temporary or local wrong that she cried out, but against the entire system which had been thrust upon her. In 1820 Naples, in 1821 Piedmont, and now Emilia and the Papal States, had risen; Lombardy and Venetia would have been the first to revolt had not their conquerors been too strong for even desperation to assail; only Tuscany seemed comparatively submissive, but she, too, though she uttered no complaint, knew that her peace was not freedom. Henceforth, no one could say that the Italians in every part of their country had not put on record by protest of word or hand their irreconcilable hatred of the bondage to which Europe had condemned them. Nevertheless, their protests, though tacitly admitted to be just, were disregarded, and the European Powers thought that they had rid themselves of the irritating Italian question by aiding the Italian despots to stuff again into Italy's mouth the gag she had wrenched away. Nervous monarchs and ministers would at least secure themselves against noise. The immediate gainer by the insurrection and intrigue was, as usual, Austria.

The Papal government, which, under Pius VII and Leo XII, had struggled to keep her at bay, now, under Gregory XVI, implored her aid. So Metternich, by patiently waiting, was acknowledged to be indispensable to the temporal existence of the Papacy, as he had formerly shown that his protection was indispensable to Ferdinand at Naples, and to Charles Felix at Turin. And he had succeeded, without striking a blow, in humiliating the only Continental Cabinet which, since Waterloo, had dared to oppose his autocratic policy in Italy. He had made the Orleanist monarchy ridiculous, and tossed its "principle of non-intervention" into the rubbish heap of Time.

BOOK THIRD.

WHILE GREGORY XVI PONTIFICATES.

> Di' oggimai che la Chiesa di Roma,
> Per confondere in sè due reggimenti,
> Cade nel fango, e sè brutta e la soma.
> DANTE, *Purgatorio*, xvi, 127-9.

CHAPTER I.

CONSPIRACY GETS ITS LEADER.

THE Revolution of 1830, ineffectual as it seemed to its promoters, was yet most significant. It failed in Italy and Poland, in Spain and Portugal; it created a mongrel monarchy, neither Absolute nor Constitutional, in France; only in Belgium did it attain its immediate purpose. Nevertheless, if we look beneath the surface, we see that it was one of those epoch-marking events of which we can say, "Things cannot be again what until just now they were." Constitutionalism, the ideal of 1789, which Napoleon abandoned for his selfish ambition, and which the Congress of Vienna thought to strangle, had risen up, not yet triumphant, but so hardy as to warn the Autocrats that they could not destroy it; and they tolerated it in France, rather than risk a decisive encounter with the demons of Republicanism and Anarchy which they saw behind it. The July monarchy was thus a compromise between the Absolutists and the Republicans: the former angry at having been forced to concede anything, the latter angry at not having gained more. Louis Philippe, with a dynasty to nurture, belonged at heart with the Autocrats, but having also his own crown to preserve, he coquetted with the Liberals. He adopted the policy of the '*just milieu*,' or golden mean, — "that doctrine," said Metternich, "which always couples a vast amount of thoughtlessness with a grain of reason;" and for nearly eighteen years he subjected France to a reign of makeshifts and disingenuousness which typified the confusion and the ebb-and-flow of the opposing forces in Europe during that period. He was shrewd enough to conceal his inmost preferences; he assumed the dress and manners of a democratic age, letting himself pass for a Citizen King and sparing no pains to ingratiate himself with the bourgeoisie. The aristocracy of the Old Régime was based on Blood; Napoleon made Talent the cornerstone of his aristocracy; since 1815 Money has been often substituted for Blood or Brains in repairing the crumbling Chinese Wall of European Aristocracy. And this is not strange; because Commercialism has been the dominant trait of our century, and it is as natural that the great social prize in a commercial age should fall to millionaires, as that, in a military age, they should fall to soldiers, or in a theologic age to churchmen. In patronizing his merchants and bankers, Louis Philippe merely acknowledged the power behind every modern throne, — the power which makes and unmakes Cabinets and gives or withholds the subsidies of war. The modern Temple of Janus is the Exchange.

Based on contradictions which were manifesting themselves everywhere, but which were most apparent in France, Louis Philippe's government existed in a constant state of unstable equilibrium: like a tilting boulder which a child can cause to vibrate, but which the mountaineers refrain from disturbing, lest it roll down the slope and crash into their village below.

In Italy, however, after the suppression of the disorderly Legations, the local tyrants and Austria redoubled their efforts to foresee and prevent all change. Round the Peninsula they drew a line of quarantine across which the dangerous ideas of progress and reform might not pass; they strove to disinfect every thought that came from abroad; they were swift to isolate every subject in whom they detected symptoms of political disease. None knew better than themselves, however, their inability to cure the predisposition to contagion; still, they were unprepared to see the epidemic take a new and more threatening form.

The late risings in the Duchies and Legations had brought no comfort to the conspirators, but had taught them, on the contrary, how ineffectual, how hopeless was the method of the secret societies. After more than fifteen years they had not gained an inch; they had only learned that their rulers would concede nothing, and that Austria, their great adversary, had staked her existence on maintaining thraldom in Italy. Innumerable small outbursts and three revolutions had ended in the death of hundreds and in the imprisonment or proscription of thousands of victims. The company of old leaders had been diminished after each failure, until now but few remained, and these were silent through discouragement or prudence. Above all, the inherent weakness of the sects had been proved by their inability to coöperate, by their lack of one central aim, by their hesitation, and by their mutual distrust. Sectional rivalry, the ancestral bane of Italy, had been in part allayed, but sectarian rivalry had too often replaced it. In this last revolution we saw, for instance, how the Romagnoles had refused to act in concert with Menotti, and we might have seen, had we examined in detail the collapse of that revolution, how those same Romagnoles treated Zucchi and his six hundred fugitives from Modena as foreigners and not as allies. Nor could the fact be blinked, that the conspiracy had failed to take root among the masses. Its promoters were soldiers and middle-class men, and a small body of the most intelligent nobles, — doubtless the best element then at hand, but too full of the doctrines of the Napoleonic period, and too much given to theory and reminiscence. Where the lower classes had joined the sects, as at Naples, they cast over all the Liberal undertakings the suspicion that violence and plunder, rather than a high principle, were their objects. That the revolutionists had so easily won their first skirmish in Naples, Piedmont, and Central Italy was due less to their own strength than to their enemy's weakness; but where had they shown the harmony and the wisdom necessary for building a better government and a strong, on the ruins of those they had cast down? Did not the brief respite between success and disaster suffice in every case to prove that their inexperience, if not their dissensions, would have prevented them, even without the inexorable veto of Austria? The forces of Liberalism lay over Italy, like the waters of a freshet in the hollows of a meadow, and they were growing stagnant because there was no channel in which they could be united and drawn off.

Just when conspiracy, through repeated failures, was thus discredited, there arose a leader so strong and unselfish, so magnetic and patient and zealous, that by him, if by any one, conspiracy might be guided to victory. This leader, the Great Conspirator, was Joseph Mazzini, one of the half dozen supreme influences in European politics during the nineteenth century, whose career will interest posterity as long as it is concerned at all in our epoch of transition. For just as Metternich was the High-Priest of the Old Régime, so Mazzini was the Prophet of a Social Order more just, more free, more spiritual than any the world has known. He was an Idealist who would hold no parley with temporizers, an enthusiast whom half-concessions could not beguile; and so he came to be decried as a fanatic or a visionary. This is the fate of those idealists who would act as well as preach. Your Kant, or Emerson, or Darwin may publish, as from a serene height, the laws of philosophy, morals, and science, and withhold themselves from the vexations of debate, in which the personality of the thinker may long distract attention from his thoughts. But the social reformer cannot divorce thought from action. The abuses which block the way of the truth he would see prevail must be attacked forthwith; it will not suffice merely to utter his message and leave it to time; society is deaf, and he must reiterate his doctrines; society is dull, conservative, timid, he must beat upon it, rouse it, fill it with unrest and shame, till it will no longer endure to uphold the bad, when good and better beckon it. Undoubtedly, physicians a century hence will have discovered remedies for many ills that now seem incurable, but this does not exonerate a physician to-day from trying to relieve the patients who appeal to him. And so the reformer can hope to bring to pass his Utopia only by removing present evils. His ideal is vast, his deeds can be only partial and restricted; and the world, comparing his promise with his performance, will pity or sneer. In judging Mazzini we must discriminate between what he aspired to do and what he actually accomplished: his acts are recorded, and they can be estimated; but a century or two may still be required to decide whether his ideal was a mere dream, or a true prophecy of the nobler order to which the world shall attain. What he proposed was clearly unrealizable at the time when he proposed it: but the question for the future to answer is, When Society shall have advanced far beyond its present condition, will it adopt the Mazzinian pattern? In so far as we shall have to deal with Mazzini in the period we are considering, we shall usually see in him the man of action, fighting for a definite and immediate end: it is all the more necessary, therefore, to remember that behind the man of action was always the idealist to whom the fact achieved seemed mean in comparison with the splendor of his aspiration.

Mazzini was born in Genoa in 1808. His father was a lawyer of repute, his mother a woman of tenderness and intelligence. Her influence over their son was deep and lasting, for he was so frail a boy that he had to be kept at home, where his physical weakness conduced to a rapid and precocious intellectual growth. He read and thought beyond his years, and he had an almost feminine organization of nerves and emotions. One day, in his twelfth year, when he and his mother were walking, — it was just after the collapse of the Revolution of 1821, — "a tall black-bearded man, with a severe and energetic countenance," approached and held out a white handkerchief towards them, merely saying, "For the refugees of Italy." That request burned into the boy's soul. "That day," he wrote long afterward, "was the first in which a confused idea presented itself to my mind, — I will not say of country or liberty, but an idea that we Italians could and therefore ought to struggle for the liberty of our country."[1] Wherever he went, the lad saw the faces of the refugees, he heard that plea, and the thought that he, too, must bear his part in his country's redemption never forsook him. His health improved, and in due time he was matriculated into the university, to fit himself for his father's profession. At the outset, he says, "in the midst of the noisy tumultuous life of the students around me, I was sombre and absorbed, and appeared like one suddenly grown old. I childishly determined to dress always in black, fancying myself in mourning for my country."[2] But soon he found among his comrades friends, few but devoted: they discussed together the largest questions, after the manner of generous and hopeful

---

[1] Mazzini: *Life and Writings* (London, 1890). i. 2.
[2] *Ibid.* 4.

collegians; they formed little groups, to smuggle in and circulate prohibited books; they wrote essays, and longed for a periodical that would publish them. Already, we see, Mazzini gave only a perfunctory attention to the law; he neglected his lessons to read Dante, and he felt within him the desire and the ability to win renown in literature. Those were the days of the war between the Classicists and the Romanticists, and that Mazzini and his young, enthusiastic companions were all Romanticists needs hardly to be said; but I must quote his own words in order to show that he, at least, though but eighteen years old, saw how much was involved in what seemed to many but a literary squabble.

"The first school," he says, "composed of Roman Arcadians and Della Crusca academicians, professors, and pedants, persisted in producing cold, laborious imitations, without life, spirit, or purpose; the second, founding their new literature on no other basis than their individual fancy, lost themselves in fantastic mediaeval legends, unfelt hymns to the Virgin, and unreal metrical despair, or any other whim of the passing hour, which might present itself to their minds: intolerant of every tyranny, but ignorant also of the sacredness of the law which governs art as well as every other thing. And it is a part of this law, that all true art must either sum up and express the life of a closing epoch, or announce and proclaim the life of the epoch destined to succeed it. True art is not the caprice of this or that individual; it is a solemn page either of history or prophecy; and when — as always in *Dante, and occasionally in Byron — it combines and harmonizes this double mission, it reaches the highest summit of power. Now, amongst us Italians, no other than the prophetic form of art was possible. For three centuries we had been deprived of all spontaneous individual life, and our existence had been that of forgetful slaves, deriving all things from the foreigner. Art, therefore, could only arise again amongst us to inscribe a maledictory epitaph upon those three centuries, and sing the canticle of the future.

"But to do this, it was necessary to interrogate the slumbering, latent, and unconscious life of our people; to lay the hand upon the half-frozen heart of the nation; to count its rare pulsations, and reverently learn therefrom the purpose and duty of Italian genius. The special bias and tendency of individual inspiration required to be nourished by the aspiration of the collective life of Italy; even as flowers, the poetry of the earth, derive their separate variety of tint and beauty from a soil which is common to all. But the collective life of Italy was uncertain and indefinite; it lacked a centre, oneness of ideal, and all regular and organized mode of manifestation. Art, therefore, could reveal itself among us by fits, in isolated and volcanic outbursts. It was incapable of revealing itself in regular and progressive development, similar to the gradual evolution of vegetable life in the New World, wherein the separate trees continue to mingle their branches, until they form the gigantic unity of the forest. Without a country and without liberty, we might, perhaps, produce some prophets of art, but no vital art. Therefore it was better for us to consecrate our lives to the solution of the problem, — *Are we to have a country?* and turn at once to the political question. If we were successful, the art of Italy would bloom and flourish over our graves. . . . The ideas awakened in April, 1821, were still burning within me, and determined my renunciation of the career of literature for the more direct path of political action. And this was my first great sacrifice. A thousand visions of historical dramas and romances floated before my mental eye, — artistic images that caressed my spirit, as visions of gentle maidens soothe the soul of the lonely-hearted. The natural bias of my mind was very different from that which has been forced upon me by the times in which I have lived, and the shame of our degradation."[1]

What is there in life comparable to the devotion of a young soul to whom the Spirit has intrusted a mission which shall be dearer to him than ease or fame, than friends' or parents' or woman's love? That command draws him with the majesty and beauty of truth; from beyond space and time, from Eternity, it shines upon him, always new, yet as old, as unchangeable as Eternity itself; it sanctifies him as the champion, not of a personal design, but of a great cause; and it endues him, being young, with unquestioning faith and the bloom and buoyancy of hope. Mazzini, having thus early beheld the message written in radiance upon his soul, renounced all to obey that. He now wrote articles which, although ostensibly only criticisms of books, were more and more impregnated by his political ideal. They brought him the acquaintance of patriots who, like himself, cherished the hope of making literature the vehicle of their political education; and then the journals in which they were published were suppressed by the too wary government. Mazzini joined the Carbonari, not without suspecting that, under their complex symbolism and hierarchical mysteries they concealed a fatal lack of harmony, decision, and faith; but, he says, they "were men who, defying alike excommunication and capital punishment, had the persistent energy ever to persevere and to weave a fresh web each time the old one was broken. And this was enough to induce me to join my name and labor to theirs."[2] After his initiation, which was simpler than usual, a friend congratulated him on his having been spared the usual terrific ordeal. Mazzini smiled, whereupon the friend asked him what he would have done had he been required, as others had been, to fire off in his own ear a pistol which had previously been loaded before

[1] Mazzini, i. 6-9.   [2] Ibid. 14.

his eyes. "I replied that I should have refused," Mazzini answered, "telling the initiators that either there was some valve in the interior of the pistol into which the bullet fell, — in which case the affair was a farce unworthy of both of us, — or the bullet had really remained in the stock; and in that case it struck me as somewhat absurd to call upon a man to fight for his country, and make it his first duty to blow out the few brains God had vouchsafed to him."[1] As he became better acquainted with Carbonarism, his conviction grew stronger that no permanent good could be achieved by it.

The approach of the revolution in France now redoubled the activity of the Piedmontese conspirators. Mazzini went on a secret mission to Tuscany, and shortly after his return to Genoa he was betrayed by a treacherous informer to the police. "Your son has a bad habit of thinking too much, and of taking solitary walks at night," was the remark made by the police to Mazzini's father, when he asked why the young man had been arrested. For many months he was confined in an upper cell of the fortress of Savona, from the little grated window of which he could look out upon only "the sea and the sky, — two symbols of the infinite and, except the Alps, the sublimest things in nature." That imprisonment at Savona was to Mazzini what the year's concealment in the Wartburg had been to Luther, — a period for self-examination whereby he classified the motives which had hitherto led him, and deduced from them the creed which he was to profess through life. The seeds of all the principles, which during more than forty years he preached and reiterated in many forms, had all taken root by his twenty-second year, when the door of his fortress-prison closed behind him.

Mazzini's political and social doctrines had their source in morals. Throughout and above all worlds he acknow-

[1] Mazzini, i. 10.

ledged one Supreme Unity, — God. Catholicism, he declared, was dead; it could no longer satisfy either the devout heart or the reasoning mind. "I felt that authority, true, righteous, and holy authority, — the search after which, whether conscious or not, is the fact of our human life, and which is only irrationally denied by those who confound it with its false semblance or shadow, and imagine they have abolished God himself, when they have but abolished an idol, — I felt that authority had vanished and become extinct in Europe, and that for the reason no power of initiative existed in any of the peoples of Europe."[1] To correspond to the divine Unity, he argued, there must be unity among mankind: the human race, distributed among so many peoples, various in hue and intelligence and faith, is yet interpenetrated and inclosed by a common humanity; those differences of feature and belief are only external, as of vessels, large or small, crooked or upright, on which diverse forms have been modeled or patterns painted, but all containing, in greater or smaller quantities, the same holy water, the same divine essence. Scanning history, Mazzini discerned that the Past had sufficed to evoke the individual from the brute shapeless mass; here and there, in different lands and ages, a few great men had risen to be the wonder and example of their fellows; but the purpose of creation is not attained in the development of a few supreme men, who live isolated from, and often at the expense of, the multitude. They are really but the first to emerge from chaos: all must follow them till chaos is blotted out. It is the sum of all the individuals, and not the value of a particular unit, to enhance which progress strains. Each tribe, each nation, is a larger individual, and just as any man singly must have freedom to exercise the powers which belong to him alone, so must a nation be free. But true freedom does not consist in selfish

[1] Mazzini, i, 36.

license to act regardless of the profit and needs of others, but in coöperation with others, deriving strength from them, and repaying it, from the store peculiar to each.

"All are needed by each one;
Nothing is good or fair alone."

The French Revolution proclaimed the Rights of Man; it warned a world in which a little group of sovereigns, nobles, and priests were masters, and all the others were slaves, that every man, however humble, has an indefeasible right to his own person and life. In brief, the French Revolution was the assertion of Individualism, which hereditary despots and privileged aristocrats had for centuries ignored or striven to repress. But Individualism is only a corner-stone on which true civilization — a society at once just and enlightened — is to be raised: above the Rights of Man are the Duties of Man, which bind the individual to the community, and teach him that his private welfare depends upon the general welfare, and that he best serves himself who serves his fellows best. Thus we rise from the plane of mere legality, which is selfish and only zealous for its own, to the sphere of morals, where the individual renounces his partial good for the sake of that general and inclusive good, wherein, if he but look deep enough, he shall see his own real prosperity. But this is as true for nations as for each several citizen; since a nation is only a larger family, and in the same way that all the families of a city make up that city, so all the nations of the earth make up the human race. Hitherto, there has been enmity among them; many have not yet reached the level of legality; none has adopted morality to be the guide of all its dealings with its neighbors; nevertheless, the solidarity of the race cannot be denied, though as yet we recognize it chiefly by negative signs. We perceive that when one nation injures another, whether by war or by commercial selfishness, all are injured; the gain that comes from unjust victory is illusive, — the robber has his gold, but at the expense of integrity; the robbed is deprived of his purse but not of his character. Servitude debases both master and slave. But this very reaction and interrelation of harm proves the underlying unity of mankind; did it not exist, the wrongs done in one hemisphere would not affect the inhabitants in the other; and since this reciprocity inheres in international evils, it must inhere in international benefits; unselfishness between one nation and another must ennoble both. To replace enmity by friendship, greed by generosity, mutual suspicion by trustfulness, and the desire to injure by the desire to help; to feel common obligations and the joy of a common service; to be suffused and quickened by the spirit which flows through all mankind, rather than to stand apart and rely upon the fitful currents of selfishness, — these should be the ideals, these are the conditions of health and progress, of the race not less than of the individual. And when Collective Humanity shall have reached this altitude, then, and not till then, can it fulfil its mission, and rise to achievements which now transcend the visions of the enthusiast and the poet's dream.

Little did the jailer of Savona suspect that the young prisoner, whom he locked in that upper cell between sky and sea, was entertaining in his solitude by day and night such companions as these thoughts: yet it was even so. Mazzini, however, could not rest in abstractions; he could not be satisfied merely to fondle in imagination that enchanting prospect, or to give his creed lip-service only. He felt the zealot's need of doing, and as he had the gift peculiar to the Italians of conceiving vastly and expressing vividly, he set him to apply his philosophy to the immediate needs of his country. "We *could*, and therefore we *ought to*, struggle," was the conviction he could not shake off. But how struggle? and for what? For independence, for liberty, and for unity. Italy could not take her place among the nations until she was independent of her foreign masters; but even though she expelled these, she might still be under the dominion of native autocrats,—therefore she must be free as well as independent; still, liberty would fail to shed its full blessing upon her, unless she were united,—therefore a federation of free Italian States would not suffice; there must be a complete union of all the Italians, before the nation could enjoy a life at once national and individual. So Mazzini adopted Republican and Unitarian principles as the bases of his system. He would have no compromise with monarchy; the tendency of the modern world being, he perceived, towards republicanism. Even were a monarchy, in spite of local jealousy and foreign interference, established in Italy, it could be only temporary; in a little while a second revolution would be necessary to create the inevitable republic. He would not deal with paltering diplomacy, that servile instrument which kings used to hide their weakness and delay their fall. Only a republic could unite all popular sentiments; federalism would subject Italy, as Switzerland was subjected, to foreign influence, revive petty feuds, "divide the great national arena into a number of smaller arenas, and by thus opening a path for every paltry ambition, become a source of aristocracy."

Having thus clearly defined his aim, Mazzini proceeded to consider the method best fitted for attaining it. The open propaganda of his Republican and Unitarian doctrines was of course impossible; it must be carried on by a secret organization. But he was disgusted with the existing secret societies: they lacked harmony, they lacked faith, they had no distinct purpose; their Masonic mummeries were childish and farcical; their irresponsible government had led to disunion and defeat; they had been now too rash and now too dilatory; they had been nurseries for the criminal, the selfish, and the vindictive, instead of for the patriotic alone; they had, at most, been able to agitate, but not to act. Therefore, Mazzini would have none of them; he would organize a new secret society, and call it *Young Italy*, whose principles should be plainly understood by every one of its members.

It was to be composed of men under forty, in order to secure the most energetic and disinterested members, and to avoid the influence of older men, who, trained by the past generation, were not in touch with the aspirations and needs of the new. It was to awaken the People, the bone and sinew of the nation; whereas the earlier sects had relied too much on the upper and middle classes, whose traditions and interests were either too aristocratic or too commercial. Roman Catholicism had ceased to be spiritual; it no longer purified and uplifted the hearts of the Italians; the educated, if they submitted to it, did so from custom, and not from faith; the ignorant accepted it blindly, and their superstitious worship debased their character. But without a religion which should be real and elevating, which should regenerate their morals and inspire in them a deep and imperative sense of duty, the Italians could not be led to a permanent political regeneration. Young Italy aimed, therefore, to substitute for the mediaeval dogmas and patent idolatries of Rome a religion based on Reason, and so simple as to be within the comprehension of the humblest peasant. One God above, and below mankind through which He embodies the Infinite Nature in the Finite; all men His creatures and His children, — therefore, all brothers, in each of whom there is some spark of His divine essence: God to be worshiped freely and directly, without the interposition of saints, and empty rituals, and arrogant priests, — to be worshiped, moreover, in men's deeds and not in mere words, and to be worshiped best by building up a noble, reverent, and unselfish character, which, ever expanding, shall afford a dwelling vaster and yet more vast for Love and Virtue. By such simple yet universal tenets, affirmed rather than argued, Mazzini hoped to arouse in his countrymen that religious sense which apprehends duty, and is at once the seat of a rational faith and the source of worthy deeds.

Recognizing in this fashion the elemental need of morals, and providing for disseminating a knowledge of them, Mazzini elaborated the political creed of Young Italy. Education and insurrection were the two means to be employed. "Education," he said, "must ever be directed to teach by example, word, and pen the necessity of insurrection. Insurrection, whenever it can be realized, must be so conducted as to render it a means of national education. . . . Convinced that Italy is strong enough to free herself without external help; that, in order to found a nationality, it is necessary that the feeling and consciousness of a nationality should exist; and that it can never be created by any revolution, however triumphant, if achieved by foreign arms; convinced, moreover, that every insurrection that looks abroad for assistance must remain dependent upon the state of things abroad, and can therefore never be certain of victory, — Young Italy is determined that while it will ever be ready to profit by the favorable course of events abroad, it will neither allow the character of the insurrection nor the choice of the movement to be governed by them."[1] Insurrection must lead to revolution, upon the successful termination of which "every authority will bow down before the National Council, the sole source of authority in the State." The true method of warfare for all nations desirous of emancipating themselves from a foreign yoke is by guerrilla bands, which supply the want of a regular army, call the greatest number of elements into the field, and yet may be sustained by the smallest number. This method

[1] Mazzini, i. 106-8.

"forms the military education of the people and consecrates every foot of the native soil by the memory of some warlike deed;" it "opens a field of activity for every local capacity, forces the enemy into an unaccustomed method of battle; avoids the evil consequences of a general defeat; secures the national war from the risk of treason, and has the advantage of not confining it within any defined and determinate basis of operations. . . . The national army, recruited with all possible solicitude, and organized with all possible care, will complete the work begun by the war of organization."[1] Every member of Young Italy, therefore, was bidden to provide himself with a gun and a dagger; the colors of the society were white, red, and green; the banner bore on one side the words, "Liberty, Equality, Humanity," on the other, "Unity, Independence." "God and People" was the watchword which summed up the Mazzinian system.

There were two degrees in the society, the "affiliators" and the "affiliated," and in order to prevent widespread treachery it was divided into groups of ten, only one member of each ten being cognizant of the members of the next group. The novice, duly informed of the purposes of Young Italy, took his oath "in the name of God and of Italy: in the name of all the martyrs of the holy Italian cause who have fallen beneath foreign and domestic tyranny: by the duties which bind me to the land wherein God has placed me, and to the brothers whom God has given me: by the love — innate in all men — I bear to the country that gave my mother birth, and will be the home of my children: by the hatred — innate in all men — I bear to evil, injustice, usurpation, and arbitrary rule: by the blush that rises to my brow when I stand before the citizens of other lands, to know that I have no rights of citizenship, no country, and no national flag: by the aspiration that thrills my soul towards that liberty

[1] Mazzini, i. 109.

for which it was created, and is impotent to exert, — towards the good it was created to strive after, and is impotent to achieve in the silence and isolation of slavery; by the memory of our former greatness, and the sense of our present degradation; by the tears of Italian mothers for their sons dead on the scaffold, in prison, or in exile; by the suffering of the millions."[1] On these solemn facts the novice vowed to further the objects of the Society, to keep its secrets, and to obey his superiors.

With the idea of Young Italy in his head, and the desire of immediate action in his heart, Mazzini was released from the prison of Savona, no sufficient evidence having been procured to warrant his longer detention. But the Piedmontese government, dimly aware that he was a young man of dangerous tendencies, insisted that he should either consent to live under police surveillance in some small Piedmontese town, or should go into exile. He chose the latter, and withdrew to Marseilles. On the accession of Charles Albert, he addressed to the young king a letter in which he stated the needs of Italy, and having exhorted Charles Albert to recognize and satisfy them, he closed with these words: "Rest assured that posterity will either hail your name as that of the greatest of men, or the last of Italian tyrants. Take your choice." The appeal, published anonymously, was clandestinely scattered through Piedmont, and coming to the notice of the King and his ministers, called forth an order to have its author arrested should he be found in Charles Albert's domains. During that same spring, 1831, Mazzini went to Corsica to take part in the proposed descent on Tuscany; but when that expedition collapsed, and Austrian intervention had crushed the revolution in the Papal States, he returned to Marseilles and set vigorously to work to organize the society of Young Italy. Fellow-exiles aided him in printing manifestoes and a newspaper, which were then

[1] Mazzini, i. 110.

smuggled in barrels of pitch or pumice-stone into Italy, and there circulated by trusty coadjutors. In Genoa, the Ruffini brothers, — the dearest comrades of Mazzini's youth, — together with Campanella, Benza, and a few other friends, undertook the work of propagandism: Leghorn was the Tuscan centre, with Guerrazzi, Bini, and Henry Mayer at its head, and there were other committees in Bologna and Rome and Naples.

The doctrines of the new sect spread, but since secret societies give the census-taker no account of their membership, we cannot cite figures to illustrate the growth of Young Italy. Contrary to Mazzini's expectations, it was recruited, not so much from the People, as from the Middle Class, the professional men, and the tradesmen; and as might be expected, it was the political rather than the religious ideas of the sect that drew adherents to it. The Carbonari and their kindred conspirators were discredited by the failure of the last revolution: it began to be felt that their methods were wrong, and their promoters superannuated; so the more zealous gladly turned to the new society, whose aims were distinct and whose members were young and enthusiastic. But the very definiteness of Mazzini's propositions helped to make clear the lines of separation, hitherto blurred, between the Liberal parties. Young Italy insisted on a republic without compromise; but there were many Liberals who, while desiring the independence and freedom of their country, were still favorable to a monarchical government or to a federation, and these refused to associate themselves with the Republicans. They came to be known as Moderates, and to be despised by the Mazzinians, who regarded them as waverers and temporizers.

The Piedmontese government soon perceived that a fresh conspiracy was gathering, and having traced it to Marseilles and to Mazzini, it requested the French government to expel him from France. This Louis Philippe consented to do. Mazzini was warned that he should be escorted to the frontier. But on the day appointed, the soldiers marched off with one of his friends who resembled him, while he remained unharmed, to continue for more than a year his editorial work at Marseilles. He and his colleagues, unable longer to resist the desire to test their principle by action, planned an invasion of Savoy, which they had to abandon, and then they concerted with their Piedmontese friends a general insurrection, which, breaking out simultaneously in many parts of the Kingdom of Piedmont, should sweep on through Northern and Central Italy. Unfortunately, before the plot was mature, two soldiers fell into a quarrel at Genoa, and, when arrested, one of them exclaimed angrily, that if he would he could tell something that would make his enemy suffer. The police were roused by this hint, and erelong they had a clue to the proposed outbreak. Many arrests followed, and the government issued a proclamation, stating that it had discovered the secret of the wicked men who aimed at destroying "the altar and the throne." The conspirators, according to this manifesto, were neither "Catholics, nor Protestants, nor Christians, nor Jews, nor Mussulmans, nor Brahmins," but new Catilines who would adopt the most hideous means — fire, dagger, poison — to accomplish their designs, and who intended to blow up the magazines of all the principal cities.[1] We suspect that the reactionaries and Jesuits who surrounded Charles Albert exaggerated the danger in order to get his consent to the terrible punishment they proposed; indeed, one of them is said to have remarked, "We must give his Majesty a taste of blood."

However that may be, sanguinary commissions were speedily appointed, and they wrought speedy vengeance. History records the names Cimella, Gattinara, and Galateri as the agents of a persecution not less merciless than

---

[1] Brofferio: *Storia del Piemonte* (Turin, 1850), part III, i, 41-3.

that of the Butcher of Modena himself. At Chambéry, Genoa, Alessandria, and smaller towns, prisoners were passed from torture to torture, to end on the scaffold or in the galleys. Some were enticed to confess by being shown the counterfeit confessions of their comrades; some were imprisoned with spies, to whom they unwittingly confided their secret; some were shaken by harmful food or drugs, till their reason tottered and their self-command deserted them; some were terrified by groans and strange sounds, uttered night after night in the corridors of their prison; some heard shots fired beneath their windows, and supposed that their friends had been executed; some were importuned by the prayers of their parents, wives, and children. One youth, James Ruffini, finding that his resolution was weakening under the strain of horrors, and dreading lest he might betray his accomplices, tore a piece of sheet-iron from the door of his cell, sharpened it on the stone floor, and cut his throat. Another victim, Vochieri, having resisted all terrors and coaxings, was led out to be shot, his executioners taking care that he should pass his own house on the way to death. In a few weeks, eleven alleged conspirators had been executed, many more had been sentenced to the galleys, and others, who had escaped, were condemned in contumacy. Among the men who fled into exile at this time were two of whom we shall hear much hereafter, Vincent Gioberti and Joseph Garibaldi. The government sealed its severity by an edict threatening any one who introduced or circulated publications hostile to the principles of monarchy with the galleys for from two to five years, or even with death, and by offering a reward of one hundred crowns to any informer.[1]

To an enthusiast less determined than Mazzini, this calamity would have been a check; to him, however, it

---

[1] Brofferio, l. c. 43-54; Poggi, ii, 92-8; Gallenga, iii, 327-8; Gualterio, iii, chap. 39.

was a spur. Instead of abandoning the expedition against Savoy, he worked with might and main to hurry it on. His countrymen at home had trusted in the coöperation of Young Italy; they had been surprised and punished: they must not be deserted. Mazzini counted upon the wrath which the recent cruelty of the government had stirred up: he felt bound to rush to the rescue of the prisoners, and he saw in Charles Albert's redoubled tyranny a stronger reason for action. He accordingly collected recruits from among his fellow-exiles, — Italians, Poles, Germans, and Magyars, — and expected aid from the French Republicans. But his nondescript forces, which one chronicler estimated at a thousand, must have a soldier at their head, and the cry being for Ramorino, that general, born at Nice, but recently conspicuous in the Polish revolution, agreed to take command of them. Mazzini, while lacking confidence in him, deferred to the popular will, and gave him forty thousand francs with which to go to Paris and buy the necessary arms. The attack on Savoy was to be made at the end of October, 1833, but, a little before the appointed day, Ramorino sent word that he needed another month's preparation; when that elapsed, he asked for a further postponement. Finally, as January, 1834, was closing, Mazzini, who suspected that the general was using the revolutionary funds at the gaming-table, sent him notice that the blow must be struck at once, for the recruits collected at Geneva were growing disheartened, the funds were nearly exhausted, and it was evident that both the Swiss and the French government had knowledge of their designs. Ramorino therefore quitted Paris, and, still protesting that it was folly to open the campaign with an ill-equipped force, he took command of one column, in which were fifty Italians and twice as many Poles, that was to enter Savoy by way of Annemasse. A second column had orders to push on from Nyon; a third, starting from Lyons, was to march towards Chambéry. Mazzini, with a musket on his shoulder, accompanied the first party. To his surprise, the peasants showed no enthusiasm when the tricolor flag was unfurled and the invaders shouted "God and People! Liberty and the Republic!" before them. At length some carabineers and a platoon of troops appeared. A few shots were fired. Mazzini fainted; his comrades dispersed across the Swiss border, taking him with them. When he recovered consciousness, he realized that the invasion had come to a ludicrous end. His enemies attributed his fainting to cowardice; he himself explained it as the result of many nights of sleeplessness, of great fatigue, fever and cold, and he charged Ramorino with wilful negligence. Ramorino retorted that he had insisted that such a gang of visionaries must inevitably fail. To all but the few concerned in it, this first venture of Young Italy seemed a farce, the disproportion between its aim and its achievement was so enormous, and Mazzini's personal collapse was so ignominious.[1]

Nevertheless, Italian conspiracy had now and henceforth that head for lack of which it had so long floundered amid vague and contradictory purposes. The young Idealist had been beaten in his first encounter with obdurate Reality, but he was not discouraged. His was a nature which, Antaeus-like, renewed its strength with every fall, and drew from defeat the conviction that he must struggle harder. Now began in earnest that "apostolate" of his, which he laid down only at his death. Young Italy was established beyond the chance of being destroyed by an abortive expedition; Young Poland, Young Hungary, Young Europe itself, sprang up after the Mazzinian pattern; the Liberals and revolutionists of the Continent felt that their cause was international, and in their affliction they fraternized. No one could draw so fair and reasonable a Utopia for them as Mazzini

[1] Mazzini, i. 355-68.

drew; no one could so fire them with a sense of duty, with hope, with energy. He became the mainspring of the whole machine — truly an infernal machine to the autocrats — of European conspiracy. The redemption of Italy was always his nearest aim, but his generous principle reached out over other nations, for in the world that he prophesied every people must be free.

Proscribed in Piedmont, expelled from Switzerland, denied lodging in France, he took refuge in London, there to direct, amid poverty and heartache, the whole vast scheme of plots. His bread he earned by writing critical and literary essays for the English reviews, — he quickly mastered the English language so as to use it with remarkable vigor, — and all his leisure he devoted to the preparation of political tracts, and to correspondence with numberless confederates. He watched the symptoms of every part of Italy; he studied the map and laid out campaigns; he shipped arms and munition to various points; he indited proclamations, concerted signals, enrolled volunteers, instigated, encouraged, and counseled. He was the consulting physician for all the revolutionary practitioners of Europe. Those who were not his partisans disparaged his influence, asserting that he was only a man of words; but the best proof of his power lies in the anxiety he caused monarchs and cabinets, and in the precautions they took to guard against him. Their spies lurked in his shadow; they even induced the British postmaster-general to open his letters, — a baseness which prevents the name of Graham from being forgotten: they sowed reports reeking with terrible insinuations against his character and methods; they bade their subjects to abhor him as a diabolical incendiary who wished to upset thrones and altars, and who, in the anarchy that would ensue, would let loose his red-handed followers to ravish and plunder. Mazzini denied the charge that he approved or condoned political assassination, although he admitted that he had given money and a dagger to a young fanatic, Gallenga, who had vowed to kill Charles Albert.[1] In friendly intercourse he was so gentle, so unselfish, so insistent in matters spiritual, that the few persons who knew him well could not believe that he would descend to criminal methods in order to compass his reforms, which were essentially moral.

Mazzini and Metternich! For nearly twenty years they were the antipodes of European politics. One, in his London garret, poor, despised, yet indomitable and sleepless, sending his influence like an electric current through all barriers to revivify the heart of Italy and of Liberal Europe; the other in his Vienna palace, haughty, famous, equally alert and cunning, with all material and hierarchical powers to aid him, shedding over Italy and over Europe his upas-doctrines of torpor and decay! Rarely, indeed, has a period rich in contrasts seen its antagonistic extremes made flesh in two such men. Then, as so often before in human history, the Champion of the Past, — arrogant, materialist, and self-satisfied, but waning — had a palace to his dwelling, while the Apostle of the Future found only a cheap lodging and an exile's welcome in a foreign land.

[1] Gallenga, iii, 338–9; Mazzini, i, 347–52.

CHAPTER II.

A DECADE OF CONTRADICTIONS, 1833–43.

Conspiracy had now its leader, its political and moral principles, and its definite aim. No member of Young Italy could plead ignorance of the cause to which he was pledged: and there dropped upon him from time to time newspapers and tracts full of brave words and ethical counsel, emanating from Mazzini. But Young Italy, which was to have been the sect of the People, failed to stir the cloddish peasantry and the lowest class of townsmen; master-artisans and professional men, and especially enthusiastic students, were the recruits it attracted. Conspiracy had its head, — but where? In London, far removed from its members. The distance between them was too great, it opened too broad a field for delays and misunderstandings. Young Italy might make converts so rapidly as to alarm the Italian governments and to cause Metternich to set spies on Mazzini; but it could not overcome that fatal remoteness between the head and the members.

Autocracy, for its part, was waking up to the unpleasant conviction that it had a permanent evil to contend with. After Waterloo, it had thought that a few years of vigilance and energy would suffice to exterminate the last offshoots of Liberalism. The French Revolution had failed; Napoleon had been beaten; what more was needed than that the Old Régime should diligently weed out the tares that had been sown between 1789 and 1815? Once clear the garden, and the old-fashioned plants would grow undisturbed. But after fifteen years of incessant weeding and trimming, the tares still flourished; and now Autocracy began to realize that it was pitted against an invisible Sower, from whose hand new seeds fell as fast as it destroyed the old. The "three glorious days of July," and the subsequent revolutions, taught the autocrats that the state of siege and political quarantine, which they had adopted as extraordinary measures against what they believed would be a passing danger, must be perpetually maintained; for the danger was chronic, and it constantly increased. Not a few turbulent men, but a Great Thought was their adversary: that Thought was Liberty, and under the guise of a desire, a need, or a duty, it kept the nations restless and their oppressors anxious.

In a government where the people has representatives to express its will and frame its laws, the personality of the sovereign is usually of secondary importance; but in an autocracy, the character of the sovereign determines not only the administration but also the social life of the people, to a degree that seems exorbitant if we reflect on the qualifications of most monarchs. And a nation proves that it deserves the curse of despotism, by the significance it attaches to every gesture and whim of its ruler. It judges, as the world in general judges, by clothes and externals: a trifling condescension, a gracious bow, a smile from its ruler, suffice for it to break out in acclamations, — as if Nero himself never smiled! A tyrannized people, living in the dread of conditions worse than the present, learns by instinct to flatter, and is an easy prey to flattery. After many deceptions, it looks forward to the advent of the present tyrant's successor. The new king may have new ideas: the change warrants hope, and hope utters itself in rejoicings. It happened that new rulers came to the throne in Naples, Rome, and Piedmont, just at the time of the revolution of 1831; and as usual, Liberals and Reactionists speculated as to the effect these unknown quantities would produce.

Of the three, Ferdinand II, who succeeded to the crown of Naples, November 8, 1830, excited the greatest enthusiasm. His father, Francis, had been so detestable that every one was glad to be rid of him, and no one believed that his infamous traits could reappear in his successor. But Ferdinand aroused more than this negative sentiment in his subjects; he had positive traits that commended him to them and justified their joyful expectations. He was young and soldierly; he seemed energetic and good-natured, and he was not charged with debauchery. He cleansed the palace of the vile creatures of both sexes who had pandered to his father's evil desires; he dismissed Vaglica and the chambermaid De Simone; he swept out the courtiers and the pet parrots; he abolished the spendthrift hunting-establishment. When he talked favorably of amnesty for political offenders, and actually allowed his soldiers to wear moustaches, — those emblems of Carbonarism, — the Liberals grew confident; when he cut down the appropriations for the civil list, and did away with the poll-tax, eulogists could not restrain their odes of thanksgiving. In verse and prose they lauded "the new Titus," whom heaven, in its mercy, had vouchsafed to them.[1]

Ferdinand propitiated the Sicilians by sending his brother, the Count of Syracuse, to rule over them. He seemed determined also to be his own master in his relations abroad. Louis Philippe, his kinsman, wrote and counseled him to conform to the spirit of the times, by taking the July monarchy, on whose friendship he could rely, as a model; the Emperor of Austria urged him to make no concessions, but to imitate his father and grandfather in following Austria's guidance. To Louis Philippe Ferdinand replied that his subjects did not need much scope for thought, as he intended to think for them; to the Emperor he expressed gratitude for the proffers

[1] Nisco: *Ferdinando II* (Naples, 1890), 5-11.

of friendship, but declared that he did not intend to be
under obligations to foreign arms?[1] These various acts
and promises made the young King so popular during the
first months of his reign that even the conspirators debated whether they could not persuade him to become the
champion of the Liberal clause. He was ambitious,
therefore let him join them and win the crown of Italy for
himself. But Ferdinand resisted the temptation, saying
that, were he to be successful, "he should not know what
to do with the Pope."[2] The older and warier Liberals
looked on skeptically during Ferdinand's honeymoon of
popularity. "A Liberal Bourbon is as unthinkable as a
stripeless tiger: let us wait," — so they mused, or whispered to each other. It is well to remember, however,
that this Ferdinand, who became in later years an abomination to the civilized world, was hailed at the outset as a
patriotic, justice-loving prince.

His true character soon began to reveal itself. He was
not in the least a reformer; he cared nothing for the
welfare of his people, and all his measures were aimed
at increasing his authority irrespective of their wishes.
His somewhat haughty attitude towards France and Austria was not inspired by a sense of dignity, but by wilfulness. He was bent on making a show in the world. So
he remodeled his army, and, when not too lazy, — indolence being one of his ruling traits, — he conducted the
military drills with a mock-martial strictness. He appointed six lieutenant-generals, thirty brigadiers, and
fourteen field-marshals, whose uniforms doubtless enlivened the dress-parades.[3] As a tribute to the Jesuits, he
created the *memory* of Ignatius Loyola a field-marshal,
and paid over to them the salary appertaining to that
rank.[4] The parasites who had defiled his father's admin-

[1] Settembrini: *Ricordanze* (Naples, 1880), i, 42.
[2] Nisco, 30.
[3] Poggi, ii, 131.
[4] Perrens: *Deux Ans de Révolution en Italie* (Paris, 1857), 449.

istration he replaced by others scarcely less disgraceful. Delcarretto, the renegade Carbonaro who had destroyed the town of Bosco and signalized himself by similar barbarities in 1828, was appointed Minister of Police, a position from which he soon rose to be the King's chief adviser. With Monsignor Cocle, the unscrupulous royal confessor, Delcarretto competed for the entire mastery of Ferdinand's actions; and now one, now the other, gained the ascendant by flattery or craft. Santangelo, Minister of the Interior, had the reputation of an embezzler, but the King, instead of investigating the charge, laughed at it.[1] Corruption was in every department. Places were bought and sold, — Delcarretto nominated his ten-year-old son to be treasurer of the bank of discount with a salary of six thousand ducats;[2] every one, from the ministers down to the turnkeys in the prison, took bribes or levied blackmail. The financial reforms proved illusory, — as, for instance, the abolition of the grist-tax, for which another impost was substituted. The King's economy was soon seen to spring from avarice.

In his private life, Ferdinand had only one virtue, — he was not profligate. Illiterate, he had a certain shallow wit that stood him in the stead of education. At times he affected great solicitude for public morals: thus he decreed that the ballet-dancers at the theatre of San Carlo should wear green tights, on the ground that that color would least excite the animal passions of the male spectators: and he ordered public prostitutes to be expelled from the capital, but winked when they bribed the police not to molest them.[3] In temper he was jovial or surly; in manners a boor. He used to amuse himself by caning a chamberlain's legs and seeing him hop about in agony: so his royal father had had the pleasant habit of dropping hot wax from a candle on the nose of one of his courtiers, and laughing at the blister he raised. Once

[1] Settembrini, i. 54-5.   [2] Perrens, 419.   [3] *Ibid.*

Ferdinand pulled the music-stool away just as his wife was about to sit down at the piano, and as she sprawled on the floor, he roared. "I thought I had married the King of Naples and not a *lazzarone*," she exclaimed indignantly.[1] That word describes Ferdinand best, — he was by instinct a *lazzarone*, by chance a king; in all things, except his apparel, akin to the beggars of the Chiaja, — a loafer, a banterer, a bully, a creature swayed by his sensations, deceitful, obstinate or cringing, quick to fly into a passion or to turn off the gravest matter with a joke.

As soon as the conspirators understood Ferdinand's real nature, they leaped from their momentary quiescence into redoubled activity. In 1831 a tumult broke out at Palermo; in 1832 a burrow of plotters was unearthed at Nola; in 1833 a cavalry officer named Rossaroll planned with several confederates to kill the King at a military review, and that same year there was frustrated an insurrection in which it was said sixty thousand conspirators would take part.[2] Chance, or a tell-tale accomplice, or the vigilance of the police, caused all these schemes to fail, but they so alarmed Ferdinand that he proposed to his fellow-monarchs to form a league for extirpating political incendiaries, and he was chagrined when they declined his proposition.[3] And now the prisons swarmed with victims, many of whom had been arrested merely on suspicion, while many more were detained one year or two after the judges had declared them innocent. What those prisons were, with their filth, their cruelty, their obscenity, equaling the worst that has ever been told of Siberia or the dungeons of the Inquisition, has been recorded by some of the brave men who suffered in them.[4] But when have arrests and persecutions strangled a movement like that which had been, for twenty years, agitat-

---

[1] Settembrini, i. 54.   [2] Poggi, ii. 134-8.   [3] Bianchi, iii. 258.
[4] Settembrini's *Ricordanza*, for instance, are vivid and trustworthy.

ing Italy? The conspirators would not surrender; they had not yet sufficient harmony and moral strength to conquer. Even those ethical precepts of Young Italy were long in taking root in a character so debased as was that of the Neapolitans, who rebelled, for the most part, for the same reason that the trodden worm turns. It seemed probable that some of the small tumults which spurted up periodically were carefully prepared by the King's ministers, in order to convince him that they were indispensable to his safety. Delcarretto and the confessor Cocle were the real masters of the kingdom, although they were satisfied to have their policy seem to be shaped by the King.

In 1835, Asiatic cholera, which had been steadily spreading over Europe from India during the past five years, appeared in Northern Italy. The following season it swept southward through the Peninsula. So devastating an epidemic had not been known for two centuries. Fifty thousand victims perished in Lombardy; five thousand four hundred in Rome, five thousand in Naples, and every town and hamlet had its heaps of dead and its crowds of panic-stricken living. Pestilence and earthquake are the two great calamities which make a general havoc of all brave and unselfish qualities; among even the stanchest races, they wrench asunder the ties of kin and friendship and common humanity, and substitute a pitiless, demoniac terror. Upon the *morale* of a people like the Neapolitans, superstitious and excitable, the effect of such an epidemic must always have been destructive, for their religion itself was based on terror; but now a political delusion intensified their frenzy. It was whispered that the pest was caused by the government, which poisoned the food and water of the people, in order to get rid of the surplus population, as well as to punish its enemies and to complete the subjection of the survivors. This suspicion of poison has added horrors to many plagues; Thucydides says that the Peloponnesians were supposed to have poisoned the Athenian cisterns in the plague of B. C. 430;[1] Manzoni describes the popular fury against the alleged *anointers* at Milan, in 1630;[2] at Naples, in 1836-7, the long infamy of the Bourbon rule gave plausibility to the assertion that the King's ministers were capable even of this crime. Ferdinand, to allay the excitement, went to a baker's shop and ate bread, but the suspicion was not dissipated; and only when cold weather came were the ravages of the disease stayed.

In the ensuing spring, 1837, the epidemic broke out with fiercer violence. Everything helped to widen its track. The minds of the Neapolitans were already terror-stricken; their bodies were ill-fed; they were housed in squalor; their streets were filthy. This time, 13,800 victims died in Naples alone within less than five months. The cholera swept on through the Abruzzi and Calabria, and passed into Sicily. Whoever could, fled; but flight was beyond the means of the masses, who remained to tremble and die. Husbands, mothers, sons, when the disease smote one of their number, forgetting their duty, their affection, and all but their terror, hid themselves. Sometimes all the members of a household were stricken together, and died with none to tend them, until the stench from their corpses warned the neighbors to come and bury them. Great ditches had to be dug, into which the tumbrils dumped their load of bodies, upon which quicklime was shoveled. The ordinary course of business was interrupted and the necessaries of life became scarce; priests no longer performed the last offices over the dying or chanted masses for the dead. The silence was at times horrible, but more horrible were the shrieks of the pestilence-stricken, and the thud of some corpse flung from an upper window to the pavement for the

---

[1] Thucydides, ii, 48. [2] *I Promessi Sposi*, chaps 31, 32.

buriers to take away; horrible, too, was that long-drawn rumble of the carts, and the shouts and unseemly laughter of the men who piled them high with the naked or half-clad bodies of men, women, and children. And, as always happens when a calamity falls upon and dehumanizes a people, many gave themselves up to desperate orgies, to drunkenness and debauch, while waiting for the plague to attack them. Nevertheless, some there were whose noble nature conquered fear and restrained brutal instincts, — some monks and priests and physicians, who would not desert the sick until their own turn came to succumb. In Palermo the cholera raged for a hundred days, and carried off upwards of forty thousand souls; as many more perished in other parts of Sicily.

To their delirium was added the horror of insurrection. The cry of poison was revived, and any unfortunate creature on whom suspicion fell was ruthlessly dispatched. An old man, who had fled from Palermo to escape cholera, was seized and burnt alive with his son. A Frenchman, who conducted a panorama at Syracuse, was torn to pieces. Woe to the person in whose house a suspicious vial or perfume was found! Sentinels guarded the wells and public fountains day and night. The delusion, like the plague, infected all classes. Cardinal Trigona exclaimed in his death-agony, "There is no remedy for this poison." The naturalist Scinà died, believing that he, too, had been poisoned. And from this strange credulity to pass to the belief that the government was the poisoner was but a step. What part the sectaries took in spreading this insinuation, we cannot say; but undoubtedly they incited the maddened people to revolt. At Penne, in Calabria, there was an outbreak, temporarily successful; then the government sent Colonel Tanfani to wreak vengeance on the town. At Gaeta, at Cosenza, and at other points on the mainland revolutionary jets were quickly extinguished, and the government turned the tables on the conspirators by charging them with the poisoning.

But in Sicily, where the hatred of the Bourbons and the desire for Home Rule needed at any time only a spark to flame up in rebellion, the agitators kindled a far more dangerous conflagration. Syracuse revolted, and declared its independence; Catania shouted for the Constitution, and then, reaction having set in, the Royalists prevailed. Palermo was in a ferment; every district was tossed by fear of pestilence and the alarms of civil war; but the force of the agitation had almost spent itself when Ferdinand, who was not a king to let part of his realm slip from him without his striving to retain it, gave full powers to Delcarretto to reduce the island to submission. Delcarretto's strength lay in punishing. To do justice, to conciliate, to make allowance for excesses committed under the frenzy caused by the pest, — such considerations as these moved him not. Within a month he had terrified the islanders into docility. Hundreds of victims were condemned to the galleys and prisons, some, no doubt, deservedly, but as there was no fair trial, there could be only guesswork in assigning the penalty; many scores were executed; and a price was set on the heads of those who had escaped. Delcarretto employed tortures that would have disgraced a Tartar khan: such as hanging men up by the wrists to the branches of trees, flogging them till blood flowed, depriving them of food and sleep, tearing out their hair in handfuls, binding them in most painful and obscene fashion: "in short," says the historian who relates these atrocities, "the cannibals of the government wished to show that they were more ferocious than the cannibals of the populace."[1] And as evidence of his insensibility, Delcarretto, whilst these outrages were in progress, gave banquets and balls at the communal palace in Catania, and required the mothers and daughters of his victims to attend them.[2] When

---

[1] Nisco, 56.
[2] Poggi, ii. 190; consult also Nisco, Turotti (ii. 133-8), Gualterio (chap. 64), and Galdi (*Ferdinando II*), for further details.

order had been restored, the King set about wiping out all trace of Sicilian autonomy, by reorganizing the administration of the island. But he could not blot the recollection of the horrors of the year 1837 from the minds of the Sicilians, nor could he, despite all his compulsion, wrench from them their desire of Home Rule.

From these facts we get sufficient insight into the nature of Ferdinand and his government, and as our present purpose is to estimate the forces which worked for and against the Liberal cause at this period, we need not describe minutely events which, Time has proved, had only a secondary and transient importance. Such, for instance, was Ferdinand's quarrel with England over the Sicilian sulphur mines, — a quarrel which he hastened to patch up, when a squadron of British men-of-war came into the harbor of Naples and unmasked their guns; such, also, were his casual bickerings with Austria or with the Pope. The great fact is that Ferdinand, by the year 1840, stood before the civilized world as a ruler not less odious than his father and grandfather had been; more vigorous than they, his tyranny was therefore more swift and skilful in persecuting; but his power, like theirs, was based on espionage and cruelty, and he maintained his hold, not because he was really strong, but because his subjects were weak, and because the autocrats of Europe tacitly supported him. The corruption of his officials, the barbarity of his judicial and penal systems, the dissoluteness of his Court, the misery of the populace in the cities and the insolence of brigands in the country, made Naples loathsome among nations, and gave to the epithet Bourbon that evil significance which will cling to it forever. The "new Titus" was seen to be a new Caligula, whose aggravated tyranny encouraged plotting. The Kingdom of the Two Sicilies continued to be a hotbed of conspirators; but though they were eager to rebel, the sects still lacked integrity and union. Young Italy itself could not quickly convert such material into a fit instrument for its patriotic enterprise, but ran the risk of being itself perverted.

Of Gregory XVI, the new sovereign of the Papal States, we have already had a glimpse during the revolution which troubled the beginning of his reign. Raised from a monk's cloister to the pontifical throne, he displayed in all his civil acts the incompetence and bigotry of a monk. His fair promises to reform his government vanished into thin air as soon as the representatives of the Great Powers had presented their Memorandum and withdrawn. In the tribunals, in the departments of police and finance, not less than in the diplomatic service and even in local administration, ecclesiastics had control. To be a layman meant practically to be cut off from all privileges and sinecures — and they were innumerable — and from all hope of preferment. Therefore it was that any man who had ambition or cupidity took orders, that he might qualify himself to feed at the papal trough; and many a vile wretch, who, in other countries would have been known only as a pot-house politician or as the corrupt tool of lobbyists, wore the livery of the Papacy, and used his holy office for private ends. Gregory had for his favorite a certain Moroni, formerly his barber and now his major-domo, — a nimble fellow, who trafficked in offices and levied bribes on petitioners, and grew rich. If Gregory was ignorant of this scandal, none of his subjects were. You will search in vain through the opinions of those contemporaries, of whatever party, who were competent to express an opinion, for any commendation of Gregory's government. "As a sovereign," said Cardinal Bernetti, the Secretary of State, "he is worth little, or perhaps nothing at all."[1] "If you wished to please the Holy Father," wrote the Piedmontese envoy at Rome, "you would have to make a present to Gaetano

[1] Bianchi, iii. 158.

Moroni, a valet who has his entire confidence. You might give him a ring or a fine piece of silver; but for that you would need to find him some pretext, that is, employ him in some matter, and then make him the present as a recompense."[1] "Among the numerous difficulties to which the position of the countries under Papal rule daily gives rise," Metternich wrote, "there is no question that the most insuperable of all is connected with the fact that the government has no idea how to govern."[2]

Nevertheless the Austrian chancellor discountenanced reforms in the Papal States, and denied that the Pope was bound to listen to any appeal for "progressive amelioration." For it was plainly Austria's interest to have at Rome a tottering and despised government, which furnished an excuse for Austria's surveillance and interference. The danger from an outbreak of Gregory's subjects would not equal the danger in the example of Papal States well governed and contented; insurrection could be put down, but the example would unsettle Austria's Lombard and Venetian vassals. Utopians were already talking of a federation of the Italian States under the headship of the Pope; for Metternich to encourage the Pope in a policy which made him detested was therefore a piece of excellent strategy, by which Gregory was easily caught. He removed Cardinal Bernetti, whom Metternich did not like, and appointed Cardinal Lambruschini, whom Metternich approved, as secretary of state; for the same reason he reorganized the body of centurions. He was, in a word, subservient to Austria in his internal administration. Lambruschini was an implacable reactionary. He called in the Inquisition to help him hunt down and punish political offenders; he dispensed justice according to whim or prejudice; he repressed every murmur, and stifled every Liberal breath. Yet in Rome itself, with all

[1] Bianchi, iii, 159.   [2] Metternich, v, 236.

its host of police and spies and Swiss mercenaries, public safety was so uncared for that bakers had to be guarded by a posse of gendarmes when they delivered their bread every morning.

The revolution of 1831 had established as a fact, — what had long been suspected, — that the Papacy could not maintain itself without foreign support. There was never a day after 1831 when an overwhelming majority of the inhabitants of the Papal States, had they been left to their own motion, would not have freed themselves from Gregory's temporal sovereignty. What more damning condemnation can the bitterest enemies of the Papal government make than simply to state this fact? The misrule of the Vicar of Christ was so iniquitous that his own subjects preferred any other rather than that. But Austria and France were pledged to prevent the Romans from throwing off their hateful incubus; and Gregory had to rely upon them and his Swiss mercenaries, many of whom were Protestants, to keep his "dearly beloved children" from driving him out of Rome.

In matters ecclesiastical, Gregory's pretensions were as extravagant as his civil power was weak. He adopted that policy, which his successors have pursued, of combating the growing Liberalism and tolerance which characterize our modern age by promulgating dogmas yet more intolerant and more retrograde. He would have blotted out seven centuries of progress, and thrust Europe back into the religious and social condition of the era of the third Innocent. Thus in human institutions as in animal organisms, when the limit of growth had been reached, there is a reversion to lower and cruder forms. Gregory asserted, in his negotiations with Catholic Powers, the right of the Church to dictate to the State, — a claim which has always been invulnerable from the Papal standpoint and which the Holy Alliance could not consistently deny: for had it not made the restoration of the feudal Past the basis of European order since 1815? Metternich, however, was never a slave to consistency, and while he propped up Gregory in Rome, and urged him to deal boldly with other rulers, he gave no scope to Papal interference in the Austrian Empire.

Thus in the States of the Church as in the Kingdom of the Two Sicilies, there were a thousand reasons why subjects should conspire, none why they should submit. But in view of the holy office which the Roman sovereign arrogated, — in view of his being the recognized representative of Christ, the corruption, the injustice, the cruelty, the deceitfulness of his government seemed far more shocking than similar crimes against civilization committed by the Bourbon barbarians at Naples. Gregory's reign was so hated that all parties, except the coterie of bigots who squatted round the Papal throne, felt that it could not long endure; in the Legations, a sect called the "Ferdinandea" actually plotted in behalf of annexation to Austria.

The third of the new rulers was Charles Albert. For ten years, except during the brief Spanish campaign, he had lived in retirement, cursed by the Liberals as a traitor, and distrusted by the Reactionists as a would-be Liberal, because of his ambiguous course in the revolution of 1821. His accession was a moment of suspense for both factions. The Liberals hoped, and the others feared, that, being now king and his own master, he would dare to retrieve his former fault; but he satisfied neither. He talked of reform, but he kept the ministers of Charles Felix, — men to whom change meant chaos. His amnesty extended only to a batch of common criminals, — no political prisoner nor exile was benefited by it. He established a Council which, having only a consultative power, was a mere echo of the ministry. And yet the Reactionists were constantly afraid that he would slip away from them, until the political turmoil of 1833 gave them a chance to implicate him in the bloody work of repression. Then they thought that they had opened an abyss between Charles Albert and the Liberals which neither would try to bridge. Erelong, it appeared, however, that although he had rigid notions of kingship, he took no ogreish delight in blood. He was stern, but not cruel.

The Italians, in and out of Piedmont, who had come to believe that their country's liberation might be achieved through the House of Savoy were most incensed by Charles Albert's apparent surrender to Austrian influence. They knew nothing of the secret pledge, extorted from him in 1824, that he would not change the fundamental character of the government. His first object was to be master at home, and as his conspiring subjects would have thwarted him in that, he naturally leaned upon Austria as the Power which excelled in the art of crushing conspiracies. And yet those who were deepest in his confidence perceived that he chafed at dependence, and that his heart was thoroughly Italian. He devoted himself to the reorganization of the Piedmontese army, which had been neglected by his predecessor, and little Piedmont again wore the aspect of a military kingdom. His court was stiff and formal: all ease strangled by strict rules of etiquette, and all movements governed by a discipline as mechanical as that which prevailed in the barracks and on the parade-ground. Soldiers and priests seemed to be numerically in the majority, as they were in influence. Charles Albert became morbidly religious, — he abstained from all but the simplest food, he wore a hair-shirt, he kept long fasts, he spent much time in pious meditation, — and the wily minions of the Church, by flattery or intimidation, played upon this morbid tendency. Jesuits controlled education and glided into every walk of life. Monasteries were crowded with lazy monks; convents swarmed with nuns. The black frock and shovel-hat of the priest, the brown garb of the friar, the starched hood or mourning veil of the sister, were met at every turn. To show his devotion to Mother Church, Charles Albert agreed upon a concordat with the Pope, and requested that a Papal nuncio should reside at Turin; and the Pope encouraged the King in his piety by canonizing several by-gone members of the House of Savoy.

To the psychologist, few royal characters of modern times offer so many interesting perplexities as this soldier-hermit of Piedmont. Like Hamlet, he continually made resolves, only to flinch when the moment came to execute them. He was the victim of after-thoughts which checked action; and his monkish asceticism aggravated that nervous-gastric temperament of his which kept his will in a flutter of irresolution. His sudden changes were due not, as his enemies charged, to insincerity, but to a diseased volition. In a moment of high spirits, he excited great hopes, which he assuredly meant to fulfil; then came the reaction, the chill, when the thing he had promised looked black and impossible; and he remained inert. Men called him "King Shilly-Shally," "King See-Saw," and they even attributed his vacillation to wilful treachery; but I find no more proof that he ever deliberately played false, than that he played the part of waverer for seventeen years in order to veil his patriotic designs from Austria. He himself felt the burden of his contradictory nature: "Am I not indeed an incomprehensible man?" he said to one whom he trusted. This sense of mystery, of being accompanied and opposed by a special, inscrutable Fate, was at all times present to him, and often inspired in him a foreboding of failure. And his outward conditions corresponded in their antagonism to the conflicts in his soul. "I live between the dagger of the Carbonari and the chocolate of the Jesuits," — in that phrase he accurately described his position. But there seems reason to believe that when the Jesuits discovered that they could do their will with him by appealing to his piety, he ran no further risk of their poison, although it has been hinted that at their instigation his physicians gave him drugs to keep him in a chronic morbid state. To the public, he seemed a man of great reserve and self-control: he was very tall, and dignified almost to haughtiness in his carriage; his countenance was serious, and not easily roused into vivacity; but despite this imperturbability, there was a certain charm in his manner that left an impression of benevolence and candor upon anyone who spoke with him.[1]

In contrast with this king who "would and would not," was his chief minister, Solaro della Margarita, a man more Royalist than his master. Count Solaro had no doubts nor hesitations; he believed in the divine right of monarchy, and his endeavor was to maintain unclipped the prerogatives of the Crown. To administer strictly the strict paternal government, to concede nothing to popular demands, to have it understood that whatever reforms were granted were due to the bounty and wisdom of the Sovereign and not to a recognition of the right of his subjects to ask for them, — these were the guiding principles of Count Solaro's life; and from his uncompromising, self-assured nature, Charles Albert's reign got its fixed hue and its uniformity. Other ministers there were, like Villamarina, who favored a wider liberty, and occasionally they almost persuaded the King to their views; but when he talked with his Foreign Secretary, the latter, who always had the last word, prevailed. In many respects Piedmont improved during this decade, in spite of the prohibition of political discussion, and in spite of the ubiquitous and domineering ecclesiastics. A uniform Civil Code was promulgated; in Sardinia, the

---

[1] For Charles Albert see Beauregard de Costa; *Prologue d'un Règne* (Paris, 1889); Cappelletti; *Carlo Alberto* (Rome, 1890); Brofferio, Cibrario, etc.

feudal system was abolished; commerce and industry revived; the King patronized the fine arts, and wished to make Turin a centre of culture. He was among the first Italian princes to discern the importance and to encourage the construction of railways; he likewise favored infant asylums and other charitable institutions, and set the fashion in humane work. But since he could overrule the law by his arbitrary decree, the new code proved less beneficial than it should have proved; and in the administration of justice, where political offenders were involved, there was but slight regard either for equity or for law. Religious intolerance showed itself in the government's dealing with the Waldenses, who were forbidden to attend Protestant colleges or even to remove from the now overpopulated valleys which had been for centuries the scene of their persecution.

In his foreign relations Charles Albert preserved friendliness towards Austria; not because he was unmindful of the hereditary ambition of his House, — an ambition which Austria's occupation of Northern Italy kept at bay, — but because he saw no present chance of expelling the Austrians, and because he recognized them as the conquerors of revolution. Nevertheless, on one occasion, at least, he was on the point of looking westward for an ally. In 1840 the Oriental Question stirred up so much diplomatic wrath that a general war seemed imminent. France, isolated through the blunders of her Cabinet, sought a league with Piedmont, holding out the prospect of the acquisition of Lombardy, should the Franco-Piedmontese army defeat the Austrians, and predicting that the Italians would rise in mass and fight for their independence as soon as the first French column appeared on Mont Cenis. Austria, on the other hand, represented to Charles Albert the danger of conniving with the revolutionary elements in Italy, and the improbability of the French being a match for the other Powers.

Charles Albert would have escaped from the dilemma by remaining neutral, but when he was shown by both sides that his neutrality would not prevent both Austrians and French from invading his kingdom, in order to come to close quarters, he weighed the chances, decided that the odds lay with Austria, and therefore he accepted an alliance with her. The war was prevented through the exertions of the same diplomats who had caused the alarm, and so Italians were spared the ignominy of seeing the only native ruler in Italy serve as an ally of Italy's inveterate oppressor.[1]

Of the three rulers whose personality and administration I have thus sketched, the Italians had come to regard only Charles Albert as a possible instrument in their redemption. From the Pope and the King of Naples they no longer expected any encouragement, — nay, they looked forward to the removal of those despots as the indispensable condition to success; but Charles Albert, despite his rigid paternalism, despite his vacillation and his failures to fulfil the hope centred in him, was still believed by many to be available as a champion of the national cause. The severity of his persecution of Liberals and his compactly organized system of repression gave conspirators reason enough to plot against him; and yet the idea was in the air that destiny pointed to him as the likeliest champion of Italy's aspirations. That strange nature of his made him still, after a dozen years of reign, an enigma; nevertheless, from little hints dropped from time to time, the enthusiastic believed that he was with them. Men remembered sayings of his that had surely a patriotic ring, and when he had a medal coined, representing a Lion crushing an Eagle, with the motto "*J'attans mon astre*," "I await my star," — they whispered that the Lion stood for Savoy and the Eagle for Austria, and that the motto was prophetic of the

[1] Bianchi, iv, chap. 5.

King's resolve. Like night-weary watchers, they hailed the first dim streak as a promise of day.

In Lombardy and Venetia the conditions of the natives remained almost unchanged, although at the death of Emperor Francis (1835) and the accession of Ferdinand they indulged in flowery hopes, which the Austrian government stimulated by festivities and pomp, as well as by releasing some of the Spielberg prisoners, who were forbidden, however, to return to their homes. Metternich's policy of encouraging the nobles and rich bourgeoisie in a life of dissipation was persevered in, and caused Italians of sterner morals to deplore the consequent sapping of vigor and integrity. Nevertheless, Austria's conduct towards her bondsmen, in all except political matters, contrasted favorably with that of every other Italian ruler except the Grand Duke of Tuscany, and thereby deceived foreigners who traveled through Lombardy and Venetia into supposing that it was just and salutary. The Duke of Modena, who employed Canosa as his chief agent, held his little duchy petrified; that, at least, he could do, having been forced to abandon his dream of wider tyranny. Modena became the oracle of reaction, and Francis, through his newspaper, *La Voce della Verità*, was the mouthpiece of the oracle, muttering warnings against Liberalism and suggesting heroic remedies for the political disease which threatened European autocracy.[1] It was his doctrine that, in a well-regulated government, the hangman should be the prime minister.

For the Liberals, Tuscany alone was an oasis amid the desert. Leopold's government was paternal, but mildly paternal, according to the standard of his minister, Fossombroni, who believed that subjects can best be diverted from political agitation when they are allowed to pursue

---

[1] He proposed, for instance, that the Czar should be subsidized to confine in Siberia all the Italian political prisoners and suspects. Bianchi, iv, 33.

their own course in social and commercial affairs. But though there was no real liberty in Tuscany, and though Leopold would have resisted any attempt to compel him to grant a Constitution, his actual tolerance drew upon him rebukes and intimidations from Austria and reprimands from the Vatican. In 1831 he was obliged to suppress the *Antologia*, in which an allusion had been made to the barbarous treatment of the Russian prisoners in Siberia; but he bravely refused to permit the Jesuits to reëstablish themselves in his domain, and he would neither surrender his autocracy to Austria, nor abolish the Leopoldine Code, which denied to the Church the right to interfere in the concerns of the State. Equally obnoxious in the eyes of his neighbors was his reform in education. He broadened the curriculum of the universities at Pisa and Siena, and, more aggravating still, he called to the professors' chairs scholars of conspicuous ability and Liberal tendencies; so that the students imbibed patriotic ideas along with their lectures in chemistry and logic. He relaxed the not over-strict censorship; he patronized charitable organizations, took measures for reclaiming the Maremme, and gave refugees an asylum. Leopold illustrated, in short, the better possibilities of Absolute monarchy, when the monarch is not made restless by ambition, nor cruel by fear, and when his subjects are content to receive the benefits which he graciously bestows, instead of fighting for ideals he will not grant. Leopold wished to be let alone; the Tuscans were thrifty and easy-going; and so Tuscany, in contrast with the rest of Italy, seemed blessed with prosperity and freedom.

Such were the salient characteristics of the decade under review as they appeared to contemporaries. If it were necessary to make a more minute study, we should undoubtedly find reason to qualify and abate some of the opinions reported concerning the men and motives of that period; but it is our object to know what the Italians regarded as intolerable grievances, for those grievances caused the struggle for independence, and they could not be offset nor soothed by measures compatible with autocratic government. An historian might with truth declare that the American Colonists enjoyed in 1775 a large number of benefits from British rule; but he would not accurately portray the condition of the Colonists unless he stated that all those benefits could not compensate for the lack of representation. Nothing but that would satisfy the Americans, and it was idle for Britain to expect gratitude from them for favors which they spurned. The Italians, likewise, had reached a point where only independence could appease them; and this they craved, not merely as the realization of a fair dream, but as an escape from the torments and iniquities they had to endure from their worst masters, and the enervating restrictions from their best.

Among the significant results of this decade of diverse tendencies were the formation of a copyright league by all the Italian States except Naples, the negotiation of a customs-union, and the establishment, at the suggestion of Prince Charles Bonaparte, of an Italian Scientific Congress, which held its first session at Pisa in 1839. The annual gathering of several hundred Italian men of science helped to quicken the national feeling. After Pisa, Turin was chosen as the meeting-place; then Florence, Padua, Lucca, and Naples in turn. The Pope alone refused to let the Congress assemble in his territory, and forbade any of his subjects to attend it elsewhere. His keen nostrils scented Jacobinism and revolution; his Papal instinct recoiled from those devotees of Reason and Knowledge as from a brood of scorpions.

From the world outside Italy received no material encouragement during these years. Czar Nicholas was leagued with Austria; Prussia still took instructions from

Vienna; France had a Constitution with which Louis
Philippe played battledore and shuttlecock, but so badly
that Europe laughed and his subjects hissed at him.
Only in England was Liberalism triumphant, and since
1832, when the English envoy, Seymour, had declined to
guarantee the temporal sovereignty of the Pope, England's sympathy was in the main on the side of the
oppressed Italians; but sympathy unseconded by official
support brought them no improvement. The exiles plotted and chafed. Mazzini from London discharged Young
Italy's shafts. The revolutionary committees in Paris
deliberated; refugees perched along the Swiss frontiers
and were ready at the first favorable signal to swoop
down into Lombardy. It would be superfluous to enumerate the abortive plans and pricked bubbles of insurrection, or to mention all the smaller sects, — such as
the Tyrannicides, the Demonolatri or Devil-worshipers,
which existed or were alleged to exist; or to describe the
guerrilla warfare which the Sanfedists and other partisans of Absolutism waged against them. It was a world
in transition, — a time of cross-tides and contradictions.
Despots like the Pope and the King of Naples were concentrating, as in a sac of venom, all that made the Old
Régime abhorred. Despots like Charles Albert and the
Grand Duke of Tuscany, under the influence of the New
Spirit, were unconsciously veering from the Past and
drifting away from the abyss. Only Metternich was immovable, deeming himself superior to wind or wave.
You know his policy at any moment: that was the one
fixture amid the eddies of change. Austria must predominate in Italy, — that was his ruling idea. Not only
did he keep shrewd diplomats at each of the little Courts
and pension a horde of spies, but he also subsidized some
member of each of the cabinets. Lascarena at Turin,
the Prince of Cassano at Naples, — not to speak of those
cardinals who were his servants in the Sacred College at

Rome. When an emergency arose, he employed still baser arts. In 1836, for instance, believing that his information from Naples was incomplete, he dispatched his agent Smucker thither, and Smucker soon became the paramour of the Queen-Dowager, a woman of loose morals, and learned through her the royal secrets, which he duly reported to the Chancellor.[1] Greedy Austria's spoon was in every broth. The Grand Duke of Tuscany had no heir, and he was informed that at his death Austria would appropriate Tuscany; fortunately for his ambition, however, his wife died, and he married another, who bore him a son.[2] Again, when it was rumored that Charles Louis of Lucca had turned Protestant, Metternich proposed to disinherit him and to absorb Lucca; but Charles Louis gave sufficient proof of his orthodoxy to frustrate this scheme.[3] In spite of casual opposition, Metternich was still master in Italy, and he deemed himself arbiter of Europe. He alone, among all the politicians of the century, could have said, — as he did say to the Piedmontese minister in 1842, — "I have the good fortune to foresee everything, to foretell everything, to bring a sound judgment to bear upon the whole future."[4] Other self-satisfied professors of statecraft may have thought this about themselves, but modesty or a sense of humor kept them from uttering it.

[1] Bianchi, iii, 280.
[3] Poggi, ii, 219.
[2] Ibid, iv, 7-10.
[4] Bianchi, iv, 90.

CHAPTER III.

THE POLITICAL REFORMERS.

THRIFT is a principle rooted in the heart of the Universe: in human affairs we see its working in those reactions when society turns back to glean the last straws of an institution which has already had its harvest. Progress is not a straight line joining the New with the Old, but a diagonal, the resultant of the effort of conservatives to hold society back and of radicals to drive it ahead. The Present zigzags between the Past and the Future. Thus the French Revolution aspired, as we have so often repeated, to break wholly from the Past, and to begin life with a new heaven above and a new earth beneath; as Noah, when the Deluge subsided, looked upon a world unprejudiced by any yesterdays. Feudalism, Monarchy, orthodox Religion, — these were declared abolished by the dare-all revolutionists. But soon it appeared that to blot out institutions which are the inveterate habits of society, society itself must be blotted out, — and that was a task too vast for even the guillotine. True reform was seen to be transformation, — a slow process, but the only sure one, by which the hateful institution is gradually sloughed off, and a better grows in its place. So the mad onset of the revolution was followed by a pause, when the inertia of the Past checked advance, and then reaction set in. Monarchy and feudal survivals again dominated Europe. But the revolution, though checked, was not spent: it rallied in turn, this time with less dash but more persistence, and gained inch by inch on its antagonist. The revolution of 1830 and the July monarchy marked, as we saw, the turn of the political tide.

Meanwhile a similar conflict was in progress between the champions and opponents of religious orthodoxy. Catholicism and Protestantism were alike on the defensive; for rationalists had everywhere proclaimed that the old creeds based on supernaturalism had served their purpose, had ceased to be spiritual, and must forthwith be abandoned as inadequate to the soul's true needs. Especially did they assert this of Catholicism, whose mediaeval ceremonies and dogmas most offended an age which declared liberty of conscience to be every man's right, and which was beginning to substitute historical comparison and criticism for blind faith and theological command in matters religious. But frugal Providence never throws away an institution which has not exhausted every potentiality latent within it: and now there was a Catholic revival. Sensitive minds looked again into Catholicism, and reported what they saw. Some of its apologists, like Chateaubriand and Lamartine, were sentimental, and painted with poetic fervor the sweet and admirable qualities of the venerable Church; some, like De Maistre, would yield nothing to her assailants, but restated boldly, in language that the time could understand, the preposterous dogmas on which she rested; some, like Lamennais and Lacordaire, assigning second rank to dogma, magnified ethics, and showed how she might be the chief uplifter of conduct; some, like Döllinger, with critical knife cut away the overgrowth of fungi and rank vines which choked her, and revealed the original Tree of Faith in its simplicity; some, like Newman and his disciples, were drawn to her because they craved a religious authority upon which their bewildered souls might repose.

This revival, to which historians have hitherto given less attention than its interest and importance as a general religious movement merits, had its supporters in Italy also, and it might seem strange that the ablest of them were unattached to the hierarchy, did we not re-

member that for a long time past no vital spiritual word
had been uttered by pope, cardinal, or prelate. It was
from laymen, and from Churchmen whom the Inquisition
suspected of heresy, that the impulse came to make Catholicism once more a dominant religious force among
the Italians. Rosmini (1797-1855), a profound thinker,
erected a vast philosophical temple in which to celebrate
the marriage of Scholastic Theology and Modern Metaphysics, — a union of incompatibles from which no lasting concord could be predicted. But whatever may be
the ultimate value of Rosmini's philosophy, he persuaded
some of the elect of his countrymen of its truth, and he
forged for them weapons by which they could repel their
own doubts concerning the incomprehensible mysteries of
Catholicism. Manzoni was his lifelong friend if not his
disciple, and Manzoni, as we saw, was a devout Catholic.
Silvio Pellico, released from the Spielberg in 1830, had
published his book, "My Prisons," which first apprised
the world of Austria's savage treatment of political offenders, and which also displayed Pellico's broken spirit
nestling in pious resignation on the dogmas of the Church.
Balbo, Tommaseo, and many others there were who believed that Italy's regeneration could best be effected by
reviving the spiritual forces at the heart of Catholicism.
"On the ruins of sophistry," says Cantù, "was erected
the world of science and truth; we ceased to be ashamed
to say the *Ave* and the *De profundis*, and not only women
attended mass; a generation seemed preparing which,
respecting 'the holy obscurities of faith, should be char-
acterized by her, as the preceding generation by incre-
dulity.'"[1] The advocates of these views came to be
known as Neo-Guelfs; they were, to quote Cantù again,
"religious democrats, not conspirators, but still less courtiers, for whom the liberty of Italy was a moral question. 'Do you complain that foreign domination corrupts

[1] *Cronistoria*, ii. 631

you?' they asked of their countrymen. 'He alone becomes corrupt who allows himself to be corrupted.' "[1]

But in Italy all questions were drawn into the orbit of politics, and presently, early in 1843, there appeared a book, "On the Moral and Civil Primacy of the Italians," that was hailed by the Neo-Guelfs as their confession of faith, and that surpassed in immediate influence any other political work ever written in Italian. Its author was Vincent Gioberti, who, banished from Piedmont in 1833, had spent his exile chiefly at Brussels, earning his bread by teaching in a small college, and devoting his leisure to the acquisition of multifarious knowledge and to the publication at rapid intervals of thick treatises on many subjects. He was a philosopher, a theologian, a social reformer, and above all a patriot. To fuse all his learning and energy into a work which should benefit his country, — that was his highest ideal, his constant desire, which he realized in his book, "On the Primacy."

Reading that work now, after a lapse of fifty years, during which the problems it discussed have been solved, and the generation it addressed has passed away, it requires an effort of the imagination to conjure back a frame of mind similar to that upon which Gioberti's prolix rhetoric and vague suggestions fell with the majesty and splendor of Eternal Truth. As old love-letters read by a stranger have no longer the glow, the enchantment, whereby they once thrilled one heart, so there are epoch-making books from which a nation at a particular crisis extracts all the pith and juice, — say rather it literally devours them, — and leaves only their rind for posterity. To this class Gioberti's "Primacy" belongs; it is a relic of great historic interest, but unlike Demosthenes's "Orations," or Pascal's "Lettres Provinciales," or Burke's "Reflections," it lacks those qualities which insure permanence among the masterpieces of political

[1] *Cronistoria*, ii, 657.

thought. But this does not detract from its importance
as a symptom and landmark, nor make it any less truly
one of the most opportune books ever published.

Even in choosing a title, Gioberti showed his daring.
At a time when the Italians were in bondage to native and
foreign tyrants, when they had not for centuries enjoyed
any genuine civic life, when foreigners believed them to
be debased and flaccid beyond hope of regeneration, when
their own moralists reproached and strangers taunted
them, when to recall their glorious Past was to accuse
their shameful Present, Gioberti boldly announced to
them, like a Hebrew prophet to the Jews in their decadence, "Behold, ye are the chosen people!" He scoured
the records of history, science, religion, literature, and
art for facts to support his thesis, and when these failed,
his vivid imagination supplied ready assumptions. Very
plausibly did he show how the Pelasgians, Etruscans,
and Romans, and all the earlier races in Italy, had been
agents in the hands of Providence to prepare for the
coming of the modern Italians, — the consummate product
of the "Hindo-Germanic" stock. Twice already had
this chosen people held the primacy of the world: once
politically, when the Roman Empire was supreme, and
once religiously, through the Catholic Church; and it
still contained all the elements necessary to a third and
greater supremacy. The forces were latent, not dead;
the ground was fallow, and needed only to be tilled and
planted. For Italy's inheritance of genius could not
perish, though it might lie dormant, for more than one
generation. The bed-rock of all civilization is religion;
Italy possessed the Catholic religion, the only true one,
and she had, therefore, the indispensable corner-stone of
civilization. In the past, her greatness had coincided
with the union of Church and State; she began to decline
when the Ghibellines in politics and the Nominalists in
philosophy sowed their errors among the Guelfs, who

were Realists. To restore the Papacy to its former eminence was, therefore, the sure and simplest way of lifting the Italians to their commanding place among the nations.

But how was this to be done, in view of the actual feebleness of the Papal government, and of the division of the Peninsula among half-a-dozen petty sovereigns? Let the princes form a federation with the Pope as its president; then all might live peacefully together, like brothers under the care of an all-wise and a benign father. The absolute authority by which those princes ruled was in itself advantageous to the scheme; for surely, five or six individuals could be brought more easily to consent to what their duty and interest advised, than could a majority of their subjects, if they were allowed to choose. The unification of Italy might indeed be a delightful ideal, but it was an abstraction, whereas the plan of federation was concrete, real, and above all feasible.

This is the germ of Gioberti's "Primacy," its one definite and positive suggestion, wrapped about with disquisitions upon theology, history, and politics, from each of which he drew illustrations to confirm his position. Perhaps no other revolutionary treatise has so unrevolutionary, so meek and conciliatory an appearance as this. You might read it and never suspect that it was more than an extravagant eulogy on the very system and men that had degraded Italy, and kept her degraded. For the ingenious Gioberti takes care always to praise in particulars and to condemn in generals. If, for instance, he speaks of the Jesuits, it is to commend their vigor and devotion, — in Paraguay; he does not attack the Jesuits by name for the evils they cause in Italy; he merely deplores in general terms the pernicious effects that spring from clerical intrigues and unscrupulousness. Again, he extols the ideal monasticism as dreamed by

St. Benedict and St. Francis, only allowing himself to
remark that should monks ever be lazy, ignorant, and
dissolute, they ought to be severely corrected. And,
since absolute wickedness is as rare as perfection, Gioberti finds traits in the nobility, the priesthood, the people, and the princes that he can honestly approve. He
rarely hazards concrete advice: rulers ought to love their
subjects, and subjects their rulers; freedom of speech is
wholesome, but a liberal censorship is also wholesome, —
these are specimens of his non-committal method. Only
against violent revolution and the fretfulness of exiles
does he speak in censure; yet he has kind words for their
intentions. In short, the "Primacy" is a work so subtle[1]
that the ablest casuist in the Company of Jesus might be
proud to say he wrote it; it was certainly not by accident
that the Jesuits immediately detected its hidden purpose
and proceeded to assail Gioberti at a time when other
orthodox Catholics were rejoicing that they had won over
so valiant a champion.

A significant parallel might be drawn between Gioberti's "Primacy" and Dante's treatise "On Monarchy."
Gioberti's book proved to be a funeral oration on the
temporal Papacy, and, as is proper in such effusions, it
abounded in praises of the dead: Dante, on the other
hand, eulogized the Holy Roman Empire, and declared
that through it alone could peace and harmony be restored to Italy; and even as he wrote the power of the
German emperor ceased in Italy. Yet both Dante and
Gioberti demonstrated by history and religion: the one
that the Emperor, the other that the Pope, had been pre-
destined by God to bring redemption to Italy.

Gioberti's book, published at Brussels in June, 1843,
soon made its way into Italy; for what ruler would be so

---

[1] The subtlety was intentional; see, for instance, Gioberti's letter to
Mamiani quoted in V. G.'s sketch of Gioberti, No. 47 of the series, *I Con-
temporanei Italiani* (Turin, 1862), 56–7.

harsh as to forbid his subjects to read what was clearly a panegyric on himself? Would the Pope, whose temporal sovereignty was so eloquently defended? Would Charles Albert, who was hailed as the right arm of the patriotic cause? Would Leopold, of whose mild paternal government the "Primacy" might be considered a eulogy? Would Ferdinand of Naples, who was placated by Gioberti's rebuke to conspirators? Even the Austrian frontiersmen let the book pass into Lombardy and Venice, until officials with keener scent perceived that, like a rose sprinkled with poison, that fair-seeming volume concealed revolution among its leaves. But even where it was prohibited, the "Primacy" was surreptitiously circulated; all educated Italians read it, discussed it, were thrilled by it, — the clerical class most of all. To have their manifest destiny pointed out in language so rich and so persuasive, to have obstacles so deftly smoothed away and the achievement of their desires described as so easy, to have their noble qualities trumpeted, and their defects hushed, made the book irresistible. Criticism might pick many flaws in the arguments and cite many misstatements of facts; but Gioberti addressed the emotions and not the reason; he was a special pleader, skilled in every art by which a jury can be captivated. The very vagueness with which he suggested the means, the very clearness with which he affirmed that the end was attainable, disarmed opposition. Each reader, applying the eulogistic passages to himself and the general censures to his neighbor, exclaimed, "How wise and virtuous this Gioberti is! He agrees with me at almost every point!"

The Neo-Guelfs, who had begun to turn their eyes towards the Papacy as the one power that might guide Italy to independence, quickly adopted Gioberti's "Primacy" as their gospel. The Piedmontese, believing in the high mission of their dynasty, likewise cherished it because it justified their secret hopes. More than this, there was forming in every part of Italy a body of Liberals, determined but reasonable, who insisted that it was time to have done with the conspiracies and violence, which, as the experience of nearly thirty years had shown, only exasperated the princes, sacrificed many lives, caused patriotic motives to be confounded with criminal or selfish ambitions, and perpetuated local and factional discords. Thus the Moderate Party, representing the common-sense and sober second thought of Italy, was also attracted by Gioberti's glowing yet temperate words, which prophesied the new era of unity, liberty, and independence, — blessings which, as he had artfully demonstrated, could be had, "without wars, without revolutions, without offending any public or private right; that is, the first two by means of a confederation of the various States under the Presidency of the Pope, and the last by means of the internal reforms of each province, feasible by their respective princes, without imperiling or diminishing their own power."[1]

Gioberti's scheme, therefore, being the first in the field, was hailed on many sides with applause, although no one deemed Gregory XVI the pope to seize the glorious opportunity for making himself immortal and his countrymen happy;[2] but fortunately he was now old, and his successor might soon have the chance which he neglected. Meanwhile, "Confederation" and "The Pontiff for President" were the mottoes of the Neo-Guelfs and of a majority of the Moderates.

But books beget books, and within less than a year after the publication of the "Primacy," Count Caesar Balbo, a Piedmontese noble of unusual scholarly attainments, brought out a treatise on "The Hopes of Italy."

---

[1] Gioberti: *Primato* (Venice, 1848), i. 262.

[2] "I would subscribe entirely to your *Primacy*," wrote Borsieri to Gioberti, "if it were possible for once for you to become pope, and for me to be, unworthily, your secretary of state." V. G. 58.

Balbo was Gioberti's counterpart; he addressed the judgment rather than the emotions. "This is eloquent," you exclaim, at the best of Gioberti's outbursts; "This is sensible," you can say of Balbo's work throughout. Gioberti had prudently refrained from taking up the question of Austria's domination in Italy; only, by his very silence and by his dedication of the "Primacy" to Pellico he gave a clue to inference. Balbo, on the other hand, boldly announced that Italy's most pressing need was independence, and he proceeded to discuss the possible means by which she might free herself from Austria. No confederation, he said, could be effectual, so long as each of its princely members were the tool of Austria. Why talk of Papal primacy, he asked, when the Pope himself is hampered and directed by Metternich? He dismissed as abhorrent the suggestion that the entire Peninsula might be united into one Austrian kingdom; he dismissed also the proposition that a group of little republics, or that one large republic, — the Mazzinian scheme, — might be established; he admitted that a confederation was, at the moment, the most rational plan, but since this could be achieved only through independence, he urged that Italians ought to devote all their energy to solving that problem. He offered four possible solutions: — first, the Italian princes might unite and repel the Austrians, — but this would be more improbable than that they should form a federation; second, there might be a national uprising, — but could twenty-three millions of people be brought more easily than six princes into concord? Third, a foreign Power might be induced to espouse the Italian cause, — but the only Power likely to be so induced was France, and what would be the gain of exchanging Austrian for French despotism? Finally, international complications might arise, during which Italians might seize a favorable moment for winning their independence. Of such complications, three were previsible, — a general democratic conflagration and an attempt at universal monarchy, both of which Balbo declared to be equally improbable, or a partition of States, which, he thought, was both possible and imminent. For the Ottoman Empire was fast falling asunder, and before long Europe would step in to divide the property of the Sick Man at Constantinople; in this division, it would plainly be for Austria's interest to strengthen her position on the Danube and to extend her dominion over the Balkan provinces, — acquisitions which would more than compensate her for voluntarily giving up Lombardy and Venetia, and withdrawing her influence from the rest of the Italian Peninsula.

Balbo, we see, had something more definite and more practical than Gioberti's iridescent scheme. He did not deceive himself into supposing that it was sufficient to describe to Pope, Princes, and People the millennium they might bring to pass by merely agreeing to love each other. Gioberti's message, reduced to lowest terms, was, "Be virtuous and you will be happy;" but this maxim, like many another equally true, was too vague, and susceptible of too many interpretations, to be generally serviceable. Balbo took human nature and the European political condition into account: he deemed it more important to try to see things as they were rather than to glorify the past or to predict primacy for the Italians in the future. And so his book, also, had a deep effect on his countrymen, and acted as a corrective and check to the too extravagant expectations kindled by Gioberti's enthusiasm. "The Hopes of Italy," although denied a license in Piedmont, issued from a foreign press, and was sold with the tacit knowledge of the government in most parts of the Peninsula; Charles Albert, while officially prohibiting the book, allowed its author to live unmolested at Turin. Such tolerance had been unknown for thirty years.

These two books had in some measure to serve the purpose which, in free countries, is served by the press, public discussion, and representative legislatures. They seemed, indeed, but slim wedges to drive into that huge trunk of injustice and corruption whose branches, like the fabled upas-tree, shed a black shadow of ignorance and a pestilence over Italy. But the first wedge is the most important, and a book is a seed from which a revolution or a new religion may grow. The soil on which Gioberti and Balbo sowed was quick; they had not long to wait, therefore, to see their ideas take root.

Meanwhile, the party of action was not idle. Mazzini, also, had been flinging his doctrines broadcast, and was preparing to garner his crops. We saw how his influence stirred the Sicilian revolters during the terrible cholera year. Thereafter his emissaries made the Kingdom of the Two Sicilies the special field of their intrigues. No season passed without some abortive uprising. At Aquila, in 1841, the conspirators were accused of assassinating Colonel Tanfano; a hundred and fifty of them were arrested, many of whom were condemned to the scaffold or the galleys. The next year, all was ready for a simultaneous revolt in Naples and the Papal States. Mazzini's agitators swooped from their eyrie at Malta, to alight among the malecontents in the Abruzzi and Romagna; exiles who had fought in the Carlist campaign, in Spain, were eager to return to their native land, and to teach their countrymen how to manage a guerrilla warfare; the Central Committee at Paris levied assessments on its members to equip the fighters; and all the while Mazzini from London showered exhortations, warnings, and commands. An "Italian Legion," whose purpose was similar to that of Young Italy, — if indeed it was not an offshoot of that sect, — was organized, and its leaders, Ribotti and Fabrizi, glided up and down the Peninsula to beat up recruits. But, despite these formidable preparations, the year 1842 passed inactive, and 1843 was more than half spent when the police took the precaution, July 31, of arresting above a hundred suspects in the province of Salerno. A week or two later, alarming symptoms broke out in the Legations. At Ravenna, Cardinal Amat, a mild and comparatively just man, allayed the excitement by giving passports to a few of the alleged leaders; but at Bologna, where Cardinal Spinola, a legate of the retrograde brood, governed, greater severity bred more ominous tumults. Three bands of guerrillas tramped through the Legations, venturing occasionally into the towns and then escaping to the Apennines, but without being able to provoke a general insurrection. At length, after six weeks of confusion and fruitless anxiety, Cardinal Spinola authorized Freddi, Fontana, and other servile minions, to conduct a military tribunal; and they, by wholesale arrests and condemnations, in a short time restored order.

Mazzini, not sobered by this failure, planned another attempt in 1844. He adopted the same tactics: the Neapolitans were assured that the Romagnoles were on tiptoe to rebel as soon as word should come to them that the Neapolitans were up; the Romagnoles were urged to emulate their Neapolitan brothers, who waited but for a sign from them. But at the first ripple of restlessness in Calabria, the government arrested twenty-one suspects, seven of whom were summarily shot and the rest sent to the galleys; while Delcarretto, for greater security, imprisoned on suspicion the most prominent Liberals in Naples. This rebuff only exasperated the chief conspirators, who wove their plots in safety in Paris and London, to a more vigorous effort. They decreed that the mighty insurrection should astonish the world and rid Italy of her despots during the month of May. A thousand volunteers were to fly over sea from Corsica; Malta was to contribute her quota of banished patriots; the

Spanish allies had promised their aid; the Ticinese were to descend upon Lombardy and Piedmont, where the populations were as tinder, needing but one spark to ignite them. In his imagination, Mazzini already saw the fires of Liberty engirdling his beloved land; he already saw the purifying flames sweep from north to south, reducing thrones and principalities to ashes, through which the tender blades of the Republic already pierced. But he did not see that at his very elbow was a traitor, Partesotti, who duly reported to Prince Metternich the glowing hopes and careful arrangements of the Great Conspirator; nor did he learn until too late that his letters were opened by the British Postmaster-General, and that their contents were communicated to the governments against whom Mazzini was plotting.

Unfortunately, these delusive expectations seemed facts to many fervent minds, among others to Attilio and Emilio Bandiera and to Domenico Moro, three young Venetian officers in the Austrian navy. The Bandiera were sons of that admiral who, in 1831, had captured the ship on which the refugees set sail from Ancona and had brought them to Venice. But the sons, fired by patriotism and Mazzini's appeals, yearned to show their love for Italy. They proposed to seize an Austrian frigate, — which they believed might easily be done, since the Austrian marine was manned chiefly by Venetians, — and sail into the port of Messina, where, they were told, the Sicilians were ripe for rebellion. But failing to incite a mutiny, the two brothers and Moro deserted from the Austrian service and met at Corfu. There they soon gathered a little band with which to cross the Adriatic and begin the glorious war of redemption. The Bandiera scorned the offers of pardon and reinstatement that Austria made to them through their mother; they resisted her entreaties; they heeded only the seductive letters of Mazzini, and the reports which emissaries spread, and casual sea captains confirmed, that the Neapolitan and Papal masses were but waiting for a leader. Mazzini declared afterwards that he tried to dissuade the generous youths, but they wrote to him that it was necessary that the few who were born to martyrdom should plunge into the vortex of even a foolhardy attempt in the hope of drawing the wavering and timid after them.[1] At length, brooking no more delay, they and their comrades, twenty in all, set sail from Corfu on the night of June 12–13, 1844, and landed three evenings later (June 16) near the mouth of River Neto, in Calabria. A peasant undertook to guide them to Cosenza, about forty miles inland, where they intended to liberate a large batch of political prisoners and to fire the revolutionary train. For three days they wandered among the wooded Calabrian mountains; then, as they halted in a ravine near S. Giovanni in Fiore, they were surrounded and attacked by Royalist troops. After a brief skirmish, in which two of them were killed, they were forced to surrender; and then they learned that Boccaciampe, who had lagged behind on a previous day under the pretense of weariness, had hastened to Cotrone, betrayed them to the police, and brought them to this disaster. They were tried at Cosenza and condemned to death, but, as was the habit with the Bourbon government, only nine of them — half the number of captives — were executed. Early on the morning of July 25 they were led to execution. They went singing the patriotic song,

"Chi per la patria muore,
Ha già vissuto assai,"[2]

and conscious heroism was in their gait and on their countenances, as they passed through the heavy-hearted

---

[1] Nisco: *Ferdinando II*, (edit. of 1884), 68.
[2] He who for his country dies,
Has yet lived long enough.

crowd, which did not dare to show its sympathy for them. Ranged in line, they shouted, "Long live Italy!" and awaited the death-volley. When the smoke cleared, only one of them, Lupatelli, remained standing: "Fire again!" he cried to the soldiery, and a moment later he, too, fell.

Thus was quenched, as if it had been a penny taper, that torch of heroism wherewith the Bandiera brothers thought to kindle Mazzini's noble conflagration. Nine corpses huddled into a grave; eight living bodies cast into a Bourbon dungeon, there to rot slowly; the traitor Boccaciampe alone to escape, — such the pitiful but inevitable ending to such an exploit. And yet from that grave there exhaled a light of glory. All Italy had followed the prisoners during their trial, had hoped for their reprieve, had been moved to admiration by the courage with which they had at last faced the muzzles of their executioners. Even their defense before the tribunal — they declared that they had hoped the King would wink at their expedition and put himself at their head in a war of independence — was not cited to tarnish their memory. Ferdinand became more than ever execrable, — had he not willingly played the executioner for Austria? — and thereafter no sane man believed that he could be enticed, for the sake of dynastic ambition, to ally himself with the Liberals. But Mazzini also, and those other promoters of insurrection, who from their own safe shelter spurred impetuous and brave youths on to perdition, were bitterly condemned by that growing body of Moderates, who had come to see that conspiracy was inadequate and therefore harmful. Mazzini tried to exculpate himself by writing an account of his dealings with the Bandiera,[1] but he did not abandon his revolutionary apostolate: on the contrary, he assailed the Moderates as lukewarm time-servers, and he inveighed against them as the worst enemies

[1] Mazzini, iii, 262-324.

of Italy. In his great scheme, a few failures meant nothing; the blood of martyrs would but sanctify the cause; examples of devotion were needed, — victims to tyranny who should make tyranny odious; proofs to the Italians that they were engaged in no holiday revel, but in the sternest and noblest of undertakings. Idealist that he was, he listened unmoved to critics who accused him of wilfully neglecting to reckon with human nature. "You set up a sordid and selfish standard," he replied, "and you call that human nature. But all reforms have been wrought by men who believed that mankind, at their worst, are meliorable to an unknown degree. Calculate only on selfishness, and only selfishness responds; appeal to the best instincts, and these leap forth invincible." So Mazzini held fast to his trust in the virtue of the masses, and in the efficacy of his methods for rousing that virtue. Few reformers have been great enough to resist the pride which is born of a strong intellect, — the pride which persuades them that they are indispensable, if not infallible; and we may in part attribute Mazzini's stubbornness to this desire to appear to himself and to others as one that could not be wrong. Such self-confidence is the badge of all fanatics, — whether of those who succeed, and are called benefactors of the race, or of those who fail, and are called visionaries or blunderers.

The pathetic fate of the Bandiera and their few comrades had, therefore, the effect of opening many eyes to the futility of conspiracy, without causing the conspiring leaders to relax their propagandism. From London, Paris, and Malta, their agents sped shuttlewise through the Peninsula to weave a new web of revolution. Hearkening to them, the republican convert imagined that, although he could count but few confederates in his own district, all the rest of the country was swarming with them; as would be proved to him when the signal for the general insurrection should be fired. To the Moderates this procedure seemed cowardly and fraudulent; but there is no more evidence that the incendiary leaders held themselves aloof from danger out of cowardly or deceitful motives, than that the zealous directors of the Board of Foreign Missions, who, from their comfortable quarters in London or New York, send out young missionaries for cannibals or jungle fever to devour, have any other than the most pious intent. Indeed, what surer proof of self-abnegation can you give than this, — that you step back and allow your comrade to win martyrdom and glory at the cannibal's or the cannon's mouth in a cause which you esteem more precious than fine gold, or than life itself? And would not that commander-in-chief be deemed culpable, who should risk his person in the front file of his army?

The fusillade at Cosenza caused the conspirators to reflect and to apologize, but it did not make all of them prudent. Against the States of the Church and Naples the sects redoubled their machinations, hoping to secure from the Pope reforms which Austria would not veto, and to hasten in Ferdinand's kingdom a revolution which France and England would allow to take its course. But Ferdinand was too vigilant, and the attempts against his tyranny failed; whereas, in the Papal States, and especially in the Legations, a faction of the conspirators kept up so active an agitation that the Holy Father resorted to his favorite instrument — a Military Commission — for suppressing it. At Bologna, it speedily condemned a few suspects; and then passed on to Forlì, where, however, the new legate, Cardinal Gizzi, would not appeal to it. At Ravenna, Cardinal Massimo, a prelate who made rigor his watchword, availed himself of the Commission's willingness to chastise; but its zeal was so excessive that when the sentences were published, the Pope ordered that they be mitigated. So the spring and summer of 1845 saw martial law set up at several points in Gregory's dominion, yet without restoring tranquillity or allaying the fear that a still more formidable eruption might at any moment befall. A group of sectaries had, indeed, planned an insurrection, but after reconnoitring the country and recognizing that the conditions were immature, they issued from Tuscany a manifesto in which they called the civilized world to witness the hideousness of the Papal government and the justice of those who protested; and they stated the reforms without which no peace nor compromise could be reached. This "Manifesto of Rimini," of which Charles Louis Farini was the principal author, is one of the most damning indictments ever drawn up by intelligent and fair-minded subjects against the wickedness and incompetence of their ruler. Its very sobriety makes the grievances and the accusations more horrible, and bespeaks sympathy for the demands. The petitioners asked that the promises of 1831 and the changes suggested in the Memorandum of that year be fulfilled; that amnesty and civil and criminal codes be granted; that laymen be allowed to fill those offices which citizens have a right to administer; that the foreign mercenaries be dismissed, and a Civic Guard organized; that education and the press be unshackled; that municipal liberties be revived. Exorbitant favors, indeed, to ask, in 1845, of Gregory XVI, who had for fourteen years been insisting that such demands were instigated by Beelzebub, and that merely to think them was heresy, while to utter them was high-treason.[1]

There was another group of sectaries, however, whom this mere Declaration of Wrongs could not satisfy, men of action, who were determined to precipitate a conflict. About a hundred of them, at the instigation of Peter Renzi, roused the populace at Rimini on September 23, and, without difficulty, took possession of the city. For three days they ruled tranquilly, awaiting

[1] Text in Farini, i. 98–112.

news from their confederates of similar success in the neighboring towns. Then a detachment of Papal troops bore down on Rimini, and Renzi, with his supporters, beat a retreat, some to embark for Trieste, others to cross the Apennines and seek refuge in Tuscany. A second squad of insurgents, after a brief skirmish near Faenza, also withdrew across the Tuscan frontier. The affair was trivial enough in itself, but its sequel caused intense excitement; for the Papal government clamored for the extradition of Renzi, and the Grand Duke, instead of complying, gave him a passport for France; whereat the Liberals everywhere rejoiced.

Presently there issued a pamphlet, "On the Recent Events in Romagna," that was eagerly read by the Italians and attracted wide attention beyond the Alps. The author of this, the third significant political treatise, was Marquis Massimo d' Azeglio, who, like Gioberti and Balbo, was a Piedmontese. In the variety of his natural gifts he resembled the great Italians of the Renaissance, and he added to this rare combination of talents commonsense, integrity, and charm. He was born (1798) into the stiff, punctilious aristocracy of Piedmont, amid which a prosperous career lay open to him either in the government or the army; but a sense of humor, a love of independence, and, above all, a desire to achieve fame as a painter, made a treadmill life, whether at court or in camp, intolerable to him. When he announced to his family that he had resolved to adopt the profession of painter, they were as much shocked as if he had expressed the intention of becoming a bootblack or a burglar. For a young noble to prefer a studio to the royal antechamber seemed madness; but the youth persisted, and his father reluctantly acquiesced. Massimo went to Rome, spent several years in hard study, lived frugally, and gradually earned reputation and a livelihood from his paintings. Having removed to Milan, where he married Manzoni's daughter, he wrote two historical romances, "Ettore Fieramosca" and "Nicolò de' Lapi," which brought him a literary popularity second only to that of Manzoni himself. He was inspired by patriotism, but a rational and temperate patriotism, which despised rant and abhorred the dagger. He was sympathetic, without being in danger of losing his individuality; he kindled enthusiasm, admiration, love, without being himself too heated to "think clearly and see straight." This happy balance between heart and head, this genial temperament and knightliness of manner, made friends of all who knew him; while his romances endeared him to thousands who had never seen his face.

By a happy chance, he had made a journey of inspection through the Papal States and Tuscany in this very month of September, 1845. He went to canvass public opinion, and there was at that time no other Italian so well fitted for that work. His reputation, his contacts with men of all ranks, his alertness and insight, his downright honesty and freedom from prejudice, gave him unique advantages. Unattached to any sect, he had friends and confidants in all sects. He found the majority of Liberals disgusted with the incendiary methods which had proved so futile and ruinous, and he tried to lead them to regard Charles Albert as the redeemer in whom they might trust. But they remembered Charles Albert's defection in 1821 and persecution in 1832, and were skeptical. So D'Azeglio reasoned with them: "If we asked the King to do something against his interest, out of pure heroism to aid Italy, we might well doubt him; but we ask him to benefit himself and us, — to allow us to assist him to become greater and more powerful than he now is. If you invite a robber to be honest and he promises, you may doubt lest he prove false; but to invite him to rob, and then for you to be afraid that he will not keep his word, — truly, I see no sense in it."[1] Argu-

[1] D'Azeglio: I Miei Ricordi, ii. 435.

ments like these show how deeply rooted was the distrust of Charles Albert, — a distrust which D' Azeglio himself still felt, although he believed in the destiny of Piedmont, and that the King might be swept by the popular tide to the accomplishment of that destiny. Preaching caution and patience, he was gratified to find that the majority acknowledged the wisdom of his counsels.

The turbulence of Renzi and his accomplices furnished D' Azeglio with the text for his pamphlet. He wrote, as he had spoken, frankly, fearlessly, repudiating the insurgents for their rashness, pointing out that the time had gone by when such ebullitions were justifiable, and declaring that they harmed the patriotic cause by rousing dissensions and involving crueller repression at home, and by giving foreigners ground for believing that the Italians were a violent, fickle people, unworthy of sympathy and incapable of self-control. But having reproved the sectaries and their methods, he went on to describe the Papal government, not abusively but calmly, laying bare its rottenness, its iniquity, its senile feebleness, its greed and hypocrisy. That civilized men should revolt against such an administration was, he said, inevitable, and Europe, which abetted that monstrous misrule, ought not to blame those who, in a spasm of anguish, tried to emancipate themselves from it. When a sufferer cries out, "I can endure this no longer!" it is not for the healthy to say, "You can." But the sufferers had by this time learned that by their outbursts they only increased their pain; it behooved them to devise other means: to abandon physical for moral protests, to be strenuous but temperate in publishing their grievances, until the public opinion of the world should plead in their behalf. That was a power which no king, nor the Pontiff himself, could long resist. "With your hands in your pockets you can win the public opinion of the world to your cause," D' Azeglio told his countrymen.

His tract, first printed at Florence, roused immense enthusiasm. Gioberti's "Primacy" had filled two octavo volumes; D' Azeglio's pamphlet could be read in an hour, and thereby had a great advantage. It slipped past customs-officers and policemen; it was reissued clandestinely from many presses; it was read and discussed everywhere. The Grand Duke took alarm at it. His aged adviser Fossombroni was dead; dead also was Neri Corsini, who had, like Fossombroni, warded off the encroachments of Rome and Austria; and the new minister, Cempini, who succeeded them, was either timid or honestly retrograde. D'Azeglio, therefore, was commanded to quit Tuscany. This silly harshness only increased the demand for the little book and added to its author's popularity. The Florentines gave him a farewell banquet, and well-wishers from all parts of Tuscany flocked along the route he traveled to the frontier; so his journey into exile resembled a triumphal progress.

Other ill-advised and unpopular acts gave warning that the Grand Duke was falling back into the ranks of Absolutism. He handed over Renzi, who, contrary to his promise, had returned from France, to the Papal government; he listened to overtures from the long-excluded Jesuits; and when the Pisan professors protested against the establishment of a convent of the Sisters of the Sacred Heart at Pisa, his ministers formally reprimanded them. But in proportion as the Grand Duke lost, Charles Albert gained in popularity among the Liberals during the early part of 1846. They were encouraged by the report of the interview which D' Azeglio, returning from his canvassing tour, had had with the King. After D'Azeglio had given the gist of his conferences with the leading Moderates whom he had sounded on his journey, Charles Albert uttered these memorable words: "Inform those gentlemen to remain quiet and not to move, as there is at present nothing to do; but let them be assured that, when the occasion presents itself, my life, the life of my sons, my arms, my treasure, my army, — all shall be expended for the Italian cause."[1] A little later, a dispute arose between Piedmont and Austria over the transportation of salt through Piedmont to Switzerland. Austria would have coerced the King, but he did not quail, although Metternich threatened, and took reprisals by doubling the duty on Piedmontese wines exported into Lombardy. Liberals who had with good reason distrusted Charles Albert now began to see in him the possible fulfiller of Italy's hopes. His subjects greeted him with acclamations wherever they saw his tall figure and melancholy face. He basked in an April sunshine of popularity. But he was still hemmed in by ministers, courtiers, and priests unconverted to Liberalism; he was still, and must always be, limited by his Hamlet nature, — quick to wish, slow to will, — and though he had daunted Austria over a matter of salt and wine, could he be relied upon to break irrevocably with the Past and declare a national war? Rigid Count Solaro, at least, would never consent to see his sovereign embark on the deceptive stream which flowed into the whirlpool of revolution. So there followed petty official acts which threw the Piedmontese into suspense concerning Charles Albert's sincerity of purpose. He seemed fated to be a puzzle, a weathercock, to the end.

But the wide circulation of the political writings of Gioberti, Balbo, and D'Azeglio was a symptom of impending change. Hitherto, patriotic tracts had issued from the secret societies, and had been read on the sly; the works of these three responsible and temperate men prevailed, in spite of reluctant censors, in securing a quasi-legitimate circulation, and in awakening a healthy discussion. They were theoretical, — "The Primacy," indeed, was but a fantastic dream, — but theories invari-

[1] D'Azeglio: *Ricordi*. ii. 462.

ably precede acts, as the vague nebula antedates the star. Treatises of all sizes, and freighted with divers suggestions or nostrums, were launched in the wake of these pioneers. Gioberti himself dashed off a volume of "Prolegomeni" to his "Primacy," and then, changing his attitude towards clericalism, he poured out five volumes of diatribe on "The Modern Jesuit." Durando, a military officer, proposed that, the Austrians having been expelled, Italy should be divided into three Kingdoms, two to be ruled by Charles Albert and Ferdinand of Naples, while the Pope and the Dukes ruled the third.[1] Ricciardi, an ardent Mazzinian, showed how easily independence and a republic could be won.[2] "A Sicilian" discoursed on the strength of national sentiment; Canuti and Capponi drew fresh pictures of the outrageous Papal government. Less popular, but not less valuable, were the contributions of two men who understood how tightly the economical question was bound up in the political. Petitti, writing on the extension of the railway system, and Cavour, writing on railways and England's tariff reforms, aided the great cause. Henceforth, the Italians had no lack of printed counsel, wise or foolish. But they must be patient, for the moment to convert counsel into deeds had not come. Gregory XVI still lived. At the Vatican, they knew, was the source of that evil system which corrupted the entire Peninsula, and with prayers on their lips and yearning in their hearts they watched for news from Rome. That ancient compact of the Papacy with Mammon had borne this hideous fact, — a whole people believed that neither justice nor happiness nor virtue could proceed from Gregory, the representative of Almighty God and the Vicar of Jesus Christ; therefore they prayed that Gregory might die.

[1] Giacomo Durando: *Della Nazionalita Italiana* (Lausanne, 1846).
[2] *Conforti all' Italia* (Paris, 1846).

www.ingramcontent.com/pod-product-compliance
Lightning Source LLC
Chambersburg PA
CBHW032002300426
44117CB00008B/871